REGIONAL INTEGRATION AND INDUSTRIAL RELATIONS IN NORTH AMERICA

Proceedings of a conference held at the
New York State School of Industrial and Labor Relations,
Cornell University

MARIA LORENA COOK AND HARRY C. KATZ, EDITORS

Institute of Collective Bargaining
New York State School of Industrial and Labor Relations
Cornell University

Library of Congress Cataloging-in-Publication Data

Regional integration and industrial relations in North America /
    edited by Maria Lorena Cook and Harry C. Katz.
            p.   cm.
    Includes bibliographical references.
    ISBN 0-87546-851-9 (acid-free paper) :
    1. Industrial relations--America--Congresses.   2. America--
Economic integration--Congresses.   I. Cook, Maria Lorena.
II. Katz, Harry Charles, 1951-   .
HD8045.R44   1994
331' . 097--dc20   94-23338
                                                             CIP

Copies may be ordered from

ILR Press
New York State School of
Industrial and Labor Relations
Cornell University
Ithaca, NY 14853-3901

Telephone: 607-255-3061

Contents

The Transformation of U.S. Industrial Relations—An Overview of
Recent Developments, *Harry C. Katz* 1

Industrial Democracy, Total Quality, and Mexico's Changing Labor
Relations, *Enrique de la Garza Toledo* 19

Current Developments in Canadian Industrial Relations,
Mark Thompson 37

The Mexican Model of Labor Regulation and Competitive Strategies,
Graciela Bensusán Areous 52

Economic Integration and Labor Law Policy in Canada, *Gilles Trudeau
and Guylaine Vallée* 66

The Social Dimension of Freer Trade, *Roy J. Adams and Lowell Turner* 82

How Will the North American Free Trade Agreement Affect Worker
Rights in North America?, *Ian Robinson* 105

The Mexican Dual Transition: State, Unionism and the Political
System, *Alberto Aziz Nassif* 132

Regional Integration and Transnational Labor Strategies Under
NAFTA, *Maria Lorena Cook* 142

Free Trade and Its Implications for Industrial Relations and Human
Resource Management, *Morley Gunderson and Anil Verma* 167

The Restructuring of the Automobile Industry in Mexico and the
Repercussions for Labor, *Arnulfo Arteaga García* 180

Industrial Relations in the Maquiladora Industry: Management's
Search for Participation and Quality, *Alfredo Hualde* 207

The Effects on Labor of the Restructuring of Petróleos Mexicanos:
1989-1993, *Rafael Loyola Díaz and Liliana Martínez Pérez* 218

NAFTA and AFTA: Regional Integration and Industrial Relations in
Southeast Asia, *Sarosh Kuruvilla and Adam Pagnucco* 233

Appendix: Summary of Paper Presentations and Discussion 254

Preface

This volume includes papers presented at a workshop on "Regional Integration and Industrial Relations in North America," held at the New York State School of Industrial and Labor Relations, Cornell University, on October 1-2, 1993. The conference was organized by Maria Lorena Cook and Harry C. Katz of the School of Industrial and Labor Relations, Cornell University. Garciela Bensusán Areous of the Universidad Autónoma Metropolitana-Xochimilco in Mexico City played a key role in conceptualizing the workshop and coordinated the group of Mexican researchers who participated.

The papers in this volume are written by leading scholars from Mexico, Canada, and the United States in the fields of industrial relations, labor law, sociology, and political science. These essays provide a rare North American comparative perspective on industrial relations developments and the effects of regional economic integration on labor and industrial relations in the three countries. Recent passage of the North American Free Trade Agreement increases the relevance of the analyses presented here. Particularly noteworthy are the contributions of leading scholars from Mexico who present unique perspectives on both the broad changes occurring in their country and on developments in the key auto, petrochemical, and maquiladora sectors.

The essays in the first section of this volume analyze the recent evolution of industrial relations systems in each of the respective countries and set the stage for the subsequent consideration of the implications of regional and trade integration. The North American Free Trade Agreement was approved by the United States Congress shortly after the workshop, and the papers were subsequently updated to account for the implications of the trade agreement. The volume also contains a compilation of the lively discussion that followed presentation of the papers at the conference. This discussion highlights the many controversies surrounding regional integration and includes an agenda for future research.

Not all of the papers presented at the conference were included in this volume as these papers were already committed for publication. In addition, the paper by Gunderson and Verma was prepared especially for this volume and was not presented at the conference.

Financial support for the workshop was provided by the ILR International Initiative and the ILR Institute of Collective Bargaining. The editors wish to thank Alison Cable of the International Initiative for her help in organizing the conference and Jackie Dodge of the Institute of Collective Bargaining for her assistance on this volume.

A Spanish language version of this volume will be coordinated by Arnulfo Arteaga Garcia and Graciela Bensusán Areous and published jointly by the Universidad Autónoma Metropolitana-Iztapalapa and the Facultad Latinoamericana de Ciencias Socioles (FLACSO) in Mexico City.

The Transformation of U.S. Industrial Relations—
An Overview of Recent Developments

Harry C. Katz

Introduction: A Transformation in Industrial Relations?

Tom Kochan, Robert McKersie, and I (KKM) claim that a major transformation is occurring in American industrial relations. (Kochan, Katz, and McKersie, 1986 and 1994). There are many dimensions to this transformation including a shift in the focus of industrial relations activity away from the "collective bargaining" to the "strategic" and "workplace" levels. Perhaps most controversial is our assertion that in a number of unionized settings a new system of industrial relations is emerging. The new system includes more contingent compensation, team systems of work organization, employment security and retraining programs, and enhanced worker and union participation in decision making. In contrast to the traditional arm's-length, formal nature of collective bargaining, the new system involves more continuous and informal relations between workers and managers.

The new industrial relations also involves changes in the *bargaining process*. Process changes include a decentralization in bargaining structure, more direct communication between management and the workforce, and a more direct role for financial and operating managers in the negotiation and administration of work rules and labor contracts.

In the section to follow, recent labor relations developments in the auto industry are used to illustrate the transformation occurring in parts of the American economy. The paper then analyzes the decentralization of bargaining structures occurring in many industries and the resulting implications for union and management roles. I then examine some of the debates surrounding the transformation thesis and analyze developments in those American firms and industries where a transformation in industrial relations is not apparent. Developments in the human resource practices of nonunion firms and union organizing trends are reviewed in the final sections of the paper.

An Illustration: The Automobile Industry

The American automobile industry provides a rich illustration of new industrial relations practices and is often cited in the debates concerning the new practices. The auto industry receives so much attention from the press and academics because the industry has long served as a pattern setter and innovator within American collective bargaining (Katz 1985; Katz and MacDuffie forthcoming).

The following discussion focuses on developments within the Big Three (General Motors, Ford, and Chrysler) and the United Auto Workers, although similar changes have occurred in the independent auto parts sector.

Contingent Compensation

From 1948 until 1979, Big Three contracts with the UAW always included annual cost-of-living increases (providing 90-100 percent protection from inflation) and annual improvement-factor wage increases (since 1955 these were 3 percent per year). Auto worker earnings were made more contingent on corporate performance when profit sharing was introduced into the Big Three contracts with the UAW in the early 1980s and continued in subsequent contracts, including the 1993-96 agreements. The profit sharing plans provide annual payouts that vary as a function of company profits.

The introduction of profit sharing has led to sizable differences in pay across workers in the different companies. In 1993, Chrysler workers received payouts that averaged $4,300 while Ford workers received $1,350 and GM's profit-sharing plan provided no payout to hourly workers.[1] Most of this variation was due to differences in the financial performance of the companies, with GM suffering substantial declines in market share from the mid-1980s on.

The introduction of profit sharing was accompanied by the use of lump-sum wage increases. Annual lump sum have been paid in the Big Three contracts negotiated since 1982. The lump-sum increases have varied between 2 and 3 percent. In some sense, the lump sum wage increases also are a form of contingent pay in that they are not automatic and their size varies somewhat as a function of how well the auto companies are doing financially at the moment a new labor contract is negotiated.

At the shop-floor level in a number of auto plants, another variant of contingent pay has been introduced through the introduction of pay-for-knowledge schemes linking worker pay and skill competence. Under these pay systems, workers receive more pay (often $.50 cents per pay step) as they prove competence in a wider variety of jobs in their respective work area. In the past, a worker's wage was set strictly on the basis of the job classification of the worker. There had been very little variation across work areas in a plant, across plants, and across companies in the wage rates assigned to particular occupations. Thus, in the past assembly line workers across the Big Three all received nearly identical wage rates. Currently, as a result of pay-for-knowledge, some assemblers earn up to $2.00 per hour more than other assemblers.

Teams

Team systems of work organization have spread throughout many of the Big Three plants. Although the form of teams varies substantially across plants, all the teams involve a shift away from the traditional numerous job classifications. A typical team requires workers to perform some machine maintenance, housekeeping, repair, and inspection duties in addition to normal tasks. In some teams, workers rotate across job tasks and some teams use pay-for-knowledge. In some extreme cases, teams are led by UAW represented hourly "team coordinators" who perform many of the tasks that were traditionally carried out by supervisors, although the roles performed by "supervisors" varies substantially across teams and plants. The operation of teams is closely linked to greater worker and union participation in decision making and employment security programs.

Employment (and Income) Security and Retraining Programs

In the traditional auto industrial relations system, workers were laid off when recessions produced declines in auto sales. The UAW had negotiated a number of programs to provide income protection to employees during these temporary layoffs, the most important the supplemental unemployment insurance benefits (SUB) paid in addition to government-provided unemployment insurance benefits.

In the 1980s and early 1990s, the Big Three-UAW contracts were extended to include a number of employment (and income) security and retraining programs. The Jobs Bank, introduced in the 1984 contracts, was one of the major innovations. The Jobs Bank provides that if workers are laid off for reasons that were in the control of the company (layoffs due to technological change, corporate reorganization, outsourcing, or negotiated productivity improvements) the workers receive full compensation while placed in a "jobs bank." Notably, the Jobs Bank program in the 1984-87 and 1987-90 contracts did not protect workers laid off due to volume-related reasons. As a result, in the mid- and late 1980s, when GM's market share fell, many GM workers were laid off and did not qualify for the Jobs Bank (although many received SUB benefits or transfer opportunities).

For workers covered by the Jobs Bank and other new employment security programs, there is less frequent recourse to layoff (even in the face of business downturns) and more secure career attachment to the firm. In GM's Job Bank program, for example, workers displaced by new technology sometimes are placed in retraining programs. The degree to which this new program actually provides valuable retraining to the workforce varies substantially across auto plants. Nonetheless, the Job Bank and other programs provide covered workers in the auto assembly firms with work careers that look more like the traditional employment security possessed by white collar workers in the United States.

The 1990-93 contract made a major change by extending the Jobs Bank to workers laid off for volume-related reasons. The 1990-93 contracts provided (and the 1993-96 contracts continue to provide) that during the term of the three-year agreement, a worker cannot be laid off for longer than 36 weeks. Once a worker has been on layoff, they are to be recalled to work or receive full pay while placed in a Jobs Bank.

The 1990-93 and 1993-96 contracts also increased the compensation provided to workers affected by layoff or plant closings. SUB and early retirement benefits, for example, were greatly expanded, although even the allocated benefit funds were not always adequate to cope with the layoffs that were occurring. GM exhausted the $4.2 billion that had been allocated for income and employment security protections in the 1990-93 contract and in the winter of 1993 had to provide supplemental funding for the SUB funds. The 1993-96 contract at GM replenished the SUB funds and provided an additional total of $4 billion to cover the income and employment security package.

The latest income security programs should be seen as a mixture of insurance and severance payments. In part the programs compensate workers for giving up pay or other potential contract improvements and provide substantial severance benefits to those workers who are laid off. Meanwhile, the auto companies do not have to make payouts in these programs if they manage to avoid extensive layoffs and plant closings (as occurred at Ford and Chrysler).[2]

The parties also hoped that these programs would reduce workers' fears that productivity improvements would lead to worker displacement and this would spur workers to agree to restructure work. The companies and the UAW created various committees operating at the plant level to develop more effective work practices.

It is, of course, possible that income and employment security programs have an effect that goes exactly in the opposite direction from what the companies hoped. These new (and expanded programs) reduce the hardships workers face if companies lose market share and close plants. Thus, it is possible that the reduction in these hardships leads workers to be more complacent and less enthusiastic about changing work practices. In the face of the new programs, workers have less to lose if they maintain traditional work practices. As a result, the productivity effects of the programs depend heavily on the shopfloor dynamics of worker-management relations.

Participation Processes

Workers and union officials have acquired increased participation through a number of channels in the new industrial relations system. Team systems, for example, involve workers in a broader variety of tasks. Some teams workers even have become involved in budget and planning. In a number of auto plants, hourly workers now have the authority to contact vendors and parts suppliers directly, and some workers make regular trips to these vendors to resolve complaints.

Workers and union officers also participate in strategic issues in the auto industry through a number of other committees and joint activities. These range from plant-level committees concerned with productivity and quality enhancement to quarterly forums where the companies report their business plans. In some plants union officers are now a part of the management committees that provide plant input into corporate strategic planning.

GM's Saturn plant represents an extreme case. At Saturn, a traditional managerial hierarchy does not exist, as union representatives serve as "partners" to management. A similar deepening of union and worker participation in business decision making has occurred at a number of other firms and industries. At Xerox, for example, management and ACTWU representatives now openly discuss investment decisions.

Another pathway for greater participation has occurred in industries outside the auto sector as a result of the adoption of employee stock ownership plans (ESOPs) as part of a package of concessions, often to avoid bankruptcy. Usually in these plans, the unions involved, for example the steelworkers and airline unions, gain the opportunity to nominate board members.

The extent of union involvement in business decisions that is obtained in organizations following the participatory path belies the claims of the critics of participation who mistakenly suggest that worker and union participation programs necessarily lead to the weakening of unions and ultimately to union avoidance. While the latter may well be occurring at some work sites in the United States, this has not been the trajectory at those sites that have engaged in a full-fledged partnership approach.

The Decentralization of Collective Bargaining

The bargaining outcome changes (contingent pay, team systems, employment security programs, and participation processes) appeared in a number of unionized industries from the mid-1980s on. A frequent and important bargaining process change that was often linked in a complex manner to these bargaining outcome changes was the decentralization of bargaining structures.

At the beginning of the 1980s, the structure of bargaining affecting unionized employees in the United States was a mixture of multiemployer, firmwide, and plant-level bargaining. During the 1980s the structure of bargaining in the United States underwent changes that were similar to the types of decentralization underway in many other countries (Katz 1993). Multi-employer bargaining in the United States in some cases ended, as was the fate of the basic steel agreement in 1986. In some other cases, the number of firms and unionized employees covered by a multifirm agreement declined as some companies withdrew from master agreements, as in trucking (where the Master Freight Agreement negotiated by the Teamsters and an employers' association set terms for intercity truck drivers) and in the underground coal mining sector (where the United Mineworkers negotiated a master agreement with the Bituminous Coal Operators Association) (Kochan, Katz, and McKersie 1986:128-130; Katz and Kochan 1992:195-197).

In many industries there were also reports of a shift to the plant level away from companywide agreements. Frequently, as in the auto, tire, and airline industries, this involved the negotiation of local pay or work rule concessions. Often these negotiations involved whipsawing by management, with local unions and workers being threatened with the prospect of a plant closing if adequate concessions were not granted (Cappelli 1985; Katz 1985:63-71; Kochan, Katz, and McKersie 1986:117-127). In the winter of 1992, a well-publicized illustration of this process entailed competition between the local unions at the Arlington and Willow Run assembly plants in the face of General Motors' threat to close one of the two plants as part of its downsizing. In some other plants, concessions on work rules were accompanied by new arrangements that provided extensive participation by workers and local union officers in decisions that had formerly been made solely by management (Kochan, Katz, and McKersie 1986:146-205). In these cases, local bargaining took on the form of the "wildcat cooperation" Streeck (1984) had predicted.

Even where company-level collective bargaining continued, negotiations in the 1980s and early 1990s produced a diversity of agreements across companies that replaced strong pattern bargaining in some industries (which informally had served to centralize the bargaining structure to the multiemployer level). Erickson (1992), for example, documents the emergence of significant inter-company variation in the aerospace industry, while Katz (1985) and Katz and Meltz (1991) describe similar variation across the auto assembly companies. Interindustry as well as intra-industry pattern bargaining weakened. Budd's 1992 analysis reveals that the influence of a key auto contract settlement had "considerably smaller" effects in 1987-90 than in 1955-79 on the contracts the UAW negotiated in industries other than auto assembly (such as aerospace, auto parts, and agricultural implements).

The Factors Spurring Decentralization

There are three major explanations as to why this decentralization is occurring. One explanation for bargaining structure decentralization is that it is a product of an increase in management's power. In this vein, bargaining structure is viewed both as a reflection of the parties' relative power and as a determinant of power.

Recent bargaining structure decentralization can be interpreted as a reversal of unions' previous success in using centralized bargaining to take wages out of competition. As management has acquired more bargaining leverage, a change itself caused by intensified international competition and declines in union membership and political strength, management pushed to decentralize the structure of bargaining with the expectation that this would produce bargaining outcomes more favorable to management.

Management need not be using more decentralized bargaining solely to win lower <u>wage</u> settlements at the bargaining table for this hypothesis to hold. For example, Pontusson and Swenson (1992) argue that Swedish employers were particularly interested in widening skill differentials and felt unable to gain such a widening in the traditional centralized structure. The main point in this hypothesis is that decentralization is used by employers to achieve more favorable bargaining outcomes and was sought primarily for that purpose. In this account, employers have used the bargaining power advantage they gained from shifts in the economic environment to promote a change in the *process* of bargaining (decentralization), which then enables employers to gain advantages at the bargaining table.

A "temporary" variant of this hypothesis sees decentralization as a useful tool through which employers have gained bargaining power advantage. The idea here is that it is the *process* of decentralization that is most important. Employers seem to benefit most from the ability to play plants (and local unions) off against one another; that is, to whipsaw local unions. Yet after gaining lower wage outcomes or wider skill differentials through whipsawing, employers may in the future prefer to return to centralized bargaining because of the advantages it provides (stability, predictability, and economies of scale).

In this temporary account, employers need decentralized bargaining to gain concessions because central unions are unwilling to grant the concessions employers desire, while local unions are more willing to do so.

It is also possible to view decentralization as a product of the decline of the bargaining power held by *both* management and unions (that is, a decline in the absolute level of power) and not as a product of the *relative* decline of labor's power. This explanation extends the argument contained in previous quantitative analyses of the determinants of bargaining power (Hendricks and Kahn 1982: Deaton and Beaumont 1980; and Greenberg 1967). These analyses find that in earlier periods among multiplant firms with single-firm agreements, collective bargaining tended to be more centralized in concentrated industries (that is, where there were greater economic rents to be shared).[3] Following this logic, recent increases in economic competition and international trade have reduced the economic rents available to labor and management and thereby spurred decentralization in bargaining structures.

A second explanation claims that it is the rise in the importance of work organization and shop floor issues that has led to decentralization in collective bargaining. As Streeck (1984) noted, economic pressures and more flexible technologies have led labor and management to restructure the workplace. At some sites these negotiations have proceeded to the point that local unions and workers have become "comanagers of the internal labor market." As a result of these pressures, non-wage issues have been elevated in importance and negotiations over these "qualitative" issues in contributing to decentralization. Thorough documentation of the existence of shop floor bargaining over work restructuring is found in a wide range of recent industrial relations research, including Turner 1991, Thelen 1991, Locke forthcoming and Mathews 1989.

Decentralization may follow from local bargaining because the identification of innovations and the implementation of new forms of work organization requires direct participation by workers and local union officials. A central union, for example, cannot come up with a new method of teamwork that is negotiated centrally with management and then applied across local work sites because the process of identifying an efficient (or acceptable) teamwork system and the successful implementation of the new practices requires the active participation of local actors.

A related claim is that the new work organization involves changes in a variety of employment practices including teamwork, performance-based pay methods, participatory programs, extensive training, and in some cases, employment security (Katz and Kochan 1992:331-341). Thus, what the parties at the local level are doing is discovering, and then implementing, new packages of employment policies.

Furthermore, there are many different appropriate new packages of employment practices that make the central negotiation of these matters impractical and inefficient. As a result, it is not possible for centralized negotiations to develop new practices and then enforce standardized local adoption of new practices. This rationale for decentralization assumes that the new work organization involves an honest dose of worker involvement, and it implicitly disagrees with critics of "joint processes," who assert that participation is largely a ruse or a device to coopt workers and unions.[4]

There is also a "temporary" version of the work organization account of bargaining decentralization. The point here is that the intensified local bargaining over work restructuring is a product of the parties' struggles to identify new practices that work well. In effect, local bargaining has followed from a process of experimentation through which labor and management are searching for effective new practices. Bargaining is occurring locally so as to provide a range of experimentation and diversity, because centralized negotiations would be too sluggish and too limited. This sort of local experimentation, however, may well be only a temporary phenomenon that will recede once labor and management have identified successful new work practices. Under this temporary scenario, local bargaining was necessary only as a learning process, and central unions and employer groups may eventually become the negotiators of qualitative issues once they have learned from their more innovative local branches.

But, there is little, if any, evidence suggesting that, as predicted in the "temporary experimentation" explanation for decentralization, the negotiation of work restructuring has begun to shift upward after local parties identify successful strategies.

Another explanation for the decentralization of bargaining structure focuses on increased diversification in both corporate structure and worker interests. On the corporate side, this explanation views decentralized bargaining as a product of corporations' decentralization of their internal organizational structure, which has increased the independence of business units or profit centers. Bargaining decentralization is seen as a natural consequence of a process in which more direct responsibility for industrial relations is being passed to lower-level managers in the decentralized corporation (Purcell and Ahlstand 1989; Marginson et al. 1988:183; Kochan, Katz, and McKersie 1986:62-65).

The push for corporate diversification and decentralization itself is said to be a product of such economic pressures as volatility and uncertainty in the economic environment, the shift from mass to specialized product markets, and increased variation in economic pressures across business lines. These economic pressures combine to put a greater premium on flexibility as the corporation searches for ways to more quickly respond to rapidly changing and competitive environments (Piore and Sabel 1984).

Evidence in support of the hypothesis that increased management power has led to decentralization comes from the fact that it is management that has pushed most aggressively for decentralized bargaining while central unions have most often opposed decentralization. Support for this hypothesis also comes from the fact that in many cases decentralized bargaining has been associated with the negotiation of pay and work rule concessions at the plant level. Such concessions are commonplace in the United States and have been noted in many other countries.

My reading of the qualitative evidence suggests that both the long and temporary versions of the bargaining power hypothesis have some credibility. Unions clearly have been on the defensive in the United States and elsewhere, and the decline in union bargaining power appears to have contributed to their inability to resist employer efforts to decentralize bargaining.

At the same time, the increase in management's power does not appear to fully explain recent events. For one thing, it is not obvious that traditional centralized bargaining was so advantageous to unions (and disadvantageous to employers) in the first place. As Weber (1961) and others have noted, centralized bargaining was useful to some employers as a mechanism through which they avoided union whipsawing. And if centralized bargaining did not favor unions, then it is less clear why employers would seek to eliminate it now that they have more bargaining power.

Another problem with the bargaining power hypothesis comes from the fact that local unions and workers often have supported the decentralization of collective bargaining. It is conceivable that local unions' support for decentralization derives solely from the fact they are trapped in a fight for survival and agree to decentralization in order to grant the concessions that keep their own plant in business. But, the case study accounts of the productivity coalitions that are formed in the now widespread local bargaining discussed earlier in this paper suggest that more than this is at stake. Local unions and workers at many sites appear to enjoy the participation in shop floor and strategic business decisions they have gained and also benefit from some of the more flexible work schedules that have been negotiated. Recognition that local unions and workers may be gaining through local bargaining implies that more than just shifts in power is causing decentralization.

My reading of the evidence suggests that there are clear advantages gained by both labor and management in the work restructuring that is underway in so many workplaces, which supports the second decentralization hypothesis. More local bargaining seems to be a natural product of the increase in worker and union participation in enterprise and shop floor decision making. It also appears that local bargaining is essential for the identification and implementation of new, more flexible forms of work organization. Thus, I am led to the view that work reorganization has played a significant role as a cause of bargaining structure decentralization.

While decentralization in corporate structure and diversity in worker preferences may also have played a role in spurring bargaining structure decentralization as predicted by the third decentralization hypothesis, there is little evidence that these factors are widespread enough to explain the extensive decentralization in bargaining that has occurred. Furthermore, although the literature on corporate decentralization and diversification is extremely informative, it is difficult to tell if the bargaining decentralization researchers are attributing to corporate decentralization is in fact a product of the factors associated with the other two decentralization hypotheses discussed above.

The decentralization of collective bargaining calls into question the traditional role of central unions. As power shifts to local unions they become more difficult to control, and the potential rises for political challenges to central union authority. Streeck (1984) and Katz and Sabel (1985) suggested early on that central unions would be hard-pressed to define new roles as decentralization proceeded, and experiences in the late 1980s and early 1990s have validated their warnings.

Corporate industrial relations staffs also face major changes in their roles as a result of the decentralization of collective bargaining. On the one hand, influence has shifted from corporate to plant or division industrial relations staffs (Storey 1992; Kochan, Katz, and McKersie 1986:197-201). This shift has had pluses and minuses for local industrial relations managers. Although the power of local industrial relations staffs rises as they acquire more direct responsibility for bargaining as it decentralizes, they also bear the burden of the increased financial pressures, and in some cases, the more explicit cost controls that accompany this responsibility. At the same time, even where the formal structure of bargaining has shifted to plant or business unit levels, corporate staffs may continue to set guidelines or exercise informal influence on the negotiations occurring at local levels (Marginson et al. 1988:183, 151).

In addition, managerial industrial relations staffs at a variety of levels have seen their influence decline as more direct authority and responsibility for industrial relations (and human resource) issues has been shifting to operating and line managers (Kochan, Katz, and McKersie 1986:131-132). Corporate industrial relations managers face many problems that parallel the issues confronting central union staffs. As bargaining has been shifting to local levels and focused more on qualitative issues concerning work restructuring, corporate staffs were initially caught off guard by the diminution of their influence. These corporate managers, like central unions, are searching to find new roles for themselves through which they can provide guidance to local bargaining and serve a coordinating function to local initiatives. Although whipsaw advantage now most frequently lies with employers given economic pressures, over the long term there are likely to be cases when aggressive unions can use the decentralization of bargaining to whipsaw employers. Examples of union-led whipsawing appeared at various GM plants in the spring of 1994 as a sales rebound put management under pressure to maintain output flows. Central as well as local management staffs will be pressed in the future to find ways to respond to these challenges without the assistance provided formerly through central bargaining structures and the standardization of employment conditions that typically followed from this centralization.

The Debate Surrounding the New Practices

A serious challenge to the KKM thesis comes from those who believe that we completely mischaracterize the nature of new industrial relations practices. According to these critics, the current period *does* amount to a transformation, but it is a transformation defined by a substantial increase in management's *control* of industrial relations (Parker and Slaughter 1988; Grenier 1988). KKM claim that there are new experiments (and possibilities) involving greater worker and union involvement in decision making. In contrast, the critics argue that new practices produce hyper-Tayloristic practices, a speedup in the pace of work, and the weakening of worker rights. KKM see the emergence of team systems as a shift toward higher skill work and mechanisms to involve workers in the coordination and direction of work tasks. The critics claim that teams are a device to eliminate traditional worker protections and introduce a system of "management-by-stress" (Parker and Slaughter 1988).

Academics are not the only parties arguing about whether the restructuring of industrial relations is focused on a speedup in the pace of work and the avoidance (or weakening) of unions. In the auto industry, the "New Directions" movement reflects these sentiments and there are similar militant groups opposing joint labor-management programs in other industries. Although the New Directions candidates failed in their efforts to win executive positions in the UAW, support for their positions on the shop floor is not trivial.

How Widespread is the Transformation of Industrial Relations?

Recent evidence shows that there has been widespread *experimentation* with a variety of participatory techniques and substantial changes in work rules. (Eaton and Voos 1992; Osterman 1994; Appelbaum and Batt 1993). However, the data also show that often the extent of work restructuring is limited.

There is clearly considerable diversity in the patterns of adaptation and the practices that result as the parties seek to move away from the traditional system of industrial relations. More use of contingent workers, even stronger managerial opposition to unions, and efforts to compete with a low-wage strategy exist alongside broader and deeper union-management partnerships in industries as diverse as paper, steel, autos, clothing, airlines, glass, copper, electronics, and communications. Although a significant number of union-management relationships have moved in a participatory direction, almost as many have moved toward conflict or retained traditional rigid rules.

Even where management has chosen to pursue or at least to try participatory restructuring, great difficulties have been encountered at many sites. While the various data mentioned earlier track the often piecemeal introduction of new work practices, there is a more subtle, although even more harmful, form of piecemeal adaptation. The problem is that management often is unwilling to, or unaware of the need to, make complimentary changes in managerial practices and production methods. Without these changes in management practice, changes in work practices or labor-management relations have yielded limited payouts.

Research from the auto industry demonstrates the drawbacks of piecemeal changes. In this case, work practice changes, such as the introduction of team systems and the involvement of workers in shop floor problem-solving groups, produce improvements in productivity and product quality only if they are accompanied by managerial changes. These changes include closer coordination between design and manufacturing engineering, a delayering of management, and the creation of direct channels of communication that can exploit the innovative ideas surfacing on the shop floor (MacDuffie 1992; Katz, Kochan, and Keefe 1987). In the absence of any decentralization of managerial authority (as a complement to work practice changes), workers become frustrated by the appropriation of, or lack of attention to, new ideas generated on the shop floor and also feel aggrieved by a perceived inequality of sacrifice.

American labor and management have faced many difficulties in transforming their relationships and work practices. The immediate obstacles range from pressures to cut costs (often leading to layoffs), to conflicts at the bargaining table, to changes in key leaders, and to a plateauing of employee interest in participatory processes. The parties appear at times to be on a yo-yo, oscillating between new forms of participation and a return to arm's-length and rule-bound relations (Hammer and Stern 1986).

A clear illustration of this cycle appeared at Eastern Airlines where conflicts ultimately led to the demise of the company. At some of the auto plants of GM, Ford, and Chrysler, a similar yo-yo-like oscillation appeared involving an initial, almost naive, euphoria after the quick identification of substantial benefits from worker suggestions—a euphoria that ends (in some instances shortly thereafter) when traditional labor-management conflicts reappear.

Management often avoids participatory workplace restructuring because an alternative low-wage option is readily available. In this option investments can be shifted to nonunion alternatives or moved out of the country, or union representatives can be decertified. KKM spoke of a choice between a low-cost/high-volume business strategy and a high-productivity/high-wage strategy based on product quality and product differentiation (Kochan, Katz, and McKersie 1986:241). There has been much discussion of this choice. A well-publicized report in 1990 referred to a choice between high skills or low wages, while a number of union leaders have begun speaking about the choice between the "low road and the high road" (*America's Choice* 1991). It is noteworthy that candidate Bill Clinton occasionally made mention of this choice in his presidential campaign speeches. However one refers to it, the point is that one explanation for the slow diffusion of participatory industrial relations is the fact that management can easily pursue a very different strategy. There are few incentives inducing American management to pursue work restructuring of the participatory mode.

The lack of sufficient commitment or breadth to management's restructuring efforts is by no means a problem only in unionized settings. This factor has worked to slow diffusion in many of the most sophisticated nonunion employers. In fact, in many of the successful restructuring cases unions have served a positive role through the pressure they have placed on management to follow through on its commitments, or as the slang goes; "to walk the talk."

Another factor that has slowed the diffusion and deepening of work restructuring has been the fears held by union leaders regarding the roles that they as individuals and the union as an institution will play in a restructured workplace. Although the leading edge cases discussed above illustrate the major changes that are possible, many unions have only belatedly developed the educational programs and internal discussions that can give union officers a sense of these possibilities. Contrary to the claims of the critics of participatory processes, frequently the core problem is not that participation enables management to marginalize the union by dealing directly with employees, rather it is the unions' lack of views regarding how work restructuring should proceed that has slowed the diffusion of a work restructuring that can benefit all stakeholders.

There also has been inadequate support for workplace innovation from governmental bodies. Since the 1980s the federal government more often than not has taken the position either that industrial relations and human resource issues are largely irrelevant to economic outcomes or deserve benign neglect out of a belief that best practice will naturally be created by competitive pressures. The slow diffusion of innovative work practices can be interpreted as evidence of the weak role that competitive pressure plays in bringing about *sustaining* organizational innovation.

The "Low Road" in the American Economy

In part, union fears spring from the frequent recourse management makes of the low wage "low road." Much evidence has surfaced in recent years revealing a bifurcation in the American job and income distribution as the rich get richer and the middle class shrinks. The slow pace of workplace restructuring has contributed to this bifurcation by generating incentives for the movement of production abroad, particularly in the manufacturing sector, thereby limiting the success of efforts to recapture a significant number of middle class jobs from our trading partners.

Now more than ever, the U.S. labor market is a place where any and everything goes. One can find examples of participatory work relations where employees and their union representatives engage in unprecedented involvement in decisions that traditionally have been under the purview of management. At the same time, one can find firms that compete on the basis of low wages and have work practices that exhibit the sort of managerial autocracy common to the early twentieth century. And in other cases companies are using part-time workers, independent contractors, and consultants to perform work that in the past was done by full-time employees.

In a number of instances multinational corporations recently have expanded investments in the United States in order to gain access to low wages and passive employees. This factor may have contributed to the high rates of migration of manufacturing from Canada to the United States in the 1990s. Even some Japanese electronics companies have located low-wage, labor-intensive manufacturing in California and adopted low-wage, nonunion personnel practices rather than the prototypical Japanese management systems associated with large firms in Japan or with NUMMI and Japanese joint ventures in the auto and steel industries (Milkman 1991). While this may lead to employment growth in the United States, it is noteworthy that much of this industrial migration is motivated by efforts to escape high labor costs in Canada or Japan and to take advantage of low wages in the United States and does not appear to be driven by access to highly skilled American workers. While the high wage-low skill dichotomy may be overly simplistic, it is helpful in understanding an ominous trend underway in North American industrial development.

The Sophisticated Human Resource Model

A higher, although also nonunion, road has been pursued by those firms described in KKM that follow the "sophisticated human resource model". In recent years these nonunion employers have had great difficulty maintaining the employment stabilization policies that had been a hallmark of their employment systems. The late

1980s and early 1990s have seen unprecedented layoffs at some of the leading nonunion employers, including IBM, Digital Equipment Corporation, and Kodak. It is noteworthy that layoffs in these and so many other firms in this period have extended into the ranks of white collar (including managerial) employees.

There is some evidence that layoffs have created substantial fears among employees and weakened their commitment to their employer (Katz forthcoming; Keefe and Boroff forthcoming) But, it is telling that even in the face of these layoffs and the apparent weakening of employee loyalty, unions have had little success in organizing the sophisticated nonunion employers.

Union Organizing Trends

The last fifteen years have seen a further decline in the percentage of the private sector workforce that is unionized. A number of unions recently have initiated serious efforts to modernize and expand their organizing strategies with the comprehensive saturation approach of SEIU being an especially prominent example. New research shows that these efforts, in particular what Bronfenbrenner terms a rank-and-file intensive strategy, have had somewhat greater organizing success (Bronfenbrenner 1993). Furthermore, the AFL-CIO Organizing Institute and various internal national union efforts have worked to spread a rank-and-file organizing approach. While a number of unions and the AFL-CIO are working on new organizing methods, new approaches have yet to be widely adopted. At this point in time, there is no sign of any sizeable increase in union membership ranks, and not even a hint that such regeneration is imminent.

Unions continue to face difficulties in organizing for a number of reasons, not the least of which derive from continuation of the employer strategies and sophisticated human resource policies identified in KKM. And yet a continuation by most unions of the traditional representation approach (with its focus on the grievance procedure and formalized work rules and seniority rights) has not proven to be attractive to employees who express concerns for issues such as day care and career development, and desire to exert influence over corporate reorganization that is taking place at an accelerating pace. Union efforts along these lines are hampered by the widening demographic diversity within the American workforce, which makes it difficult to form coalitions bridging the wide spectrum of interests that exist among unorganized workers.

Furthermore, union organizing efforts continue to be hampered by the ability of employers to pursue low-wage alternatives, including moving production offshore.

While there is has been much talk in the new Clinton administration about addressing the disadvantages the existing labor laws and their administration provide for union organizing, to date there has been no evidence that union organizing has benefited greatly from the election of a Democratic president. The most significant effort in this vein involves the appointment of a commission (the Commission on the Future of Worker Management Relations) given the task of reassessing the nation's labor and employment laws.

Final Thoughts

There is no easy way to summarize the recent evolution of employment practices in either the union or nonunion sectors of the American economy. Perhaps most striking is the wide diversity in trends and the repercussions that diversity exerts on the process of bargaining (particularly the decentralization of bargaining structures) and the roles played by unions and industrial relations managers.

Endnotes

1. Profit sharing bonuses were also very large for executives at Ford and Chrysler in 1993. In 1993, two hundred Chrysler executives received bonuses that amounted to 100 percent of their annual salaries (Lavin 1994).

2. Ford and Chrysler, because of expanding sales, from the mid-1980s on made little use of the income and employment funds that were included in their contracts with the UAW. The auto companies also utilize attrition to create job openings that workers can be placed into and thereby avoid the need for income security payouts. The contracts, however, do require the companies to replace one-half of all the jobs lost through attrition. This latter requirement is quite novel within American collective bargaining.

3. Note, these statistical analyses also found that multifirm agreements were more commonly found in industries with low degrees of concentration.

4. For criticism of worker participation and joint activities, see Parker and Slaughter 1988.

References

America's Choice: High Skills or Low Wages. 1991. Rochester, N.Y.: The National Center on Education and the Economy.

Applebaum, Eileen, and Rosemary Batt. 1993. *The New American Workplace: Transforming Work Systems in the United States*. Ithaca, N.Y.: ILR Press.

Bronfenbrenner, Kate L. 1993. "Seeds of Resurgence: Successful Union Strategies for Winning Certification Elections and First Contracts in the 1980s and Beyond." Ph.D. diss., NYSSILR, Cornell University.

Budd, John W. 1992. "The Determinants and Extent of UAW Pattern Bargaining." *Industrial and Labor Relations Review*, 45, no. 3 (April): 523-39.

Cappelli, Peter. 1985. "Competitive Pressures and Labor Relations in the Airline Industry." *Industrial Relations*, 24 (Fall): 316-38.

Deaton, D. R., and P. B. Beaumont. 1980. "The Determinants of Bargaining Structure: Some Large-Scale Survey Evidence for Britain." *British Journal of Industrial Relations*, 18 (July): 202-16.

Eaton, Adrienne E., and Paula B. Voos. 1992. "Unions and Contemporary Innovations in Work Organizations, Compensation, and Employee Participation," In *Unions and Economic Competitiveness*, L. Mishel and P. Voos, eds., pp. 173-216. Washington, D.C.: Economic Policy Institute.

Erickson, Christopher L. 1992. "Wage Rule Formation in the Aerospace Industry." *Industrial and Labor Relations Review* 45, no. 2 (April): 507-22.

Greenberg, David H. 1967. "The Structure of Collective Bargaining and Some of Its Determinants." In *Proceedings of the Nineteenth Annual Winter Meeting*, Gerald G. Somers, ed., 343-53. Madison, Wis.: Industrial Relations Research Association.

Grenier, Guillermo J. 1988. *Inhuman Relations*. Philadelphia: Temple University Press.

Hammer, Tove, and Robert N. Stern. 1986. "A Yo-Yo Model of Cooperation: Union Participation in Management at the Rath Packing Company." *Industrial and Labor Relations Review* 39 (April): 337-49.

Hendricks, Wallace E., and Lawrence M. Kahn. 1982. "The Determinants of Bargaining Structure in U.S. Manufacturing Industries." *Industrial and Labor Relations Review* 35, no. 2 (January): 181-95.

Katz, Harry C. 1985. *Shifting Gears: Changing Labor Relations in the U.S. Automobile Industry*. Cambridge: MIT Press.

-----. 1993. "The Decentralization of Collective Bargaining: A Literature Review and Comparative Analysis." *Industrial and Labor Relations Review* 47,no. 1, (October): 3-22.

Katz, Harry C. Forthcoming. "Downsizing and Employment Insecurity" In *The Changing American Economy*, P. Cappelli, ed. National Planning Association.

Katz, Harry C., and Thomas A. Kochan. 1992. *An Introduction to Collective Bargaining and Industrial Relations*. New York: McGraw-Hill.

Katz, Harry C., Thomas A. Kochan, and Jeffrey H. Keefe. 1987. "Industrial Relations Performance and Productivity in the U.S. Automobile Industry." *Brookings Papers on Economic Activity* 3: 685-715.

Katz, Harry C., and John Paul MacDuffie. Forthcoming. "Collective Bargaining in the U.S. Auto Assembly Sector." In *Contemporary Collective Bargaining in the Private Sector*, Paula Voos, ed. Madison, Wis.: Industrial Relations Research Association.

Katz, Harry C., and Noah Meltz. 1991. "Profit Sharing and Auto Workers' Earnings: The United States vs. Canada." *Relations Industrielles* 42, no. 3: 513-30.

Katz, Harry C., and Charles F. Sabel. 1985. "Industrial Relations and Industrial Adjustment in the Car Industry." *Industrial Relations* 24 (Fall): 295-315.

Keefe, Jeffrey H., and Karen Boroff. Forthcoming. "Telecommunications Labor-Management Relations after Divestiture. "In *Contemporary Collective Bargaining in the Private Sector*, Paula Voos, ed. Madison, Wis.: Industrial Relations Research Association.

Kochan, Thomas A, Harry C. Katz, and Robert B. McKersie. 1986. *The Transformation of American Industrial Relations*. New York: Basic Books, 1st ed.

-----. 1994. *The Transformation of American Industrial Relations*. Ithaca, N.Y.: ILR Press. 2d ed.

Lavin, Douglas. 1994. "Chrysler Aides to Get Bonuses Equal to Salaries." *Wall Street Journal*, p. A-3.

Locke, Richard M. Forthcoming. *Rebuilding the Economy: Local Politics and Industrial Change in Contemporary Italy*. Ithaca, N.Y.: Cornell University Press.

MacDuffie, John Paul. 1992. "Beyond Mass Production: Organizational Flexibility and Manufacturing Performance in the World Auto Industry." Unpublished paper, Wharton School, University of Pennsylvania. September.

Marginson, Paul, et al. 1988. *Beyond the Workplace: Managing Industrial Relations in Multi-Establishment Enterprises.* Oxford: Blackwell.

Mathews, John. 1989. *Tools of Change: New Technology and the Democratization of Work.* Sydney: Pluto Press.

Milkman, Ruth. 1991. *Japan's California Factories: Labor Relations and Economic Globalization.* Los Angeles: Institute of Industrial Relations, University of California, Los Angeles.

Osterman, Paul. 1993."How Common Is Workplace Transformation and Who Adopts It?" *Industrial and Labor Relations Review* 47,no. 2 (January): 173-188.

Parker, Mike and Jane Slaughter. 1988. Choosing Sides: Unions and the Team Concept. Boston: South End Press.

Piore, Michael J., and Charles F. Sabel. 1984. *The Second Industrial Divide.* New York: Basic Books.

Pontusson, Jonas, and Peter Swenson. 1992. "Markets, Production, Institutions, and Politics: Why Swedish Employers Have Abandoned the Swedish Model." Paper presented at the Eighth International Conference of Europeanists, The Council for European Studies, Chicago. March 27-29.

Purcell, John, and Bruce Ahlstrand. 1989. "Corporate Strategy and the Management of Employee Relations in the Multi-divisional Company." *British Journal of Industrial Relations*, 27, no. 3. (November): 396-417.

Storey, John. 1992. *Developments in the Management of Human Resources: An Analytical Review.* Oxford: Blackwell.

Streeck, Wolfgang. 1984. "Neo-Corporatist Industrial Relations and the Economic Crisis in West Germany." In *Order and Conflict in Contemporary Capitalism*, John H. Goldthorpe, ed., 291-314. Oxford: Oxford University Press.

Thelen, Kathleen A. 1991. *Union of Parts: Labor Politics in Postwar Germany.* Ithaca, N.Y.: Cornell University Press.

Turner, Lowell. 1991. Democracy at Work: The Changing World Market and the Future of Unions., Ithaca, N.Y.: Cornell University Press.

Weber, Arnold B. 1961. "Introduction," in *The Structure of Collective Bargaining.* Arnold Weber, ed., New York: The Free Press, pp. sv-xxxii.

Industrial Democracy, Total Quality and Mexico's Changing Labor Relations

Enrique de la Garza Toledo

This paper explains how Mexico's presidency is forging a new ideology as an alternative to what is known as the "Mexican Revolution" ideology. The old ideology prevailed in the Mexican state, the Institutional Revolutionary Party (PRI), and the trade unions up to 1982. The new ideology is called social liberalism, and the labor relations component of the new ideology is becoming known as industrial democracy. The new ideology of industrial democracy is related to employers' efforts to improve total quality. The new focus on industrial democracy and total quality has taken specific shape in the National Agreement for Increased Productivity and Quality (ANEPC), and in the union education programs offered by the National Solidarity Institute.

We will now analyze the links between neoliberalism, industrial democracy and trade-union neocorporatism. We will also examine whether the new ideology coincides with the actual changes that have occurred in labor relations over the past decade in Mexico.

Social Liberalism, Industrial Democracy, and Total Quality

Until a few years ago, the symbiotic relationship that prevailed between the Mexican state and the trade unions gave them a common ideology, the "Mexican Revolution." That is, the state and the unions considered themselves heirs to the Mexican Revolution of 1910-17, and adhered to its component ideologies. Those ideologies were nationalism (linked to a well-defined national identity and to the idea that national development would be directed by the state), statism (the state as the great articulator of identity, development, and social justice, and thereby determining the direction taken by national history), and populism (in a highly unequal society, the state should be the tutor of the poor and should carry out a form of social justice by restoring usurped rights) (Cordova 1976).

The Mexican revolution included an ideology with a powerful body of ideas that contributed to Mexico's cultural identity and state domination up to the beginning of the 1980s. Nonetheless, there were no explicit links between the revolutionary ideology and the forces of production. On the one hand, the revolutionary ideology was linked to a concept of economic development involving partial state involvement and a mixed

20

economy. On the other hand, production problems and workers' rights were not addressed directly by the ideology of the Mexican revolution.

In 1982 a rupture began between the state policies and the Mexican revolution ideology. This split did not occur overnight, nor was a new ideology generated instantaneously. The rupture began as an economic one with the state defining the economic crisis as a fiscal one. The split continued in the midst of a debate concerning state intervention in the economy. An alternative focus for state policies was developed over a decade's time. The emphasis here involved an economic policy of privatization and deregulation and, in the social arena, through the development of a National Solidarity Program (PRONASOL), a program of assistance for the poorest sections of society.

Finally, on March 5, 1992, on the anniversary of the PRI's founding, the new state ideology was baptized by President Salinas as "social liberalism." The new state ideology proposed enhanced economic relations without political integration and explicitly opposed a nationalist program based on fears of foreign entanglements. The new state ideology included the following key platforms:

> 1. Instead of a proprietary state, the new ideology proposed a "solidary" state that regulates and compensates in response to imperfections in the market. The state, however, no longer plays a principal role in economic development.

> 2. In opposition to a populist notion of social justice, the new ideology seeks a non-paternalistic model by seeking to incorporate those who benefit from state policies. The new ideology does not promise what it cannot deliver, nor does it sacrifice the economy for social justice. In addition, the new ideology combines individualism with communitarianism (Salinas de Gortari 1992).

The fusion of economic neoliberalism with the new concept of a "solidary" state (the National Solidarity Program) had two components (Mayer 1993). There is neoliberalism for efficient firms, with some direction of the external and the domestic market. In addition, economic development is left to the initiative of individual investors, and the needs for efficiency are satisfied by balancing commercial logic with the solidarity state. The latter helps support those individuals whose problems are not solved by the market, originally by supplying indispensable goods, and currently by providing support for inefficient producers.

The two components of the new, social liberal ideology are not equally important. The most important objective is development of a commercial sector. Economic policy and legislative changes are directed toward this objective. Social concerns are subordinated to neoliberal economic needs. The fact that social liberalism has a dualistic conception of society does not mean that there are no points of compromise and accommodation between economic and social concerns. For instance, PRONSOL is funded in part by the sale of state enterprises and plays a key role in the search for the sort of social peace that will allow for the continuation of market reforms, economic growth, and economic modernization. Labor policy places a subordinate role within the economic model. Labor markets, far from being liberalized, are controlled by the state much more firmly than in any previous periods of corporatism. Nor has the political system—in particular, the electoral process—opened up to full democratic procedures.

The form of social liberalism introduced included corporative liberalism for the trade unions, but authoritarianism remained in the political sphere (Enrique 1993). Social liberalism also included the discarding of egalitarianism as a political objective, an objective that previously had contributed to the rhetoric of the Mexican Revolution. In the new social liberalism, the abstract concept of market freedom predominated over concepts concerning democracy and equality. All this translated into a state become less dominating in the economic sphere, but no less strong in policies and labor relations than in the past (Garza 1992 and Crozier et al. 1975).

The key aspect of the rupture between the Mexican Revolution ideology and social liberalism was a movement away from the conception of the state as the center of the economic process, or the party responsible for social justice. Nevertheless, the state continued to regulate the economy, although in the end economic development will be determined by individual investment decisions. Further, the state no longer claims to be the universal benefactor. The determination of income and employment conditions is commercialized, while social assistance programs are maintained for those who are unable to subsist by their own means.

With regard to labor, on May 1, 1990, President Salinas outlined the following as key characteristics of the new unionism in Mexico:

1. Decentralization of the firm and shopfloor— level labor relations. Workers and management are now free to confer and reach agreement, and there is to be decentralization in the decision-making processes within trade union confederations.

2. Decentralization, however, does not mean pluralism in a political-theory sense, but rather, its purpose is to preserve the "historical alliance between trade unions and the state," or, in other words, to promote corporatism.

3. The new unionism will no longer maintain a confrontational relationship between capital and labor, but, rather, negotiation will predominate and unions are to have common cause with management in efforts to improve productivity.

4. For all this to happen, a new labor culture is needed among workers and in unions. That is, a culture of productivity must prevail and there must be more representative unions that are capable of productively mobilizing their members (Salinas de Gortari 1990).

A new unionism consistent with social liberalism would have to be a state-corporative one, instead of a pluralistic one, so as to establish a corporatist link with employers, with a common concern for productivity. (Schmitter might call this a combination of macro and micro-corporatism.)

The presidential speech that formulated this new brand of unionism coincided with the founding of a new trade union federation (the Federation of Goods and Services

Unions, FESEBES). The founding statutes of FESEBES expressed concepts very similar to those in the president's speech, summarized below : (Estatutos 1990)

1. Unions should be aware that a new model of economic development exists and they should be active participants in the new economy;

2. the constitutional political pact should be maintained;

3. unions should be active and take initiatives in the production process;

4. the union should be based on formal agreements with management, but continue to use all legal forms of struggle;

5. unions should be more democratic with no automatic reelection of leaders and no intervention of FESEBES in political parties. Workers should be free to choose their own political affiliation.

FESEBES concurs, in general terms, with the new corporatism proposed by President Salinas. The coporatism includes a macro level, with participation by unions alongside the state in the design of economic policy, a micro level, and with participation by workers in the ownership, organization and administration of companies.

The presidential speech and ideas expressed by the FESEBES formulate the outlines of the "industrial democracy" strategy. This strategy involves shared decision making in organizations and in administration. The strategy includes macrocorporatism, since the state, together with the large trade union confederations and business associations, delineates the general outlines of the tripartite agreements. These outlines are then made more specific at the company level. Furthermore, the doctrine of industrial democracy in Mexico implies that some portion of the company shares should be owned by the workers or the unions (Giugni et al. 1978).

The concepts of social liberalism, the new unionism, and industrial democracy were crystallized together for the first time by the signing of the ANEPC by the heads of union, business, and state organizations (STPS 1992). It was hoped that the ANEPC would serve as the concrete starting point of a new corporatist pact and be unaffected by electoral politics or political parties and focus primarily on productivity concerns. The ANEPC combines the ideologies of social liberalism, the new unionism, and industrial democracy with a management doctrine concerning total quality. The latter involved abandoning the previous acceptance of Taylorism and Fordism. New production and quality concepts recognized a radical separation between conception and execution and between production, maintenance, and quality control. The total quality movement admitted that traditional work practices of workers' initiative and involvement and prevented work that was individualized, segmented, monotonous, repetitive, and standardized. Traditional work practices were linked to mass production. The ANEPC establishes that the concept of productivity should be seen as problematic. Productivity should not be conceived simply as the relation between product and input, but as a result of the interaction of several factors, that is, as a social relation.

The total quality movement claimed that in order to increase productivity, the work process had to be humanized. It should be participative and collective, with permanent, rather than routine, retraining. Work systems would be more flexible. Productivity bonuses would be better distributed and the unions explicitly recognized as the intermediaries between management and the workforce and their role would be enhanced through productivity-based pay. All this was intended to promote cooperative worker-employer relations and increase productivity.

The ANEPC is much more than a program to raise business productivity through the collaborative efforts of unions and workers. It is a neocorporatist model (both state and business corporatism). This program does not coincide with either of Schmiter's two pure models (of state or of society). In the new Mexican model, the State does not remain on the sidelines. Rather, it is committed to promoting a national labor policy based on agreement, and to creating a productive social labor movement and a new culture of labor, as well as promoting the signing of a national agreement and agreements between unions and business.

The ANEPC conforms to the most advanced ideas of the management doctrine of total quality by adding a role for the new unionism and industrial democracy. The latter two concepts give this form of corporatism greater specificity in terms of the roles of management and the state.

To summarize, Figure 1 shows that via the doctrines of social liberalism, the new unionism, industrial democracy, and total quality, an ideology is being forged. On the level of industrial relations, the new ideology can be seen as an alternative to that of the Mexican Revolution. On a macropolitical and macroeconomic level, the state remains the great coordinator and supervisor. In this sense the state has no reason to cease being authoritarian regarding labor, inasmuch as the state is still thought to truly know which direction the country should take. On a macro level, the state promotes labor policies which, it is hoped, will guide labor relations at the work place level. The State's coordinating and supervisory role is consistent with a decreased role for the state in economic policy where public funding is no longer the force behind capital accumulation. The neocorporatism promoted by the State, with its new industrial democracy, implies a decentralization of decision making, without the state giving up its authoritarian control in the political sphere.

The new ideology renewed worker representation, without allowing democracy to become an intrinsic value. It has been instrumental in achieving a consensus on productivity, eliminating confrontation with capital, and replacing confrontation with agreement (and here the state does not hesitate to be authoritarian with those who have not understood that times have changed and class struggle is a thing of the past).

Macrocorporatism is intertwined with, and induces, a microcorporatism through industrial democracy. The new culture of labor includes bilateralism and a distribution of benefits between workers and employers. This microcorporatism is consistent with the new need of businesses to ensure their market position. Faced with the globalization of the economy, business relies on the total quality focus to improve competitiveness. Neoliberalism in the market, state macrocorporatism, and company microcorporatism together form a consistent discourse.

This process can also be interpreted as an attempt to reconstruct the system of industrial relations while meeting economic constraints by taking up old state-corporatist traditions, as well as new management doctrines of total quality. In this new model, the relationship between unions and the PRI disappears. The social security system becomes less important as remunerations and private insurance plans are decentralized. The focal point of the system becomes the pact promoted by the state and the authoritarian use of labor legislation to constrain the participants within the model. I have given the name of neoliberal corporatism to this constellation of macro, micro, political, productive and economic relations involving the state, businesses, and unions.

Industrial Democracy and Changing Labor Relations in Mexico

Industrial democracy, an ideological and programmatic formulation of trade unionism, usually originated with labor movements and with social democratic political forces. In Mexico, industrial democracy was never taken up by the social authoritarian state or by corporatist trade unions. It has no precedent and there is no history of labor demands unified around an industrial democracy formulation, with the exception of a few, very short singular episodes that did not leave traditions.

These episodes include the workers' administrations in the railways and in Pemex, the state oil concern, during President Lázaro Cárdenas's official term. In addition, there are a few factory committees in the 1970s that were motivated by independent union movements: Dina (autos), Nissan and Constructora de Carros de Ferrocarril (railway-carriage construction).

Mexican unions have been, above all, state unions, either allied with, or against, the state. The state has provided their main arena of struggle and negotiation. Any interest the unions may have shown in the production process or in their management has been, at best, defensive. Rather, Mexican unions have focused on the protection of working conditions, health and preservation of their representation monopoly. That is, the unions have concerned themselves principally with employment conditions (their demands center around the conditions under which the workforce is bought and sold, employment security issues, and working conditions). Unions have also been patrimonial, an important aspect of their domination of the workers. In particular, this domination has manifested itself in the exchange of permits, certificates of leave, low workloads, and so on, in exchange for the consensus granted to union leaders.

To summarize, the doctrine of trade union democracy as it has existed in Mexico has been invented by the state hierarchy in an attempt to provide the ideological foundation for industrial relations. This is the function unions previously fulfilled by pursuing the Mexican Revolution ideology.

The doctrine of total quality has a different history in Mexico. It made its first appearance in business discussions in the 1970s. In the 1980s it became the dominant management doctrine for production. Later, the state adopted the total quality doctrine and some unions tried to incorporate some of its tenets into their strategies. In Mexico, management efforts to improve total quality have been linked to privatization, deregulation, and antibenefactor state currents of thought. The goals of total quality have been strictly limited to achieving greater productivity and higher quality at the company level by making use of labor flexibility. This did not require broad changes in the "system of industrial relations." The focus was on the need for flexibility in labor legislation, the privatization of social security, and opposition to union corporatism.

Up to 1990, the presidency of the country attempted to reconstruct the "system of industrial relations" and labor relations, as well as corporatism. The language of "industrial democracy" was used to create a new discourse. But a discourse in social relations can have various functions. It can express part of a nondiscursive reality (epistemological content). It can signify a project to be carried out through the actions of subjects (utopian content). Or it can conceal a reality that goes against the discourse (concealing content).

Labor relations in Mexico, understood as worker-employer relations within the production process, have a codified level (contained in collective contracts, internal rulings on labor, or special agreements signed by employers and unions). Labor relations also have an informal level which, by whatever manner, recognize practices sanctioned by custom.

Labor relations have been undergoing radical change since 1981. The first of these changes coincided with the economic crisis of the early 1980s. They were erratic and circumscribed. They probably began with the opening of the General Motors and Chrysler plants in Ramos Arizpe. These plants were intended to serve foreign markets with new organizational practices and a collective contract that was remarkable for the auto sector because of its flexibility. In 1982, the management of Dina, then a state-owned auto company, proposed making the collective contract more flexible, something it has yet to achieve.

After 1985, when the state and the auto and other companies recognized the need for industrial reconversion in the face of new market conditions, along with the steady movement of the State toward neoliberalism, collective contracts began to become more flexible in many large and medium-sized companies. This trend continues today. Contract changes are still being made, but the focus has been clear from the beginning—flexibility.

Labor flexibility in Mexico means the ability to rapidly adjust the number of workers, their activities in the working process, and, to a lesser degree, their salaries, according to the daily needs of production and the market. To achieve flexibility, worker-employer relations have been altered along with organizational policies, often under the label of total quality policy.

Companies vary greatly in the extent of labor flexibility they have achieved. In the first place, one must recognize that only 28 percent of salaried workers over the age of fourteen are unionized in Mexico. Without a union, there is no collective contract (Garza 1993). Furthermore, employees in positions of confidence (such as supervisors and those working in planning, administration, and control) are legally prevented from joining blue-collar unions. Unionization by economic activity is very unequal. It is almost non-existent in farming, trade, and traditional services. It is prevalent in the state bureaucracy, large industry, and modern services, and is particularly high in state-owned companies and large private companies. Unionization is modest in medium-sized businesses and virtually nonexistent in small businesses. The factors that influence the degree of contract flexibility in Mexico include the geographical area, the previous nature of the contract, the nature of the union, government labor policy for that particular sector, management modernization strategies, and management and worker cultures.

I now examine the degree to which and how flexibility has been increased in collective contracts and corporate policies across different economic sectors since 1982.

In-bond Processing (Maquiladoras) on the Northern Border

This sector has been the most dynamic sector in the Mexican economy over the past ten years. It employs half a million workers, predominantly women, who have an average of six years of education. Most of the workers are between the ages of twenty-two and twenty-six. This sector's productive processes consist mainly of assembly lines. New organizational practices have spread faster in the maquiladoras than in any other sector in Mexico. Fifty percent of border establishments use a just-in-time system. Sixty percent of the personnel of these establishments are organized into work teams. Functional mobility exists among 40 percent of the workers and there is internal rotation among 30 percent of the employees (Carrillo 1991).

Two different situations exist with respect to collective bargaining contracts (Quintero and Eugenia de la O 1992). Contracts in Tijuana and northern Sonora provide management with unilateral flexibility. In this region, the unions are "protection unions." This is the term given in Mexico to rubber-stamp unions that are "arranged" between employers and trade union confederations as a way of preventing the workers from unionizing themselves. In these unions the workers are usually unaware that they belong to the organization because they never see the collective bargaining contracts nor their union "leaders."

A typical contract from the northern Sonora has fifteen clauses. Management enjoys almost complete flexibility in hiring and firing, in the use of casual labor or subcontracted workers, the filling of positions of confidence, transferring of workers within the labor process, or work-hour adjustments (such as making employees work during public holidays).

In the Chihuahua region, two types of contracts exist. Some, like those in Tijuana, are highly flexible. They are designed in discussions with the Regional Confederation of Workers and Peasant Farmers. Others, such as those used in Tamaulipas, are agreed upon with the Confederation of Mexican Workers (CTM). These contracts are flexible, but contain a certain degree of bilateralism.

The type of contract common in Matamoros, in the state of Tamaulipas, contains some rigidities which originate with the CTM's interest in maintaining its representational monopoly. This translates into almost total unionization, as well as well-defined conditions and significant benefits, such as a forty-hour work week and the absorption of social security taxes by the company. Nonetheless, as Carrillo (1991) states in his representative survey of the maquiladoras, "in general, there are no rules for the regulation of employment, promotion and mobility, and the unions do not participate in decision-making regarding the labor process."

In brief, with the exception of Matamoros, the northern maquiladoras show a high level of labor deregulation, in favor of, and at the demand of, management. Labor relations, in spite of the extensive use of new organizational and production policies, are very far from any sort of post-Fordist utopia (Taddei 1992; Pozas 1992; Carrillo 1991; Lara 1992).

Large State-Owned Enterprises, Private Companies, and Transnationals

State-owned enterprises, both those remaining state-owned and those that have been privatized over the past five years, have probably shown the greatest degree of unilateral flexibility in their collective contracts (Bensusan and Garcia 1990). The airlines of Aeromexico and Mexicana have the highest level of flexibility. Pemex and the Federal Electricity Commission are found lower down the scale. At the other extreme, in what is something of an anomaly, the Central Light and Power Company, for political reasons, has not made its collective contract flexible at all. In transnational companies there is also a clear tendency toward unilateral flexibility. Nevertheless, those plants that have opened since the 1980s (such as Ford in Hermosillo) were highly flexible at start-up. Older plants owned by transnationals are generally still engaged in various stages of this process of change (Mora et al. 1990).

Areas targeted for flexibilization by the management of large companies in Mexico are:

1. Freedom by management to employ casual or subcontracted labor to perform tasks within the plant.

2. Freedom to employ new staff with a minimum of union involvement.

3. Fewer restrictions on management in the disciplining of workers.

4. The establishment of internal mobility across positions, categories, departments, shifts, and workplaces.

5. Pay scales incorporating functional mobility.

6. Promotion by qualification instead of by seniority.

7. Reductions in the number of unionized workers through the transfer of laborers to positions of confidence (that is, management).

The larger companies have more extensively introduced certain aspects of total quality, such as quality-control circles, statistical control of production, and just-in-time systems. This is most evident in export companies and transnationals, followed by private national companies, with enterprises still owned by the state bringing up the rear (Arteaga et al. 1989).

"Standard" Contracts

In Mexico it is possible for one ("standard") contract to govern an entire sector, whether or not this sector contains a variety of companies and unions. Sectors that have these contracts include rubber, radio and television, sugar, and textiles. The latter is divided into the subsectors of stiff fibers; cotton; wool; synthetic fibers and silk; knitwear; ribbons; elastics; and lace and tape. Standard contractors are probably the most complex and rigid in the country. Generally, they have not changed much in the last ten years, despite a level of management that has generated prolonged strikes. Standard contracts do not all have the same degree of rigidity. At the top of the scale (most rigid) are those for radio and television, rubber, and knitwear. The rest of the textile industry follows, while sugar occupies the bottom of the scale.

The lack of change in standard contracts is probably due to the strength of corporatist union control, which has protected unions and workers. In the face of these obstacles, management has opted for a "termite strategy" of flexibilization. This strategy

28

includes the signing of single-company contracts that violate the standard contract, or the establishment of flexibility in practice, although not in formal contract language (Mondragón 1993; Román 1992; Covarrubias 1992).

Contracts in the "Sham Unions"

In Mexico, "sham unions" are those that depend directly on the employers without state mediation. These unions do not belong to the Workers' Congress, nor are they connected to the independent left-wing unions. Monterrey is their stronghold, although they have also spread to Guadalajara, Guanajuato, and Puebla. They account for 8.7 percent of all unions, and most of the companies involved are linked to the one-time "Monterrey group."

In sham union contracts flexibility tends to be high. Subcontracting is permitted as is casual hiring, internal mobility, and cutbacks in order to modernize production. The working week is long (often forty-eight hours). Management is free to fill positions of confidence. The hours of work can be changed to adapt to the company's production needs, and the unions are committed to supporting production plans, including an explicit commitment for productivity increases. In recent years the flexibility provisions in these contracts have not been significantly modified.

Despite the fact that total quality has become almost an official doctrine in the large companies of Monterrey, only a minority (2 percent) have experienced systematic application of total-quality programs. Most of these companies experience high levels of conflict between employers, middle managers, and workers.

Labor Contracts in Small and Medium-Sized Businesses

In these sectors labor contracts range from those that are very flexible and similar to contracts of the nothern maquiladoras, to contracts that are more similar to the protective contracts found in the larger companies. In general, however, prior to the wave of flexibilization, contracts in this sector were either highly or moderately flexible. Recent changes have been less drastic here than in the large companies.

Collective Contracts in the Universities

There are sixty-five collective bargaining contracts in Mexican universities. University unions are grouped into five large organizations: the Single National Union of University Workers (twenty-three unions), the National Coordinator of University Unions, the National Confederation of University Workers (which in turn, is comprised of the National Association of Associations and Unions of University Academic Personnel, with seventeen unions), and the Single Federation of University Administrators' Unions (twelve unions). There is also a National Federation of Unions of University Academic Personnel, and one independent union.

Furthermore, a distinction must be made between those contracts governing labor relations for academic staff and those applying to administrators and service personnel. In the first case, the following significant changes were made in the 1980s: 1) union exclusion from the admission and promotion of academic personnel, and 2) the institution of productivity-related incentive plans for research and teaching which are not included within the collective contract.

By contrast, the contracts governing administrators and service personnel have not changed. They continue to be extremely rigid. The union recommends new employees and controls casual labor and positions of confidence. The cataloge of positions is agreed upon bilaterally. Neither functional nor internal mobility are stipulated. The use of overtime is regulated, as are disciplinary procedures. There are joint commissions on hygiene, safety, and retraining. Promotion is based on seniority. In contrast to academic personnel, incentives for administrators and service personnel have so far been negligible, being confined to punctuality and attendance bonuses. In these contracts, however, there is no room for union initiatives concerning new technology or organizational restructuring.

The State Bureaucracy

State employees, not to be confused with those who work in state-owned enterprises, are governed by special legislation (Paragraph B of Article 123 of the Constitution; the Federal Law on State Employees; the Law on the Social Security Institute for State Employees; the Organic Law on Public Administration; the Federal Law on the Responsibilities of Public Services and the Law on Civil Bonuses, Incentives, and Compensations). In addition, each government department has what are called general working conditions (CGT). The CGT establish the manner in which workers are expected to perform their tasks. The legislation prohibits collective contracts, and the CGT are not legally binding. Instead, they are issued by the corresponding authority after taking into account the views of the union.

The CGT combine unilateralism and flexibility with elements of rigidity that originate in the legislation listed above. These CGT protect state employees from being removed from their posts, prevent employees from being fired except for serious offenses, and restrict internal mobility. In recent years, the government has been trying to homogenize the CGT and promotion scales by means of the Civil Service Careers System. This has been foiled, however, by the heterogeneity of public administration functions and the efforts of public administrators to make labor relations flexible in concrete situations but not standardized. Thus, the Civil Service Careers System remains an unfinished project, focused only on specific issues and often disregarded by authorities in the various governmental departments (Tiburcio 1992).

Final Reflections

The presidency of the country has in just a few years constructed an alternative discourse to the one that prevailed in the postrevolutionary state up to 1982—that is, the previous Mexican Revolution discourse. The new discourse is about social liberalism. It combines a liberal doctrine with a supposed concern for market imperfections. The Mexican state, for its part, has been forging a specific "system of industrial relations" at the center of which are tripartite negotiations that are mediated by the State and subordinated to political and economic policies. That is, at the center of the new industrial relations is a state-corporate relationship. This relationship subordinates unions to the state and promotes the resolution of industrial relations conflicts. The system of industrial relations and the political system have become intimately related, forming part of the corporatist net spread by the state and unions over the workers. This net embraces both industrial relations and employment issues including: social security, the negotiation of labor disputes, the electoral-political system, government posts, and positions of popular representation (Covarrubias and Solis 1993).

The system of labor relations has undergone significant change in the face of the restructuring of large companies and the process of state reform. Important matters have been settled without union involvement or settled with unions in a ritualistic manner. The state had two alternatives. One option was to abide by the neoliberal premises upheld by large sectors of the business community stating that consensus should ultimately be left to the market. That is, it should not be necessary to resort to special mediators or representation of interests outside the processes of citizen democracy. But, the Mexican political elite, including its current neoliberal component, have been unwilling to rely solely on the market and have found it useful to uphold traditions that have helped these elites maintain political power.

Thus, although it is still an unfinished project, an attempt is being made to forge a neocorporatist discourse that would not come into conflict with neoliberal economic policies. To achieve this, the management doctrine of total quality has been incorporated into the corporatist relationship. That is, by means of neoliberal corporatism, an attempt is being made to preserve a macro-level pact between the state, unions, and business organizations. This pact is partially macroeconomic (controlling the principal macro variables), but it is also a productivity pact intended to increase business competitiveness in the context of a deregulated and globalized economy. A pact of this kind cannot, like the previous one, be restricted to the state; it must include middle and micro-levels if it is to provide competitive production.

The pact offers business a stable macroeconomic environment—above all, low inflation and attractive exchange and interest rates. It also promotes a state and unions that adjust their policies for the benefit of business productivity through agreement instead of conflict, and a culture of labor that embraces total quality. The corporatist pact offers survival to unions (defying predictions that unions would be excluded from the highest levels of state power), wage increases linked to productivity increase, job growth generated by a growing economy spurred by the North American Free Trade Agreement, and "industrial democracy." The pact also offers unions participation in the plans being made for modernization, and in the processes of economic organization and administration. Furthermore, unions are offered a stake in company ownership as part of a micro-level alliance never before seen in Mexico. The new "system of industrial relations," far from leaving all outcomes to market forces, requires that a pact be forged at the level of economic production, and therefore, has been extended to middle and micro-levels through worker involvement. For the moment, the pact leaves aside social security, party politics, and union intervention in public administration. The market is being used to reward the most efficient players, including workers, even if to be more efficient, they have to become neocorporatist.

Nonetheless, not only is there a considerable distance between discourse and reality, but the principal players may not be fully convinced of the benefits of the new corporatist pact. For the moment, the success of the corporatist pact and its extension to other levels appears to depend largely on the capacity of businesses to modernize. In fact, there has been a polarization of the productive apparatus. On one side stand a minority of companies that have modernized by becoming efficient exporters, (these are mainly large industrial-financial groups). On the other side are the majority of medium-sized and small businesses that have not made significant changes. If these conditions persist it is unlikely that the new corporatist pact will give equal treatment to either salaried employees or unionized workers.

In addition, the new pact has so far delivered little of substance in terms of material benefits to workers. Several neocorporatist pacts have been signed since 1987, but real wages have not recovered. Over the past ten years real wage increases have not, in fact, kept pace with productivity increases, and collective contracts have undergone modifications that, apart from a few exceptions, show a strong tendency towards unilateral flexibilization. In practice it seems that management continues to regard workers as undesirable players who must be excluded from questions of production. The dominant type of flexibility in Mexico can be characterized as neoliberal (understood as giving employers a free hand). This goes against the discourse of industrial democracy.

After 1992, when the ANEPC was signed, the situation apparently changed, with the State pressing for company-by-company productivity agreements. Nonetheless, two factors suggest that the drastic increase in the flexibility of labor relations has not been reversed. With a few exceptions, single-company pacts provide that unions give their approval to the employers' production policies in return for negligible productivity bonuses. In these cases, the union is very far from becoming a real joint partner even in companies espousing the doctrine of "industrial democracy."

Furthermore, after the signing of the ANEPC in May 1992, there have been several serious labor disputes whose settlements, pushed by business and the state, have gone in a direction opposite to that of industrial democracy. One of these was the strike at the Volkswagen plant in Puebla, which ended with the union being forced to submit to management through a belligerent intervention by the Ministry of Labor. The contract was made significantly more flexible, and the local union was defeated and divided, while the FESEBES (the model industrial democracy union) gave its support to the process. The other telling conflicts concerned revisions to the standard contracts governing the cotton industry (in September 1992), and the rubber industry (at the beginning of 1992). In these cases the intentions of management were clear: to remove the legal standing of the standard contracts governing the respective industries in order to reduce union strength by negotiating single-company contracts. It was also quite clear that the sympathies of the Ministry of Labor lay with the employers. Solutions that would have been in keeping with industrial democracy were never even considered.

Management-directed change has been reinforced by the total-quality programs found in most Mexican companies that have often included just-in-time programs and statistical control of production. The new organizational policies appear to delegate little power to work teams. They are combined with Fordist production methods and function more as instruments providing self-regulation to production decisions. Total quality without industrial democracy is particularly evident in decision-making processes that completely ignored unions.

Total quality efforts in Mexico are not being combined with better salaries or job security. The design of total quality programs has little union involvement, and unions in the end simply rubber-stamp company decisions. Mexican employers show little consistency with regard not only to the discourse of industrial democracy, but also to that of total quality.

In short, the discourse concerning industrial democracy in Mexico only expresses certain aspects of the changing relationships between companies and unions. It conceals the fact that the modernization of the economic system, is a polarizing force that is characterized by low salaries, heavy workloads, and a lack of job security. As an idea, industrial democracy has not fully taken hold among either employers, unions, or the state. Up to now, the discourse has been promoted by the state hierarchy and is not linked to previous traditions in the system of industrial relations. The only continuity with the past is the strategic use of discourse by the rulers on the subject of the ruled.

Table 1
The Evolution of Ideology

	Ideology of the Mexican Revolution	Social Liberalism
Statism	The state is the economic, political, and cultural basis of society	Free market with some state regulations
Nationalism	The nation in the face of foreign dangers	A rhetorical and ambiguous nationalism, open to foreign countries
Social Justice	To restore the conditions of deprived lives, for the entire population	Segmentation by Pronasol for actors that don't require "social justice" and those for whom the market does not work (subject to Pronasol)
Agrarianism	The state acts as a third route between capitalism and socialism	The countryside caters to the market completely
Education	The state's universal obligation	Basic education the only obligation. Pressure from commercialization for other educational levels
Tutor State	It recognizes the division between social groups that are asymmetrical and tutorial to those that are helpless	The state treats the modern social groups equally and assists those in extreme poverty with basic necessities

34

Table 2
Principles of Neoliberal Corporative Relations

1a. Macro-corporative level
1b. Alliance with the state
1c. Coordinator, supervisor, and sanctioner
1d. Corporative and authoritarian
1e. Promotion of labor policy
1f. Not based on public funds or subsidies, market openings

2a. Induction
2b. New unionism
2c. Decentralization of labor relations
2d. Union representation
2e. No class struggle
2f. Economic model

3a. Micro-corporatism
3b. Industrial democracy
3c. Productivity as a sociotechnical problem: depends on multiple factors
3d. Restructuring of production (modernization, flexibility, new forms of organization; work teams, retraining; productivity commissions); globalized market
3e. New culture of labor (humanization, motivation, incentives, retraining)
3f. Bilateralism in production changes; organization; share ownership
3g. Distribution of benefits (productivity commissions)

References

"Acuerdo Nacional para la Elevación de la Productividad y la Calidad." 1992. STYPS.

Arteaga, Arnulfo. et al. 1989. *Transformaciones Tecnológicas y Relaciones Laborales en la Industria Automotriz.* FES, Working Paper No. 19.

Bensusan, Graciela, and Carlos Garcia. 1990. *Cambio en las Relaciones Laborales: Cuatro Experiencias en Transición."* FES, Working Paper No. 32.

Carrillo, Jorge. 1991. *Mercados de Trabajo en la Industria Maquiladora de Exportación.* STYPS.

Carrillo, Jorge. 1992 "Relaciones Laborales en la Industria Maquiladora ante el TLC." *Revista Mexicana de Sociología,* Vol. 3 (July-September): 235.

Cordova, Arnaldo. 1976. *La Ideología de la Revolución Mexicana.* Mexico: ERA.

Covarrubias, Alejandro. 1992. *La Flexibilidad Laboral en Sonora.* Colegio de Sonora.

Covarrubias, Alejandro, and Vicente Solis. 1993. *Sindicalismo, Relaciones Laborales y Libre Comercio.* Colegio de Sonora.

Crozier, M. J., et al. 1975. *The Crisis of Democracy.* New York: New York University Press.

Garza, Enrique de la. 1992. "Neoliberalismo y Estado." In *Estado y Políticas Sociales en el Neoliberalismo,* edited by A. C. Laurell. UAM-X.

..... 1993a. "El Futuro del Sindicalismo en México." Albuquerque. University of New Mexico Press.

..... 1993b. "La Restructuración del Corporativism en México." In *The Politics of Economic Restructuring in Mexico.* La Jolla: UCLA.

Giugni, W., et al. 1978. *Democracia Política, Democracia Industriale.* Bari, Italy: E. Spa.

Lara, Blanca Esthela. 1992. "Tecnologias Flexibles y Flexibilidad en el Trabajo: Nuevos Retos para los Trabajadores," mimeograph, Colegio de Sonora.

Mayer, Lorenzo. 1993. "Neoliberalismo Antiliberal," *Excelsior,* P-1, February 14, 1993.

Mondragón, Ana Laura. 1993. "La Reconversión en las Ramas Sujetas a Contratos Ley." Masters thesis in Political Science, UNAM.

Mora, Felipe, et al. 1990. *Modernización y legislación Laboral en el Noreste de México*, Colegio de Sonora.

Pozas, María de los Angeles. 1992. "Reestructuración Industrial en Monterrey." Ebert Foundation, Working Paper No. 40, Mexico.

Quintero, Cirila, and Maria Eugenia de la O. 1992. "Sindicalismo y Contratación en las Maquiladoras Fronterizas." *Frontera Norte* (Colef, Tijuana) 4, no. 8: 7-48.

Román, Sara. 1992. *Relaciones Laborales en la Industria del Hule.* FES, Working Paper No. 38.

..... 1992. "El Liberalismo Social," *Perfil de la Jornada*, March 5, 1992.

Salinas de Gortari, C. 1990. "Discurso 1o. de Mayo de 1990." *La Jornada.*" Estatutos de la FESEBES."

Taddei, Cristina. 1992. "Las Maquiladoras Japonesas: Modelo de las Maquiladoras Postfordistas? Un Analisis Empírico." *Estudios Sociales* (CIAD-Colegio de Sonora) 3, no. 6: 99.

Tiburcio, Jesús Armando. 1992. *Relaciones Laborales en el Sector Público.* FES, Working Paper No. 37.

Current Developments in Canadian Industrial Relations

Mark Thompson

Canadian industrial relations superficially resemble those in the United States.[1] The two nations have similar legal regulation of industrial relations, unions with formal organizational links, and plant-level collective bargaining. However, Canadian industrial relations has many distinctive features. It is extremely decentralized, with relatively high levels of conflict, stable union membership, management strategies based on the existence of collective bargaining and frequent legislation to deal with labor problems.

The Environment of Industrial Relations

The economic, social, and political contexts of Canadian industrial relations are different from most other developed nations. Canada enjoys a standard of living equal to the more prosperous nations in Western Europe, but depends heavily on the production and export of raw materials and semiprocessed products—mineral ores, food grains, and forest products. Although it has a comparative advantage in the production of most of these commodities, their markets are unstable and these industries generate limited direct employment. A large manufacturing sector does exist in Ontario and Quebec, but its contribution to gross national product is less than 20 percent. After a sharp decline in the early 1980s, traditional Canadian manufacturing industries, such as clothing, automobiles, and electrical products, were hit by a second slump in 1990-91. The result of these two recessions has been a contraction of the manufacturing sector. Canada usually exports about 28 percent of its gross national product and imports almost as much. These transactions are dominated by the United States, which is Canada's largest trading partner. Apart from proximity and a natural complementarity of the two economies, Canadian-American trade relations are encouraged by extensive U.S. ownership in many primary and secondary industries, the Canada-U.S. Free Trade Agreement (FTA) covering most economic sectors, and the North American Free Trade Agreement (NAFTA).

Compared to the United States, the role of government in the Canadian economy is high. Public enterprises exist in transportation, public utilities, liquor distribution, and natural resources. Education and health services are almost exclusively in the public sector. There is no consistent rationale to explain the patterns of public and private ownership. Canada is fundamentally a market economy, but the role of government has also been defined by the need to provide necessary services when the private sector was absent, the promotion of economic development and nationalistic goals—the limitation of foreign (principally U.S.) influence. A number of government enterprises and operations were privatized in the 1980s and 1990s, reducing the role of the state without fundamentally altering the basic role of government.

Canada's most pressing economic problems in the 1990s have been unemployment and slow economic growth and government deficits, difficulties it shared with most other developed nations. After a period of inflation in the mid-1970s, unemployment, always substantial by international standards, rose sharply and remained high, as can be seen in Table 1. Fears of renewed inflation caused the central bank to restrain demand by raising interest rates. The combination of low inflation and high unemployment pushed wage settlements down to the lowest levels ever recorded in 1993.

Table 1
Earnings, Prices, and Unemployment
1974-1993

Year	Effective wage increases	Annual rate of unemployment	Annual rate of change, consumer price index	Annual rate of change, gross national product
1974-78	11.5	7.1	9.2	13.5
1979-83	10.6	9.0	9.7	10.9
1984-88	3.4	8.9	4.2	8.1
1989	5.2	7.5	4.8	8.3
1990	5.6	8.1	5.6	2.9
1991	3.6	10.3	1.5	1.7
1992	2.1	11.3	1.5	1.6
1993	0.7	11.2	2.5	-

Source: Bank of Canada Review, Winter 1993; Canada Bureau of Labour Information, unpublished data.

After a period of inflation (and wage and price controls) in the 1970s, the national bank adopted a modified monetarist economic policy early in the 1980s. Interest rates rose, growth in the supply of money was restrained and the bank attempted to maintain a relatively stable exchange rate with the United States. When the recession of the period grew more serious, federal and provincial governments re-imposed wage controls for the public sector only in an effort to reduce government spending and divert revenues to the private sector. These policies provoked scattered labor disputes and held public sector compensation down, but did little to reduce deficits or stimulate the private sector.

Politically, Canada has a modified two-party system. The Liberal Party has dominated federal politics for the past fifty years, occasionally forming a minority government or yielding power to the Conservatives, who won two large majorities in the 1980s but were almost eliminated from the federal Parliament in 1993. The Liberals are a pragmatic, reformist party, with a traditional base of support in Quebec. The Conservatives are a right-of-center party, normally drawing votes from the eastern and western regions, and occasionally strong in Quebec. Despite its market orientation, the Conservative government did not embrace the social and economic policies of the Thatcher or Reagan administrations. The New Democratic Party (NDP), with a social democratic philosophy and strong union support, traditionally has a small number of parliamentary seats and 15 to 20 percent of the popular vote. It too lost heavily in the national election of 1993. Other parties appear from time to time. After the 1993 election, a pro-independence party from Quebec was the official opposition. A conservative populist was party from the western provinces also had a substantial number of seats. None of the federal parties is strong in all the provinces, and purely provincial parties have often governed in Quebec and British Columbia. A large provincial pro-independence party exists in Quebec, though both French- and English-speaking citizens voted to remain in Canada in a 1980 referendum.

Official efforts to deal with economic problems have been hindered by the nation's political structure. Canada is a confederation with a parliamentary government. Ten provinces hold substantial powers, including the primary authority to regulate industrial relations, leaving only a few industries, principally transportation and communications, under federal authority. The political structure reflects strongly held regional sentiments, accentuated by distance and language. Predominantly French-speaking Quebec is the second most populous province and has strong separatist tendencies. Other provinces, often led by Quebec, not only have resisted any efforts to expand federal powers but periodically demand greater provincial authority.

In an effort to establish certain guarantees for Quebec, the nation's first written constitution was signed in 1982. It included a "Charter of Rights and Freedoms" that contained a number of protections for individuals and groups from government action. Among these are freedom of association and speech and the right to live and work anywhere in the nation, all of which have potential impact on industrial relations law and practice.

Participants in Industrial Relations

The Labor Movement

The Canadian labor movement has displayed steady, though unspectacular, growth since the 1930s, despite a long-standing tradition of disunity. Membership reached 4 million in 1990 and has been stable since then. Union density has varied between 36 and 39 percent since 1976. This membership is divided among three national centers and a large number of unaffiliated unions.

The greatest penetration of unionism is in primary industries, construction, transportation, manufacturing and the public sector. The early development of unionism paralleled that of the United States, beginning in the late nineteenth and early twentieth centuries with craft unionism in construction and transportation. During the 1930s and 1940s, industrial unionism spread to manufacturing and primary industries, without including white-collar workers in the private sector. Since the late 1960s, the major source of growth in the labor movement has been the public sector. By 1980, virtually all eligible workers in the public sector had joined unions. Table 2 shows the relative rate of unionization by industry.

Approximately 280 unions operate in Canada, ranging in size from under 50 to over 400,000 members. Two-thirds are affiliated with one of the central confederations discussed below, with the remainder, principally in the public sector, independent of any national body. A variety of union philosophies are represented. Most of the old craft unions still espouse apolitical business unionism. A larger number of industrial unions see themselves fulfilling a broader role and actively support the NDP and various social causes. A few groups, principally in Quebec, are highly politicized and criticize the prevailing economic system from a Marxist perspective. But rhetoric aside, the major function of all unions is collective bargaining.

The role of U.S.-based "international" unions is a special feature of the Canadian labor movement that has affected its behavior in many ways. Most of the oldest labor organizations in Canada began as part of American unions—hence the term "international." The cultural and economic ties between the two countries encouraged the trade union connection, while the greater size and earlier development of U.S. labor bodies attracted Canadian workers to them. For many years, the overwhelming majority of Canadian union members belonged to such international unions, which often exerted close control over their Canadian locals. But the spread of unionism in the public sector during the 1960s and 1970s brought national unions to the fore, as internationals were not active among public employees. As a result, the proportion of international union membership declined from over 70 percent in 1966 to under 45 percent in 1982.

Persistent complaints about the quality of service in Canada, American labor's support for economic protectionism, and increased Canadian nationalism created pressures for change within the labor movement. During the 1970s, a few unions in Canada seceded from internationals, and the largest international in Canada (the United Auto Workers) separated in 1985. Other internationals granted special autonomous status to Canada. While the influence of American-style business unionism continues in the internationals, the impact of policies originating in the United States is low and seems destined to decline further.

The most important central confederation in Canada is the Canadian Labour Congress (CLC), with about one hundred affiliated unions that represent 60 percent of all union members. CLC members are in all regions and most industries except construction. It is the principal political voice for Canadian labor, but has no substantial powers over its affiliates. The CLC's political role is further limited by the constitutionally weak position of the federal government, its natural contact point, in many areas the labor movement regards as important, such as labor legislation, regulation of industry, and human rights. In national politics, it officially supports the NDP.

The Confederation of National Trade Unions (CNTU) represents about 5 percent of all union members, virtually all in Quebec. It began early in the twentieth century under the sponsorship of the Catholic Church as a conservative French-language alternative to the English-dominated secular unions operating elsewhere in Canada. Beginning in 1949

Table 2
Union Members as a Percentage
of Paid Workers, 1991

Industry group	Percent unionized
Public administration	77.9
Transportation, communication, and other utilities	55.2
Construction	64.2
Forestry	65.4
Fishing and trapping	41.9
Manufacturing	36.2
Service industries	36.1
Mines, quarries, and oil wells	28.4
Finance, trade, and agriculture	17.5

Source: Ministry of Supply and Services: 1993. Annual Report of the Minister of Industry, Science & Technology under the Corporations and Labour Unions Returns Act, Part II. Ottawa: Ministry of Industry, Science & Technology.

the Catholic unions abandoned their former conservatism and moved into the vanguard of rapid social change in Quebec. In 1960, the federation adopted its present name and severed its ties with the Catholic Church. Since then, ideological competition has prevailed in the Quebec labor movement, and the CNTU has become the most radical and politicized labor body in North America. It has actively supported Quebec independence and has adopted left-wing political positions. Unlike the CLC, it has a centralized structure gives officers considerable authority over member unions. Because of its history, current political posture, and the large provincial public sector in Quebec, the CNTU membership is concentrated among public employees.

42

A third labor central emerged in 1982. A group of construction unions had left the CLC a year earlier over the issue of greater autonomy to Canadian sections of international unionism and the CLCs, the social and political activism. Ten of the dissident unions, representing over 5 percent of all union members, formed the Canadian Federation of Labour (CFL). The new group is apolitical, though it quickly established ties with the federal government. Both the CLC and the CFL have avoided any open hostilities since the latter appeared, but the issues separating them remain and so is the potential for conflict.

Management

Most Canadian managers have limited commitment to collective bargaining. Nonunion firms strive to retain that status, some by matching the wages and working conditions in the unionized sector, others by combinations of paternalism and coercion. A small number of firms have union substitution policies, which replicate many of the forms of a unionized work environment with grievance procedures, quality circles, or mechanisms for consultation. Although the majority of unionized firms accept the role of labor grudgingly, open attacks on incumbent unions are rare. Moreover, in industries with a long history of unionism for example—manufacturing, or transportation-unionism is accepted as a normal part of the business environment.

In the late 1980s, employers in manufacturing and parts of the service sector sought to improve employee relations. These efforts included increased communication with employees and unions, employee involvement programs, and work teams. These innovations appear to have been conferred to fewer than 20 percent of unionized enterprises and often met with resistance from unions in these firms. In several industries, government-sponsored joint committees were formed to recommend and implement policies to deal with job loss and industrial restructuring.

The high degree of foreign ownership in the Canadian economy affects general management, but seldom industrial relations. Over 20 percent of the assets of all industrial firms are foreign-owned, chiefly by U.S. corporations. Foreign ownership clearly affects a number of strategic managerial decisions, such as product lines or major investments. But the impact of non-Canadians on industrial relations decisions appears to be slight. Foreign owners prefer to remain in the mainstream of industrial relations for their industries rather than imposing corporate policies.

The organization of employers varies among regions. No national organization participates directly in labor relations, although a number do present management viewpoints to government or the public. Since most labor relations law falls under provincial jurisdiction, few industries have national bargaining structures. In two provinces, Quebec and British Columbia, local economic conditions and public policy have encouraged bargaining by employer associations, normally specialized bodies for that purpose. Elsewhere single plant bargaining with single unions predominates, except in a few industries with many small firms, like construction, longshoring, and trucking, where multiemployer bargaining is the norm.

Government

The government in Canada has a dual role in industrial relations—it regulates the actors' conduct and employs large numbers of people both directly and indirectly.

Government regulation of industrial relations is very specific, although it rests on an assumption of voluntarism. Each province, plus the federal government, has at least one act covering private sector labor relations in the industries under its jurisdiction. Most governments also have other separate public sector labor relations statutes. Although the details vary considerably, labor relations legislation combines many features of the U.S. National Labor Relations Act of 1935 (Wagner Act) and an older Canadian pattern of reliance on conciliation of labor disputes. The statutes establish and protect the right of most employees to form trade unions, and sets out a procedure by which a union obtains the right of exclusive representation for groups of employees. The employer is required to bargain with a certified trade union. A quasi-judicial labor relations board administers this process and enforces the statute.

Labor relations legislation imposes few requirements on the substance of a private sector collective agreement, though the exceptions are significant and expanding. For many years, Canadian laws have effectively prohibited strikes during the term of a collective agreement, while also requiring that each agreement contain a grievance procedure and a mechanism for the final resolution of mid-contract disputes. More recently, statutes have added requirements that the parties bargain over technological change and that management grant union security clauses. The federal labor code and a few provinces also provide rights of consultation for nonunion workers.

Separate legislation exists federally and in eight of ten provinces for employees in the public sector. These statutes normally apply to government employees and occasionally to quasi-government workers, such as teachers or hospital workers. They are patterned after private sector labor relations acts except for two broad areas. The scope of bargaining is restricted by previous civil service personnel practices and broader public policy considerations. For example, the introduction of technological change is often outside the scope of bargaining. In a majority of provinces, there are restrictions on the right to strike of at least some public employees. Police and firefighters are the most common categories affected by such limits, but there is no other common pattern of restrictions. Employee groups without the right to strike have access to a system of compulsory arbitration. Although a statute requires arbitration, the parties normally can determine the procedures to be followed and choose the arbitrator.

Industrial Relations Processes

The major formal process of Canadian industrial relations is collective bargaining, with union power based on its ability to strike. Joint consultation is sporadic and generally confined to issues such as safety, although, in some areas, these are quality of working life activities, which consist of consultation in the work area on production methods. Other formal systems of worker participation in management are extremely rare. Arbitration of interest disputes is largely confined to the public sector.

Collective Bargaining

Collective bargaining in Canada occurs on a decentralized basis. The most common negotiating unit is a single establishment-single union, followed by multi-establishment-single unions. Taken together these categories account for almost 90 percent of all units and over 80 percent of all employees. Companywide bargaining is common only in the federal jurisdiction, where it occurs in railways, airlines, and telecommunications. The importance of provincial legislation and practice impedes the formation of wider bargaining units. Despite the decentralized structure of negotiations, bargaining often follows patterns. Although there are no national patterns in bargaining, one or two key industries in each region usually influence provincial negotiations. In larger provinces, such as Ontario and Quebec, heavy industry patterns from steel or autos tend to predominate.

The results of bargaining are detailed, complex collective bargaining agreements. Grievance procedures are a legal requirement and invariably conclude with binding arbitration. In the workplace, agreements regulate behavior rather closely. Negotiated work rules are numerous and many parties are litigious, so rights arbitrations are frequent and legalistic. In turn, this emphasis on precise written contracts often permeates labor-management relationships. Another outcome of collective bargaining is labor stoppages, the most controversial single feature of Canadian industrial relations. There have been frequent allegations, never really proven, that the nation's economic growth has been seriously hindered by labor unrest. These concerns were especially notable because Canadian society generally has low levels of social conflict. Historically, strike levels have moved in cycles. There was a wave of unrest early in the twentieth century, another around World War I, a third beginning in the late 1930s, and a fourth in the 1970s. After 1981, the number and size of strikes fell sharply, and by the early 1990s, the proportion of working time lost due to strikes fell to the lowest levels since World War II. By international standards, the two salient characteristics of Canadian strikes are their length and the concentration of time lost in a few disputes. Involvement is medium to low (7 to 12 percent of union members annually), and the size of strikes is not especially large (350 to 450 workers per strike, on average). The largest five or six strikes typically account for 35 percent of all time lost. In recent years, the average duration of strikes has been 15 to 20 days. These characteristics have not been fully explained, but may be due to the existence of major companies, such as General Motors or International Nickel, and large international unions taking strikes at individual production units incapable of inflicting major economic loss on the parent organizations.

Outside of the public sector, compulsory arbitration of interest disputes is rare. However, special legislation to end particular disputes is not uncommon in public sector or essential service disputes. Back-to-work laws are extremely unpopular with the labor movement and have contributed to the politicization of labor relations in some areas. In the public sector, interest arbitration is common. Arbitrators are usually chosen on an ad hoc basis from among judges, lawyers, academics.

45

Table 3
Strikes and Lockouts in Canada, Selected Years

Year	Number	Workers involved	Days lost (000)	Average length	Percent of working time
1966-70	572	291,109	5,709	19.6	0.35
1971-75	856	473,795	7,309	15.4	0.38
1976-80	1105	618,743	7,824	12.6	0.35
1981-85	709	296,950	5,203	17.5	0.22
1986-90	561	397,663	4,929	12.3	0.18
1991	399	253,486	2,530	10.0	0.09
1992	353	149,551	2,115	14.1	0.08
1993	325	101,745	1,603	15.8	0.06

Source: Labour Canada. Strikes and Lockouts in Canada, various issues; unpublished data.

Current and Emerging Issues

Although the Canadian industrial relations system has been more stable than the other national systems in North America, major questions about its future development remain.

The Role of Collective Bargaining

The future of collective bargaining is being questioned in most industrialized countries. In large measure, this issue revolves around the ability of unions to retain, or even expand, their traditional bases of strength in heavy industry and blue-collar occupations. Union density in these industries in Canada has not declined materially and is consistently twice as high as that of the United States, for instance. However, Canadian unions have had the same difficulty as their counterparts elsewhere in extending their membership base into the more rapidly growing areas of the service sector and technologically advanced industries. As employment shifts from the goods producing sectors to the service sectors, the traditional base of collective bargaining gradually shrinks. Historically, the organized elements of the labor force have led the nonunion employers in the expansion of employee rights and improvement in wages and conditions of employment. If collective bargaining becomes confined to declining sectors of the economy, this role will also diminish.

The immediate future of collective bargaining will be a function of the actions of government and management in the face of trade union economic and political power.

46

Both federal and provincial governments continue to respect the legitimacy of collective bargaining and an active labor movement. Legislation and other public policies reflect that commitment, even when most right-of-center parties govern. Few major changes in labor legislation occurred in the 1980s. The most important exception to this generalization was in British Columbia, where a conservative government enacted sweeping changes in the basic labor relations statute. These changes provoked vigorous reaction from the labor movement, which is especially strong in that province. Ultimately, the government was replaced by the NDP, which returned most legislative provisions to their previous state and added a number of protections for the labor movement in 1992. At about the same time, the NDP government of Ontario, the largest and most industrialized province, passed a new labor law assisted organized labor substantially. Both of these statutes aroused strong opposition from employers and will undoubtedly be amended if the NDP is defeated. On balance, it is not clear that the legislative support for collective bargaining will change markedly, but further gains by labor are unlikely in the remainder of the 1990s.

Management and Collective Bargaining

Canadian employers have faced strong market pressures to reduce their costs for virtually all of the period since 1982. The manufacturing sector faced growing foreign competition. New entrants in the service sector, such as retailing, challenged traditional market leaders. Public sector employers were required to at least limit the growth of labor costs and often had to reduce expenditures absolutely in this area. The Canada-U.S. Free Trade Agreement and NAFTA increased competitive pressures. Many employers' responses to these pressures have been traditional. Layoffs have dramatically reduced employment in many industries. The use of part-time workers rose substantially. But there was no substantial movement to escape unionism.

A combination of cultural and legal forces have caused Canadian employers in traditionally - unionized industries to respond to these competitive pressures by working through the collective bargaining system. Major employer organizations support cooperative relations with unions and have not called for "deregulation" of labor markets. Thus, surveys of industrial relations and human resource managers show little interest in unseating incumbent unions. Instead, employers have pushed to decentralize bargaining structures in the private sector, effectively putting wages into competition. Negotiated changes in work rules were frequent, and in the 1990s, the incidence of wage freezes and concession bargaining rose substantially. In industries such as pulp and paper, and brewing, the parties have negotiated collective agreements with terms as long as six years, incorporating wage freezes followed by modest wage increases and employment guarantees for most members of bargaining units. The resistance of employers to unionism in the small business sector and traditionally nonunion industries remains strong.

At the level of the workplace, adoption of work organization based on high levels of employee commitment has been slow, in part because of union resistance. Labor generally regards these initiatives as having the effect, and perhaps the goal, of weakening workers' allegiance to their unions. The results of collective bargaining, including the wage settlements summarized in Table 1, changes in collective agreement provisions and the like, seem to have reduced some of the pressures for other innovation in the organization of work. In addition, the decline in the value of the Canadian dollar beginning in 1990 reduced cost pressures from foreign competitors.

If the labor movement's base of strength falls, and the commitment of Canadian workers to their unions declines, the willingness of Canadian employers to work with their unions to address economic problems may diminish. Canadian employers generally resist the unionization of new bargaining units within the limits of the law, but they seldom welcome the arrival of a union. Should legal restraints weaken while competitive pressures continue, management's resistance to unionization may rise.

Public Sector Industrial Relations

An area of industrial relations under strong pressures to change is the public sector. Since the mid-1960s, Canada has developed mature systems of industrial relations in all provinces and the federal government. Although public sector collective bargaining has been an established feature of Canadian industrial relations since the 1960s, the conduct and results of bargaining was restricted in 1982 and 1983. Governments in several jurisdictions sought to combat the prolonged recession by reducing the size of their expenditures. A politically acceptable means was to cut the number and compensation of public employees (at least in real terms). Many governments chose to make these cuts by legislation, rather than through bargaining, leaving public sector unions with very little to negotiate. By 1987, however, all jurisdictions had removed formal restrictions on collective bargaining, though spending limitations remained. Early in 1991, the federal government and five provinces introduced new restrictions on public sector compensation increases. Similar measures were adopted in the remaining five provinces. In 1993 and 1994, a majority of all provinces imposed restrictions on public sector bargaining as part of efforts to restrain government spending.

Public sector unions protested, but generally in vain. Governments continue to face serious fiscal pressures, and restrictions on public sector wages and bargaining have proven to be safe policies politically. The willingness of the federal and provincial governments to dictate the outcomes of bargaining puts the entire process into question. Governments have been unwilling to use the techniques developed in the private sector and negotiate changes to meet economic needs. For their part, public sector unions have seen their members as victims of changing political priorities. The result is a growing sense of alienation by major organizations in the public sector and reports of low morale among employees affected by these restrictions. If governments persist in their restraint policies, the eventual reaction of public sector labor organizations in those provinces where they are most strongly organized, such as Quebec, Ontario, and British Columbia, will be political. In the 1980s public sector unions in those three jurisdictions organized major demonstrations and work stoppages that brought pressure on governments to moderate their policies. Strikes in other provinces where public sector workers are regarded as less militant have demonstrated the resistance of public sector workers to restrictions they regard as unfair. Whether these unions could organize similar campaigns in the less militant climate of the 1990s is still to be determined.

Constitutional Protections

Another issue arises from the Charter of Rights and Freedoms proclaimed as part of the new Canadian Constitution in 1982. Previously, an 1867 act of the British Parliament had established the structure of Canadian government, and Canada relied on the British tradition of an unwritten constitution and the supremacy of Parliament to protect individual and collective rights. Several provisions of the new charter with potential implications for industrial relations were included without much debate. Thus, their impact will not become clear until complaints are reviewed by the courts. These rights include: freedom of association, freedom of speech, the right to pursue a livelihood in any province, and protection against discrimination on the basis of age, sex, and race. It is almost inevitable that the courts will apply elements of the charter to industrial relations.

Several issues have already arisen. Restrictions on the scope of bargaining and the right to strike that governments impose on their own employees may be challenged as a violation of the right of citizens to equal treatment before the law. Employer communications during a union organizing campaign may fall under the protection of freedom of speech, thereby strengthening management's hand in antiunion campaigns. The right of public sector unions to spend dues money for political purposes has been challenged. Despite the significance of some of these issues, the initial decisions under the Charter did not upset existing industrial relations practices, however.

Whatever the outcome of these or other issues arising from the charter, one result has been increased litigation and the remaking of certain long-standing policies entrenched in labor law and the parties' practices.

Political Role of the Labor Movement

Although many Canadian unions and union leaders are active in partisan politics, the labor movement has no defined political role. The CLC official support for the NDP has created two problems. Federally, the NDP has been unsuccessful in raising its share of the popular vote (and legislative seats) beyond about 20 percent. The CLC is thus left to deal with governments whose election it has opposed. This dilemma was heightened in 1993, when the NDP was reduced to 8 seats (out of 295) in the Parliament and lost official party status. Second, the labor movement has been unable to deliver large blocs of votes to the NDP, though financial contributions and the diversion of staff to the party are invaluable. As a consequence, when the NDP has governed provincially, it has not been a "labor" party in the British or Australian modes. An NDP government in Ontario imposed reductions in the terms of public sector collective agreements as part of a fiscal restraint program. This action outraged the unions affected and caused the provincial federation of labor to withdraw support from the party.

The practical result of these problems is that the CLC has vacillated between wholehearted commitment to the NDP and a more independent posture as workers' lobbyists before governments of any party. To further complicate the situation, many public sector unions avoid political endorsements and the CFL is strongly apolitical. The founders of the NDP had the British Labour Party as a model, but were unsuccessful in achieving their goal. The American tradition of labor acting as an independent political force has adherents in Canada, despite limited relevance in a parliamentary political system. It thus appears that the labor movement will continue to search for an effective political role.

Labor Disputes

Historically, a major issue in Canadian industrial relations has been time lost due to strikes. In 1982, the incidence of strikes fell sharply as the economy suffered a severe recession and unemployment rose, though the number of strikers declined much less. Time lost and the number of strikes remained low throughout the 1980s. Despite public concern about strikes, there have been few efforts to deal with their underlying causes or even to understand them better. Certainly, the fragmented structure of bargaining is one factor that contributes to the pattern of strikes. Yet the causes of fragmentation lie in the nation's governmental structure and politics. Provincial governments resist virtually any effort to limit their powers and the paramount importance of Quebec separatism on the national political agenda has restrained any impulses of the federal government to extend its authority over economic issues. Employers traditionally preferred to seek political solutions rather than work actively to improve industrial relations.

Governments have attempted to deal with labor unrest in a variety of ways. One model is the encouragement of consultation. During the 1970s there were a number of initiatives directed at establishing tripartite systems of consultation on economic issues, as practiced in Western Europe. At the level of the firm, companies under federal regulation and in several provinces are required to establish a joint planning committee, with half of its members elected by the employees, to minimize the impact of redundancies, when the company is planning to terminate fifty or more employees. None of these initiatives had any impact on industrial relations.

Conclusions

Industrial relations has seldom been a major issue in Canadian life, but the system is caught up in the central concerns of the nation - the division of powers between provinces and the national government, the relative importance of the public and private sectors, relations with the United States and other trading partners, and economic performance. The outcomes of each of these issues will be in doubt for the remainder of the century. While industrial relations will contribute to the resolution of these issues, the future direction of the system is likely to be determined by broader trends in Canadian life. Canadian governments have been conciliatory in their dealings with labor in the private sector. In dealing with public sector employees, however, the growing tendency of the 1990s is to avoid bargaining in times of fiscal restraint and impose wage freezes or cutbacks on organized workers.

Endnotes

1. An earlier version of the introductory portions of this chapter appeared in Greg J. Bamber and Russell D. Lansbury, eds. *International and Comparative Industrial Relations: A Study of Industrialized Market Economies*, 2d ed. Sydney: Allen & Unwin, 1993.

References

Anderson, John, Morley Gunderson and Allen Ponak. 1989. *Union-Management Relations in Canada,* 2d ed. Toronto: Addison-Wesley.

Arthurs, H. W., D. D. Carter, and H. J. Glasbeek. 1988. *Labour Law and Industrial Relations in Canada*, 3rd ed. Toronto: Butterworths.

Chaykowski, Richard P., and Anil Verma, eds. 1992. *Industrial Relations in Canadian Industry*. Toronto: Dryden.

Hébert, Gérard, Hem C. Jain, and Noah M. Meltz, eds. 1989. *The State of the Art in Industrial Relations*. Kingston: Industrial Relations Centre, Queen's University, and Centre for Industrial Relations, University of Toronto.

Kumar, Pradeep. 1993. *From Uniformity to Divergence: Industrial Relations in Canada and the United States*. Kingston, Ont.: IRC Press, Queen's University.

Riddell, W. Craig, Research Coordinator. 1986. *Canadian Labour Relations*. Toronto: University of Toronto Press.

Swimmer, Gene, and Mark Thompson, eds. In press. *Public Sector Industrial Relations: The Beginning of the End or the End of the Beginning?* Kingston, Ont.: IRC Press, Queen's University.

Thompson, Mark, and Gene Swimmer, eds. 1984. *Conflict or Compromise: Public Sector Industrial Relations*. Montreal: Institute for Research on Public Policy.

Weiler, Paul. 1980. *Reconcilable Differences*. Toronto: Carswell.

The Mexican Model of Labor Regulation and Competitive Strategies

Graciela Bensusán Areous

The purpose of this paper is to reflect on the importance of labor institutions as instruments that can reorient business strategies toward both productivity and equity within the framework of the North American Free Trade Agreement (NAFTA). The paper is based on the premise that the possibilities for achieving this reorientation under conditions of regional integration depend, among other factors, upon the existence of appropriate links between national regulations and those that form part of NAFTA. In other words, international commitments should induce the governments of each country to formulate policies and regulations that create an internal equilibrium that would allow them to develop cooperative labor relations and shared benefits for the social partners. This entails recognition of the need for new types of regulation and state intervention, within companies and at the level of macroeconomic decision making, which aim at discouraging authoritarian and exclusionary solutions (Banuri 1990).

By placing the analysis of the history, regulation, and structural determinants of the capital-labor relationship at the center, this approach challenges others that are limited to a simple comparison of each country's labor standards. Such limited approaches have been used to justify proposals for upward or downward harmonization, depending on their theoretical focus.[1] They have frequently neglected other key aspects of the system of domination which prevent changes to the rules of the game.

A comparison of Mexican, U.S., and Canadian labor rights illustrates the shortcomings of North American economic integration. During the initial phase of negotiations, which concluded with the signing of NAFTA by the governments of the three countries on December 17, 1992, the "advanced" character of Mexican labor legislation served, paradoxically, to support neoliberal arguments in favor of not making the adoption of common labor standards a condition of the agreement. Given that free trade would, in itself, generate benefits and improve living and working conditions in the three countries, the impact of integration on labor was excluded from the trilateral negotiations.[2]

During a second phase, however, it was established that levels of protection for workers in Mexico, which are formally higher than those contained within U.S. law, cannot be viewed as obstacles to competitive strategies based on low Mexican labor costs and the possibility of lowering labor costs in the other two countries. In this way, the problem of breaches of legality, principally in Mexico, was highlighted as a topic to be considered alongside the signed NAFTA text.

Nonetheless, although the question of legal enforcement remains, the advances achieved in the labor side agreement are not sufficient to change the course of those low-wage competitive strategies. They responded more to an interest in obtaining the votes necessary for NAFTA's ratification by the U.S. Congress than for the purpose of identifying and correcting institutional factors (legal and political) that have hindered the defense of workers' interests in the three countries during the recent years of crisis and productive restructuring.

The creation of a trinational arena in order to oversee compliance with the law, as well as the increased exchange of information concerning labor matters, will provide an opportunity to evaluate the advantages and disadvantages of contrasting models of protection for workers. For decades, the marked differences between Mexican and U.S. labor laws were justified by differences in levels of development. In Mexico's case, these developmental differences were based on the internal market. However, Mexico's economic opening in recent years has led to more of a convergence in the changes experienced by labor relations in both countries.

For this reason it is necessary to explain how both state and corporatist solutions, as well as liberal and individualist ones, may be devised to protect worker rights. We will approach this question from the perspective of the Mexican model of labor regulation. First, this model will be analyzed in terms of its unique features, taking into account the historical circumstances from which it emerged, and the type of competitive strategies that sustain this model. Secondly, I argue that the labor side agreement is limited, and I present the minimum requirements for national institutional change that could support a new type of competitive strategy.

Worker Protection and Control: The Legacy of the Mexican Revolution

The constitutional recognition of high labor standards for Mexican workers can be seen as a case of premature institutionalization, which preceded the establishment of levels of economic development that could sustain such standards. The "revolutionary" solution to the labor question had three distinct objectives: 1) The achievement of consensus among workers in the face of the new state, and the creation of mechanisms capable of resolving class conflict; 2) the prospect of creating a capitalist consumer market; and 3) a desire to obligate employers to replace the methods characteristic of extensive capital accumulation (low salaries and nonmonetary remuneration) with other, intensive methods, through the imposition of legal exploitation limits (Bensusán 1992a).

In short, the modernization of labor relations took place via institutional channels, through high levels of state protection and intervention on behalf of workers. The advantages derived from this situation have often been emphasized. In particular, analysts have highlighted the importance of Article 123, which set out a range of labor rights, since it provided arguments for the legitimization of the post-revolutionary Mexican state and for new social bases of support. However, less has been said of the unintended consequences, such as employers' open resistance and the intense union mobilization (which centered on compliance with the new rights), that immediately complicated the exercise of domination.

At a formal level, the adoption of this order implied an abrupt leap, both qualitative and quantitative, with respect to the terms of the worker-employer relationship that had existed in prerevolutionary Mexico. The majority of the new rights were taken from protective laws derived from European social reforms. Nevertheless, the Mexican solution was a radical one. Those countries that had experienced early industrialization imposed restrictions on capital for the gradual and selective acquisition and employment of the workorce. They paid close attention to workers' suitability for the technological and organizational characteristics of the work process and, consequently, to the productive levels of the workforce.

Mexico's revolutionary legacy helped to reshape these laws. A complete cataloge of workers' rights was adopted in the Constitution. These rights consisted of a maximum workday of eight hours, prohibition of child labor, protection for women, minimum wages that would meet the needs of a head of household, profit-sharing, the right to housing, security, hygiene, and other fundamental rights, such as freedom of association and the right to strike.

The adaptation of these high labor standards to the accumulation process was only achieved after a complex process of legal and political institutionalization. A corporatist agreement (the Calles-CROM alliance between 1924 and 1928) gave rise to the regulatory criteria of Constitutional Article 123. These criteria underlay the Federal Labor Law of 1931 and their essential features are still in force today. This instrument was adopted in the midst of a severe political and economic crisis, when limits to state autonomy vis-à-vis capital interests demanded a greater realism than that what had been envisioned by the 1917 Constituent Congress. Thus, a new regulatory model emerged. It was based on the power of state intervention to satisfy the claims of workers and employees. Later on, this satisfaction would depend less upon the letter of the law than on expediency.

The most important characteristics of this regulatory model were: 1) minimal interference of employers in the organization of workers; 2) the importance of collective rights (the right to organize, to bargain collectively, and to strike) over individual liberties; 3) strong state involvement in the regulation of union organization and resolution of grievances; 4) the consolidation of a tripartite system of labor justice that depended on the executive branch; and 5) guaranteed stable employment and promotion based on seniority.[3]

Nonetheless, this model had important limitations. It created the mechanisms for a corporatist system of interest representation, but it did not implement that system. While the registration procedure for unions and their leaders made state intervention in organizational activity possible, this was not necessarily the cause of the subordination of workers' interests to government policies nor of the establishment of monopolies of representation without regard for the wishes of the rank and file. Union plurality was formally permitted. However, the practice of granting the bargaining contract to the union with majority representation, in cases where there was competition among unions, and the legalization of exclusion clauses (the obligation of workers to join the union that held the collective contract and their loss of employment as a result of resignation or expulsion from the union) favored monopolistic organizational structures.[4] Such structures served to transform minorities into majorities and inhibited the emergence of alternative union choices.

Regulation of the right to strike facilitated state intervention. However, obligatory arbitration was never imposed, making it indispensable to obtain the acquiescence of the strikers. This was a significant limitation, since in Mexico a legal strike entails the absolute suspension of work (with the exception of emergency services) and is imposed on employers as well as non-strikers. This explains the importance of seeking permanent links between the state and the unions as a means of avoiding the interruption of the productive process or of bringing such interruptions to a rapid end. Another reason for the importance of state-union ties was due to the legalization of solidarity strikes, which the labor movement could draw on in order to increase its strength independent of state support.

But, the tripartite nature of the labor justice system favored alliances with the executive and encouraged workers to settle their claims via this route. Thus, a broad arena for state discretion was created, particularly in the area of collective conflicts (collective suspension and termination of labor relations or modifications to collective bargaining agreements). In such cases, the conciliation and arbitration boards were authorized to alter working conditions, and even the number of jobs, either upward or downward, as long as they did not violate the legal minimums.

As demonstrated by the experience of workers in the years that followed the adoption of the Federal Labor Law, the law by itself did not determine the course of worker actions or organization. Political agreements were needed. These further strengthened the state's role in the arbitration, and, above all, the prevention of conflicts. The corporatist model of regulation of labor-capital relations was consolidated by political agreements, which were characterized by a law that bore the mark of the state and by an alliance between the state and unions. Political agreements were also significant in the consolidation of the political system and its distinctive features: presidentialism, the creation of the "official" political party (PNR-PRM-PRI), and the incorporation of workers as a sector into the party, which occurred in 1938.

Employers, on the other hand, demanded the withdrawal of legal protection for workers in order to adapt to the economic reality of the country, and the reduction of coercive union powers (unionization, collective bargaining, and strikes). Nevertheless, employers finally accepted that these alternatives had limited political feasibility for a state that sustained its legitimacy more through its revolutionary origins and commitment to its dominated subjects than through an attachment to legal forms.

The alliances between unions and the government became institutionalized within the framework of an authoritarian political regime with few limits on the exercise of presidential power. Consequently, from the mid-1940s onward, unions also became a key element in the system of domination.

Corporatist Flexibility

The term "corporatist flexibility" refers to the particular means of adapting recognized levels of protection for the worker to the imperatives of capitalist accumulation. In the Mexican case this adaptation is carried out through violations of the law, state discretion, and union complicity. It is aided, as we have seen, both by legal regulation and by the political system within which this regulation operates. It is worth observing that, as an instrument of an industrialization project that focused on the domestic market, "corporatist flexibility" generated an unequal distribution of the benefits of industrialization, but it also led to a relative balance between the interests operating in the Mexican labor arena.

During the years of economic growth, some areas of relatively greater protection for workers emerged. These were located principally in state firms and in the large private enterprises, where what Enrique de la Garza has defined as the "contractual model of the revolution" was firmly rooted. The relative stability in the relations between the social partners implied by this model was partly explained by the state's support of labor's ties to the PRI, as well as the consolidation of an organizational structure with monopolistic features and a subordinated union leadership. Open or covert breaches of legality occurred at the margins of this state-union exchange, but they were tolerated by the government and unions. These breaches of legality occurred mainly in small and medium-sized businesses where many workers were employed under conditions that were inferior to the minimum protection levels established by the legal system.

Economic and state restructuring in the 1980s produced significant changes in the relationship between the state, capital, and labor. These changes altered the old rules of the corporatist game. The change in the development model (trade liberalization, privatization, and the reorientation of production toward the foreign market) was accompanied by a new form of state intervention. This intervention aimed to restore the power of employers, dismantle the most important collective bargaining agreements, lower wages, and weaken the unions (de la Garza 1990). This strategy, implemented without changes to the labor laws, relied on "corporatist flexibility," and resulted in the further subjection of the official union leadership (those who held these collective contracts and who negotiated with the state over wage policy) in favor of the new economic project.

The new economic model favored competitive strategies that entailed reductions in labor costs. Until 1982, the corporatist and statist features that characterize Mexico's labor institutions (National Commission for the Minimum Wage, Conciliation and Arbitration Boards, unions and collective contracts, and others) operated both as a useful mechanism for improving working conditions and as a means of freeing small and medium-sized businesses from many of their restrictions. In contrast, the new institutional arrangement served to impose, without affecting traditional controls on labor, a change in the worker-employer relationship in the direction of a less protectionist and more discretionary model. In other words, this was a model that entailed less of a role for unions in the mobility of workers within the firm, a less stable employment, fewer direct and indirect wage costs, and so forth.

But, this means of adapting to the new regime of accumulation discourages other types of strategies, namely those that are oriented toward the formation of a trained workforce that would be endowed with the skills necessary for confronting and participating in the challenges posed by the new structure of production. Nor can the workers, consensus be obtained through a corporatist flexibility that permits not only a lowering of labor standards but an authoritarian management style as well. The latter is demonstrated by the fact that employer commitment to employee training and to new methods of worker involvement (which would increase worker participation in productivity and quality) remains weak.

When union leaders, bereft of the power to negotiate and unable to adequately represent the interests of their membership, are faced with state-supported firm management, the ostensible result is an unbalanced exchange. This imbalance is damaging to workers who, in addition to experiencing a reduction in their purchasing power and a deterioration in their working conditions, encounter obstacles within the legal and political system that prevent them from reorganizing their system of representation or from choosing their own union leadership. In addition, the weakening of the role that these leaders traditionally played in channeling the negotiation of labor claims has accentuated their authoritarian practices. As a result, the legitimacy of the union leadership has been eroded, a factor that in the future could place the control of labor at risk, especially when one considers the strong tradition of collective defense of workers' interests that exists in Mexico.

The characteristics of the different models of labor flexibility established during the recent process of restructuring reflect this imbalance. One model, characterized by Ludger Pries as neo-Taylorist external flexibility, consists of unilateral change by the firm, the elimination of employment security (the use of temporary workers, subcontracting, high turnover of personnel) and a reduced number of areas for union intervention. At the same time, the flexibility of the workforce and pay-for-knowledge schemes are absent or play a limited role in this strategy. Another model, known as renewed paternalism, centers on the search for greater participation of individual workers through training and consultation, even though the addition of quality control and flexibility to the tasks of production is just as unilateral as in the previous model. Moreover, compensation packages in this model often do not match the increased skills and training required of the workforce.[5]

Finally, those strategies that promote "concerted flexibility" through union and management agents who are prepared to negotiate organizational and technological changes, sharing risks and benefits alike, are extremely rare (Pries 1993; Montiel 1992).

While the first two models rely on corporatist union complicity, the last one demands the presence of a union agent with genuine powers of representation and with specialized training. These characteristics would allow the agent to participate with independent proposals in the search for productivity and quality, themes that have traditionally been foreign to the concerns of corporatist union leaders. Nonetheless, the existence of a corporatist apparatus of control was a key element in reducing real protection levels and conserving peace in the labor arena (de la Garza 1992).

It is worth noting, had that the laws currently in force, been fully enforced, management's room for maneuvering would have been limited. For instance, this would be the case with laws governing the duration of employment contracts, which would limit the use of temporary contracts. Another point of law states that revisions of collective agreements cannot produce changes that are less favorable to the workers than those which preceded them: the rights that have been acquired are irrevocable.

In any case, these laws also block workers' ability to recreate their unions as representative institutions and leave all negotiation in the hands of the official recognized leadership. Some of the most important conflicts linked to restructuring, such as those which occurred in the Ford Motor Company or in Volkswagen de México, illustrate the significant role labor leaders have played as accomplices of unilateral management strategies, as well as the authoritarian responses to workers' resistance to restructuring (Bensusán and León 1991; Bensusán and García 1992).

These conditions of imbalance in capital-labor relations extend to the macroeconomic level. There, adjustment policies are imposed with sacrifices unequally divided among the social partners, and with the endorsement or tolerance of the corporatist union leader. For instance, the traditional tripartite institutions, together with the various pacts agreed on by management, labor, and the government from December 1987 onward, made it possible to sustain an anti-inflationary strategy, which was based on both minimum and contractual wage reductions (Bensusán 1992b).

However, this strategy of high-level negotiation was ineffective in the areas of productivity and quality. Agreement on such issues was sought through a National Accord on Productivity and Quality, which, to date, has not resulted in significant advances at the firm level. The national accord was supposed to consolidate commitments between management and unions. While the agreement calls for generating shared benefits through productivity-related incentives, and for worker training and participation in technological and organizational changes, reality has been quite different. The absence of even a minimum balance in the bargaining power of the participants is one of the factors obstructing the transition toward forms of mediation other than authoritarianism.

While corporatist flexibility has its costs, these are tolerable in the eyes of employers as long as they can avoid dealing with a genuinely representative union leadership, and as long as they are able to continue the restructuring that in itself alters the role of unions as disciplinary tools within the firm (through work teams, human resource policies, the individualization of work relationships, and so forth.)

This explains why it has been possible to postpone the incorporation of employers' demands (principally those of the Confederation of Employers of the Republic of Mexico [Coparmex]) in Mexican labor legislation reform. President Salinas committed himself to the promotion of a new federal labor law during his electoral campaign. During the first months of his term, he established a tripartite commission to discuss the necessary changes. But resistance by the Confederation of Mexican Workers (CTM) halted this process. At the same time, pressures for reform from employers did not cease during the Salinas administration. Nevertheless, labor, employers, and the government did eventually reach consensus on some issues, such as the national agreement on productivity, in anticipation of NAFTA's ratification.

The union bureaucracy fought the revision of labor legislation for three main reasons: First, the law provided the bureaucracy with the legal mechanisms to sustain monopolies of representation. Second, the more flexible legislation that employers proposed would accelerate the collapse of corporatism. A third factor was the labor leadership's symbolic/ideological commitment to the revolutionary origins of this model.

The government obtained significant benefits in exchange for its acquiescence on the issue of labor law reform. These benefits included labor complicity in macroeconomic adjustments and in firm-level restructuring, labor's support for the government's decision to negotiate NAFTA, and the possibility of using the labor standards in the current law within this negotiation as proof of the state's commitment to the protection of workers in Mexico.

Employers, for their part, while agreeing through their various organizations on the necessity for reform, have displayed divergent positions, mostly with regard to the possibilities for change in the labor scenario. While the Coparmex and the Confederation of National Chambers of Commerce (CONCANACO) were in favor of liberalizing the rules of the game (less state interference and a reduction of coercive union powers), the Confederation of Chambers of Industry (CONCAMIN) adopted a more conservative position. That position was rooted in the fear of losing control in areas where there were high levels of unionization, particularly in the industry's largest companies.

The new regulatory model proposed by Coparmex in 1989 contained the following characteristics: greater discretionary powers for employers, particularly with respect to the duration of the work contract, dismissals, and internal mobility; a lower level of protection for workers (individualization of wages, reduced employment security, and so on); a greater emphasis on individual liberties of employment and unionization; a redefinition of the function of the union (cooperation); greater state control over the exercise of the right to strike (obligatory arbitration upon request of either party); and the conservation of tripartism as a method for resolving individual and collective labor conflicts. In this model there is also a notorious absence of alternatives aimed at obtaining the consensus of workers.

With these adjustments, Coparmex intended to introduce economic realism into the legal arena and diminish the risks of a transition toward more independent forms of representation, once the factors that made political alliances between the state and unions necessary were removed. In July 1993 a new proposal was advanced by the Board for Management Coordination and Coparmex. Some key principles of the former proposal were ratified, although any change in the rules of the game where unions were concerned appears to have been rejected (Bensusán, Areous 1993).[6]

National Regulation and Trilateral Supervision: The Labor Side Agreement

One conclusion that can be drawn from the parallel labor commitments agreed to as part of NAFTA is that the future fortunes of Mexican workers will depend principally on external factors. Supporting this hypothesis is the fact that the Mexican government promised to change the means used to determine increases in the minimum wage, and that efforts to increase the effectiveness of Mexican labor legislation did not originate primarily from the demands of the official union movement. On the contrary, these advances—which are as yet unclear and dubious, especially in the area of wages— were a result of the initiatives of U.S. negotiators and the president of the United States.

The social dimension of integration, which had been absent from the NAFTA text signed on December 17, 1992, was finally approached as a topic of consideration as a result of pressure from unions and civic organizations in the U.S. In order to defend their own labor standards and jobs, they placed restrictions on a free trade sustained by the major comparative advantage of low Mexican wages. Although the Mexican Action Network on Free Trade (an independent coalition of labor and civic organizations) insisted on including this social dimension, it was political developments in the United States that permitted the re-opening of negotiations on labor and the environment.

For Mexican workers, the impact of the labor side agreement may well be positive. In particular, the greater transparency which is likely to ensue by making each country's compliance with the labor laws in force a trinational issue, could well contribute to discouraging those management strategies that violate workers' rights in their efforts to adapt to new economic circumstances.

According to the draft text of the side agreement produced on August 12, 1993, each of the governments committed themselves to compliance with their own laws.[7] This international commitment explicitly includes a collection of labor-related principles shared by the three countries: freedom of association, the right to strike, and collective bargaining, together with other principles that have great relevance for Mexico, such as the protection of migrant workers. Although the agreement has been defined as one of cooperation, its content surpasses this goal, and borders on international supervision. This is demonstrated by the fact that, along with the specific obligations governments undertake in order to enforce national labor legislation, evaluations of national "standards of conduct" are contemplated. These evaluations (as well as resolution of conflicts, which could result in the adoption of trade sanctions) will be the responsibility of independent expert committees.

Nevertheless, there are at least three types of limitations that could weaken and even suppress the agreement's ability to restrict or, where necessary, correct violations of each country's labor laws by those companies whose exports will make them competitors in the new arena of the NAFTA. These limitations are the following: a) Only those violations of law related to minimum wages, occupational health and safety, and child labor, and which affect competing companies in North America can result in trade sanctions, and only in instances where the companies resort to "repeated, systematic, and unjustified" violations of these laws. This relatively restricted scope of the labor side accord is likely the result of an implicit agreement among the official negotiators to exclude those labor standards that are more often violated on both sides of the border. Such is probably the case for collective rights and freedom of association, and, in the United States, for the protection of migrant workers. b) As Mexican negotiators have consistently explained, the application of trade sanctions would only occur after the completion of a long and complex procedure, and could be halted not only by complying with the law, but also by making a financial contribution.[8] Some say that the advantage of this model is that it protects Mexico and exporters based in this country from disputes and sanctions provoked by protectionist claims. c) The Trinational Labor Commission is under the direction of the labor ministers of the three countries (Council of Ministers -- International Coordinating Secretariat). The National Administrative Offices (NAOs) are set up by each country and are entrusted with receiving correspondence from the public and carrying out preliminary evaluations. Because breaches of legality may emanate from the labor authorities themselves, the commission's abilities to act independently as both judge and participant are obviously limited.

It remains to be seen whether the labor side accord reflects each government's interest in seeking genuine solutions to the problem of labor rights in the region, or whether, on the contrary, it represents an effort to defend the status quo, and especially the tendencies associated with the restructuring of the last decade: wage decline, the reduction of employment security, and the weakening of unions.

In any case, even with NAFTA's ratification, there will still be a long way to go before these competitive strategies can be reoriented, in spite of the fact that this reorientation is one of the aims of the labor side agreement. This is so for several reasons: First, because the side agreement is restricted to seeking an improved compliance with the standards and labor laws in force in each country, which means that institutional change is not seen as a condition for achieving equity in the resolution of conflicts of interests. Second, because it does not contain any expression of a desire to link the process of integration with democracy in the political arena, at the firm level, and within the union organizations of the three countries. These gaps are especially significant in the case of Mexico. Without institutional change in the capital-labor relationship and without democracy, authoritarian responses will continue to dominate in the process of adaptation to new competitive conditions.

It is worth outlining, therefore, some of the requirements for domestic institutional change that could secure both the effectiveness of Mexican legislation and the possibility of reaching a more balanced exchange between capital and labor. Moreover, these factors should be key considerations in any trinational strategy for institutional innovation and reform.

a) It is essential to push for and consolidate a state based on legal foundations and principles of justice, so that violations may be adequately punished through the appropriate national channels. Government commitment to the reinforcement of the current labor justice system, as demanded by the parallel labor agreement, is not an adequate response to the problem of the inefficacy of the legal order. On the contrary, the restructuring of this system ought to form part of an extensive judicial reform that would strengthen the autonomy of the judiciary vis-à-vis the executive. This should be done in such a way that full compliance with workers' rights would not depend on political or economic expediency. An intermediate solution, which would immediately discourage the more common labor law violations, might be to grant Mexico's National Commission on Human Rights jurisdiction over matters relating to labor, at least insofar as they refer to freedom of association. Having the president offer to invite the International Labor Organization (ILO) to observe whether Mexico complies with its national labor laws and with the many international treaties (approximately seventy-three) ratified by Mexico could be another alternative. The recommendations to date by the specialist committee of the ILO on the subject of Agreement No. 87 on freedom of association have been limited essentially to the suggestion that there be a revision of legislation related to federal employees (in whose case the system of one union per department is imposed and pluralism, a principle established by the treaty, is prevented). In any case, current circumstances may demand that there be an evaluation of whether Mexican laws may be adapted to reflect the principles of international treaties, whether these laws are enforced, and the legal and political obstacles to their enforcement. However, the tripartite nature of the ILO does not guarantee its neutrality in evaluating the efficacy of each country's recognized labor standards, including freedom of association.

b) The reform of Mexican labor legislation with the aim of endowing worker-employer relations with an institutional framework that would restore the balance between the interests at stake, would produce greater and more widespread compliance. The main aspects of this reform would be: 1) a strengthening of the principle of legality (that is, less room for state discretion); 2) a balance between individual liberties and collective rights; 3) the creation of spaces for the participation of workers in the running of the company, and workers' right to information and consultation on technological and organizational changes; 4) regulation of productivity and reinforcement of employer commitments to the workforce (training, incentives, and so on) and 5) a new labor justice system. A reform of this nature demands the creation of a suitable sociopolitical context in which agents with genuine representative powers could have access to reliable information and debate the dimensions and consequences of violations of the laws in force, and the way to correct these violations. If, until now, change within companies has emanated from a "corporatist flexibility" consisting of violations of labor rights, discretionary powers, and complicities that permitted the lowering of labor costs and the imposition of the will of employers, it is now necessary to devise an institutional framework that will promote a new type of flexibility. This would be a flexibility based on the education and training of the workforce and workers' cooperation in productivity strategies, in exchange for a more equitable sharing of sacrifices and benefits. This option cannot be developed within the framework of precarious labor relations nor with agents -- either management or union--who are trapped in a corporatist and authoritarian inertia. The freedom to organize unions and freedom of affiliation are, then, essential conditions for this equilibrium. Consequently, the ambiguous and interventionist legislation which currently supports coercive monopolies of association should be replaced.

c) It is necessary to have socially and politically independent union agents who are prepared to demand compliance with the law. These agents also would need to participate with feasible proposals to change those practices and regulations (both legal and contractual) that currently aim for higher productivity without benefits for the members they represent. In general, workers' disatisfaction with their union leadership is not openly expressed for many reasons, and a fear of losing their jobs, legal obstacles, the absence of alternative union options, and a preference for individual solutions. When conflicts do break out, however, they are increasingly costly, and it is ever more difficult to reestablish consensus within the company. The costs derive more from an insistence on retaining leaders who have been opposed by the rank and file, than by the threat that alternative union leaders might represent for management interests. Moreover, the greater part of such conflicts are not resolved, but postponed without an effort to deal with their root causes.

The above scenario outlines the possible pathways toward institutional change in the domestic labor arena. The prospects of such institutional change will depend as much on what occurs in the Mexican political transition as on the tendencies that develop within the capital-labor relationship in the other two countries. For this reason, an analysis of the evolution of labor relations in the current process of integration demands approaches that transcend national borders and which contribute to a delineation of the requirements for a new institutionalism in both the national and trinational arenas.

Endnotes

1. These positions have been classified as neoclassical and neoinstitutional. The lack of agreement between the two lies principally in the type of labor standards and labor market policies that should be adopted in order to increase economic growth and productivity. While the neoclassical viewpoint is concerned with the distortions that could be generated by an early adoption of labor standards, its opposite (neoinstitutionalism) sees these standards as "instruments which could have an influence on social development, in a positive or negative fashion, depending on how they are formulated and applied," Herzenberg and Pérez 1990, p. 4.

2. However, two bilateral instruments for cooperation on labor issues were negotiated, one between Mexico and the United States (May 1992) and another with Canada (May 1992). See Bensusán 1992.

3. Worker participation in the management and administration of firms was not contemplated in this model.

4. Exclusion clauses, often found in Mexican collective bargaining agreements, obligate an employer to dismiss any worker who leaves or is expelled from the union for any reason.

5. In the case of Japan, where these new organizational models originated, compensation included lifetime employment, forms of remuneration linked to seniority, the formation of internal labor markets would allow relatively rapid upward mobility, and strong investment in training (Coriat 1992).

6. In spite of the fact that this new proposal was presented to the minister of lbor, the government of President Salinas publicly rejected the possibility of advancing in this direction before the next presidential succession (Aziz 1993).

7. The summary of this provisional text can be found in Excelsior, August 14, 1993.

8. On this subject, see statements of Herminio Blanco, Underscretary for International Affairs of the Ministry of Trade and Industrial Development, La Jornada, August 21, 1993. One of the unclear aspects of the agreement is who will pay these contributions. Although there is a reference to "the party" which gave rise to the conflict, government officials have explained that this "party" of the areement refers to the country in question and,therefore, it would appear that the responsibility of payment does not fall on the companies or authorities causing the violation.

64

References

Aziz, Alberto. 1993. "La doble transición Mexicana: Estado, sindicalismo y sistema político," paper presented at the research workshop on "Regional Integration and Industrial Relations in North America," Cornell University, October.

Banuri, Tariq. 1990. "Comments on Fields." In *Labor Standards and Development in the Global Economy*. Stephen Herzenberg and Jorge F. Perez-Lopez, eds. Washington, D.C.: U.S. Department of Labor.

Bensusán Areous, Graciela. 1992. "Institucionalización Laboral en México, Los Años de la definición" Doctoral thesis, FCPyS, UNAM, México.

..... 1992b. *La Concertación Social en los Tiempos del Ajuste Estructural*, Occasional Papers, ILO, Geneva.

..... 1993. "Los empresarios y la legalidad laboral." *Revista Sociológica* no. 22 (UAM-Azcapotzalco, May-August).

Bensusán Areous, Graciela coord. 1992. *Las Relaciones Laborales y el TLC*. México: Editores Porrúa.

Bensusán, Graciela, and Carlos García. 1992. "Entre la Estabilidad y el Conflicto: Relaciones laborales en la Volkswagen de México." In *La Industria Automotriz en México*, Arnulfo Arteaga, corrd. México: UAM-Iztapalapa, FES.

Bensusán, Graciela, and Samuel León, coord. 1991. *Negociación y Conflicto Laboral len México* (Mexico: FLACSO/FES).

Coriat, Benjamin. 1992. *Pensar al Revés*. Siglo 21. México.

"Estilos de Desarrollo y nuevos patrones de relaciones laborales." 1993. In *Trabajo industrial en la transición: experiencias de América Latina y Europa*, Ranier Dombois and Ludger Pries, coord. Venezuela: Editores Nueva Sociedad, Venezuela.

Dombois, Rainer. 1993. "Modernización Empresarial. Reto para las relaciones industriales en América Latina." In *Trabajo industrial en la transición: experiencias de América Latina y Europa*. Ranier Dombois and Ludger Pries, coord. Venezuela: Editores Nueva Sociedad.

de la Garza, Enrique. 1990. "Reconversión industrial y cambio en el patrón de relaciones laborales en México." In *La modernización de México*, Arturo Anguiano, coord. México: UAM.

Herzenberg, Stephen. 1993. "In from the Margins: Morality, Economics, and International Labor Rights." Mimeo.

Montiel, Yolanda. 1993. "Experiencias de modernización y flexibilidad en tres empresas mexicanas." In *Trabajo industrial en la transición: experiencias de América Latina y Europa*, Rainer Dombois and Ludger Pries, coord. Venezueva: Editores Nueva Sociedad.

Pérez, Jorge. 1990. *Labor Standards and development in the Global Economy*. Washington, D.C.: U.S. Department of Labor.

Pries, Ludger. 1993. "El reto de la flexibilidad y las relaciones obrero patronales en México." In *Trabajo industrial en la transición: experiencias de América Latina y Europa*, Venezuela: Editores Nueva Sociedad.

Economic Integration and Labour Law Policy in Canada

Gilles Trudeau and Guylaine Vallée

North America constitutes a more and more integrated economic continent. The Free Trade Agreement (FTA) between Canada and the United States came into effect on January 1, 1989, and, when fully applied, should eliminate most of the remaining commercial barriers that presently exist between the two countries.[1] The free trade zone will also include Mexico when the North American Free Trade Agreement (NAFTA), signed on December 17, 1992, comes into effect.[2] These agreements, however, formally recognize an economic integration that has to a large extent existed for several years.

Through this paper, we will discuss the evolution of Canadian labor policy and labor law in a more economically integrated continent. We start by discussing the assumption that continental *economic integration* already constitutes a factor in the evolution of our labour law. We will discuss to what extent the *formalization* of this economic integration through free trade agreements constitutes an additional factor in the evolution of our national labor law policy. We assume that, with this formalization, it will become much harder to modify social and economic trends that have taken place as a result of the economic integration.

The Nature of Economic Integration and Its Effect on the Development of Canadian Labour Law

Economic integration between the United States and Canada on the one hand and between the United States and Mexico on the other hand is not the result of the FTA and NAFTA. Rather, they confirm and formalize a situation that has existed for years and that has already largely affected the shaping of Canadian labour policy.

Economic Integration Based on Dependency

The continental integration that has taken place in North America with the application of the FTA and NAFTA is essentially commercial. These accords create a large continental market formed by the three countries in which goods, services, and, to some extent, capital originating from any one of the three countries will be allowed to circulate freely, without commercial barriers imposed at the border of the other countries. However, when we consider the state of trade links between Canada, the Unites States and Mexico rather than the formal object of these free trade agreements, we are able to see that this economic integration already existed and that it was an integration founded on economic dependency.

The Canadian economy is largely dependent on exterior markets. In 1989, Canada was the second-largest exporting nation among the principal G-7 countries.[3] More than 70 percent of Canada's total exports in 1989 were to the United States and 65 percent of imports by Canada came from the United States.[4] Canadian-United States relations have intensified since the middle of the sixties. They have been controlled, however, by a limited number of enterprises and have developed for a large part within transnational enterprises.[5] These commercial relations have taken place in the context of a relatively free market.[6] Before the achievement of the FTA., 73 percent of Canadian imports from the United States were duty- free, as were 71 percent of American imports from Canada.[7] Furthermore, when tariffs were imposed by Canada and the United States on goods and services from the other country, they were very low.[8]

A similar commercial relationship can be observed between Mexico and the United States. The United States constitutes Mexico's most important trading partner. Seventy-five percent of Mexican exports are shipped to the United States, about the same proportion as for Canada.[9] Mexico represents the third largest partner for the United States, after Canada and Japan.[10] On the Mexican side, the bargaining for NAFTA must be seen as a part of a liberal economic policy that has guided other decisions of the Mexican government : participation in GATT, unilateral reductions of tariff barriers, and massive privatization of publicly owned enterprises.[11] As in the case of Canada, negotiations between the United States and Mexico were based on important bilateral relations between the two countries.

The same cannot be said of relations between Canada and Mexico. Direct commercial exchanges between the two countries are limited, even if they have increased in recent years. In 1987 Canada exported U.S. $418 million worth of goods to Mexico and imported United States $882 million worth of goods from Mexico. Trade with Mexico represented only 0.4 percent of total Canadian exports in 1987.[12] Mexico represents Canada's seventeenth largest trading partner.[13] The Economic Council of Canada has found that two-thirds of Canadian exports to Mexico in 1987 consisted of agricultural products or products with a high natural-resource content. The other third consisted of machinery and transportation equipment.[14] The nature of Mexican exports to Canada has changed over the last few years. Today, 70 percent of Mexican exports to Canada consist of machinery and transportation equipment requiring no specialization. Most of this trade takes place within transnational companies.[15]

These figures indicate that Canada and Mexico share a common dependence on the United States with regard to their exports. Even though a large part of their exports were different, the Economic Council of Canada noted that, in 1987, 34 percent of Canadian exports were comparable to Mexican exports. This "similarity index" between the exports of the two countries rose from 16 percent in 1971 to 34 percent in 1987. According to the Economic Council of Canada, this would indicate that the Mexican economic structure is becoming more and more similar to that of Canada.[16] This conclusion of the Economic Council of Canada is confirmed by more recent figures. Thus, the similarity of Canadian and Mexican exports to the United States increased from 30 percent in 1985 to 43 percent in 1990, or by almost 50 percent.[17] This is one of the reasons that Canada, after a long period of hesitation, decided to participate in the trilateral negotiations in order to preserve its privileged access to the American market, a market also coveted by Mexico. In the NAFTA negotiations, Mexico and Canada were not allies but rather competitors. It also indicates that there was no true trilateral bargaining among Canada, the United States and Mexico, but merely bilateral negotiations conducted in parallel.[18] At least, the state of trade relations among these countries gives some support to this analysis.

The same disproportionate relations among the three countries can be found concerning foreign investments. Among the parties to NAFTA, Canada is the country with the most direct foreign investments.

Figures indicate that the FTA and NAFTA confirm rather than create a continental capitalism, which is characterized not by the globalization of trade in the world, but by the free circulation of goods, services, and investment within a continental bloc, itself in competition with other international integrated markets.[19] This North American continentalism has not been based on equal interdependence among Canada, the United States and Mexico, but rather on the "asymmetrical interdependence" of Canada and Mexico towards the United States.[20] Inside this North American continental economy, some fear the reinforcement of labor division among the three countries: resources in Canada; technology and capital in the United States; cheap labor in Mexico.[21] This labor division would encourage strategies of delocalization that have already begun with maquiladoras. Such a "continentalization" of the economy would confirm the renunciation, by Canada and Mexico, of an international multilateral trade policy.[22]

Development of Canadian Labor Law Institutions

Part A shows how Canada and the United States had joined in an integrated economic and commercial zone long before the implementation of the FTA in 1989. It is also clear that the trade links between the two countries are characterized by Canada's strong economic dependence on the United States. This economic integration appears to be an important factor in explaining similarities in labor legislation in the two countries.

In Canada, the main legislative jurisdiction over labor policy belongs exclusively to the provinces, the federal government retaining authority only over labor policy that applies to specific industries of national importance such as radio and television, railways, airlines, banking and grain handling.[23] Despite this decentralization in jurisdiction over labor policy in Canada, only one model of labor legislation prevails, a model largely borrowed from the American Wagner Act. In the last years of World War II and in the following decade, most of the ten Canadian provinces and the federal legislature enacted collective bargaining legislation embedding to a large extent the model of labor relations that had been formalized by statute in 1935 in the United States.[24]

In addition to economic integration between the two countries, it must be kept in mind that the adoption of the American legislative model in Canada was preceded by the appearance of a labor movement very close to American labor organizations. Although the first labor unions in Canada were Canadian, just a few years after the conclusion of the Treaty of Reciprocity of 1854, the first international American labor unions appeared in Canada.[25] Lipton explains the development of American trade unionism in Canada as follows:

Why affiliation to U.S. unions? Here are some reasons : The undeveloped condition of the Canadian economy; its interflow with the U.S. economy; Canadians' need for jobs in the United States; trade solidarity; the Canadian workers' desire for organization, and their readiness to use anything to get it-east, west, north or south of the border.[26]

In 1911, 89.7 percent of unionized Canadian workers were members of international unions.[27] Since that time, in spite of a significant trend toward the "Canadianization" of unions, international unions have always been an important part of the labor movement in Canada. In 1989, 32.4 percent of unionized workers in Canada were still members of international unions.

In the two countries, collective bargaining plays the same role, at a very decentralized level. The framework of the system, the nature and functions of the social actors, and the institutions within the system are highly similar, if not the same, on both sides of the border. Moreover, a set of general labor standards legislation, including health and safety and workers' compensation regulations, has the same function in both countries mainly with respect to the non-union part of the labor force.[28]

It has been said that Canadian collective bargaining legislation has been much more favorable to the union movement than has its American counterpart.[29] This characteristic of Canadian legislation has even been presented as one of the factors explaining the significantly higher union density in Canada.[30] American-legislated labor standards have also been perceived as being "much less restrictive for employers ... as compared to [those in] Canada."[31] However, these differences in the two sets of national labor legislation do not change the fact that American and Canadian labor and employment laws are much alike. It would be very difficult to find two other countries in the world with such highly similar labor legislation.

It is also interesting to note that in sectors where economic integration between the two countries has been more accentuated, such as in the automobile industry and professional sports, there has been some transnational collective bargaining.

The above factors cannot explain all aspects of the convergence of and divergence between two different systems of labor policy. Other factors, such as political institutions and backgrounds, can also play an important role. Thus, it should not be forgotten that a number of important differences exist between the Canadian and American models, such as a higher degree of protection for workers and unions under Canadian legislation. These divergences may also be explained by the differences in political institutions in each country.[32] Such factors certainly contribute to explaining the more important divergences that can be seen between the Mexican and the American models of labor legislation.

Specific Effects of the Formalization of Economic Integration

As shown in part I, the economic integration of North America was to a large extent realized before the FTA and NAFTA were concluded. This integration can be perceived as an explanation of the importance of the American influence in shaping Canadian labor law and the industrial relations system.[33]

This does not mean that the formalization of North American economic integration through the FTA and NAFTA will not affect the development of Canadian labor policies. In order to assess these effects, we will first analyse how the FTA and NAFTA formalized the existing economic integration in North America.

The Content of the FTA and NAFTA

The FTA established a free trade zone between Canada and the United States. The agreement is essentially commercial and does not deal with social matters and the social regulation that would apply to the enlarged market. When fully in force, the FTA will allow the free circulation of goods, services and, to some extent, investments between Canada and the United States.[34] The FTA does not provide for free circulation of persons, except businesspersons.

The agreement preserves the complete sovereignty of the two participating countries. No centralized agency is created and no centralized binding regulations can be elaborated within the existing framework. However, one chapter of the agreement sets up a mechanism to settle implementation and compliance disputes (Chapter 18) and another deals with disputes concerning antidumping and countervailing duty cases (Chapter 19). In Chapter 19 cases, the decisions of the binational panel are binding upon the governement concerned.[35]

The agreement concluded between Canada, the United States and Mexico in December 1992 creates a larger free trade zone comprising the three countries. As under the FTA, this agreement provides for the free circulation of goods and services within the free trade zone. Moreover, it guarantees more open conditions governing investment. NAFTA does not allow the free circulation of persons, except businesspersons.[36]

Even though NAFTA is essentially commercial, it deals to some extent with social matters. This is done exclusively in the preamble of the agreement, which states that the three signatories resolve to "create new employment opportunities and improve working conditions and living standards in their respective territories" and to "protect, enhance, and enforce basic workers' rights." These provisions remain very general and are not enforceable as such. This is in striking contrast to the route that European integration has followed so far.[37]

More extensive provisions on social matters are now found in a side accord, concluded in August 1993. This accord resulted from intensive negotiation among the representatives of the three countries over labor and environmental issues related to the implementation of a free trade zone. The new Clinton administration has made the conclusion of this and another side accords a prerequisite to the ratification of NAFTA in order to prevent a "race to the bottom" in environmental and labor standards.

This side accord, constituting the social aspect of NAFTA, sets out very ambitious objectives and obligations. But although the consultation and cooperation mechanisms it establishes cover a wide range of subjects, very few are subject to the binding dispute resolution mechanism.

Objectives and Obligations. The objectives of the side accord are set out in very general terms in Article 1. It is intended mainly to improve working conditions and living standards in each of the three countries, and to encourage cooperation and the exchange of information among the three on their respective labor legislation. More specifically, the accord is also intended to promote a wide range of labor principles, including freedom of association, the right to bargain collectively, the right to strike, minimum employment standards, prevention of occupational injuries and illnesses, and so on (Annex 1). The parties also wish to promote the effective enforcement by each party of the labor legislation in force in its territory, and foster transparency in its administration.

It must be emphasized that right from the beginning of the side accord, in the reference to Annex 1, it is very clearly established that no minimum common standard will be adopted. The objectives of the accord are to be pursued with total respect for each party's national sovereignty and subject to the legislation in effect in each of the three countries.

These objectives are given concrete form in a number of obligations in Part II of the Accord. Article 2 establishes a general obligation in these terms:

> Affirming full respect for each Party's constitution, and recognizing the right of each Party to establish its own domestic labor standards, and to adopt or modify accordingly its labor laws and regulations, each Party shall ensure that its labor laws and regulations provide for high labor standards, consistent with high quality and productivity workplaces, and shall continue to strive to improve those standards in that light.

This provision explicitly illustrates and confirms several of the inherent limitations of the social aspect of NAFTA, that is, the lack of common standards, complete respect for national sovereignty and legislation, and nonbinding obligations reliant on moral suasion.

The other obligations are more specific. Each of the parties agrees to "promote compliance with and effectively enforce its labor law through appropriate government action" (Art. 3). This article refers in particular to the establishment of an adequate system for receiving complaints from different labor representatives and bodies, an inspection system, mediation, conciliation and arbitration services, and procedures for applying sanctions or obtaining redress for violations of labor law.

Each party also agrees to ensure that any person with a legally recognized interest has access to judicial or quasi-judicial tribunals for the enforcement of that country's labor law and collective agreements (Art. 4). Proceedings of these tribunals must be fair, equitable, and transparent, and must offer adequate redress (Art. 5). Finally, the Parties are also obliged to ensure that the labor legislation in effect in each country is published or otherwise made available (Art. 6) and must promote public awareness of its labor laws (Art. 7).

Consultation and Cooperation Mechanisms. The side accord establishes a consultation mechanism with the general mandate of overseeing the implementation of the accord, facilitating consultations between the parties, addressing questions by any party, and handling any complaints that may be submitted (Part III of the accord). This mechanism is embodied in the Commission for Labor Cooperation, itself consisting of a council and a secretariat.

The council comprises the labor minister from each country. It will promote cooperative activities among the three countries in the many areas listed in Article 11, that is, occupational safety and health, child labor, human resource development, labor statistics, labor-management relations and collective bargaining procedures, employment standards, and so on .

The secretariat, made up of representatives of each of the three nations, provides the administrative support necessary for the implementation of the side Accord.

In addition, each of the parties is to establish a National Administrative Office (NAO), mainly to provide the commission with requested information relevant to the accord, in particular as concerns the legislation and administrative procedures relating to labor in effect in the country in question.

Dispute Resolution Mechanism. Any matters concerning the application of the side accord must be settled as much as possible through cooperation and consultation by the parties. The dispute resolution mechanism is designed primarily in this light (part IV of the accord).

Accordingly, one country may request consultations at the ministerial level regarding any matter within the scope of the side accord. The parties concerned must make every attempt to settle the question through consultation. At this step, the accord gives a very wide definition of subjects that may be addressed through ministerial consultations. Note, however, that only the three parties to the accord, and not the various social actors in a country, can request such consultations.

If a matter has not been resolved after ministerial consultations, a party may request that an evaluation committee of experts (ECE) be established (Art. 23). The ECE is to analyze "patterns of practice by each Party in the enforcement of its occupational safety and health or other technical labor standards as they apply to the particular matter" considered by the ministers. Nevertheless, no ECE may be convened to consider a matter that is not trade-related or is not "covered by mutually recognized labor laws."[38]

Thus it is clear that at the point where matters are dealt with by the ECE, the parties have considerably limited the application of the dispute-resolution mechanism. In fact, only matters relating to occupational health and safety and other technical labor standards may be submitted to the ECE.[39] Furthermore, an additional restriction has been introduced at this step, concerning the relation of the issue to international trade and to labor laws mutually recognized by the two parties to the complaint.[40]

The ECE is made up of three members selected by the council from a roster of experts drawn up in consultation with the ILO. It must submit a draft evaluation report within 120 days after it is established, and a final report within 60 days after the presentation of the draft report. Each of the three parties will have the opportunity to present its views to the ECE on the draft report.

After the final report is submitted, each of the two countries not covered by the report may request consultations to determine whether there has been "a persistent pattern of failure" by the third country "to effectively enforce" the standards that are the subject of the ECE report, bearing on "occupational safety and health, child labor or minimum wage technical labor standards" (Art. 27). At this and the following steps, the field of application of the dispute resolution mechanism becomes quite narrow.

If such a matter remains unresolved after these consultations, a party to the accord may request a special session of the Council to attempt to reach a mutually satisfactory resolution of the dispute (Art. 28). If the matter still has not been resolved within 60 days after the council has been convened, any consulting party may request that the council, by a two-thirds vote of the Council members, convene an arbitral panel to consider the matter.

The terms of reference of the panel are firstly to determine whether the alleged persistent pattern of failure is trade-related and covered by mutually recognized labor laws (Art. 29). If so, then the panel is to:

> examine . . . whether there has been a persistent pattern of failure by the Party complained against to effectively enforce its occupational safety and health, child labor or minimum wage technical labor standards, and to make findings, determinations and recommendations in accordance with Article 36(2). (Art. 33(3))

The panel is made up of five members appointed by the parties to the complaint, in accordance with the procedures set out in the accord. It must submit an initial report within 180 days after the last panelist is selected (Art. 36). The final report is to be submitted within 60 days after presentation of the initial report, and must take account of any comments by the disputing parties on the initial report.

If the panel determines that there has been a persistent pattern of failure by the party complained against to effectively enforce its occupational safety and health, child labor or minimum wage technical labor standards, the disputing parties may agree on an action plan. If no such plan can be agreed on or if the plan is not fully implemented, the panel may meet again to establish an adequate plan or to determine whether the plan adopted has been fully implemented (Art. 39). In both cases, the panel may impose a monetary enforcement assessment.[41] The panel is responsible for ensuring that the plan is implemented and that any such assessment is paid.

If the party complained against fails to pay a monetary enforcement assessment, the complaining parties may suspend the application to the party complained against of NAFTA benefits in an amount not exceeding the monetary enforcement assessment (Art. 41). This suspension of benefits may be extended from year to year until the assessment has been paid or the action plan fully implemented. The resolution of disputes concerning these matters falls under the jurisdiction of the panel.

One specific procedure concerns Canada, with regard to the enforcement of a panel determination imposing a monetary enforcement assessment or requiring the full implementation of an action plan. Rather than suspending NAFTA benefits if Canada fails to comply with the determination, a complaining party may request that the commission take proceedings in a domestic Canadian court to have the determination executed. When filed before such a court, the panel determination shall become an order of the court and shall be enforceable as such (Annex 41A of the side accord).

Note also that the application of the side accord as it relates to labor standards gives rise to constitutional problems in Canada. Although the accord was signed by the federal government, it deals with issues that are to a large extent under exclusive provincial jurisdiction. Consequently, for the accord to be fully implemented in Canada, the agreement of the provinces must be obtained, as stipulated in Annex 46.

In the following section, we will see to what extent this formalization will modify the development of Canadian labor policy.

Potential Effects of the Formalization on Canadian Labor Policy

In this section, we will first examine the effects of the formalization of economic integration on the raison d'être of labor law (1).[42] Then we will discuss the potential effects of the formalization on the content of labor legislation (2).

Effects on the Raison d'Être of Labor Law. From a historical perspective, labor law originated from the excesses of the laissez-faire and free-market policies that prevailed in western countries during the industrial revolution.[43] The state first defined some basic labor standards in order to ensure human dignity in the workplace. Some rules were enacted regarding child labor, hours of work, and sanitary conditions.[44] The state also gradually legitimized the existence of coalitions of workers and, later on, even promoted peaceful mechanisms to settle labor disputes and to foster unionism and collective bargaining.[45]

The original raison d'être of labor law was twofold. First, it had a protective function in favor of the working class, by imposing some minimum labor standards and giving workers the possibility of counterbalancing employers' bargaining power in establishing working conditions.[46] However, this legislation had another raison d'être, namely as a guarantee of stable conditions for the production of goods and services. Furthermore, the gradual improvement of working conditions enhanced mass consumption, which permitted the development of mass production.

It appears that these traditional raisons d'être of labor law are not taken into account either by the FTA or by NAFTA. This is even more obvious when one considers the side accord to NAFTA dealing with labor standards. This omission could very possibly alter the future development of labor law.

In the context of the FTA and NAFTA, labor seems to be a commodity. Labor law is perceived as an obstacle to free trade among the participating countries. In the debate on North American free trade, national labor laws have been reduced to one of the elements of commercial competition among the producers of the participating countries. The social legislation of a country, depending on its content, may be seen either as a cost of production that unduly affects the competitiveness of an enterprise with regard to its foreign counterparts or, on the contrary, as a state subsidy that amounts to an unfair commercial practice.[47]

This reduction of national labor legislation to its commercial dimension could first be seen in the FTA. This agreement was completely silent on social matters. However, it provided for a resolution mechanism for disputes concerning antidumping and countervailing duties that could take social matters into account. For example, would it not be possible to challenge the right-to-work laws in force in some American states through this mechanism, arguing that they amount to an unfair state subsidy?[48] And the same applies to NAFTA. It is our view, for reasons stated below, that the side accord on labor standards contains major flaws that will prevent it from changing this trend significantly.

The emphasis that the free trade agreements place on the commercial dimension of integration will certainly affect the future development of labor law. Rather than being on the protective aspect of a given labor standard, the focus will be on its possible effects on the competitiveness of enterprises. In the context of divergent national labor laws, it seems obvious that this consideration will not lead to a general improvement in national labor standards.[49]

Potential Effects on the Content of National Labor Law. If free trade does not produce a general improvement in national labor legislation, could it bring about a "race to the bottom" in social standards among the three countries? This question has been examined by several authors and was at the center of the debate on the FTA and NAFTA, at least in Canada.[50] No definite answer has been proposed so far, given the complexity of the question. However, the inclusion of Mexico, and eventually of other Central or South American countries, in the free trade zone has enlivened the debate. While there is less fear of a decline in national labor standards when labor conditions are equivalent in the countries involved, the threat is amplified when labor conditions and legislation differ sharply from one state to another in the new integrated market.[51]

A "race to the bottom" would result from the mobility of capital. In selecting a location, a multinational firm can take advantage of differences in the costs of production that would result from establishing a plant in one country rather than another. This possibility adds a new source of pressure both on the negotiation of working conditions and on national legislation.

The formalization of economic integration brought about by the FTA and eventually NAFTA gives new credibility to the argument. Even though it does not create the mobility of capital, it facilitates and fosters plant relocation.[52] This argument has already been widely used in Canada, mainly in collective bargaining, and the first effects of a "race to the bottom" may well be seen in collective agreements. This threat will also be used to prevent the state from enacting any new social legislation or to convince the government to downgrade existing legislation.[53]

Moreover, the mechanism provided by the side accord to NAFTA on social legislation will not decrease the risk of weakened social policy in Canada. Aside from the fact that the side accord imposes no uniform and centralized labor standards, it contains major flaws that defeat the purpose for which it was negotiated. First, the enforceable provisions of the accord deal only with health and safety, child labor and minimum wages. It leaves aside important parts of Canadian social legislation such as those dealing with freedom of association, the right to organize, the right to bargain collectively and the right to strike, and minimum labor standards on such issues as unjust dismissal, pregnancy leave, hours of work, job security and so on. It is worth stressing the fact that, just like the first labor laws adopted more than a century ago, the side accord addresses only matters related to basic human dignity in the workplace.

Secondly, and perhaps most importantly, the side accord contains no provision preventing any of the three countries from deregulating its labor market. No enforcement mechanism that would ensure any upgrading and harmonization of social legislation is included. On the contrary, NAFTA promotes competition among states on the basis of labor costs and nothing in the side accord prevents this competition from leading to deregulation in areas of social policy. Even under the FTA, NAFTA and the side accord, it is the logic of the market that will prevail in shaping the social dimensions of North American economic integration.

76

Endnotes

1. In Canada, the agreement was ratified by *An Act to Implement the Free Trade Agreement between Canada and the United States of America,* S.C. 1988, c. 65.

2. In Canada, the agreement was ratified by 2. *An Act to Implement the North American Free Trade Agreement* (Bill C-115), adopted on May 27, 1993.

3. See Department of Finance 1991.

4. See D. Brunelle and C. Deblock 1991.

5. Ibid.

6. Expressed as a percentage of imports, the tariffs collected by Canada fell from more than 10 percent in 1955 to less than 4 percent in 1990. See Department of Finance, *L'Accord,* n. 3, p. 8.

7. Brunelle and Deblock, *Libre-éxchange,* n. 4, p. 12.

8. For example, the average of the Canadian tariffs on goods imported from the United States was 3.8 percent before the FTA took effect. The average of American tariffs imposed on Canadian goods was only 0.7 percent. See M. A. Moreau and G. Trudeau 1992.

9. See Economic Council of Canada 1992.

10. See T. Thomas 1990.

11. Ibid., pp. 9, 12.

12. Economic Council of Canada, *"Le libre-échange,"* n. 9, p. 14.

13. Thomas, *Le libre-échange* , n. 10, p. 14.

14. Economic Council of Canada, *Le libre-échange* , n. 9, p. 14.

15. Ibid.

16. Ibid., p. 15.

17. Department of Finance, *L'accord,* n. 3, p. 33.

18. See G. Vallee 1993.

19. See D.Brunelle and C. Deblock 1989.

20. See D. Brunelle and C. Deblock 1992.

21. On the concentration of cheap labor in Mexico, see D. Maschino 1992.,

22. Thomas, *Le libre-échange*, n. 10, p. 17.

23. The judicial precedent on this question is *Toronto Electric Commissioners v. Snider* [1925] A.C. 396. On this subject, see G. W. Adams 1985.

24. See A. Adams, n. 24, pp. 12 et seq.

25. See E. Theroux 1991.

26. See C. Lipton 1969.

27. See M. L. Coates, D. Arrowsmith, and M. Courchene 1989.

28. On the comparison between Canadian and American labor legislation, see G. Trudeau 1991.

29. See B. Langille 1991.

30. See P. C. Weiler 1983.

31. Langille, "Canadian Labour Law Reform", n. 30, p. 594.

32. For instance, the New Democratic Party, a political party that is very close to the labor movement, has played a major role in shaping Canadian labor policy. See P. G. Bruce 1989.

33. Moreau and Trudeau, "Les modes de véglementation," n. 8, pp. 375, 376.

34. The FTA entered into effect on January 1, 1989, and will be gradually implemented by January 1, 1999.

35. The FTA, s. 1904 (9). On the mechanism set up by Chapter 19, see E. Saucier 1991.

36. For an overview of NAFTA, see among others, S. Globerman 1993.

37. See Moreau and Trudeau 1985, H. Smit 1985, E. Vogel-Polsky and J. Vogel 1993, G. Guery 1991, N. Catala and R. Bonnet 1991, G. Lyon-Caen and A. Lyon-Caen 1991.

38. An independent expert must rule on whether a matter is covered by mutually recognized labor laws. See Annex 23 of the side accord.

39. This expression is defined in Article 49 of the side accord, and refers to laws and regulations directly related to the prohibition of forced labor, labor protection for children and young persons, minimum employment standards, elimination of employment discrimination, equal pay for men and women, prevention of and compensation for occupational injuries and illnesses, and protection of migrant workers. The definition also

specifies that the establishment of standards and levels concerning minimum wages and union protection for children is not subject to the side accord; in these two areas, only the application of the general standards is subject to the accord.

40. As defined in Article 49.

41. Annex 39 of the side accord describes the limits and items to be taken into account by the panel in determining the amount of the assessment payable.

42. The term "labor law" is used here in a very broad sense, including "employment law" as well. On the distinction between labor law and employment law, see B. Langille 1981.

43. See, for example, Privy Council Office 1968.

44. See particularly the legislation adopted in Great Britain, Ontario, and Quebec in the nineteenth century to impose some basic labor standards in factories. On the Quebec legislation, see particularly A. C. Côté 1985.

45. For a general discussion, J. M. Weiler, "The Role of Law in Labor Relations," a text prepared for the Research Advisory Group in Law, Society, and the Economy, Royal Commission on the Economic Union and Development Prospects for Canada.

46. This is true at an individual and collective level since labor law has challenged the presumption of equality of the contracting parties stated by private law.

47. On the concept of state subsidies, see J. Stanford 1991.

48. This hypothesis is presented in Stanford, *Going South*, n. 49, p. 28.

49. For example, in Quebec, the government announced an economic action plan. According to the Minister of Industry and Trade, this plan is centered on a deregulation of the labor market mainly by giving up some vested rights in collective agreements, collective agreements extended by government decrees, and in the Labor Code ("La relance économique passe par l'abolition de certains acquis", *Le Devoir*, August 30, 1993, p. 2.)

50. For a detailed account of this debate, see Langille, "Canadian Labour Law Reform," n. 30.

51. In Canada, where the provinces have the most jurisdiction over labor law, it does not seem that a "race to the bottom" has occurred between the provinces, even though they are already largely integrated. See Langille, Canadian Labour law Reform," n. 30..

52. For instance, the phenomenon of maquiladoras in Mexico, which can be seen as both a manifestation of the mobility of international (mostly American) capital and of economic integration with the United States, appeared even though no treaties between Mexico and the United States have formalized it. On maquiladoras, see S. Peters 1990.

53. This argument is more likely to be considered in the context of the changing role of the state in Canada. Some studies, even though not in labor law, have shown that North American economic integration accompanies a fundamental transformation of the role of the state in Canada. Since the end of the 1930s and until recently, the role of the state in Canada was based on Keynesianism. In the last decade, an evolution toward a neoliberal conception of the role of the state has been noted. According to this new conception, the market plays a larger role both in economic and social regulation. The idea of a free trade agreement with the United States gained momentum at the same time mainly through the recommendations of the Macdonald Commission. Moreover, it is to be noted that, in the same decade, the Canadian Charter of Rights was entrenched in the Constitution, guaranteeing thereby the supremacy of neoliberal individualist values. See D. Brunelle, "Le rapport des "sages" et la Loi constitutionnelle de 1982: une analyse régressive," in *Le droit dans tous ses états*, edited by R. D. Bureau and P. Mackay, Wilson et Lafleur 1987, pp. 35-53. This evolution in the role of the state undermines our earlier assertion that there exists a fundamental difference between the role of the state in Canada and the United States.

References

Adams, G. W. 1985. *Canadian Labor Law* (Aurora, Ont.: Canada Law Book), 100.

Bruce, P. G. 1989. "Political Parties and Labor Legislation in Canada and the U.S.," *Industrial Relations* 28: 115.

Brunelle D. and C. Deblock. 1992. *Libre-échange et continentalisation: le cas du Canada* (Montréal: Groupe de recherche sur la continentalisation des économies canadienne et mexicaine, *Cahier de recherche* 91-1, January), pp. 12 and 34.

..... 1992. "Canada, Mexico, and Continentalism: Analysis of the New Parameters of Integration," p. 14.

..... 1989. *Le libre-échange par défaut* (Montréal: vlb éditeur), pp. 242-45.

Coates, M. L., D. Arrowsmith, and M. Courchene, *The Current Industrial Relations Scene in Canada* (Kingston: School of Industrial Relations/Industrial Relations Centre, Queen's University), p. 20.

Catala, N. and R. Bonnet. 1991. *Droit social européen* (Paris).

Côté, A. C. 1985. "L'Acte des manufactures de Québec, 1885, un centenaire," *Relations industrielles* 40: 623.

Department of Finance. 1992. *L'Accord de libre-échange nord-américain. Evaluation économique selon une perspective canadienne.* (Ottawa: November): 6.

Economic Council of Canada. 1992. "Libre échange: Canada - Etats-Unis - Mexique" *Au courant* 13, no. 1, p. 14.

Globerman, S. 1993. "Canada's Interests in North American Economic Integration," *Canadian Public Administration* 36: 91 et seq.

Guery, G. 1991. *La dynamique de l'Europe sociale* (Paris: Dunod).

Langille, B. 1991. "Canadian Labor Law Reform and Free Trade," *Ottawa Law Review*, 23 (1991): 587.

..... 1981. "Labor Law Is a Subset of Employment Law," *University of Toronto Law Journal* 31: 200.

Lipton, C. 1969. *The Trade Union Movement of Canada 1827-1959*, 2d ed. (Montreal: Canadian Social Publications) p. 23.

Lyon-Caen, G. and A. Lyon-Caen. 1991. *Droit social international et européen*, (Paris: Dalloz).

Maschino, D. 1992. "Salaires et relations du travail dans un contexte de libre-échange nord-américain. La comparaison Mexique-Québec," *Le marché du travail* (October): 6 et seq.

Moreau, M. A. and G. Trudeau. 1992. "Les modes de réglementation sociale à l'heure de l'ouverture des frontières: quelques réflexions autour des modèles européen et nord-américain." *Cahiers de Droit* 33: 375.

Peters, S. 1990. "Labor Law for the Maquiladora: Choosing Between Workers' Rights and Foreign Investment," *Comparative Labor Law Journal*, 2: 226.

Privy Council Office. 1968. *Les relations du travail au Canada*, Report of the Staff Relations Task Force, H. D. Woods chairman, December, pp. 13-14.

Saucier, E. 1991. "Les aspects procéduraux du mécanisme de règlement des différends en matière de dumping et de subventionnement," 25 *Revue juridique Thémis* 523.

Smit, H. 1985. "The Relevance of the EEC Experience to Additional Prospective Sectoral Integration between Canada and the United States," 10 (1985): *Canada-United-States Law Journal* 53.

Stanford, J. 1991. *Going South, Cheap Labor as an Unfair Subsidy in North American Free Trade* (The Canadian Centre for Policy Alternatives, December), pp. 12 et seq.

Theroux, E. 1991. "Du traité de réciprocité à l'Accord de libre-échange," *Revuw juridique Thémis*, 25: 227.

Thomas, T. 1990. *Le libre-échange entre le Mexique, le Canada et les Etats-Unis: le contexte et les enjeux* (Ottawa: Library of Parliament, Research Branch), p. 11.

Trudeau, G. 1991. "L'impact de l'accord de libre-échange canado-américain sur les relations du travail au Québec et leur encadrement juridique," *La Revue juridique Thémis*, 25: p. 279.

Vallee, G. 1993. "L'intégration économique nord-américaine et le droit du travail au Canada," paper presented at the International Congress of the Sociology of Law, Mexico, July 1992, published in *Document de recherche* 93-04, École de relations industrielles, Université de Montréal, August, pp. 6-8.

Vogel-Polsky, E. and J. Vogel. 1991. *L'Europe sociale: illusion, alibi ou réalité*, (Brussels: University of Brussels.

Weiler, P. C. 1983. "Promises to Keep: Securing Workers' Rights to Self-Organization under the NLRA," *Harvard Law Review*, 96: 1769.

The Social Dimension of Freer Trade

Roy J. Adams and Lowell Turner

Introduction

In recent times there has been a general global movement toward freer trade. Notable developments include the single European market, the negotiation of a Canada-U.S. trade agreement subsequently expanded into the North American Free Trade Agreement (NAFTA), and most recently, the completion of Uruguay Round GATT negotiations resulting in both a worldwide lowering of trade barriers and the establishment of a new world trade organization. Although the primary objective of these initiatives has been to remove trade barriers, changing one aspect of an economic system can have broad impacts. Because freer trade has implications not only for business and consumers but also for labor, the "social dimension" of free trade has attracted a good deal of international attention.

The objective of this paper is to review the general reasons for including a social dimension in free trade agreements and to discuss approaches both actual and suggested to the social side of trade. While many reasons have been cited for the inclusion of social and labor protections in trade agreements, we argue that the primary driving force for a social dimension is to build political support for freer trade. As evidence for this proposition, we review the development of both the European single market and NAFTA. If our argument is right, then free trade negotiations should be viewed not as a curse by labor but as an opportunity to push for higher labor standards and new protections, in more and less developed countries alike.

The rationale for a social dimension to free trade

One of the most widely noted justifications for the establishment of a social dimension as part of any free trade agreement is to avoid "social dumping." The basic idea is that no partner in such a trade agreement should derive competitive advantage from inadequate labor standards. While the concept is straightforward, interpretation is not.

Some countries in Europe, notably Portugal, Spain and Greece, are at a level of development that is considerably below that of more advanced countries such as Germany and France. Because they are not as rich, firms in the less developed countries cannot afford to provide the same level of wages, benefits and social security as firms in the wealthier countries. To insist that they do so is simply unrealistic, a position that is accepted as such by all members of the EEC. The same holds true for Mexico in the emerging North American Free Trade area. Table 1 provides estimates of average hourly compensation costs for production workers in manufacturing.

The table indicates that differences among countries in the European Union (Germany, Greece, Spain, Portugal) are quite substantial, as are differences between the members of the North American Free Trade Zone. Although the data in Table 1 suggest that the gap between Portugal and Germany is about the same as the gap between Mexico and the United States, other comparisons indicate an even larger gap in North America than in Europe. In the steel industry, for example, Hufbauer and Schott (1992, p.244) report that U.S. compensation is approximately eight times that of Mexico.

Table 2 provides an estimate of differences in per capita GNP. The difference between Mexico and the United States in dollar terms is substantially greater than the difference between Portugal and Germany. However, one study that attempted to estimate the purchasing power of GNP concluded that the differences between Mexico and the United States, while considerable, were not so great as the raw figures would suggest. Variation in estimations of economic differences has made it very difficult to achieve consensus about the viability of North American free trade and the relevance of European experience in evaluating the likely impact of a Canada-United States-Mexico pact.

Although it is generally recognized that partners to a free trade agreement cannot be expected to have identical social conditions, it is also considered improper for any country deliberately to maintain poor conditions in order to gain a trade advantage. Such an approach has recently been likened to a form of government subsidy, while the elimination of such subsidies is a major object of trade agreements (Stanford 1992). Adopting a social charter in which all parties to a trade pact affirm a set of social standards, with some form of unbiased adjudication to enforce adherence to the accepted standards, is one way to address the problem of social dumping. In the European Community, the Charter of Fundamental Social Rights provides the standards, while the European Court of Justice provides the adjudicatory tribunal (see, for example, Springer 1992).

A second issue giving rise to the need for a social dimension is the growth of the multinational firm. When enterprises were national in scope they could be effectively regulated by national governments. As they have become increasingly multinational, it has become more difficult to establish effective regulations on a national basis. As a result, international organizations such as the International Labor Office and the Organization for Economic Cooperation and Development have evolved standards of conduct for such firms, standards that are used as benchmarks in the negotiation of multinational trade agreements.

A third reason for a social dimension to free trade agreements has to do with the overall objectives of any democratic society. In such a society, the nation pursues an efficient economy not for its own sake but rather to improve the general welfare. Attaching a social charter to an international trade agreements, for example, is a way of ensuring citizens within a free trade area that the ultimate objective of the exercise is to improve the conditions of work and life for the average individual, as opposed to improving the conditions of certain groups to the disadvantage of others.

The final reason for promoting a social dimension is to achieve social consensus. This is a primary rationale for the attention given to the issue by the European Commission. The belief is that over the long run (or even medium run), an important condition for the smooth functioning of an efficient market is a high level of acceptance by all relevant parties of the rules and regulations guiding the substance and process of that market. High levels of conflict and social unrest are major reasons for market dysfunction. This has been demonstrated both by micro- and macro-level studies. At the macro level, countries with a cooperative labor-management culture (such as Germany and Japan) have generally outperformed those with a confrontational culture (such as the United Kingdom and the United States) over the past several decades (see, for example, Adams 1992; 1994b). At the micro level the same holds true for individual enterprises. Most experts have concluded that Japanese economic success in recent decades is in large part due to the ability of Japanese firms to establish labor-management "productivity coalitions"—that is, labor-management cooperation at the enterprise level in pursuit of higher productivity (see, for example, Womack et al. 1990).

A social charter is a means of securing labor's cooperation in the implementation of freer trade. Such cooperation has been achieved in Europe where labor movements almost unanimously have supported the move toward a single European market (Springer 1992). In North America, by contrast, labor's opposition to freer trade (Jackson 1992; Cowie 1994), although ultimately unsuccessful, has resulted in the inclusion in NAFTA of quite modest yet new international labor protections. While the latter are weak and viewed as a defeat for labor (Cowie and French 1994), we suggest an alternative perspective: to see the new provisions as a platform upon which labor can build, especially in budding efforts at cross-national union collaboration. This is especially relevant within the context of contemporary labor policy reform debates in the United States and Mexico.

Although social charters are generally seen to be something of value to individuals and labor organizations, a working party of the European Commission, established in 1988 to develop a Community position on the social dimension, concluded on the basis of considerable evidence that social clauses in trade agreements were of positive benefit not only to labor but also to industry (Commission of the European Communities 1988). Similar conclusions have been reached by analysts of NAFTA (see, for example, Hinojosa-Ojeda and Robinson 1992).

The Development of the Social Dimension in Europe

The European Coal and Steel Community

In 1950 a proposal for establishing a European common market in coal and steel was formulated. A major factor giving rise to the proposal was the onset of the cold war (see, for example, Collins, vol. 1, 1975; Kerr 1987). By 1950 both Czechoslovakia and Hungary had become communist; the threat of open conflict between the Soviet Union and the West appeared real. Although there was a perceived need to meet the threat there was also fear of a rearmed Germany. In order to forestall the emergence of another Western European internal conflict, a common market for coal and steel—the essential war industries—was set up. In 1951, the Treaty of Paris established the European Coal and Steel Community, composed of the following agencies:

a. The High Authority had primary administrative responsibility. Although made up of appointees from the six original countries (France, Germany, Italy, Belgium, Netherlands, and Luxembourg), allegiance was supposed to be supranational. The primary function of the High Authority was to establish a free market in coal and steel (including the free movement of workers), and, toward that end, to help inefficient producers modernize and ease the social problems of transition. It was given the power to impose a levy on the coal and steel companies, to make loans, and to collect information with a view toward establishing common standards.

b. The Council of Ministers was composed of relevant ministers from the six countries. With some exceptions the council had to approve the initiatives of the High Authority. Its main function was to protect the sovereignty concerns of the nations involved. Because critical decisions had to be unanimous, each country had an effective veto over decisions of the ECSC.

c. An advisory body composed of equal numbers of management and labor representatives, along with others such as professionals and farmers. This body was set up in part as a response to the fears of trade unions concerning a fall in wage levels and a rise in unemployment resulting from the new freer trade. As an additional means to address union concerns, it was agreed that at least one member of the High Authority would be representative of union views.

d. An Assembly composed either of members appointed from the parliaments of each country or individuals directly elected to the ECSC. This body was largely advisory.

e. A Court of Justice whose function was to settle disputes with respect to the interpretation and operation of the legislation creating the ECSC.

There was no social charter built into the Treaty of Paris which created the ECSC. Nevertheless, the treaty did declare that a basic purpose of the Community was to promote better conditions of living and work for workers in all of the affected industries. The treaty also asserted a need to safeguard the continuity of employment. Means for reaching these general goals were to be worked out by negotiation between the various institutions involved with the operation of the coal and steel market. In 1967 the ECSC was absorbed into the broader European Economic Community and continues to exist today as a department of the European Community.

In the years prior to its merger with the EEC, the ECSC carried out a good deal of research on training, health and safety, and on the reintegration of redundant workers. The ECSC also made substantial grants to assist redeployment and for the construction of housing, which after World War II was particularly problematic. At the same time, ambitious proposals by worker representatives for social advances such as a "Miners Charter," to provide common standards for pensions, guaranteed wages, regularity of employment, vocational training rights, and the like, failed to win the support of either governments or employers (Collins 1975: 73-78).

In the mid 1970s, subsequent to the first oil price shock, world demand for steel fell significantly. One result was that the ECSC began to manage steel production more actively than it had in the past. Establishing country output quotas and pushing for vigorous restructuring, the new approach became known as the Davignon plan, named after Etienne Davignon, the commissioner for industrial policy. To assist restructuring, substantial funds "were made available for: voluntary early retirement, short-time working, tide-over allowances, training and retraining, severance pay, and other benefits" (Bain 1992: 45). This assistance "made the restructuring process more acceptable by reducing the costs to the government and the firms." It also "created a better climate for the unions to accept restructuring" (Bain 1992: 47). Some countries (such as Germany) were, however, more vigilant in implementing the ECSC's restructuring plan than were others (such as Italy), giving rise to some controversy. Nevertheless, on the whole the initiative was considered to be a success.

The European Economic Community

By the mid-1950s fears of the reemergence of internal conflict within Western Europe as a motive for economic integration had subsided. Nevertheless some countries continued to push for broader integration. In 1955 an intergovernmental committee was established to look at the possibilities of further supranational integration. The primary theme of the resultant Spaak report concerned the economic advantages of a larger general market. The report argued that "the resulting increase in economic strength would enable Europe to acquire a political and economic stature comparable with that of the United States and the United StatesSR" (Collins 1975, vol. 2: 7; see also Addison and Siebert 1991). The report paid little attention to social matters and did not foresee "any large transfer of responsibility to a supra-national field." The theory embraced by the committee was that the free movement of workers ensured that market forces would even out social disparities.

The Spaak report was endorsed by the same countries that had entered into the ECSC. With the Treaty of Rome, signed in 1957, the European Economic Community came into being.[1] Although there were six founding members of the EEC, the Franco-German rapprochement was central to the agreement; the original EEC was founded most essentially upon a deal between French agriculture which would be protected, and German industry, which would get the open export markets that it needed.

The institutions of the EEC followed the pattern of the ECSC. From the outset the "European Assembly" (later to become known as the European Parliament) and the Court of Justice served both bodies. Instead of a High Authority, the Rome Treaty established a Commission. As with the ECSC there was a Council of Ministers (in which each country had a veto over issues seen as critical to national sovereignty; less critical issues could be decided by a qualified majority) as well as a tripartite advisory body. Unlike the ECSC, the European Commission was given no levy powers. The EEC Treaty did, however, establish a Social Fund which enabled the Commission to support initiatives to overcome the social effects of restructuring. Money from the fund has been allotted to training, recruitment and wage grants, resettlement assistance, and job creation (Springer 1992).

The commission, after complicated consultations with the other institutions, may issue several kinds of statements. First it can adopt regulations, binding on all member states in a manner similar to national legislation. Member states, however, have to apply the regulations; the commission has no enforcement administration. Directives are also binding on the member states; in this case, however, the means for making the directives effective are left to the states. In other words, each state may have different legislation as long as that legislation meets the intent of the directive. Both regulations and directives must be approved by the Council of Ministers, where each country has veto power for issues of importance. The commission may also issue recommendations, opinions, memoranda, and communications, none of which are binding but which provide a framework for intergovernmental negotiations and, in some cases, guidelines for corporate and union actions. The commission may also make Decisions on issues of immediate concern such as aid to West Africa. Although it is up to individual national governments to implement the first two sorts of instruments, community law does give individuals rights that they may make effective by resort to either national courts or the European Court of Justice. Depending on the issue, rights may be enforced "vertically" against member states or "horizontally" against other persons, such as employers. For example, equal pay for men and women has been held by the Court of Justice to be enforceable both vertically and horizontally (Hepple 1990).

For the most part the nations involved have conformed to requirements established by the EEC, although enforcement has been variable. EC regulations have impacted some countries to a much greater degree than others. In Britain, for example, approximately three quarters of British regulation with respect to occupational health and safety derive from EC regulations and directives (Addison and Siebert 1992: 496). It should not be surprising that enforcement of EC regulations has not been entirely uniform. Research on the administration of labor standards indicates that such standards are generally honored by large firms more than by small to medium-sized firms (Starr 1981). This observation is true not only in poorer countries but also in highly advanced countries like Canada and the United States (Adams 1987). Indeed government administration of labor standards in small to medium-sized firms, for example, through inspections and response to complaints, has not been very effective anywhere. This is one reason for the development of the so-called internal responsibility system in which labor-management committees are responsible for the implementation of legislation.

The veto power of the European Council of Ministers has provided insurance that no legislation seen to be critically averse to the interests of any of the member countries can be passed. Requirements for unanimous agreement have also had the effect of ensuring that movement toward common social standards has been very slow.

Initially France was concerned that its substantial legislated benefits would place it at a competitive disadvantage in a free market. As a result it pushed for and won a few social clauses in the Rome Treaty such as equal pay for men and women as well as specific standards on a few issues (for example, paid leave). As noted above, however, no general charter was included in the treaty.

In the late 1960s Europe entered into a period of social upheaval. Strikes, demonstrations, and demands for social change rose in incidence and volume. One result was that the EEC began to look more closely at social issues. In 1972, the commission developed its first "action program," which went into effect in 1974. That program produced directives on collective redundancies, employee rights company ownership changes, and protection of employees in the event of company insolvency (Hepple 1990; Addison and Siebert 1991). In addition the equal pay issue was revitalized, resulting in an equal pay directive in 1975 (providing equal pay for work of equal value), an equal treatment directive in 1976, and a directive on equal treatment for men and women in social security in 1978. Legislation was also passed with respect to health and safety and an action program to put the new requirements into effect was initiated.

Wolfgang Streeck (1991) has shown well how the European Commission enlarged its mandate by moving into new and "open" areas such as gender pay equality and environmental protection, areas for which national governments had not yet developed adequate rules or institutions. It is also quite clear that the EC's "social activism" of the 1970s followed directly upon the social unrest and "resurgence" of class conflict (Crouch and Pizzorno 1978) of the late 1960s and early 1970s.

Several draft directives on labor issues were also formulated and strongly promoted during this period. One proposed regulation, for example, would have allowed the incorporation of a European company. The draft provided for workers' participation in enterprise decision making modeled on German practice, including works councils with rights to information, consultation, and co-decision on certain issues. This proposal met with considerable opposition from employer groups and from some governments. Other proposals giving employee representatives the right to information, consultation, and participation, such as the Vredeling directive were also proposed and hotly debated (Turner 1993a: 51-54). Although none of these directives were successful in the 1970s or 1980s, the commission continues to consider this issue crucial to the maintenance of a long-term consensus within the EEC. It is now widely expected that a directive on consultation and participation rights (requiring "Euro-works councils" at multinational firms) will soon be implemented as the result of the ratification of the Maastricht Treaty, which expands the area of qualified majority voting (as opposed to unanimity; see below) for social legislation.[2]

In the early 1980s, as the European economy sank into a deep recession, movement toward social innovation slowed down. The new focus was on competitiveness, flexibility, and relieving high levels of long-term unemployment. In addition, by this time the Community had grown: Britain, Denmark, and Ireland joined in 1973, Greece became a member in 1981, and Spain and Portugal would join in 1986. By the early 1980s, the antiregulatory government of Margaret Thatcher in Britain was regularly vetoing (or just as effective, threatening to veto) any attempt by the Commission to introduce new social legislation. Nevertheless, in a few areas there were new initiatives.

Considerable progress was made in the area of health and safety. Two new action programs in the 1980s led to directives on several aspects of industrial health and safety including major accidents, lead, ionizing radiation, asbestos, hazardous agents, noise, heavy loads, personal protective equipment, and the effects of VDUs. Initiatives were also taken on training, new information technology, local employment creation, the rights of disabled people, employment growth, training for young people, and vocational training for women. Several directives were adopted on equal treatment of men and women.

The situation changed again in the late 1980s. In 1985 the commission decided, in a context of increasing competition from Asia and economic inertia in Europe, to move vigorously toward removing remaining barriers to competition. A Single European Market Act was passed in 1987 which adopted the goal of removing all barriers to trade by 1992. Little regard was paid to the social dimension until the Commission took up the issue in 1988. According to some observers this was a belated attempt to placate labor, but according to the commission, the intention from the outset was to include a social dimension in the single market. In 1989 a Charter of Fundamental Social Rights was accepted by the heads of state of all member governments except Britain (Hepple 1990).

The charter denotes the following fundamental social rights: freedom of movement, freedom to choose and engage in an occupation and to be fairly remunerated, the improvement of living and working conditions, the right to social protection, the right to freedom of association and collective bargaining, the right to vocational training, the right of men and women to equal treatment, the right of workers to information, consultation, and participation, the right to health protection and safety at the workplace, the protection of children and young persons, the rights of the elderly, and the rights of disabled persons.

Even though the charter is not a legally binding document, the eleven approving member states did commit themselves to take the steps necessary to make the terms of the charter a reality. Toward that end, the commission put an action program into effect which contained 49 proposals. By the end of 1992 most had been adopted or seemed likely to be adopted (Addison and Siebert 1992). Thirty-two of the 49 proposals required a decision by the council, and 17 of these had been adopted. These included seven directives on health and safety (temporary workers, medical treatment on ships, temporary and mobile construction sites, drilling, mines and quarries, health and safety signs and asbestos); two directives having to do with employment rights (proof of an employment relationship and collective redundancies); one directive on pregnant women; decisions having to do with the initiation of a vocational training and with action for the elderly; recommendations on social protection (two); childcare and financial participation of employees; and one regulation on freedom of movement.[3]

Several draft proposals were derailed by the continuing opposition of the British government. Early in 1992, however, eleven of the twelve member states (with Britain dissenting) adopted the Treaty on European Union at Maastricht in the Netherlands. The primary focus of this initiative was the achievement of a monetary union and movement toward a more unified political system. In addition, however, the eleven agreed to permit qualified majority voting on many of the social issues that previously required unanimity. In a new protocol, the Community adopted as formal objectives the promotion of employment, the improvement of living and working conditions, social protection, and the promotion of dialogue between labor and management.

By the end of 1992 all members of the EEC had ratified the treaty except for Britain and Denmark. Initially defeated in Denmark, after further negotiations the Maastricht Treaty was ratified there by popular vote in the spring of 1993. The British House of Commons voted in favor of the treaty (excluding the Social Protocol) in May of 1993. With the treaty ratified by all twelve member states and signed into law in the fall of 1993, social dimension prospects are enhanced by the replacement of unanimous voting on the Council of Ministers with the qualified majority principle. In particular, the imminent implementation of a Euro-works council directive (mandating cross-national information committees at large multinational firms) increases the likelihood of new initiatives for cross-national union collaboration (Turner 1993b).

Informed and perceptive analysts are in many cases quite pessimistic about the substance of a social dimension and its capacity to regulate the European single market in a way that affords workers and their unions much protection at all (Streeck 1991; Keller 1993). On the other hand, this is the first time in history that cross-national labor standards and union collaboration have developed as far as they have; it may be quite premature to be overly pessimistic so early on.

NAFTA

In June of 1990 the United States and Mexico agreed to discuss the possibility of a free trade agreement between the two countries. This event was the culmination of a series of U.S. initiatives toward freer trade in North America. Between 1985 and

1989, Mexico and the United States had signed three major trade accords, and in the same period the United States had signed the Canada-U.S. Free Trade Agreement (Hufbauer and Schott 1992). The United States action was prompted in part by the growing competition from both Europe and Asia and the belief that expanding North American trade would improve the efficiency and productivity of American enterprises. Another U.S. objective was to promote economic growth, political stability and progress toward democracy in Mexico—not just for altruistic reasons but because illegal immigration from Mexico had become a serious problem in the U.S. Southwest. Moreover, a prosperous Mexico would "become a thriving market for U.S. exports" (Hufbauer and Schott 1992: 11). Although Canada had little independent interest in a free trade pact with Mexico, it felt compelled to become involved in order to protect its interests. As a result, the NAFTA agreement was signed by all three countries in 1992.

Initially NAFTA, like the European Common Market Accord, did not have a social dimension, and it was strongly opposed by organized labor in both the United States and Canada. The major voice of labor in Mexico, the Confederation of Mexican Workers, (CTM) is closely tied to the party in power, the Institutional Revolutionary Party (PRI) and, as a result, accepted the accord. The opposition of labor in Canada and the United States was based on the expectation that American and Canadian companies would move plants to Mexico for the low wages and the health, safety, and environmental standards well below those to the north (Jackson 1992; Friedman 1992). In the process, Canadian and American jobs would be lost. In effect, Canadian and American employers would receive a social subsidy from Mexico, to the detriment of American and Canadian workers.

That analysis has caused a good deal of controversy. Econometric studies on the effects of the pact suggest that it will produce more, rather than fewer, net jobs (see Hufbauer and Schott 1992; Lustig et al. 1992), although there will be winners and losers. Economists generally expect jobs to grow the most in Mexico, but they also expect growth to the north. That research, however, is based on models that make controversial assumptions; as a result, a consensus position has not yet developed. There is, however, general agreement that many lower-skilled jobs in Canada and the United States will disappear in the foreseeable future under pressure from low labor costs in other countries; and NAFTA is expected to exacerbate this development. For workers who lose their jobs, the United States lacks the infrastructure to ensure smooth resettlement in new productive work. The system of labor adjustment in the United States is in fact, among the worst among industrialized countries (Hufbauer and Schott 1992: 113). The Canadian system, by contrast, is considerably more developed and continues to improve with recent initiatives at the federal and the provincial level. Nevertheless, the threat of job loss with expanded free trade remains a major concern in both countries.

The debate more recently has shifted its focus to skilled jobs. In some industries, American companies have been able to establish technologically advanced production operations in Mexico comparable to those in Canada and the United States (Shaiken 1990). The question is whether that success can be repeated on a broad scale. If so, then not only low-skill, low-pay jobs may be in danger in the North but also the jobs of the highly skilled as well. In general, lower education, poorer health, and inadequate infrastructure mean that Western companies operating in less developed countries cannot approach the same levels of productivity as in the home country even with identical technology. Integrated steel mills in the United States, for example, need only one-third as many hours to produce a ton of steel as do comparable mills in Mexico (Hufbauer and Schott 1992: 244).

The threat of massive job loss, even if accompanied by equal or larger levels of new jobs, is a particular problem for organized labor in the United States. As capital mobility increases, the jobs lost in the United States are in many cases high-wage, union jobs. Because the playing field is no longer level and it is now so difficult for unions to organize new workplaces, employment shifts foreseen to accelerate under NAFTA, in the absence of substantial labor law reform, may well contribute to the continuing downward trend in union membership in the United States.

In the United States presidential election of 1992, Bill Clinton, running with the support of organized labor, promised that if elected he would add side agreements on labor and the environment to the NAFTA Treaty (Cowie 1994). Those talks began in March, 1993. Among the objectives of the U.S. negotiators were the establishment of cooperative mechanisms for assessing the impact of the agreement and devising means for addressing problems that arise. Negotiators also sought more and better data sharing and technical assistance. The United States, in addition, sought better enforcement of general labor standards as well as particular national laws and pushed for tripartite commissions to oversee the implementation of any side agreement. Enforcement mechanisms built into the intellectual property agreement were put forth as a potential model for labor standards enforcement. These include the ability of an injured party to win substantial damages in court and to be accorded immediate injunctive relief. Also considered were provisions allowing border guards to confiscate goods produced illegally under intellectual property laws or produced in factories operating contrary to the provisions of the labor side agreement, and due process guarantees for workers.[4]

A background paper prepared by the Congressional Office of Technology Assessment (1992) to assist Congress to formulate a satisfactory policy, provided additional options including the following (noted particularly in Robinson 1993a):

A North American Social and Environmental Charter, to be developed, monitored, and enforced by a North American Commission for Labor and Social Welfare.

A continental Auto Pact.

A continental investment policy aimed at preventing bidding wars for private investment among the federal, state, and local governments of the three countries.

Making access to NAFTA markets for apparel contingent upon respect for worker rights through provisions located in the GATT revisions to the Multi-Fibre Agreement, or in an OAS-level agreement.

A Binational Commission of U.S.-Mexico Border Environment and infrastructure.

The provision of technical assistance to Mexico on matters relating to workplace health and safety.

92

The provision of loans and aid for balanced economic development in Mexico, including the creation of a North American Development Bank.

Establishment of North American works councils in firms employing more than 1,000 employees and more than 100 employees in each of the three countries, to provide a mechanism for negotiated resolutions to labor tensions among the three countries.

A reduction of the continental work week; and

A Commission on the Future of Political Democracy in North America.

These options drew on European experience but were also directed toward the elimination of problems specific to North America. In the social area, in fact, Mexican standards are in many respects quite progressive. On a number of issues they exceed formal requirements in the United States. With respect to health and safety, for example, Mexico has ratified 72 ILO conventions while the United States has adopted only ten (Hufbauer and Schott 1992: 119). A comparison of several standards is provided in Table 3. The problem with labor standards in Mexico is not that they are formally so poor but rather that enforcement is lax. As noted above, however, enforcement of labor standards in small to medium-sized firms is a serious problem in many countries, including the United States and Canada. Generally, large, highly visible firms voluntarily abide by the formal rules. But they are more likely to do so if there is an employee representative body resident in the firm.

Respect for human rights has also been problematic in Mexico. It is widely recognized that the 1988 presidential election was rife with irregularities and that if a fair election had been conducted the Institutional Revolutionary Party (PRI), in power in Mexico for much of the twentieth century, may have been defeated. In addition, in the years after that election there was considerable repression of leaders opposed to the PRI; the murder of more than 100 of those leaders has been reported (Robinson 1993a). Sheldon Friedman, of the AFL-CIO, reports the case of labor leader Agapito Gonzales Cavazos who was arrested in 1992 on charges of tax evasion while negotiating a collective agreement with several companies operating in the maquiladora export processing zone. Although the charges did not hold up in court, Gonzales was held in jail for several months, during which time the workers involved in the negotiations settled for wage increases considerably below the rate of inflation (Friedman 1992). It is because of such irregularities that the U.S. Congress's Office of Technology Assessment recommended the establishment of a commission on political democracy in North America.

Elements of a North American Social Charter

Drawing on the above review, we suggest that an effective North American social charter, beneficial to all concerned, might include the following elements.

An affirmation of general social rights. Drawing in part on the European Social Charter, these might include all of the following:

1. The right of workers to be fairly remunerated.

2. The right of workers to expect improvements in living and working conditions as a consequence of the positive economic returns of freer trade.

3. The right of workers to freely choose an agent to represent their employment interests to the employer.

4. The right of workers to training appropriate to their jobs and necessary for advancement.

5. The right of men and women to equal treatment with respect to all aspects of employment.

6. The right of workers to information, consultation, and participation in the making of decisions critical to their employment status.

7. The right of workers to health protection and safety at the workplace.

8. The right of workers who become disabled to appropriate care and support and, if possible, continued employment.

9. Equal employment opportunity for workers of all national and racial groups.

In addition to the charter it would also be beneficial to have:

1. Elected works councils whose job it would be to receive information about the prospects of the firm and consult with management about decisions critical to the welfare of the workforce. The councils might also have the responsibility to ensure the effective implementation of health and safety regulations, employment equity, and other labor standards. In multiplant and multinational firms, there might be enterprisewide committees to discuss concerns common to the company as a whole. Mandatory health and safety committees are already established by law in both Mexico and Canada, while a bill requiring them in the United States is currently working its way through Congress. Several North American labor analysts have recently proposed the universal establishment of councils with a wider mandate to provide a forum for labor-management consultation and worker participation (see, for example, Weiler 1990; Freeman 1990; Adams 1986).

2. A trilateral commission with either levy power or income from a border tax whose job it would be (a) to carry out research and recommend to labor, management, and government ways that the charter could be made more effective internationally; (b) to make loans and grants likely to improve the economic well-being of firms and employees; and (c) to make policy recommendations to governments. Several analysts have pointed to the critical need for an agency with this sort of a mandate as part of the broader NAFTA agreement (see, for example, Hinojosa-Ojeda and Robinson 1992).

3. An adjudicatory tribunal whose function it would be to settle disputes over the interpretation of all aspects of the free trade agreement, including the social charter. Over time such an agency could be expected to develop a body of jurisprudence similar to the "arbitral jurisprudence" that has accumulated under collective bargaining in Canada and the United States. That body has provided a fairly clear set of behavioral rules for the guidance of labor and management and is generally considered to be one of the most positive accomplishments of the North American pattern of collective bargaining.

The Labor Side Accord

The actual labor side accord that was negotiated by the Clinton administration did not result in a package of rights and duties as rich and well articulated as the one discussed above nor as advanced as the European Social Charter with its accompanying implementation mechanisms. Nevertheless, it did include among its objectives the promotion "to the maximum extent possible" of the following labor principles:

1.   Freedom of association and protection of the right to organize.

2.   The right to bargain collectively.

3.   The right to strike.

4.   Prohibition of forced labor.

5.   Labor protections for children and young persons.

6.   Minimum employment standards.

7.   Elimination of employment discrimination.

8.   Equal pay for women and men.

9.   Prevention of occupational injuries and illnesses.

10.   Compensation in cases of occupational injuries and illnesses.

Each country, in signing the agreement, publicly promised to abide by and promote those principles and to "promote compliance with and effective enforcement" of labor regulations designed to achieve those ends (p. 3). However, as with most international labor standards, the *North American Agreement on Labor Cooperation* specifically recognizes the right of each party to put the principles into effect in its own way: "affirming full respect for each Party's constitution, and recognizing the right of each Party to establish its own domestic labor standards, and to adopt or modify accordingly its labor laws and regulations..." (p. 3). Because the complex enforcement mechanism included in the agreement applies only to disputes over child labor, occupational health and safety, and minimum wages, critics dismiss as meaningless the inclusion of most of these principles. Most dialogue since the passage of NAFTA has either dismissed or completely ignored the affirmation by the three governments of these principles. Indeed some (Robinson 1993b; Cowie and French 1994) have suggested that the side accord is a step backward because it makes inoperative the option (by the United States) of using trade sanctions as a threat to pressure delinquent governments into complying with generally accepted labor standards.

Although we understand the apprehension of those concerned with labor's welfare, we are more optimistic about the potential of the agreement. We too would have preferred a stronger commitment by all three parties to support the principles with common substantive regulations and adjudicatory procedures likely to ensure compliance with the regulations. Nevertheless, we suggest that formally strong enforcement procedures are no guarantee that the principles they are designed to support will be honored and that strong adherence to principle can occur even in the absence of supposedly strong enforcement procedures.

Two examples are illustrative. First, the National Labor Relations Act in the United States includes very strong enforcement procedures. In the last resort, managers who fail to comply with the directives of the National Labor Relations Board to bargain collectively in good faith with labor organizations freely chosen by their employees can be jailed for contempt of court. But that formally strong enforcement procedure has not thwarted large segments of the business community from contemptuously trampling on the principles that the law was intended to support (see, for example, Adams 1993). On the other hand, employers in Britain "voluntarily" recognized and bargained with trade unions representing their employees despite the absence of compliance mechanisms because, from early in the 20th century until the advent of the Thatcher regime, British governments steadily but firmly leaned on employers to respect the principle of freedom of association and the right of workers to bargain collectively (Adams 1994). In fact, few European countries have active legal mechanisms in force to compel respect for basic labor rights. They are held in place instead by a strong social consensus; by a "culture" (in currently popular parlance) fostered and vigilantly defended by the labor movement.

The problem for North American labor from all three countries is to formulate a strategy designed effectively to move society toward a public consensus, making it impossible for employers to escape from their responsibilities to conform to universally acclaimed labor rights. The public affirmation of those rights by the governments of each of the three countries could be used as an instrument for the achievement of that end. In short, how effectively the principles above are adhered to is dependent on the behavior of those who have an interest in them from this point in time. In its campaign against the passage of NAFTA, the American labor movement devoted most of its efforts to the defeat of any legislation and very little effort to the achievement of an effective social dimension (Cowie 1994). If labor continues to dismiss the accord as window dressing and a sham, then it will hardly be a surprise if the principles that the accord affirms are ignored. On the other hand, if labor vigilantly insists that those principles be respected, then there is some probability that progress will be made.

Conclusion

With momentum resulting from the passage of NAFTA, the United States helped to push through the successful conclusion of the Uruguay Round of GATT negotiations, which, along with trade barrier reductions, established a new World Trade Organization

(WTO) to monitor implementation of the agreements. In the spring of 1994, the United States made a major effort to have a social dimension (guaranteeing minimum labor standards) included in the jurisdiction of the WTO. Although enough governments opposed the initiative to block it for the time being, a social dimension to freer trade was now on the agenda in world trade talks. In 1994 too the International Labor Office began seriously to consider linking labor standards to liberalized trade. That possibility is now being actively debated as a potential new ILO initiative (Hansenne 1994). From the point of view of organized labor, here is an issue strongly promoted by the United States and many European governments that could give unions worldwide a new basis for cross-national collaboration in pursuit of social justice.

The evidence presented in this paper points toward the following causal argument: The primary reason for inclusion of a social dimension in trade agreements or trade agreement negotiations is to build political support for freer trade. The causal linkage can be seen in the timing of four major periods of social dimension debate. The period of social activism in the European Community in the 1970s (which resulted in new Common Market legislation on gender equality and plant closings protections for employees) coincided both with the expansion of the Community and the "resurgence of class conflict in Western Europe" (Crouch and Pizzorno 1978). Social Charter adoption and activism of the late 1980s and early 1990s coincided with the "relaunched" drive toward a single European market, reflecting the need to build popular and labor support for what became known as "Europe 1992." Labor side accords in the NAFTA agreement of 1993 resulted directly from a campaign promise to organized labor made by candidate Clinton in 1992 and were intended to soften labor's opposition to the agreement. And the active promotion of a social dimension in GATT/WTO negotiations followed directly upon labor's defeat in the NAFTA debate; this highly publicized initiative was clearly intended to demonstrate to Clinton's important labor allies the administration's resolve to protect labor standards in the drive toward freer trade.

If this argument is right, worldwide and regional trade negotiations may be viewed by labor not only as a threat (and sometimes the threat is very real and immediate, especially when the drive toward freer trade is not accompanied by social protections) but as an opening to press for new rights and standards in a social dimension. Trade negotiations, as in the European Union and North America, may open the door to increasing cross-national union collaboration, an important future agenda item for labor in an increasingly global economy (Jacek 1994). While the biggest stumbling block lies in very different existing national standards, especially between more and less developed countries, Social Charter collaboration in Europe among unions from countries as diverse as, for example, Germany and Spain, suggests that progress in this area is certainly possible.

Table 1

Average Hourly Compensation Costs for Production Workers in Manufacturing,
1989, (in U.S. Dollars)

United States	$14.31	Germany	$17.53
Mexico	2.32	Portugal	2.77
Hong Kong	2.79	Greece	5.48
Brazil	1.72	Spain	9.10
Korea	3.57	Japan	12.63
Taiwan	3.53	Singapore	3.09

Source: U.S. Department of Labor, Bureau of Labor Statistics, International Comparisons of Hourly Compensation Costs for Production Workers in Manufacturing, 1975-89, Report 794, October 1990.

Note: Hourly compensation includes all payments made directly to the worker before payroll deductions, including employer expenditures for legally required insurance programs and contractual and private benefit plans.

Table 2

Comparisons of Per Capita GNP

United States	20,910 (19,851)	Germany	20,440
Canada	19,030 (17,681)	Spain	9,330
Mexico	2,010 (5,323)	Portugal	4,250

Source: World Bank, World Development Report, 1991.

Note: The open figures are for 1989 and are expressed in U.S. dollars. The figures in parentheses are from Robert Summers and Alan Heston, "The Penn World Table (Mark 5): An Expanded Set of International Comparisons, 1950-1988," Quarterly Journal of Economics 106, no. 425, (May 1991). They are expressed in U.S. dollar-purchasing power parities and they are for 1988.

Table 3

Labor Standards in Canada, the U.S., and Mexico

	Canada	United States	Mexico
Union certification	Generally on the basis of cards. Employer duty to bargain.	Secret vote always required following a campaign in which employers generally oppose certification. Emplr duty to bargain.	Provided on request of 20 employees. Employer "must enter into collective agreement with registered union."
Right to strike	Prohibited for unorganized employees and during the term of a collective agreement. Compulsory conciliation required	Permitted to both organized and unorganized unless collective agreement clause to the contrary. No compulsory conciliation	Permitted to registered unions. Compulsory conciliation required prior to implementation.
Striker replacements	Permitted except in Quebec (and as a result of recent changes in the law) Ontario and BC	Permitted	Not permitted
Checkoff of union dues	Permitted	May be prohibited in right-to-work states	Permitted

	Canada	United States	Mexico
Minimum wages	Varies by province from $4.25/hr in Newfoundland to $5.97/hr in the Yukon.	Federal rate of $4.25 United States. Small firm minimum is $3.35 United States.	Rate varies by occupation and economic zone from $3.90 Cdn/day to $5.50 Cdn/day but mandatory profit sharing and bonuses add 50-60%

100

Hours of work	Std week varies by province. Overtime rates of 1.5 times regular pay.	Federal standard work week is 40 hrs with overtime 1.5 times regular pay.	Federal standard work week of 48 hrs. Overtime rates are 2 times regular rates for the first 9 hrs and then 3 times.
Holiday provisions	Varies by province from 5 to 9 paid days.	None by law.	Federal law provides for 7 paid days.
Annual vacation	Provincial law provides for min. of 2 weeks after one year.	None by law.	Minimum of 6 paid days after one year.

Source: Labor Canada, 1991.

Endnotes

1. At about the same time a third community on atomic energy also came into being.

2. See, for example, "New European Information and consultation Draft" *European Industrial Relations Review* (June 1994): 18-23.

3. See *European Industrial Relations Review* (December 1992).

4. Testimony presented by Mickey Kantor, U.S. trade representative to the U.S. Senate Finance Committee. Reported in *Labor Relations Week*, March 17, 1993. See also Robinson 1993b.

References

Adams, Roy J. 1986. "Two Policy Approaches to Labor-Management Decision Making at the Level of the Enterprise: A Comparison of the Wagner Model and Statutory Works Councils." In *Labor-Management Cooperation in Canada*, Craig Riddell, ed. Toronto: University of Toronto Press.

..... 1987. "Employment Standards in Ontario: An Industrial Relations Systems Analysis." *Relations Industrielles* 42 (1): 46-65.

..... 1992. *Labor, Management, Government Relations and Socioeconomic Performance: Lessons from the experience of Germany, Japan, Sweden and the United States.* Ottawa. Draft Report Prepared for the Canadian Labor Market and Productivity Centre.

..... 1993. "The North American Model of Employee Representational Participation: 'A Hollow Mockery.'" *Comparative Labor Law Journal*, 15 (4): 4-14.

..... 1994a. "Union Certification as an Instrument of Labor Policy: A Comparative Perspective." In *Restoring the Promise of American Labor Law*, edited by S. Friedman et al. Ithaca: ILR Press.

..... 1994b. *Industrial Relations under Liberal Democracy.* Columbia: University of South Carolina Press.

Addison, John T., and W. Stanley Siebert. 1991. "The Social Charter of the European Community." *Industrial and Labor Relations Review* 44 (4): 597-625.

..... 1992. "The Social Charter: Whatever Next?" *British Journal of Industrial Relations* 30 (4): 495-514.

Bain, Trevor. 1992. *Banking the Furnace: Restructuring of the Steel Industry in Eight Countries.* Kalamazoo, Mich.: W. E. Upjohn Institute.

Collins, Doreen. 1975. *The European Communities, The Social Policy of the First Phase,* Vol. 1, *The European Coal and Steel Community 1951-70;* Vol. 2, *The European Economic Community 1958-72.* London: Martin Robertson.

Commission of the European Communities. 1988. "The Social Dimension of the Internal Market." *Social Europe*, special edition.

Cowie, Jefferson. 1994. "The Search for a Transnational Labor Discourse for a North American Economy: A Critical Review of U.S. Labor's Campaign against NAFTA." Duke-UNC Program in Latin American Studies, Working Paper no. 13.

Cowie, Jefferson, and John D. French. 1994. "NAFTA's Labor Side Accord: A Textual Analysis." Duke-UNC Program in Latin American Studies, Working Paper no. 10.

Crouch, Colin, and Alessandro Pizzorno, eds. 1978. *The Resurgence of Class Conflict in Western Europe since 1969*, vols. 1 and 2. New York: Macmillan.

Freeman, Richard. 1991. "Employee Councils, Worker Participation, and Other Squishy Stuff." *Proceedings of the Forty-third Annual Meeting of the Industrial Relations Research Association.* Madison, Wis.: IRRA.

Friedman, Sheldon. 1992. "Why a Bad NAFTA is Worse than No NAFTA." *Proceedings of the 1992 Spring Meeting of the Industrial Relations Research Association.* Madison, Wisc.: IRRA.

Hansenne, Michel. 1994. "The New Paths Toward Social Justice." *World of Work*, (June): 4-6.

Hufbauer, Gary C., and Jeffrey J. Schott. 1992. *North American Free Trade: Issues and Recommendations.* Washington, D.C.: Institute of International Economics.

Jacek, Henry J. 1994. "Public Policy and the North American Free Trade Area: The Role of Organized Business Interests and the Labor Movement." Paper presented at the 1994 annual meeting of the Canadian Political Science Association," University of Calgary, June 14.

Jackson, Andrew. 1992. "A Social Charter and the NAFTA: A Labor Perspective." In *North American Free Trade Area*, William Watson, ed. Kingston, Ont.: John Deutsch Institute for the Study of Economic Policy.

Keller, Berndt. 1993. "The Social Dimension of the Single Market: A Euro-Pessimistic View." Paper presented at the Fifth Annual International Conference of the Society for the Advancement of Socio-Economics, New York, March 26-28.

Kerr, Anthony J. C. 1987. *The Common Market: How It Works.* 3rd ed. Oxford: Pergamon Press.

Labor Canada. 1991. *Comparison of Labor Legislation of General Application in Canada, the United States, and Mexico.* Ottawa: Labour Canada.

Lustig, Nora, et al. 1992. *North American Free Trade: Assessing the Impact.* Washington, D.C.: Brookings Institute.

Robinson, Ian. 1993a. "The NAFTA, Democracy, and Economic Development: Continental Economic Integration as If Democracy Mattered." Draft paper, University of Michigan, Institute of Labor and Industrial Relations, January 24.

104

..... 1993b. *North American Trade as If Democracy Mattered: What's Wrong with Nafta and What Are the Alternatives?* Ottawa: Canadian Centre for Policy Alternatives.

Shaiken, Harley. 1990. *Mexico in the Global Economy: High Technology and Work Organization in Export Industries.* San Diego: University of California at San Diego, Center for U.S.-Mexican Studies.

Springer, Beverly. 1992. *The Social Dimension of 1992.* New York: Greenwood.

Stanford, Jim. 1992. "Cheap Labor as an Unfair Subsidy in North American Free Trade." Ottawa: Canadian Centre for Policy Alternatives.

Starr, Gerald. 1981. *Minimum Wage Fixing.* Geneva: International Labor Office.

Streeck, Wolfgang. 1991. "More Uncertainties: German Unions Facing." *Industrial Relations* 30 (3): 317-47.

..... 1994. "From Market-Making to State-Building? Reflections on the Political Economy of European Social Policy." In *Prospects for Social Europe: The European Community's Social Dimension in Comparative Perspective,* Stephan Leibfried and Paul Pierson, eds. forthcoming.

Turner, Lowell. 1993a. "Worker Participation in Management in the Single Market." In *Labor and an Integrated Europe,* Lloyd Ulman et al, eds. Washington, D.C.: Brookings Institute pp. 45-79.

..... 1993b. "Beyond National Unionism? Cross-National Labor Collaboration in the European Community." In *Shifting Boundaries of Labor Politics,* Richard Locke and Kathleen Thelen, eds.

Ulman, Lloyd, Barry Eichengreen, and William T. Dickens, eds. 1993. *Labor and an Integrated Europe.* Washington, D.C.: Brookings Institute.

U.S. Congress, Office of Technology Assessment. 1992. *U.S.-Mexico Trade: Pulling Together or Pulling Apart?* Washington, D.C.: U.S. GPO.

Weiler, Paul. 1990. *Governing the Workplace: The Future of Labor and Employment Law.* Cambridge: Harvard University Press.

Womack, James P., Daniel T. Jones and Daniel Roos. 1990. *The Machine That Changed the World.* New York: Macmillan.

How Will the North AmericanFree Trade Agreement Affect Worker Rights in North America?

Ian Robinson

Introduction

As the title suggests, this paper asks one central question: How will NAFTA affect basic worker rights in Canada, the United States, and Mexico? For the purposes of this paper, "basic worker rights" encompasses three distinct rights: the right of workers to form autonomous unions governed by internally democratic decision-making processes; the right of workers to bargain collectively through the agency of such unions; and the right of workers to withdraw their labor collectively—to strike—should such collective bargaining yield results that the majority of union members deem unsatisfactory.

This paper argues that NAFTA's most important direct impacts on worker rights result from the fact that it will substantially increase continental capital mobility.[1] This will have two kinds of negative effects on worker rights. First, it will encourage employers and governments to adopt strategies of international competition that combine very low wages with very high productivity. Comprehensive, well-enforced worker rights are an impediment to this strategy, so employers and governments intent on such a strategy will try to curtail or override such rights. Second, increased capital mobility and economic restructuring will reduce unions' economic and political power, thereby reducing workers' ability to resist corporate and government efforts to curtail or override their rights.

The paper is divided into five sections. The first sets out the principal elements of NAFTA that contribute to North American capital mobility. The second section links the level of capital mobility with government and corporate choices of competitive strategy. The third section examines the implications of a low—wage, high—productivity competitive strategy for employer and government attitudes toward worker rights. The fourth section considers how increased capital mobility and economic restructuring affect labor movement power. The final section considers a number of counterarguments that might be advanced against the central thesis of this paper—that NAFTA will have a negative impact on worker rights in all three countries.

NAFTA and Capital Mobility

NAFTA contributes to continental capital mobility in two basic ways. First, it eliminates all remaining tariffs among the three countries over a period of fifteen years. Most are eliminated within ten years. It also eliminates the need for import licenses and a variety of "nontariff barriers" or NTBs that have restricted the free movement of capital as well as consumer goods in and out of Mexico.[2] Reduced tariffs and NTBs make it easier for private investors to produce goods in countries other than their primary markets, secure in the knowledge that they will still have access to those primary markets. This new security enhances capital mobility.

Second, NAFTA reduces the risks associated with direct foreign investment in the NAFTA countries. It does this by creating new private property rights that will protect the value of the investments of NAFTA investors, and in some cases, all foreign investors, operating in the NAFTA countries. This also makes foreign investment more attractive, other things equal, with the largest effect in the countries where the risks would otherwise be greatest—in this case, in Mexico.

The first point needs no elaboration, so I focus here on the second. The new NAFTA private property rights are explicit in the investment chapter, the chapter on private and government monopolies and state enterprises, the intellectual property chapter, and the financial services chapter. But the restrictions on government regulation found in the standards-related measures chapter, and in the section of the agriculture chapter dealing with Sanitary and Phytosanitary (SPS) standards, can also be understood as property rights. These latter chapters make it more expensive and difficult for governments to regulate the behaviour of domestic and foreign corporations in ways that might reduce the value of private property.[3]

The most important of the new private property rights are found in the Investment chapter.[4] Under the U.S.-Canada Free Trade Agreement, American (and, in principle, Canadian) investors were granted protection against four types of "performance requirements."[5] They were also protected against expropriation without "just compensation," as determined by an FTA panel.[6] Finally, they were protected against any "nullification and impairment" of benefits that they expected to derive from the agreement, even though such disappointment might not result from the violation of any specific provision of the FTA.[7] The NAFTA incorporates these rights and extends them in a number of ways. It prohibits three new types of "performance requirements," the most important being "technology transfer" and "product mandating" requirements. These rights are granted to all foreign investors, whether or not they qualify as NAFTA investors.[8]

NAFTA also creates a new investor-state dispute process, permitting NAFTA investors to go to an international tribunal with binding arbitration powers, or to the domestic courts, whichever the aggrieved investor prefers. Under the FTA and the Tokyo General Agreement on Tariffs and Trade (GATT), by contrast, private investors must persuade their national governments to undertake such a challenge. The NAFTA investment chapter also greatly increases the number of corporations that will be able to claim these new rights and employ the new enforcement mechanism by expanding the definition of NAFTA "investors."[9]

NAFTA's chapter on Monopolies and state enterprises incorporates the FTA's restrictions on government and private monopolies.[10] In addition, it requires that all monopolies accord "nondiscriminatory" treatment to NAFTA investors. NAFTA also requires state enterprises to comply with the obligations set out in the Investment and Financial Institutions chapters when exercising any "regulatory, administrative, or other government authority."[11]

NAFTA's intellectual property chapter has no precedent in the Tokyo GATT or the FTA.[12] It applies to virtually every important form of intellectual property, in many cases granting more stringent forms of protection than were available under the domestic intellectual property laws of Canada and Mexico. The intellectual property chapter also contains novel and important enforcement procedures.[13]

The main impact of the FTA's financial services chapter on capital mobility was the waiving (for American investors) of restrictions on foreign ownership of financial institutions chartered by the Canadian government.[14] NAFTA's financial services chapter is much more comprehensive, incorporating the national treatment principle, and the investment chapter's provisions on the right to transfer profits, dividends, and the like freely across national borders.[15] It also incorporates the investment chapter's investor-state dispute mechanism to protect these rights, subject to certain qualifications.[16] Finally, financial institutions are explicitly granted the right to transfer financial data out of NAFTA countries for processing.[17]

NAFTA also strengthens FTA restrictions on government regulation by increasing the burden that governments must meet in order to defend technical and SPS standards deemed trade restrictive. Like the Tokyo GATT and the FTA, NAFTA recognizes a special class of "legitimate" regulatory objectives—the "safety or the protection of human, animal or plant life or health, the environment, or consumers"—that may be valid even if they restrict trade.[18] If a measure is found to be trade restrictive, a government seeking to defend it must first demonstrate that the intent of the measure was to realize one of these "legitimate objectives." In the FTA and the Tokyo GATT, if a trade-restrictive measure passed this first hurdle, the government had to show that this measure was also "necessary" to achieve that legitimate objective. If this second test was also met, the measure survived the challenge. NAFTA increases the difficulty of meeting this second test by requiring that governments prove that the measure chosen was the "least trade restrictive necessary" to achieve a legitimate objective.

Given the difficulty of successfully defending a regulation deemed "trade restrictive," the burden that a challenger must meet in order to show that a measure is indeed trade restrictive becomes very important. In many cases, the most promising way to meet this burden is to show that the measure violates the National Treatment principle. Under this principle, a measure is trade restrictive if it discriminates in favour of national producers or investors as against nonnational exporters or investors. Over the years, GATT panels have developed a broad interpretation of what counts as "discrimination"—the "equal competitive opportunity" (ECO) interpretation.[19] On this reading, a government measure can apply the same rule to nationals and nonnationals and still be discriminatory if the rule has the _effect_ of placing foreign exporters or investors at a competitive disadvantage.[20] Language reflecting this interpretation is explicitly included in NAFTA's financial services chapter,[21] and it may be "read into" other chapters by future NAFTA panels, investor-state arbitration tribunals, or the courts.

In all of these ways, NAFTA will make it faster and less expensive for an expanded list of eligible NAFTA investors to protect their new property rights against the depredations of NAFTA governments. NAFTA will also increase the likelihood of successful challenges to a broad range of government regulations. This will result in more such challenges, other things equal, and hence, higher regulatory costs, even if governments successfully fend off all such challenges. Where governments lose, they will have to change their behavior or pay compensation. Efforts to reduce the number and success of such challenges by ensuring that the "least trade restrictive necessary" test has been met will cost money and reduce the range of policy instruments available to governments. All this is likely to have a chilling effect on efforts to control foreign private investors in the public interest and to raise national regulatory standards in existing fields or to introduce regulations in new areas.

These changes will have the greatest impact on capital mobility where the risks of investment, without NAFTA, were greatest. These risks were perceived to be much higher in Mexico, owing to the more interventionist character of past economic policies, memories of American oil company nationalizations in the 1930s and bank nationalizations in the early 1980s, perceived economic nationalist hostility to foreign investors, the lesser legal protections offered by Mexican courts, and a range of other factors. Risks of investment in Canada were doubtless rated higher than in the United States, but they had already been reduced by the new investor property rights created in the FTA. Thus, NAFTA's impact on the foreign private investor security is much greater in Mexico than the other two NAFTA countries. But the impacts of this greater investor security, and the increased mobility to which it gives rise, will be powerfully felt in all three NAFTA countries.

Capital Mobility and Competitive Strategies

Worker rights are held against employers and governments (and, in some cases, against unions). How these actors behave thus directly affects the de facto scope and character of worker rights, whatever the content of legal documents such as constitutions, statutes, and regulations. The behavior of corporations and governments will depend, to a considerable degree, on the competitive strategies that they adopt.[22] How does the level of capital mobility affect the choice of competitive strategy by governments and corporations?

Setting protectionist responses to one side, corporations can choose one of three basic types of competitive strategy: (1) they may try to cut labor and other input (e.g., raw material) costs by locating production where these costs are at least as low as those of their competitors, (2) they may invest in new technologies and worker training in order to boost labor productivity and quality, or (3) they may do both.[23] Similarly, national and subnational governments seeking to maintain or increase current levels of investment and employment can choose one of three types of strategy: (1) they may help private employers to hold labor costs by reducing the regulatory burden, narrowing labor rights, and so on, (2) they may focus on building the physical infrastructure (that is, transportation, communication, property rights, R&D) and "human capital" (that is, high quality public education, active labor market policies) that will increase productivity and product quality, or (3) they may do both.

Where labor costs are a significant part of total production costs,[24] and worker skills are important to productivity, combining strategies (1) and (2) would seem optimal from the narrow standpoint of competitiveness, for corporations and governments alike. If it is indeed the optimal strategy, then firms and governments pursuing this strategy will ultimately prevail in a competitive market economy. Those that do not follow the strategy will perish. In that sense, within the institutional parameters of an unregulated competitive market economy, such a strategy is not merely preferable on competitive grounds, it is necessary on survival grounds.

Since the denial of basic worker rights and constant pressures to reduce worker compensation are highly undesirable on social justice and political stability grounds, and since these other values are widely acknowledged to be more important than competitiveness per se, this leaves the principled defense of unregulated competitive markets in a difficult spot. If unregulated markets give rise to the labor market equivalent of Gresham's law, in which bad wages and no rights drive out good wages and extensive rights, many would conclude that competitive markets should be regulated so as to preclude the low wage, rights repressing option. And what holds for national markets, holds a fortiori for international markets.

Unless, of course, it is impossible to combine strategies (1) and (2) effectively, so that it is necessary to choose one course or the other, and it is unclear which strategy will prevail in "head-to-head" competition. Not so surprisingly, perhaps, this is precisely what conventional neoclassical wage and trade theories assert. The argument has two components. First, businesses and corporations operating in less developed countries (LDCs) will not invest in capital-intensive, high-tech production processes, and LDC governments will have fewer resources to invest in human capital and physical infrastructure. Second, worker compensation (wages and benefits) will rise with labor productivity.

The second proposition is axiomatic for neoclassical economics, because compensation levels in competitive labor markets are supposed to be determined by the marginal productivity of labor. As Lawrence and Litan put it:

> Since wage levels tend to reflect productivity levels, the truth is that the United States like other high-wage countries, *can* compete with low-wage countries because its superior productivity compensates for higher wage rates. If developing countries had our skills, technology, and capital levels, their wages wouldn't be so low.[25]

A trade theory built upon such theoretical foundations will also assume that the first proposition is true, because rational foreign investors will see no point in pursuing capital-intensive production in LDCs. They will obtain no unit labor cost advantage, since compensation will rise commensurate with any productivity gains so obtained. Moreover, since capital is expected to be more expensive in LDCs, given higher risks in these countries, the costs of achieving high levels of productivity in LDCs will always be higher than those obtaining in OECD countries, other things being equal.[26] The moral of the story is that manufacturers in LDCs (whether foreign or indigenous) can expect to compete successfully only if they take advantage of the "natural" comparative advantage that these countries possess: their supply of inexpensive labor. This will entail the use of labor intensive, low-productivity production technologies and processes.

If these propositions were accurate descriptions of the real world, LDCs would have low wages and low productivity, and the more developed economies of the Organization for Economic Cooperation and Development (OECD) countries would have higher wages and higher productivity. As a result, "unit labor costs"—the number of worker-hours required to make a product multiplied by compensation per worker hour—would be quite similar in both sets of countries. Moreover, as barriers to the free international movement of goods, services, and capital diminished—as they have been doing over the last fifty years—unit labor costs within and between the two groups of countries should converge. In fact, however, manufacturing unit labor costs vary greatly, with those of a number of newly industrialized countries (NICs) being much lower than those of the OECD countries in recent years. Moreover, unit labor cost differences appear to be growing over time, not only in relatively labor-intensive industries such as apparel and footwear, but also in more capital-intensive, high value-added industries such as steel and autos. The principal reason for this divergence appears to be that worker wages are not rising as fast as productivity in most of the NICs, while the latter are rising very quickly.[27]

Why does the current reality conform so poorly to neoclassical predictions? Why did the earlier postwar experience of the OECD countries appear more consistent with these predictions? We must begin with some realism about market institutions and relations. There are few actually existing labor markets in which neither employees nor employers are concentrated enough for power relations to influence compensation outcomes. The modern corporation, even if it competes with other corporations for employees, is a concentration of numerous owners, possessing enormous bargaining leverage vis-à-vis any single employee. Employees often respond to such a concentration of power by seeking to organize or join unions that will enable them to face such employers collectively. Governments deriving substantial support from unions try to help them to achieve this objective through supportive legislation. Employers and conservative governments often try to frustrate these efforts through some combination of legislation, cartelization, cooptation, and coercion. Labor markets are thus arenas of intense conflicts of material interests and correspondingly intense power struggles.

Where employer and government resistance to unions largely succeeds, the inequality of bargaining power between corporate employers and individual employers ensures that workers will reap few of the rewards of productivity gains, except in rare cases of "enlightened despotism" (e.g., Lee Kuan Yew of Singapore)[28] or full (formal sector) employment.[29] Where employer efforts are less successful, corporations and employers' associations will confront organized workers in wage bargaining. Either way, labor markets do not function as imagined in neoclassical theory. Instead, compensation levels are generally determined by the balance of power among unions, employers, and governments—mediated by the effectiveness of bargaining strategies—rather than by labor productivity.

Where labor movements have been less powerful, productivity growth typically outpaces compensation growth by a substantial margin.[30] Where labor movements are relatively strong and operate in a democratic context, compensation and productivity growth rates are often closely linked. Unions are powerful enough to push up wages to this level, but don't wish to push much further because the inflationary potential of exceeding productivity growth rates is regarded as counterproductive.[31] Because OECD country unions achieved unprecedented economic and political power in the first quarter century after World War II, wage and productivity data from these countries and this time period were broadly consistent with the predictions of neoclassical theory. But the correlation between neoclassical predictions and reality was spurious, and began to diminish as labor movement power in the OECD countries began to diverge dramatically from the mid-1970s.

If compensation and productivity growth are not "naturally" linked in the fashion so glibly asserted by neoclassical theorists, the principal limits on the viability of the low-wage, high-productivity strategy are the scarcity of domestic investment capital in LDCs and the limited international mobility of foreign capital. Immediately after World War II, both constraints were substantial. But as LDC manufacturers successfully exported labor-intensive, low-tech products to booming OECD markets, they rapidly accumulated capital for reinvestment. At the same time, international capital mobility increased for various reasons. Successive rounds of the GATT increased the opportunities for transnational corporations (TNCs) to produce in foreign markets and export back to their home markets. The elimination of capital export controls freed their industrialists and bankers to invest where they pleased. OPEC created a vast pool of petro-dollars which sent the world's major banks (in which the money was deposited) roaming the globe in search of new investment opportunities. New computer technologies made it possible to move credit from one nation and one currency to another at lightning speed. New communications technologies facilitated the coordination of production across far-flung branch plants.[32]

The upshot is that a number of LDCs gained access to capital for private and public investment in quantities bearing no relation to their level of economic output. South Korean *chaebol*, for example, were able to raise the capital and technology necessary to build consumer electronics plants comparable in productivity to the best in Japan, while Korea's GDP per capita was only one-sixth of Japan's.[33] Similarly, as Harley Shaiken has documented, automobile TNCs began to build plants in Mexico using technology at least as good as that which they employed in Canada and the United States, with the result that they were very quickly able to achieve productivity levels on a par with those to the north even for products, such as engine parts, requiring high levels of precision and skill.[34] Many of the NICs then had authoritarian regimes willing and able to cooperate closely with employers to keep labor disorganized or subordinated in captive or corrupt unions,[35] while investing heavily in public education and physical infrastructures.[36] Such investment ensured that worker skills bottlenecks would not stand in the way of rapid gains in productivity; labor repression ensured that these productivity gains would not be matched by compensation gains.

The effectiveness of this competitive strategy was reflected in the export performance and consequent economic growth rates of the NICs that employed it. This success, in turn, increased the pressure on other countries to follow suit. Where this has only been possible to a limited degree—in countries where relatively high-quality democratic regimes and strong labor movements protect worker rights effectively—firms often feel compelled to shift production to countries where they are freer to adopt a low-wage, high-productivity strategy.[37]

In countries where labor repression is extensive (or has so far proved unnecessary owing to weak or accommodating unions), domestic and transnational corporations pressure governments to make full use of their "comparative political advantage," lest they go elsewhere.[38]

In sum, increasing international capital mobility is making the low-wage, high-productivity competitive strategy increasingly viable—indeed, irresistible—for an increasing number of corporations in a growing range of manufactured goods. As this process unfolds, governments concerned to maintain investment and employment in their jurisdictions come under increasing pressure to fall into line, adopting economic policies that encourage corporations to pursue such a strategy. NAFTA, by promoting North American capital mobility, will strengthen this trend in North America.

Competitive Strategies and Worker Rights

If the NAFTA reinforces existing opportunities and pressures for the widespread adoption of low-wage, high-productivity competitive strategies in North America, what does this imply for worker rights on this continent? There are precedents. The southern United States have long pursued such a strategy in an effort to sustain textile and apparel manufacturers competing with LDCs, and to attract auto and other manufacturing industries from the high-wage Northeast and Midwest. That strategy has sometimes been closely associated with state government and local employer resistance to unionization,[39] and resistance by southern democratic congressmen to federal government policies that might reduce regional wage differentials or increase the "social wage" nationally.[40]

With the creation of Mexico's maquiladora zone in 1965, American TNCs extended their southern strategy further south. Plants were built along Mexico's northern border to perform relatively labor-intensive tasks at wage rates far below those they could achieve anywhere in the United States. The goods so produced were then shipped back to the United States for sale, with duties paid only on the very low value-added associated with Mexican wages. This strategy yielded enormous labor cost savings.[41] In contrast to the indigenous Mexican manufacturing sector, sheltered from foreign competition under the "import substitution industrialization" strategy that prevailed until the debt crisis of the early 1980s, the level of unionization in the maquila sector was kept very low.[42] As in the southern United States, it took sustained if relatively low-key repression by employers, backed by government, to maintain this largely nonunion situation.[43]

NAFTA will encourage the extension of the low-wage, high-productivity strategy by making it possible to reorganize the entire Mexican economy along these lines. Firms setting up in Mexico after NAFTA will be able to locate anywhere in the country and get the same advantages as regards American (and now Canadian) tariffs and NTBs. They will also be able to sell to Mexican consumers, something that the original maquiladoras could not do. This will do great damage to the Mexican import substitution industrialization (ISI) sector, which has higher wages[44] and lower productivity levels[45] than the current maquila sector and the new plants that TNCs from the United States, Canada, and other countries will build.[46] In so doing, it will also severely damage the Mexican unions that are concentrated in the ISI sector.

There is no reason to believe that TNCs or the current Mexican regime will be any less keen to prevent the emergence of autonomous, democratic unionism in this new national context than they were in the maquiladoras. To succeed, a Mexican low-wage, high-productivity strategy must hold Mexican wages at levels comparable to those of competitors for the American and Canadian consumer markets, such as China, Thailand, Malaysia and Indonesia, unless Mexico can achieve significantly higher productivity levels in its plants. The latter possibility seems remote, given the kind of DFI going into these Asian countries at this time in response to the phenomenal growth rates that that region is expected to enjoy in the 1990s. It is true that Mexico's geographic proximity will give it some advantage in transportation costs, once its infrastructure is brought up to scratch. But wages are potentially much more important than transportation costs for many manufactured goods.

The upshot is that to succeed at this game, employers and the Mexican government cannot permit Mexican wages to rise very far above the levels prevailing in the export processing zones of their principal Asian competitors, many of whom remain authoritarian regimes with even weaker and more subordinated unions than the official PRI-affiliated unions of Mexico. This, in turn, will require holding Mexican worker compensation far below the level justified by the productivity gains that will result from the NAFTA-induced influx of direct foreign investment. Widespread underemployment will exert a powerful drag on Mexican wages in general.[47] But the experience of numerous LDCs suggests that, barring state and employer intervention, high unemployment alone will not prevent the formation of independent unions in this sector. Where such unions form, it will be difficult to deny them wage increases that reflect productivity, given their capacity to disrupt the core of the government's economic strategy, and scare away vital foreign investment. The objective of governments and employers intent on a low wage, high productivity strategy will be to prevent things from reaching this unhappy pass by nipping union organizing efforts in the bud. Thus, they can be expected to extend to the entire nation the labor relations policies that were originally confined to the maquiladora sector.

These expectations are consistent with worker rights trends during the Salinas presidency. Worker rights have seldom been respected by Mexican governments, despite Article 123 of the 1917 constitution, and they have been particularly subject to repression in the maquila sector from its inception.[48] Nonetheless, labor repression entered a new phase with the Salinas administration's decision to abandon Mexico's traditional ISI strategy in favor of an export-oriented industrialization (EOI) strategy inspired by the success of the Asian NICs. Public sector worker rights were subordinated to a massive privatization process that is still under way,[49] and steps were taken to divide and weaken several important unions—oil workers and teachers—that would otherwise have been relatively unscathed by ISI restructuring and privatization.[50]

The Mexican government's refusal to include either worker rights or a commitment to link wage and productivity growth in the labor sidedeal is consistent with this interpretation. It suggests that President Salinas believes the Mexican state must continue the labor "disciplining" role that it expanded in the 1980s. The promise to link minimum wage increases to average productivity growth—made by President Salinas on the same day as the sidedeals were announced—might seem to cut against this interpretation. But it is significant that, in spite of strong American pressures, this commitment was not located in the sidedeal itself. It remains to be seen what it will amount to.

If NAFTA encourages a substantial part of the Mexican economy to restructure along low-wage, high-productivity lines, manufacturers remaining in Canada and the United States will face increased pressure to hold down or roll back wages and benefits. In their efforts to respond to these pressures, these employers will be more likely to resort to union avoidance tactics whenever possible. These pressures have been growing for some time, owing to the international trends discussed above. The data on employer unfair labor practices in both countries show substantial increases in both countries, with the Canadian rate of increase in the 1980s even greater than the American, albeit from a much lower baseline. These trends would likely intensify under NAFTA.

For their part, Canadian and American governments will be under pressure not to permit public sector wages and benefits to undercut private sector employer efforts to hold wage and benefit growth in check. This will be more difficult for government than for private employers, because public sector workers will be less intimidated by the prospect that their jobs will be moved out of the country. Public sector unions, at least in Canada, may be more willing to strike than their private sector counterparts. This is likely to provoke governments into amendments that try to narrow public sector strike rights (where they exist), or to temporarily suspend those rights. The 1970s and 1980s witnessed a growing number of such ad hoc suspensions of worker rights in Canada.[51] In the United States, where workers' rights are more constrained to begin with,[52] it was enough to veto efforts to improve the enforcement of existing labor law principles in the private sector (for example, the defeat of Carter's 1978 reform package),[53] and to suppress efforts by workers to expand their rights through strikes or other job actions (for example, President Reagan's response to the PATCO strike).[54]

Labor Movement Power

For any given level of economic development, the scope and character of workers' rights, like the wage and benefit levels discussed above, is primarily a function of the economic and political power of unions and their political allies—taken together, the labor movement. Where labor movement power declines, it is not long before worker rights are eroded, de facto, if not de jure.[55] This holds a fortiori if employer and government hostility towards union rights increase at the same time for the reasons considered in the previous section. NAFTA will reduce labor movement power in North America in three basic ways. First, it will give many manufacturing and service sector employers a more credible threat of exit. Second, it will tend to reduce the share of the workforce belonging to unions, other things being equal. Third, it will reinforce the tendency of governments and the general public to see unions that resist corporate efforts to become "leaner and meaner" as frustrating the national interest in greater international competitiveness. Such beliefs will make governments less willing to enforce or otherwise defend worker rights in the private sector and more willing to curtail public sector worker rights in order to set a "good example."

The loss of union bargaining power vis-à-vis employers will be greatest in industries such as automobiles where the low-wage, high-productivity competitive strategy has already proven to be highly effective. In Canada and the United States, national unions—and, a fortiori, particular locals—will constantly be threatened with employer exit and membership loss.[56] Even before the NAFTA, GM employed more workers in Mexico than Chrysler did in the United States, and the Big Three planned to double their auto production in Mexico to two million by the year 2000. With NAFTA, the President of Ford's Mexican subsidiary has stated that Ford alone could be making three million cars a year in Mexico by 2000.[57]

In Mexico, employer threats to leave the country will not be as credible as in the two northern countries—at least in the short run[58]—but they do not have to be. To achieve a parallel effect, it is enough to tell local communities in the maquila zone, and the industrial area surrounding Mexico City, that unless concessions are forthcoming, industry will have to relocate to green field sites in other parts of Mexico. In this sense, the NAFTA extends American TNC's Southern strategy yet again, this time from northern to southern Mexico. The main constraint on this pressure in the short run will be the inadequacy of transportation and communications infrastructure in non-traditional areas. But this is just a matter of time.

The threat of exit will not be confined to the manufacturing sector. As already noted, the financial services chapter provisions on data transfer and processing communications permit the processing of Canadian and U.S. data in Mexico.[59] The possibility of relocating data processing functions can thus be used in bargaining for concessions in at least some parts of the service sector as well.

Union density will be reduced by three kinds of processes that NAFTA will accelerate and intensify. First, rapid economic restructuring, which will substantially reduce the share manufacturing employment in Canada and the United States, and increase the share of employment in private services. The private service sector has proved difficult to organize for a variety of reasons.[60] As a result, private sector union density has been falling in both countries, in part due to the implications of this type of structural shift for union organizing effort and success.[61] In Mexico, the share of manufacturing employment could well increase, but as noted above, the government will attempt to ensure that most of these new workplaces either remain union-free, or are "organized" by PRI-affiliated unions.

Second, many already organized plants in the manufacturing sectors of all three countries will close. As with the United Auto Workers (UAW) and the United Steelworkers (USW)[62] in the 1970s and 1980s, such closings can cause dramatic losses in absolute union membership levels as well as contributing to declining sectoral and national union densities. Mexican unions will not be immune from this kind of loss. As already noted, a substantial part of the former ISI manufacturing sector—one of the two sectors in which Mexico's unions are strongest—is likely to be destroyed under NAFTA. Those ISI firms that survive will do so, in part, by imposing substantial wage cuts—which may or may not require destroying their unions—and reorienting to production for TNCs.[63]

Finally, where unions find themselves less and less able to make significant collective bargaining gains for their members, owing to the altered balance of economic bargaining power noted, previously, demand for union membership by unorganized workers declines, and existing membership becomes more difficult to mobilize.[64] Declining demand makes organizing the unorganized more difficult and expensive. Declining capacity to mobilize existing membership exacerbates the problem of declining economic bargaining power, since the union's only real threat (barring political influence) is members willing to engage in collective job actions. A vicious circle of declining union density and declining union bargaining power is thus set in motion.

Labor movement loss of political influence will result partly from the fact that nothing but the most supine, accommodationist brand of unionism is compatible with the national interest in maintaining or increasing international competitiveness, as long as the low-wage, high-productivity strategy is perceived to be the best means to this end. It is critical to the public support and political clout of any social movement that it be able to identify its interests with those of the nation (or the world, as with the environmental movement). Otherwise, even its own members will view it as a "special interest," seeking to promote nothing but its narrow self-interest. Such a perception undermines volunteerism and commitment on the part of union activists and members, and weakens

116

public sympathy. No social movement can long thrive without these forms of commitment and support, and labor movements are no exception to this rule.[65]

Counterarguments

In laying out the argument for NAFTA's negative impacts on worker rights, I have not attempted to respond to the many challenges that might be leveled against it. This final section addresses six counterarguments that are popular, important, plausible, or some combination of these.

Side-Deal as Redeemer

Your Gresham's law argument presupposes that the North American market economy is not regulated so as to prevent the low-wage, high-productivity competitive strategy from driving out the more desirable, high-wage, high-productivity strategy for a wide range of goods and services. But isn't that what the NAFTA labor accord or "side deal" was supposed to do?

It was indeed supposed to do just that. That was what President Clinton, in his October 4, 1992, speech on NAFTA, told the American electorate must be achieved before he would support the NAFTA terms negotiated by the Bush Administration. But, the labor side deal that emerged from the negotiations conducted between February and August of 1993 fell so far short of this promise that the Canadian and American labor movements rejected it as worse than useless. As the battle over the approval of the NAFTA implementing legislation in the House of Representatives heated up, the Clinton administration tacitly conceded the point. Instead of explaining how the side deal would deal with social dumping problems, it reverted to the Bush administration's rhetoric: anyone opposed to NAFTA, whatever might or might not be in the side deals, was a Luddite, a self-interested protectionist, and a doubter of America's future. Gone was the recognition that the Bush NAFTA, taken on its own, was unacceptable.

Why was the labor side deal so inadequate? The essential objective is to take minimum labor standards and basic worker rights out of continental competition. Put another way, it must not be possible for any single national or subnational government to defect from the regulatory regime by unilaterally narrowing worker rights or lowering minimum labor standards as competitive pressures intensify. Only a supranational regime, that can be modified only by the consent of the majority or all of the parties to that regime, can perform this function. That is why the European Union, committed to dealing seriously with social dumping problems, assigns this function to the European Commission.[66]

The NAFTA labor side deal explicitly excludes basic worker rights from coverage. For the labor standards that it does cover, national laws will determine the standards to which each government is to be held. Nor is there anything in the side deal to prevent a government from lowering those standards by legislative or regulatory amendment. The national equivalent would be an OSHA law that told individual corporations that they would be held to whatever occupational health and safety standards were current corporate policy, unless they chose to lower those standards. Once this basic structural flaw is understood, criticisms of the loopholes in the enforcement language and the convoluted character of the enforcement process become redundant.[67]

Lessons from the European Union

Doesn't the case of the European Union demonstrate that continental economic integration, even when it goes beyond free trade to full-fledged economic union, is compatible with strong unions and high wages? Moreover, doesn't the export success of high-wage EU members such as Germany demonstrate that, with sufficiently high skill and capital investment levels, OECD countries can remain immune from the Gresham's law that is supposed to drive all freely trading nations toward the low-wage, high-productivity competitive strategy?

On the first point, to invoke the EU case is to demonstrate that one has missed the point. The argument here is not that any form of enhanced economic integration is harmful to unions or worker rights. Rather, it is that it will be harmful if one or more of the countries in the free trade arrangement has ready access to capital investment for the production of high productivity factories, and is willing and able to repress basic worker rights in order to drive and hold down worker compensation. None of the first nine members of the EC could plausibly be characterized in this way. All were democracies with well-defined and protected worker rights. As long as they remained democracies, there was no serious prospect of those worker rights being substantially rolled back.

The parallel to the issue raised by NAFTA arose for the EC when it considered whether or not to admit Spain, Portugal, or Greece as members while they remained authoritarian regimes. Under the generals, all three of these countries systematically violated basic worker rights. Had they been admitted to the EC in this condition, concerns parallelling those raised about Mexico would have been appropriate. But the European Community refused membership to these countries, making the restoration of democracy a necessary if not sufficient condition for admission. If, at that time, French and German firms were busily setting up factories in export processing zones just inside the borders of Franco's Spain, merely refusing admission to the EC would not have been an adequate response to the problem. But European firms were not so investing. The contrast with our situation in North America is obvious.

Even after democracy had been restored, the EC took the challenge posed by integration with substantially lower-wage countries seriously enough to substantially expand its EC-level labor standards regulations and "structural funds." The former were supposed to neutralize social dumping pressures, and the latter to help the poorer countries of the Community to increase their productivity and wages as quickly as possible.[68] This difference in approach is particularly striking when we recognize that the unit labor cost gap between the richest and poorest of the major manufacturing countries of the EC (Germany and Spain) is less than half of the size of that between Canada and Mexico and almost twice as large as that between the United States and Mexico.[69]

Turning to the second argument, Germany has indeed been a splendid example of what can be achieved with a well-regulated national labor market, an effective (and expensive) active labor market policy, and high levels of investment in the latest manufacturing technologies. It is, for this reason, a model for many who would argue that Canada or the United States can compete effectively against the NICs with a high-skill, high-wage competitive strategy. Quite aside from the fact that the balance of political forces in the American Congress is such that nothing resembling German levels of taxation or spending on education and training is anywhere on the horizon, it is unclear whether the German (or Scandinavian or Austrian) model can be sustained much longer under conditions of global free trade.

It is one thing to compete with Spain, but quite another to compete with China or even, as the deutsche mark appreciates against the dollar and real wages continue to erode, the United States. An increasing number of Western European firms are shifting production to low-wage sites outside the European Union—in the United States, Latin America, and Eastern Europe.[70] At the same time, national regulatory systems are being weakened by the processes associated with the completion of the Single European Market— itself driven by the need to increase productivity to compete more effectively with the relatively low-wage economies of the rest of the world.[71] Whether this means that the citizens of northern Europe will permit their economic systems to be reorganized in accordance with the imperatives of the new Gresham's law of wage determination, or will develop social tariffs to neutralize unfair competitive advantages possessed by authoritarian NICs is a political choice. But it is becoming clear that these countries are going to be forced to make such a choice in the not-too-distant future. So will we in North America (to the degree that we have not already made it).

Economic Growth and Democracy

By your own admission, NAFTA should substantially increase direct and portfolio foreign investment in Mexico. It should also encourage the return of much of the flight capital that Mexican elites sent out of the country in the years of economic crisis. The resulting increase in investment should stimulate more rapid economic growth than the status quo. That is bound to be good for democracy in Mexico because it will increase the size of the middle class, as well as the economic pie to be divided among Mexico's rapidly growing population. A democratic Mexico, as you have asserted, will tend to promote and protect worker rights. Failure to accelerate Mexican economic growth, on the other hand, will exacerbate zero-sum distributional struggles over a small or dwindling per capita economic pie, a political environment inhospitable to democracy or worker rights. Why can't you be more subtle and recognize that NAFTA induced economic growth, while not a straight line, is actually the shortest political distance between where we are today and strong Mexican democracy and worker rights?

This argument rests on a set of empirical claims that I have elsewhere examined at considerable—if still inadequate—length. Here I must be very brief, and can only summarize the conclusions of that inquiry. The fundamental point is that economic growth per se does not "naturally" lead to high-quality democracy, or even stable democratic institutions. What matters is the kind of economic growth that takes place, and what it implies for levels of poverty and economic inequality. The kind of economic growth promoted by a low-wage, high-productivity competitive strategy—because of its implications for worker rights, union density levels, wages, and for the size and composition of the middle class—tends to exacerbate economic inequalities and poverty, other things being equal. This conclusion holds a fortiori if governments are trying to pay off massive debts to First World banks at the same time as they are pursuing such a competitive strategy. (This was the case in Mexico and most of Latin America in the 1980s, and seems likely to be the case in the 1990s as well.) For in this context, a large part of the gains from aggregate economic growth that are captured by the government will go to paying off foreign creditors, rather than to public goods and domestic redistribution.

NAFTA thus seems likely to reduce the odds that Mexico will be able to make a transition to a high-quality, stable democracy in the foreseeable future, although other factors can always intervene. Your question is misleading in that it attributes a defense of the status quo to NAFTA critics. The best alternative to NAFTA is an approach to North American economic integration that puts the promotion of Mexican democracy at its center. Critical components of such an approach would be a North American social charter, including basic worker rights and minimum labor standards, backed by trade sanctions. Also vital is the creation of North American structural funds of the sort that the European Union has developed.

It may take some time to build the political support for EU-type structural funds, but we could begin by forgiving the lion's share of Mexico's outstanding debt, the principal of which has already been more than repaid since 1980. Then, instead of selling off its national assets to pay the debt, Mexico could fund serious credit and outreach programs to promote more efficient small holder agriculture, and improve the quality of public education and health programs, particularly for women. Such measures would not only advance the cause of distributive justice, but help to reduce the birth rate that currently results in the injection of one million new workers into the Mexican workforce each year. This is a rate of workforce growth that not even the most optimistic projections of Mexican economic growth under NAFTA can possibly keep up with.

Gales of Creative Destruction

You argue that NAFTA will destroy substantial parts of the existing Mexican labor movement, and weaken what remains. But most of the unions that make up that labor movement are allied with the ruling PRI state, and seek to prevent the emergence of a more autonomous and democratic labor movement. So why aren't you happy to see them weakened? Doesn't that clear the decks for the emergence of the kind of Mexican labor movement that might actually begin to turn things around?

I don't think we should be cavalier about the destruction of unions, even when they are not particularly autonomous or democratic, whether in Mexico or in the United States. There are usually reformists in such unions. If at all possible, it would probably be better to turn over such unions to their reform-oriented members, as was done with the Teamsters' International Executive in the United States. Moreover, it seems to me that, if the weakening of the existing Mexican labor movement takes place in the context of the kind of state and corporate competitive strategy that NAFTA encourages, it will be very difficult for new unions to establish themselves. Goons may have to be hired by companies or supplied by the government's security forces, rather than by corrupt unions, but they can presumably shoot just as straight.

NAFTA Promotes International Labor Solidarity

NAFTA gave rise to an unparalleled level of cross-border linkages among the labor movements, as well as a potent combination of social movements within Canada and the United States that surprised and worried many conservative politicians. If NAFTA had been defeated, these connections would have become less relevant and would likely have been allowed to lapse. Thus, paradoxically, NAFTA promotes the kind of international cooperation and solidarity that are essential if there is ever to be political support for the kind of continental social dimension that you advocate.

This is a common but confused view. The introduction of NAFTA was, indeed, the catalyst to the formation of many cross-border alliances among unionists. But as NAFTA supporters and detractors alike argued, the agreement only intensified and formalized a process of continental economic integration that had been accelerating under the impetus of Salinas's unilateral liberalizing reforms in the latter half of the 1980s. While many who participated in the fight against NAFTA were not so aware of this process before the NAFTA fight, by the time the fight ended they were very conscious of the fact that economic integration would continue no matter what the vote on NAFTA. This consciousness and the underlying economic process would both have continued if NAFTA had been defeated. Most of the linkages established during the NAFTA fight would therefore have been maintained and strengthened in any case.

NAFTA and the Ideology of the American Labor Movement

You are overly pessimistic about NAFTA's impact on the labor movements of the three countries. Particularly in the case of the United States, the NAFTA forced union leaders to re-think their conception of how the global political economy ought to work at the end of the Cold War, and what role American unions ought to play in that world. The "Not This NAFTA" campaign slogan symbolized an important—if tentative and partial—move away from the economic nationalism that informed most union thinking about trade policy from the early 1970s. What emerged and partially displaced this earlier frame was one that affirmed a sense of solidarity with Mexican workers, and so, framed the critique of the existing economic system in class and internationalist, rather than national corporatist, terms. The anti-NAFTA fight also demonstrated the kind of alliances with other social movements that were possible should the American labor movement adopt a more consistently critical and internationalist stance on global economic issues, and the power of such an alliance in the Congress. Looking back on things years later, historians may well argue that NAFTA helped to give birth to a new, post-Cold War moral economy for American unionism—one that promises to be much more effective in rebuilding the labor movement than the old combination of anti-Communism abroad and business unionism at home.

I agree with much of this and have written elsewhere about the positive spin-offs of the NAFTA fight.[72] I have argued that while the short-term and direct impacts of NAFTA on labor movement power and worker rights are indeed negative, the new way of framing international economic issues to which your argument points is a very important and positive development. Indeed, barring the advent of such a powerful new post-Cold War moral economy, it is difficult to see how the American labor movement's long-running slide into oblivion can be reversed.[73] Still, as in my response to the previous question, I must insist that it was the fight against NAFTA that was the catalyst to developing the new critique and the social movement alliances that were built around it. Had this alliance managed to defeat NAFTA in the House, it would have been an enormous boost to the movement, which would have pressed forward with renewed energy to insist on basic changes to the content of the Uruguay GATT.

121

As it is, some of the wind was taken out of the sails of the various anti-NAFTA groups by their failure to stop NAFTA. Still, upcoming battles over the implementing legislation for the Uruguay GATT, the revival of Super 301, and so on, are likely to strengthen the critical ideas and the alliances that made the anti-NAFTA fight so interesting and important. In this, American experience may well parallel that of the Canadian labor movement, which first developed a broad social movement alliance strategy in the course of the anti-FTA fight, and then returned to that strategy with greater conviction and self-consciousness in the NAFTA fight. In Canada, most of the alliance members are now committed to the idea of institutionalizing the "social justice" coalitions that sprang up across the country to fight not merely against a trade agreement, but for a global political economy that is consistent with the requirements of social justice. I can imagine a similar process emerging in the United States over the next five years.

Conclusions

In the short run, NAFTA is likely to weaken existing worker rights in all three North American countries, owing to its impact on government and corporate competitive strategies, and union economic and political power. However, the fight against NAFTA may prove to be the beginning of a process of moral, intellectual and strategic regeneration that will make it possible to reverse the current decline of American union density and labor movement power. Should this prove to be the case, the implementation of the NAFTA will, in retrospect, appear to have been a Phyrric victory for those who support the neoconservative model of globalization embedded in the NAFTA and the Uruguay GATT. Should such a turnaround prove possible in the United States, it will have substantial positive spillover effects for the other two countries that share the North American continent.

Endnotes

1.   This is not the only negative impact that NAFTA is likely to have.   A less direct but important longer run impact will be its tendency to increase income inequalities and class polarization.   These trends result in a deterioration in the quality of democracy (where it exists), and beyond a certain point, regime instability.   Because worker rights generally fare much better in high quality democracies, this will further contribute to the erosion of worker rights.   I have developed these arguments at some length elsewhere, and will not repeat them here.   See Ian Robinson, *North American Trade as If Democracy Mattered* (Ottawa and Washington, D.C.: Canadian Centre for Policy Alternatives and International Labor Rights and Education Research Fund, 1993).

2. For an overview of these NTBs, see Clyde Prestowitz and Robert Cohen, with Peter Morici and Alan Tonelson, *The New North American Order: A Win-Win Strategy for U.S.-Mexico Trade* (New York: University Press of America, 1991), pp. 9-13, 113-120.

3.   "Property rights" include but go beyond the exclusive ownership of a thing or an idea.   A right to the value accruing from—or expected to accrue from—the use of some thing or idea can also be considered a property right.   Government regulations can reduce the value of property even though they do not expropriate it.   Investor rights that restrict such government regulations—or provide for compensation for any lost value caused by such regulations—can thus be understood as a species of property right.

4.   NAFTA's Investment chapter is the only one that American negotiators sought to protect with a clause guaranteeing that its provisions would continue to apply for a full decade after abrogation, should any party exercise its right to abrogate the agreement. This provision was cut in the final round of negotiations and does not appear in the final text, but it indicates the unique importance attached to this chapter by American negotiators.

5. FTA Article 1603. Performance requirements are conditions that investors must meet if they are to do business in a province or nation. They often apply exclusively to foreign corporations, because the ownership of these corporations is thought to make them less amenable to other forms of government regulation, and more likely to behave in ways contrary to the public interest. The National Treatment principle would require governments to generalize performance requirements to all comparable investors, foreign and domestic.   The four performance requirements listed are prohibited even if governments impose them equally on domestic investors.

6. FTA Article 1605.

7. See FTA Article 2011. A government measure need not conflict with the provisions of the FTA in order to violate the "nullification and impairment" clause. Nor need the expected benefits be "directly" affected by the measure in question; it is enough if they are "indirectly" affected (whatever that means).

8. "Technology transfer" conditions require foreign investors to train host country workers and engineers in all stages of product development, manufacture, and sale. "Product mandating" requires the parent transnational corporations to assign its operations in a particular country the mandate to develop, produce, and market one or more products for the continental or global market.

9. Foreign investors seeking the more limited protections of the FTA's investment chapter had to own a majority of shares in, or otherwise control, the business claiming these protections. The NAFTA definition of "investment" merely requires *some* ownership or control on the part of an investor from one of the NAFTA countries. This appears to grant almost any publicly held business protection under this chapter, since most of them will have at least some shares owned by a national of one of the three countries. Protection against the performance requirements listed in Article 1106 extends even further to include all foreign investors.

10. Article 2010 of the FTA imposed constraints on the creation of new monopolies and the operation of existing ones by governments. Governments had to try to "minimize or eliminate any nullification or impairment of benefits" to U.S. investors or exporters caused by such monopolies. Further, monopolies were required to act "solely in accordance with commercial considerations" and could not use their monopoly power to engage in "anticompetitive practices," such as "the discriminatory provision of the monopoly good or service, cross-subsidization or predatory conduct."

11. NAFTA Articles 1502, 1503, and 1505.

12. There were no *intellectual property* (IP) provisions in the Tokyo GATT or the FTA. Intellectual property rights were discussed during the FTA negotiations, but no agreement was reached. See G. Bruce Doern and Brian W. Tomlin, *Faith and Fear: The Free Trade Story* (Toronto: Stoddart, 1991), pp. 67-74, 97-98, 153-57, and 281-82.

13. NAFTA Articles 1714-1718.

14. FTA Article 1703.

15. NAFTA Articles 1405 and 1401, respectively.

16. NAFTA Article 1415.

17. NAFTA Article 1407.

18. NAFTA Article 904.

19. See "United States—Section 337, Report of the Panel (16.1.89)," *World Trade Materials* 2, no. 1 (January 1990): pp. 51-53.

20. For example, Northern Telecom has recently developed a non-ozone-depleting (that is, CFC-free) way of cleaning printed circuits and microchips. Were Canada to require that all producers of such materials in that province and all exporters of such materials to that province employ a CFC-free process, this would place Northern Telecom's

124

foreign rivals at a competitive disadvantage in Canada until they licensed its clean technology or developed their own. This would be enough to qualify such a regulation as discriminatory, hence trade restrictive, on the ECO interpretation. Thanks to Frank Longo for this example.

21. NAFTA Articles 1404.5, 1404.6, and 1404.7.

22. See Michael J. Piore, "Labor Standards and Business Strategies," in *Labor Standards and Development in the Global Economy*, Stephen Herzenberg and Jorge F. Perez-Lopez, eds. (Washington, D.C.: U.S. Department of Labor, 1990), pp. 35-50; and U.S. Congress, Office of Technology Assessment, *U.S.-Mexico Free Trade: Pulling Together or Pulling Apart?* (Washington, D.C.: U.S. Government Printing Office, October 1992).

23. There are, of course, other ways in which competitive advantage can be sought: better advertising, better distribution networks, better aesthetics and quality, strategies for lowering the costs of capital, and so on. However, every firm is free to pursue all of these strategies as best it can. The contentious issue is whether it is possible to simultaneously pursue low wages and high productivity, or whether one or the other of these key components of competitive strategies must be chosen.

24. It is difficult to say exactly what share of total production costs must be comprised by labor costs before the latter become "significant," from a competitive standpoint. As important as the share of total costs that labor costs represent will be the degree to which the other cost components are (rightly or wrongly) perceived by employers and governments to be fixed, or at least, more difficult to reduce than labor costs in the short-run, during which company survival may be at stake.

25. Robert Z. Lawrence and Robert E. Litan, "Why Protectionism Doesn't Pay" 65 *The Harvard Business Review* 63, no. 3 (May-June 1987): 60.

26. Standard neoclassical labor market and trade theory assumptions are reviewed and critiqued in many places. See, for example, Mehrene Larudee, "Trade Policy: Who Wins, Who Loses?" in *Creating a New World Economy: Forces of Change and Plans for Action*, Gerald Epstein, Julie Graham, and Jessica Nembhard, eds., (Philadelphia: Temple University Press, 1993), pp.47-63; and Lester Thurow, *Head to Head* (New York: William Morrow, 1992), pp.82-83, 42-51.

27. See Walter Russell Mead, *The Low-Wage Challenge to Global Growth: The Labor Cost-Productivity Imbalance in Newly Industrializing Countries* (Washington, D.C.: Economic Policy Institute, 1990), pp. 14-26.

28. See Linda Y.C. Lim, "Singapore," in *Labor Standards and Development*, pp. 73-96.

29. See Gary S. Fields, "Labor Standards, Economic Development, and International Trade," in *Labor Standards and Development*, pp. 23-26. Fields is a strong advocate of labor market-determined wages in developing countries. That is, he strongly opposes union "monopoly" pricing. However, even Fields allows that such a labor market will

begin to raise wages for relatively unskilled workers only when something close to full employment has been reached.

30.   Hong Kong, for example, had a less repressive labor regime than the other Asian NICs until very recently, but its labor movement was nonetheless highly fragmented and politically weak. Labor productivity in Hong Kong rose by almost 60 percent between 1979 and 1988, while real wages grew by about 10 percent.   See David Levin and Stephen Chiu, "Dependent Capitalism, a Colonial State, and Marginal Unions: The Case of Hong Kong," in *Organized Labor in the Asia-Pacific Region*, Stephen Frenkel, ed., (Ithaca, N.Y.: ILR Press, 1993), p. 206.

31. Arguably, the United States met this description between World War II and the early 1970s. The relationship between labor productivity and nonfarm wage growth parallels fluctuations in labor movement power.   Between 1950 and 1973, labor productivity in the manufacturing sector rose by 85 percent (3.7 percent per annum), while real manufacturing wages rose by 53 percent (2.3 percent per annum). Manufacturing sector workers were thus able to capture about two thirds of the gains from productivity growth.   Between 1973 and 1991, union economic power in the manufacturing sector declined considerably, a trend reflected in and partially caused by a decline in manufacturing sector union density from over 42 percent to under 24 percent. In the same period, sectoral labor productivity rose by 54 percent (3.0 percent per annum), but real manufacturing wages fell by about 7 percent. The productivity and wage data are from the Bureau of Labor Statistics, *Employment and Earnings*, various years, as reported in Ravi Batra, *The Myth of Free Trade* (New York: Scribner's, 1993), p. 52. On the collective bargaining norms, practices and institutions by which wages were (loosely) linked to productivity in the American manufacturing sector for the first two decades of the postwar period, see Michael J. Piore and Charles F. Sabel, *The Second Industrial Divide* (New York: Basic Books, 1984), pp. 79-104.

32.   See Thurow, *Head to Head*, pp. 42-55; and Julie Graham, "Multinational Corporations and the Internationalization of Production: An Industry Perspective," in *Creating a New World Economy*, pp. 221-41.

33.   See Thurow, *Head to Head*, p. 42.

34.   See Harley Shaiken with Stephen Herzenberg, *Automation and Global Production: Automobile Engine Production in Mexico, the United States, and Canada* (San Diego, Calif.: Center for U.S.-Mexico Studies, 1987), Harley Shaiken, *Mexico in the Global Economy: High Technology and Work Organization in Export Industries* (San Diego, Calif.: Center for U.S.-Mexico Studies, 1990); and John Sheahan, *Conflict and Change in Mexican Economic Strategy* (San Diego, Calif.: Center for U.S.-Mexico Studies, 1993).

35. On labor repression in the NICs,, see the essays collected in Frederic C. Deyo, *The Political Economy of the New Asian Industrialism* (Ithaca, N.Y.: Cornell University Press, 1987).

126

36. On investment in education, see Stephan Haggard, *Pathways from the Periphery* (Ithaca, N.Y.: Cornell University Press, 1990), pp. 223-53.

37. Not always, however. As Graham, "Multinational Corporations," pp. 234-35, points out, the response in the American clothing industry has been to "import" third world workers, working conditions, and wages back into the United States through contracting out to the burgeoning informal sector of homeworkers. See Piore, "Labor Standards," on the factors that originally led to the abolition of the sweatshop mode of production in the American clothing industry, and why the sweatshop is now coming back.

38. For example, Malaysian workers are generally permitted to organize unions to improve wages and working conditions, but an exception was made for electronics workers (Malaysia is currently the world's largest exporter of semiconductors). The Malaysian American Electronics Industry Society told the Malaysian government that its member firms would not continue to invest in that country if unions were permitted in their sector. See Richard Rothstein, "Setting the Standard: International Labor Rights and U.S. Trade Policy," Economic Policy Institute briefing paper, March 1993, p. 23.

39. On employer and state government resistance to the CIO's early postwar organizing drive in the South, see Barbara S. Griffith, *The Crisis of American Labor: Operation Dixie and the Defeat of the CIO* (Philadelphia: Temple University Press, 1988). The South became the homeland of the right-to-work" laws—rendering closed shop agreements illegal—made possible by the Taft-Hartley Act of 1947, and average union density levels in that region remain far below the national average. It should be noted, however, that by the 1970s, certification election victory rates tended to be at least as high in the South as in other regions of the country. Moreover, state union densities in the South have remained relatively stable over the last two decades, while they have fallen in most higher density states. Thus, differences in the level of employer resistance to unions between this and other regions appear to be declining. See Michael Goldfield, *The Decline of Organized Labor in the United States* (Chicago: University of Chicago Press, 1987), pp. 139-44. Arguably, by this time regional differences in the United States were being swamped by the impact of dramatic increases in foreign competition and import penetration. On this, see Joel Rogers, "Don't Worry, Be Happy: The Postwar Decline of Private Sector Unionism in the United States," in Jane Jenson and Rianne Mahon, eds., *The Challenge of Restructuring: North American Labor Movements Respond* (Philadelphia: Temple University Press, 1992), pp. 48-71.

40. This was nowhere more evident than in the Congressional debate over the 1937 Wage and Hours Bill, which would have prohibited child labor, and authorized a national Fair Labor Standards Board with discretionary powers over wages and hours and a mandate to move gradually towards a national minimum wage and a 40-hour work week. Southern elites perceived the bill as a fundamental challenge to their low-wage strategy, and members from both parties of low-wage states voted against it in Congress. John M. Robison of Kentucky declared that the bill's proponents "in some sections of the North and East, do not disguise their purpose. They claim it will stop the movement of industries, factories, mills, and shops in the North and East, and force those that have gone South to go out of business or go back to the North and East." See Richard

Bensel, *Sectionalism and American Political Development* (Madison: University of Wisconsin Press, 1984). The quote is from p. 161. See chapters 2 and 3, generally. Thanks to Paul Pierson for making me aware of the importance of the South for the evolution of American labor market and social welfare legislation.

41. For example, Ford's Hermosillo plant, built in 1986 and employing 1,600 workers, is estimated to have an annual labor bill of about $7 million. In the United States, a plant of similar size and vintage would have a labor bill of about $100 million. See Jim Sinclair, ed., *Crossing the Line: Canada and Free Trade with Mexico* (Vancouver: New Star Books, 1992), p. 30.

42. There is substantial regional and sectoral variation in union organization levels in the maquiladoras, however. The director of the American Chamber of Commerce's Maquila program estimates that Tijuana plants have organization levels of 10 to 15 percent, while the level is 40 to 50 percent in Juárez, and 100 percent in Tamaulipas. The variation depends primarily on the prior strength of the CTM and the CROC—Mexico's two principal "official" union federations—in the non-maquila sector in these regions. It appears that most new plants are being located in "greenfield" sites where unions are less strong. Electronics maquilas tend to have particularly low rates of organization, while apparel, chemical, and auto maquilas are more organized. However, in many cases, this organization is "defensive" in the sense that employers sign an agreement with non-threatening "official" unions in order to fend off organizing efforts by more autonomous unions. See Tom Barry, ed., *Mexico: A Country Guide* (Albuquerque, NM: The Inter-Hemispheric Education Resource Center, 1992), p. 191 and endnote 49.

43. For example, Ford of Mexico recently resorted to repression to prevent the formation of independent unions in its Mexican plants. In January 1990, unarmed workers involved in efforts to form an independent union in Ford's Cautitlan plant, near Mexico City, were attacked by armed men on the payroll of the PRI-allied CTM auto union whose status was challenged by the formation of the autonomous union. The thugs were permitted into the plant by Ford management. One organizer was killed and several others were wounded. See Dan LaBotz, *Mask of Democracy: Labor Suppression in Mexico Today* (Boston: South End Press, 1992), pp. 148-160. Ford is not alone among TNCs willing to use repressive tactics. Volkswagen of Mexico recently fired 14,200 workers from its huge complex and annulled the collective agreement that it had earlier signed with an independent union. See Office of Technology Assessment, *U.S.-Mexico Free Trade: Pulling Together or Pulling Apart?* (Washington, D.C.: Government Printing Office, October 1992), p. 85.

44. The most recent wage data, for 1989, suggest that the hourly compensation costs in the ISI sector are about twice those in the maquiladora sector. See Bureau of Labor Statistics, Office of Productivity and Technology, "International Comparisons of Hourly Compensation Costs for Production Workers—Mexico" (April 1990).

45. Large manufacturing plants in the US exhibit productivity levels that are 11 times the Mexican ISI sector average. But in sectors such as auto, as already noted in endnote 42, some U.S. maquiladoras are able to operate at 80 percent of U.S. productivity levels.

See Alvarez and Mendoza, in *Crossing the Line*, p. 34, for productivity data. One indicator of what is to come may be the experience in the Mexican auto sector under the unilateral liberalization measures taken by Mexican governments in the 1980s. The exposure of Mexico's ISI auto sector to increased competition resulted in the loss of about 100,000 jobs between 1980 and 1987. In the same period, maquilas in the auto parts subsector alone increased from 53 plants and 6.3 percent of the total maquila workforce to 121 plants representing 21 percent of the maquila workforce. Yet only about 90,000 jobs were created in the new maquila auto and auto parts plants, for a net auto manufacturing employment loss of about 10,000 jobs. See Jim Sinclair, "Cheap Labor, Cheap Lives," in Sinclair, ed., *Crossing the Line*, pp. 55-56.

The picture for the manufacturing sector as a whole in the 1980s presents a somewhat rosier picture, showing a net employment increase of 38 percent (or 849,121 workers) between 1981 and 1991—that is, 84,912 new manufacturing jobs per year. Most of this growth (56 percent) took place in the northern industrial belt, suggesting that it is mainly due to the expansion of maquila employment. The implication is that net manufacturing employment in the non-maquila sector grew by only 373,000 in a decade, or by 37,300 per year. See Edur Velasco Arregui, "Industrial Restructuring in Mexico During the 1980s," in Ricardo Grinspun and Maxwell Cameron, eds., *The Political Economy of North American Free Trade* (Montreal/Kingston: McGill-Queen's University Press, 1993), p. 169.

46. Barbara Kopinak cites a study carried out by *El Financiero*—a strong supporter of NAFTA—which predicted that Mexico would lose approximately 23 percent of its manufacturing industry and 14 percent of its jobs in the first two years of the NAFTA's operation. See Kopinak, "The Maquiladorization of the Mexican Economy," in Grinspun and Cameron, eds., *Political Economy*, p. 153. Edur Velasco Arregui, a critic of these policies, argues that the acutely vulnerable element of the Mexican manufacturing sector is comprised of 135,000 small and medium companies with an average productivity of $8,000 per worker per year. These firms employ about one-third of the industrial workforce. He also notes that, owing to lack of credit availability, productivity in this sector is stagnant. Indeed, total factor productivity for Mexican manufacturing as a whole increased at an average annual rate of only 0.5 percent between 1981 and 1991. See Velasco Arregui, "Industrial Restructuring in Mexico during the 1980s," in Grinspun and Cameron, eds., *Political Economy*, pp. 171-72. Not surprisingly, many small and medium Mexican businesses have become strong opponents of Salinas's trade liberalization program. See Judith Teichman, "Dismantling the Mexican State and the Role of the Private Sector," in *Political Economy*, pp. 177-92.

47. Official Mexican statistics show unemployment at below 3 percent. But everyone who works more than one hour per week for income is counted as employed under the current Mexican government definition. See Office of Technology Assessment, *U.S.-Mexico Free Trade*, p. 69, n.16. Lawrence Whitehead estimates that in 1988, only about 20 million of a workforce of about 46 million were engaged in "remunerated employment." Of this number, probably less than half were full-time wage earners. See Lawrence Whitehead, "Mexico's Economic Prospects: Implications for State-Labor Relations," in *Unions, Workers and the State in Mexico*, Kevin J. Middlebrook, ed. (San Diego: Center for U.S.-Mexico Studies, University of California, 1991), pp. 62-64.

48. For a brief history of Mexican labor relations, followed by a detailed look at labor repression under the Salinas regime, see LaBotz, *Mask of Democracy*.

49. It is estimated that 600 Mexican public enterprises have been privatized since 1982. See Sinclair, "Cheap Labor," p. 53.

50. This is not required by NAFTA, but it is part of the same deregulation and privatization agenda that underpins President Salinas's support for the agreement. See LaBotz, *Mask of Democracy*, pp. 81-130.

51. On the erosion of Canadian worker rights in the 1970s and 1980s, see Leo Panitch and Don Swartz, *The Assault on Trade Union Freedoms: From Consent to Coercion Revisited* (Toronto: Garamond Press, 1988).

52. See Noah Meltz, "Inter-state versus Inter-provincial Differences in Union Density," *Industrial Relations* (Spring 1989).

53. See David Brody, "The Uses of Power II: Political Action," in *Workers in Industrial America*, Brody, ed. (Oxford: Oxford University Press, 1980), pp. 244-50.

54. See Kim Moody, *An Injury to All* (New York: Verso, 1988), pp. 139-41.

55. The United States provides a striking example of this phenomenon: the R-squared between declining union density and rising employer resistance to unionization efforts (measured as consent elections as a share of total certification elections) was 0.80. See Ian Robinson, "Organizing Labor: The Moral Economy of Canadian-American Union Density Divergence, 1963-1986" (Kingston, Ont.: Queen's Papers in Industrial Relations, 1992), p. 34.

56. General Motors portrays the latest round of plant closings in Canada and the United States—projected to involve the layoff of 74,000 employees in 21 plants—as downsizing to eliminate excess capacity, but it plans to build 27 plants in Mexico by 1995. GM currently has 30 Mexican plants employing 25,500 workers. See Jim Sinclair, pp. 55-56; "Cheap Labor," Timothy Koechlin and Mehrene Larudee, "The High Cost of NAFTA," *Challenge* (September-October 1992): p. 20; and John Bursos, "The Judge Who Stood Up to G.M.," *The Nation* (April 12, 1993): p. 488. More generally, see Harry Browne and Beth Sims, *Runaway America: U.S. Jobs and Factories on the Move* (Albuquerque, N.M.: The Resource Center Press, 1993).

57. See Mehrene Larudee, "Trade Policy: Who Wins, Who Loses?" in *Creating a New World Economy: Forces of Change and Plans for Action,* Gerald Epstein, Julie Graham, and Jessica Nembhard, eds. (Philadelphia: Temple University Press, 1993), p. 56.

58. This qualifier is necessary because NAFTA contains an "accession clause" (Article 2204) that facilitates the extension of the agreement to other countries. The Reagan and Bush administrations made it clear that this was an important medium-term objective of their trade policy, under the rubric of the "Enterprise for the Americas Initiative." The Clinton administration has recently signaled that, with appropriate changes in

nomenclature, it intends to pursue the same objectives. See "U.S. Shows Early Favor for NAFTA Expansion over Separate Pacts," *Inside U.S. Trade* (January 14, 1994): 1-2.

59. See NAFTA Article 1407.2.

60. See Noah Meltz, "Unionism in the Private-Service Sector: A Canada-U.S. Comparison," in Jenson and Mahon, eds., *Challenge of Restructing*, pp. 207-225.

61. Shifts in sectoral employment do not, however, explain the bulk of American union density decline. Canada has undergone a parallel shift of comparable magnitude, and yet its union density has fallen only slightly from a peak of 40 percent in the early 1980s to about 36 percent at present. See Meltz, "Unionism in the Private Sector." I have also published analyses of Canadian and American union density trends. See Ian Robinson, "Organizing Labor," and "Economistic Unionism in Crisis: The Origins, Consequences, and Prospects of Divergence in Labor-Movement Characteristics," in *Challenge of Restructuring*, pp. 19-47.

62. Between 1975 and 1987, the Steelworkers lost more than half of its American membership, which fell from 1,071,000 to 494,000 members. Over the same years, the UAW lost almost 20 percent of its American membership, falling from 1,245,000 to 998,000 members. See Leo Troy and Neil Sheflin, *Union Sourcebook* (West Orange, N.J.: Industrial Relations Data and Information Services, 1985).

63. If the TNCs will buy from them. Maquiladoras in Mexico today are estimated to buy only about 2 percent of their inputs from Mexican suppliers. See Jim Sinclair, "Cheap Labour, Cheap Lives," p. 29.

64. Recent survey-based work by Henry Farber and Alan Kreuger concludes that virtually all of the decline in union membership in the United States between 1977 and 1991 is due to a decline in worker demand for union representation. See Farber and Kreuger, "Union Membership in the United States: The Decline Continues," Working Paper No. 306, Industrial Relations Section, Princeton University, August 1992. While they offer no explanation of this decline in demand, it is consistent with the declining bargaining power of American unions. In Canada, where union density remained stable, and union bargaining power declined less (as manifest in lower levels of concessions at the bargaining table), demand for unionization remained higher. On the difference between Canadian and American union responses to demands for concession bargaining in the 1980s, see Pradeep Kumar, "Industrial Relations in Canada and the United States: From Uniformity to Divergence," School of Industrial Relations, Queen's University, March 1991, pp. 60-80.

65. On the nature and importance of membership moral commitment to the cause, see Amartya Sen, "Rational Fools," in *Beyond Self-Interest,* Jane Mansbridge, ed. (Chicago: University of Chicago Press, 1990). The importance of broader public support is nowhere more evident than in the successful use of the boycott as a weapon. For one important example, see J. Craig Jenkins, *The Politics of Insurgency: The Farmworkers Movement in the 1960s* (New York: Columbia University Press, 1985).

66. The European Union approach is summarized in Robinson, *North American Trade as If Democracy Mattered*.

67. In the last section of my monograph, *North American Trade as If Democracy Mattered*, I set out ad nauseum the inadequacies in the labor side deal. I will not inflict this tale of woe on the present reader.

68. These structural funds are not trivial. If Mexico received transfers from Canada and the United States in accordance with the EC's pre-Maastricht formula, it would amount to about $10 billion per year—that is, about the same amount that Mexico was paying out in annual debt service payments by the end of the 1980s. See Office of Technology Assessment, *U.S.-Mexico Free Trade*, p. 52.

69. The ratio between German unit labor costs and those of Spain is about 1.56, while the ratio between Canadian and Mexican unit labor costs is 3.51. It is 2.59 for the USA and Mexico. See Jim Stanford, Christine Elwell, and Scott Sinclair, *Social Dumping Under North American Free Trade* (Ottawa: Canadian Centre for Policy Alternatives, October 1993), p. 17.

70. Auto analysts estimate that, by taking advantage of lower wages and taxes in the United States, BMW could easily produce its cars for 20 percent less than in Germany. This gap can be expected to widen, given the continued strength of Germany's metal workers' union, and the growing weakness of the UAW. BMW has already announced its intention to build a $1 billion auto plant in South Carolina or Omaha. Its CEO, Eberhard von Kuenheim, warns that "The exodus of German industry is getting under way." Daimler Benz, which already builds trucks in the United States, has announced plans to build Mercedes cars in Mexico for export both to Latin and North America. Small and mid-size German auto parts companies known as "mittelstand" are also expanding their North American investments to maintain their supply lines with the German assemblers, and to secure better access to the North American producers. Other German corporations are buying into American firms or acquiring them outright. See "The Exodus of German Industry is Under Way," *Business Week* (May 25, 1992): 42-43.

71. This argument is most fully developed in an unpublished paper by Wolfgang Streeck, "The Social Dimension of the European Firm," A discussion paper prepared for the 1989 Meeting of the Andrew Shonfield Association, Florence, Italy (September 14-15, 1989). For published work by Streeck that makes similar points in less detail, see "Skills and the Limits of Neo-Liberalism: The Enterprise of the Future as a Place of Learning," *Work, Employment and Society*, 3 no. 1 (1989): 92-97, and "More Uncertainties: German Unions Facing 1992," *Industrial Relations* 30, no. 3 (Fall 1991): 317-49.

72. See Ian Robinson, "The NAFTA, Social Unionism, and Labor Movement Power in Canada and the United States," *Industrial Relations/Relations Industrielles* (forthcoming).

73. See Robinson, in *Challenge of Restructuring*.

The Mexican Dual Transition:
State, Unionism and the Political System

Alberto Aziz Nassif

A Problem from Three Angles

At the end of July 1993, when passage of the North American Free Trade Agreement (NAFTA) was uncertain, the Mexican government announced to business corporations that at least for the remainder of 1993, and perhaps until late 1994, any proposed modifications of either the Federal Labor Law or fiscal regulations would remain "frozen". (El Financiero July 30, 1993). The government's announcement had nothing to do with productivity needs, nor with the government's efforts to have NAFTA approved. Rather, government policy was motivated by concerns surrounding the 1994 presidential succession. The Mexican government did not want to open a new area of conflict which the opposition might use to its advantage against the PRI.

Although the Mexican political system is not yet a fully democratic system, it has become ever more costly to maintain electoral authoritarianism. The period from July 1993 to the 1994 elections entailed great governmental weakness as the Mexican government had to confront the risks associated with the ballot box and the public's evaluation of Salinas's policies.

Why did the government not want to face a new area of conflict, such as that surrounding labor reform? The government wanted to avoid confronting a labor sector that is dissatisfied with the lack of improvements in the pervailing low salaries, and - with exceptions - a discontented business sector.

Constitutional reforms of the Federal Labor Law and other employment regulations have been occurring in Mexico as part of a long and pragmatic adjustment process since the early 1980s. This paper analyzes the relationships that exist between unions, the state, and the political parties and assesses the effects imposed on these relationships by NAFTA and other steps toward economic integration.

The central hypothesis in this analysis is that the labor movement has been a dependent force and has been under pressure from the following three key factors:

1. The political system has begun to shift from its former authoritarian corporative-style, under which the Mexican worker's movement was constructed and enjoyed it greatest moments, toward a system involving greater democratic citizen involvement. This has caused a shift away from unions that were formerly integrated within a state party and a noncompetitive electoral system. In the process, unions' social influence has changed.

2. The reforms underway in the Mexican government modified the bases on which ideological discourse and constitutional legislation were conducted. The reforms promoted the opening of borders, the privatization of a large share of the public sector, and reforms in agriculture, the education sector, and the church. Revolutionary nationalism ceased to be the hub of discourse and a discourse of "social liberalism" was created. Thus, unions' political influence also changed.

3. The new economic model caused fundamental changes in the relationships that prevailed among economic agents. This occurred over a period of a few years and during one of the country's gravest crises. The country's formerly closed borders experienced accelerated opening and a globalized integration radically modified production regulations and labor relations. In the process the country's culture surrounding labor issues changed.

In the mid-eighties, when the crisis was at its worst, several students of unionism wondered whether there would be a reaction from the labor movement to the economic restructuring and whether and how corporative unionism would end. It was clear that corporative unionism would be affected by the changes occurring in the political and economic systems.

We can now see that the change process has accelerated and the labor movement has experienced a difficult period of transition. Labor confronted the following changes:

A.) With labor's defeat in the 1980s, it ceased to be one of the state's privileged interlocutors. The labor movement went from being part of a permanent negotiation to an obedient follower of regulations.

B.) The arrival of greater electoral democracy went along with the promotion of the idea that the labor movement was an inefficient entity in the face of competitive pressures.

C.) The changes occurring in the economic model reduced the importance of the political control that had been exercised over workers. The central focus turned to productivity issues and the labor movement had little to contribute to these debates.

Labor Flexibility: From Control without Productivity to a Unilateral Dismantling of Labor's Influence

We now focus on the substantive core of the change process, which involved the effects the changes in economic relations exerted on labor rules. Since we retain a political perspective, our analysis recognizes the role played by the economic globalization that helped create a new work culture focused on productivity. In the old system union gains came through the collective legal work contracts. The 1982 economic crisis led international financial bodies and the government team that came to power with Miguel de la Madrid to conclude that painful economic restructuring was necessary. One of the central aspects of this process was the destruction of collective work contracts, which was accomplished through the promotion of labor flexibility as an indispensable requirement for the attainment of productivity. As Zapata (1992) describes,
"in questions as crucial as upward mobility, which for many years was a union prerogative based on the recognition of seniority as a basic criterion for promotion, the union loses authority in that this mobility today results from training. At the same time, the union loses authority over horizontal mobility since all transfers, exchanges, replacements and so on, tend to be administered unilaterally by the company. Also, employment levels cannot be effectively defended and they must frequently accept cuts

in personnel, which remove their representative power. The new categories of subcontracting also introduce a weakening of the unions' capacity for collective representation by removing the possibility of speaking in the name of all those who work in the company. The imposition of salary levels based on productivity increases and ever fewer guaranteed salaries commits the worker to the indiscriminate use of overtime and to a significant erosion, which is reflected in turnover and the appearance of occupational illnesses."[1]

A key point in the savage restructuring has been the creation of new labor rules, with which mangement gained greater discretion. Labor relations have become much more authoritarian because unions lost their capacity to negotiate, interact, and apply pressure. Most importnt has been the dissappearance of worker protections. In recent years, a completely pragmatic labor program has been implemented in which the logic of management and productivity has been imposed. When labor relations or work rules are adjusted the changes adhere to the needs of the company in question.

Market Logic and Authoritarian Control: Toward a New Model

This section traces how relations between the state and unions have been modified since the introduction of greater labor flexibility. The Mexican State's relationship with unionism was a founding part of the national postrevolutionary project, and obeyed the logic of incorporating popular coalitions within the state project as a counterpart to the prevailing class structure. This relationship passed through the following stages: alliance, subordination and defeat.[2]

Today the relationship is passing through a complicated transition in which both written and informal regulations have been used to encourage a highly authoritarian and vertical process of modernization. This has resulted in the destruction of the union model, which functioned up until 1982. The key features of the traditional union model were: bilateral work relations; the right to strike; mobilization of the masses in favor of the official party; privileged interaction with the state; an authoritarian and vertical culture for the control of the rank and file; wages by negotiation based on normative criteria; stable employment; political representation for associations; a revolutionary discourse creating linkages between leaders, functionaries, and the rank and file; and a distancing from the business world.

The state, union and business interaction, had a political and corporate logic. Mexican labor relations, from the end of the 1930s up until the crisis of 1982, operated according to the following key parameters:

a) limited margin for employer intervention in exchange for the acceptance of state intervention;

b) the loss of individual liberties in exchange for the use of collective rights, and political control in exchange for improvements in welfare conditions (salary, health, education, housing);

c) homogenization of labor conditions;

d) a tripartite system of labor justice which depended on executive powers and a wide margin of discretion in the application of judgements.[3]

One by one, the above-mentioned parameters have been altered. Unilateral labor relations now exist in which the company decides the timing, rhythm, and contracting of production. There is an effective loss of the right to strike. Salaries are based on productivity and job positions, and are flexible in both function and type. There is a new neoliberal discourse providing a new interpretation of history and the revolution. Workers' identification with unions is weakening which is beginning to destroy the old monolithic scheme of corporative unionism. The logic of business has been accepted as the only route to productivity. There are closer relationships between company unions and government functionaries and weaker ties between these two and the old union bureaucracy.

Working conditions seriously deteriorated from the early 1980s on. There was a drastic change to the rules of the game, and the process of change was largely unilateral in nature. In 1989, the Confederation of Employers of the Republic of Mexico (Coparmex) made a proposal that served as the basis for the new labor model. The new model consisted of "employers' discretion; lower levels of protection for salaried employees; greater individual choice regarding work and association; a redefinition of unions with state control of strikes; and the conservation of tripartitism as a means of conflict resolution."[4]

The State Party and Mass Politics during the Transition

In Mexico, the only relationships that exist between political parties and unionism are those that still exist between the PRI and the Congress of Labor (Congreso del Trabajo). The other parties do not have effective links with labor organizations. For the Acción Nacional (National Action Party or PAN) links with labor are precluded by the party's principles and liberal roots. PAN prefers to link to individual workers and not to unions. The PRD (Revolutionary Democratic Party) has relationships with social organizations, but it does not have a structure that allows for corporative links with labor.

Another important factor in party-union relations is that with growing democratic demands there is an increasing need for links and affiliations between political parties and individuals. In fact, the 1989 constitutional political reform established in Article 35, Paragraph III, that one of the prerogatives of the citizen is: the possibility of "free and peaceful association to participate in the political affairs of the nation." This simple reform weakens one of the key principles of Mexican state corporativism, in force since 1938, namely, the complete full incorporation of the Confederación de Trabajadores de México (CTM) into the official party (the Party of the Mexican Revolution, PRM. In the old political systems peasants were incorporated into the CNC, where the corporative logic was established, and the logic of citizenship was ignored. Even the military was incorporated into the same corporative structure (although they remained only in this position for only a few years).

The PRI's Fourteenth national assembly (1990) tried to link up with the previous reforms. It promoted a new relationship between citizens and other economic and social groups, although the internal struggles over this process continue within the PRI. Each time the role of social groups in the PRI is quesioned, corporative unionism is put on guard and begins to reclaim its traditions. At the end of the PRI's fifteenth assembly (1992) the reformist "excesses" of the fourteenth assembly were corrected, and Fidel Velázquez achieved the reinstitution of the labor sector within the PRI.

A central part of the changes in the state's relationship with corporative unionism concern the weight of unionism in the official party evident in the reduction of the labor movement's influence in electoral politics.[5]

136

The old labor movement is no longer an asset to the party because it has not been effective in the electoral arena. However, it remains tied to the party. For political maneuvers the PRI has used the National Education Workers' Union (SNTE), which has played a strategic role in territorial organization and in election campaigns. In our view, the National Solidarity Program, initiated at the beginning of Salinas de Gortari's six-year term, has become the key to the PRI's links to the rank and file.

The change in the rules of the game has produced two transformations in the political role of corporative unionism. Posts now have to be won by vote and are no longer provided through appointment.[6] In addition, salaries are no longer negotiable for labor leaders, but form part of a rigid pact. In the future wages will depend solely on the company's performance and ability to pay.

In spite of the profound nature of these changes, some important traditions remain. Not even in the worst repression of Miguel Alemán's six-year term (1946-52), did corporative unionism occupy as disagreeable a role as it does with the Salinism of today. Unions have been converted into the promotor of a project that unions themselves consider a mistake. Corporative unionism continues to be powerful because it still provides control over workers under new circumstances. Furthermore, an alternative model of unionism does not exist.

Salinism destroyed resistant union leaders and weakened opposition to its modernization project. Key events were the removal of la Quina and Jonquitud, who had been, respectively, leaders of the petroleum and teachers' unions in the first years of Salinas' six-year term. The first was imprisoned and the second was simply dismissed. Not only have the obstacles to authoritarian modernization been removed, in addition, a modification is occurring within the old political class. The modification includes the modernization of leadership, the removal of obstacles to the modernization process, and destruction of any counterweights to presidential powers.

One of the new strategies, which replaced the political-electoral role previously fullfilled by the traditional sectors (workers and peasants) was the National Solidarity Program (Pronasol). This program channeled the state's social spending and served various functions during Salinas de Gortari's term. These functions include provision of the state's social policy in an era of great economic readjustment, and a mechanism to address social discontent over the crisis and recover legitimacy and votes for the PRI.

Pronasol is a model of the new political class, not only for the votes that the PRI can gain through social spending, but because the program's operators, in many cases, have become the PRI's most viable candidates. This strategy also affects corporative unions' power, which is no longer the only means of mass control between the state and workers.

Pronasol and the state social policy are not the democratic alternative to corporative unionism. Rather, in accordance with the hypotheses of Bolívar, Méndez, and Romero (1992) what is "social" now acts as a political limit on what is "liberal." They are the resources of a new centralizing presidentialism, with an authoritarian and paternalistic nature. It is one of the links that makes the implementation of the new economic model possible. In this way, we now have two complementary routes for mass politics, corporative unionism and presidential "pronasolismo," and neither has a democratic orientation.

Strengths and Weaknesses of Corporative Unionism

The roles that corporative unionism and the CTM play in the political process can be described by the following two scenarios:

a) The "agreement without pacts" whereby the government and business groups make the decisions and the labor sector signs on has been a key ingredient of stabilization pacts. This was begun in December 1987 and continues today. If we look at only this side of the coin, it is easy to think that corporative unionism has lost almost all its power.

b) On the other hand, it is useful to contemplate what would have happened to the Salinas project if it did not have the discipline provided by corporative unionsim. To begin with, stabilization pacts would have been impossible to achieve. If instead unions had mobilized to pressure the government over its projects, economic and financial stabilization would have been greatly complicated. The source of the strength held by the upper echelons of the labor movement is in the discipline and conformance with state policies.

This is ullustrated by the recent position of the CTM. In August 1993 during preparation of the Pact for Stability, Competitiveness, and Employment (PECE), and in the face of the presidential succession, Fidel Velázquez affirmed that the CTM would refuse to renew the next phase of the pact if the wage limits imposed by governmental authorities persisted. In addition, the ninety-three year old leader surprisingly declared that the workers were to be included in the pact through obligation and not by agreement (El Financiero, August 3, 1993).

The CTM's strength lies in its capacity to control workers and in the veto rights it can exercise over the economic policy of Salinas's government. The potentially destructive power of corporative unionism depends on many factors, including: whether Fidel Velázquez is able to remove salary limits during his negotiations with the economy cabinet; the positions gained in the presidential succession by functionaries of the CTM and the other labor organizations; and the role unionism will play within the workplace of the future.

The process of negotiation between the state and the unions continues and the possibility of conflict persists. If there is one moment of government weakness during which the CTM, and corporative unionism, can achieve sinecures and favors, it is when the end of a presidential term is approaching and the creation of a new government is underway.

The Long Road of Productivity Regulation

Without a doubt, labor reform is the major outstanding feature in Salinas's new economic model. In this sphere there is an unresolved struggle between the government, which wants to complete the adjustment with constitutional regulation; the business boards, which have directed the adjustment process to serve their interests; and a corporative labor sector that clings onto the current legislation like the survivors of a shipwreck clinging to a life raft.

The adjustment process has included down-sized collective contracts, which are but a shadow of their former selves. The new rules of the game which President Salinas defined clearly on May 1, 1990, include an end to confrontation and cooperation in productivity improvement efforts. Corporative unionism has largely accommodated to the new rules.

Step by step, labor flexibility is being imposed. In 1992, the CTM and Fidel Velázquez accepted the postponed National Agreement for Increased Productivity and Quality. They agreed to help create a new labor culture in which the business sector would promote a program of technical aid and stimulation; the labor sector would work to improve productivity; all sectors would support training and human resource development programs; in each company, organizational modernization, administrative development, and human resource and technological improvement would be coordinated; the government would maintain a macroeconomic climate to promote productivity increases; and there would be an evaluation and follow-up commission. As yet, the agreement appears to be just another political discourse.

The Mexican Transition: An Era of Uncertainty

The future of the relationship between the state, unions, and political parties depends to a great extent on international eceonomic forces. Labor relations are likely to enter a highly politicized phase due to the 1994 presidential succession. Actions taken by corporative unions will likely have a short-term rationale and involve efforts to conserve power in the whirlwind of the 1994 succession.

In the 1994 presidential succession, the following factors will be at stake:

1) The profound changes that have been emerging in the country in the last three decades, including urbanization, greater levels of education and information, high civic participation, significant advances in electoral participation, modifications to the party system, and electoral processes.

2) Another important factor is the expectations held by political actors.

3) Recent political uncertainty is in part a product of the economic ills experienced by broad sections of the population.

4) The current parties lack social articulation and the power to impose a democratic agenda. A number of political factors are critical, including:

a) We have emerged from two extraordinary federal elections in 1988 and 1991.

b) We have a highly diversified party system whose territorial strongholds spring from highly diverse traditions in the political terrain. The existing single political process is on the brink of changing to a multiparty system.

c) We are experiencing a wide-ranging modification of ideological positions and values. Intense political discourse has revolved around a revolutionary axis involving a broad-based state, welfare institutions single-party corporativism, authoritarian modernization, and closed borders. The new political model revolves around modernization, a closed state, competition, the international market, electoral democracy, the party system, and integration into North America.

d) Radical changes have also occurred in popular culture whereby the mythology that accompanied post-revolutionary Mexico has disappeared. We are witnessing an explosion and fragmentation of regional and local cultures that coexist alongside globalization. The old Mexico was represented by the novels of Pedro Páramo and the union leadership of Fidel Velázquez. Today we have a network of cultural industries that limit the role of mythology.

Corporative unionism will necessarily have to learn to live within a dual transition. On the one hand, the political system is changing and there is an increase in electoral competition. Opposition parties have emerged and adjustments have occurred in the PRI which diminish the influence of traditional sectors. On the other hand, the labor system finds itself in a period of profoud adjustment as a result of the enormous economic changes occurring within Mexico after 1982. The central elements of the new labor system are:

—A new culture of competitiveness which regulates labor relations

—The logic of the international market and economic integration including NAFTA

—A crisis in the state corporative model, and the absence of a model to replace it.

Endnotes

1. Zapata 1992.

2. On the political structuring of the State and popular coalitions, see Aziz et al. 1990

3. The old labor model is described in the paper by Graciela Bensusán in this volume.

4. ..... Ibid.

5. As an example, one can look at the decrease in popularly elected posts that the labor sector of the PRI has held: in 1982 it had 25 percent of the party candidates and in 1991 only 16 percent. Data from Camillo, 1992.

6. There are many types of electoral competition in Mexico today including multiparty and biparty regions, dominant campaigns, and soleparties. See Aziz (1992). Las elecciones federales de 1991. Mexico: Miguel Angel Porrua and the CIIH-UNAM.

References

Aziz Nassif, Alberto. 1992. *Las elecciones federales de 1992*. Mexico: Miguel Angel Porrua and the CIIH-UNAM.

Aziz Nassif, Alberto, et al. 1990. "El Estado Mexicano y la CTM." Casa Chata Editions, no. 32, Mexico.

Bolívar, A., L. Méndez, and M. A. Romero. 1992. "El naimiento del Estado liberal social, 1982-1992," *El Cotidiano*, 12.

Camillo, Juan Reyes del. 1992. "PRI: del nacionalismo revolucionario al liberalismo social." *El Cotidiano*, Universidad Autónoma Metropolitana, no. 50 (September-October): 77.

Zapata, Francisco. 1992. Francisco "La crisis del control sindical sobre la dinámica del mercado de trabajo en México." In the collective book, *Ajuste estructural, mercados laborales y TLC*, 70-71 Mexico: Colegio de Mexico, Fundación Friedrich Ebert, and the Colegio de la Frontera Norte.

Regional Integration And Transnational Labor Strategies Under NAFTA

Maria Lorena Cook

Introduction

The globalization of the economy and the recent trend toward the formation of regional trading blocs pose a fundamental challenge to national labor movements. The mobility of capital offshore and across national borders to take advantage of lower labor costs has threatened jobs in higher-wage countries and raised charges of labor exploitation in poorer nations. Critics contend, furthermore, that regional trade pacts such as the one recently created for the North American area grant transnational corporations greater autonomy and power at the expense of states and citizens. Labor movements, confined within national boundaries by legislation, tradition, and political institutions, are at a special disadvantage in defending their interests in this new international environment. Nonetheless, global production provides the incentive for labor unions to seek out new, collaborative strategies with labor in other countries. And regional integration, by providing possibilities for direct and regular contact between labor unions, may make such transnational strategies more feasible.

Together with the internationalization of the economy, another related yet distinct global trend is the internationalization of domestic politics. This phenomenon has been described as the "interpenetration of domestic and international spheres" and the "blurring of domestic and external issues," and involves the increased influence of international actors on states at multiple points in the political process (Chalmers 1991; Pastor 1992; Sikkink 1993). The internationalization of domestic politics has also begun to reshape understandings and definitions of national sovereignty in ways that reflect the increasing pressures and influences of international actors on states and their policies (Sikkink 1993). The issue-areas of human rights, and to a lesser extent, environmental protection, are examples where this internationalization and the reshaping of traditional concepts of sovereignty are most evident. In formally constituted regional economic blocs, such as the European Community (later the European Union) or the North American Free Trade Area, the pressures for the internationalization of domestic politics would appear to be even greater.

This paper argues that while the internationalization of the economy has tended to weaken national labor movements, the internationalization of domestic politics may expand the traditional arenas for strategic action for labor unions. In particular, the

North American Free Trade Agreement has been portrayed by some of its many critics as representing the consolidation of a neoconservative or neoliberal project that will not only shape the future economic development of the region, but also constrain its social policies and limit its political options (Grinspun and Cameron 1993: Chapter 1). However, these same critics have also noted that the debate surrounding NAFTA in Mexico, Canada, and the United States has led to a broad range of contacts and cooperative efforts among labor, environmental, women's, religious, and educators' groups in the three countries. This process is not only itself an expression of the search for new strategies in the context of regional integration, it has also altered the traditional ways in which U.S.-Mexican relations have been carried out and shaped the political process within Mexico. While the constraints to transnational labor collaboration remain strong, these new dimensions of the international and political environments nonetheless potentially offer new opportunities to weakened labor movements in all three countries.

This paper will begin with a discussion of the contours of this new international political environment—in particular, the internationalization of domestic politics—and how this environment differs from traditional, nationally bounded notions of domestic politics and state action. I then discuss how both the transnationalization of politics and regional economic integration change the arena for strategic action by labor groups, how this new environment affects the labor movement in Mexico, and the kinds of strategies Mexican and U.S. labor unions have begun to pursue in this context. Finally, I consider whether the side agreement on labor standards that was developed as a complement to the NAFTA represents an example of institutionalization of this political internationalization, thus potentially facilitating further transnational collaboration among unions, or whether, alternatively, the side accord buttresses national institutions and state autonomy in ways that could constrain labor's strategic use of the international arena.

The Internationalization of National Politics: Shifting the Strategic Arena

Several authors have tried recently to describe and reconceptualize what appears to be a new global phenomenon, variously described as the "interpenetration of international and domestic spheres" or the "internationalization of domestic politics." They argue that what is emerging in domestic and international politics is not adequately captured by existing theories of international relations, which tend to maintain the "hard division" between domestic and foreign policies and stress the role of the state in defining and determining these policies (Chalmers 1991; Sikkink 1991). While the literature on "interdependence" comes closer in its acknowledgment of the multiple influences on state policies, it tends to ignore the role that nongovernmental organizations (NGOs) and transnational social movements play in favor of the role played by foreign governments, international organizations, and transnational corporations (Sikkink 1991:36). In contrast, the "internationalization of domestic politics" refers to the pressures and influence of multiple international and domestic actors (acting in concert with international allies) on the domestic political process. These actors include international organizations and foundations, international and domestic nongovernmental organizations, and social movements, as well as foreign governments. Thus, in contrast to traditional notions of the role of states in international relations, multiple nongovernmental groups, and not just states, engage in "international relations" (Chalmers 1991).

Those who argue that the internationalization of domestic politics is a new, important phenomenon in the world today are quick to point out that states remain important and are in most cases the key determinants of domestic and foreign policies. Nonetheless, the numerous other groups that act in the international arena and that act to influence other nations' domestic policies must increasingly be taken into account in order to understand the political processes shaping particular issues in many countries. These international influences are also reshaping traditional notions of national sovereignty, generally understood as a state's exclusive right to determine what happens within its national borders. One issue-area that represents an obvious challenge to conventional definitions of national sovereignty is human rights. As Kathryn Sikkink (1991, 1993) has pointed out, an individual citizen's appeal to universal standards of human rights in challenging his or her own government is probably the clearest example of the undermining of national sovereignty. A very different but important example is provided by the European Community, where member states have voluntarily ceded some degree of sovereignty to supranational institutions within the community.

In the case of human rights, a range of international actors, including international organizations, foundations, and NGOs, as well as foreign governments, have been influential in pressuring governments to alter their practices or to investigate individual cases of rights violations. Often, these international actors provide support to domestic NGOs, granting them a leverage vis-à-vis their own government that they would not have otherwise had. The confluence of pressures from international organizations, foreign governments, and domestic NGOs/social movements was especially clear during the 1970s in Latin America, when, for example, the U.S. administration of Jimmy Carter, Amnesty International, U.S. solidarity committees, and domestic groups such as the Mothers of the Plaza de Mayo generated limited but significant pressure on the repressive Argentine military regime to halt human rights abuses.

Another issue-area where international actors increasingly shape domestic politics is the environment. Again, international organizations such as Greenpeace, acting in alliance with domestic environmental groups and some foreign governments, are creating important pressures on states to address the problem of environmental degradation (Keck 1991). Whereas the appeal in the case of human rights is primarily a moral one, and the assumption is that all individuals, regardless of nationality, possess certain rights, in the case of the environment the assumption is that the planet's natural resources are the responsibility of all and that states do not have exclusive rights to determine how these resources are exploited. In Latin America, moreover, environmental preservation is increasingly tied up with the cultural and even physical preservation of indigenous groups. The rights of indigenous groups is fast emerging as an issue-area drawing the attention of international actors. In these cases, a multiplicity of international and domestic NGOs and social movements have pressured national governments to change the way they address both sets of issues and have helped to place these issues on the agenda of states and international agencies.

The issue of labor rights shares some of the characteristics of both the human rights and environmental issues. The labor rights conventions of the International Labor Organization, for example, treat labor rights as human rights in their universality, even though signatories to the ILO conventions have often belied this by their actions. Such conventions as those concerning forced or child labor may not be followed by all nations, yet governments that permit such practices are universally condemned. Still, developing country governments in particular have frequently argued, on both national sovereignty and economic backwardness grounds, that they have a right to exploit the environment or to violate labor rights in the interest of national economic development. They and others argue that it is unfair for advanced nations to restrict developing countries' ability to exploit their environmental and human resources in order to pass through the same stages of development as the wealthier countries. Such an expectation, goes the argument, constitutes the imposition of advanced countries' standards on poorer countries and has raised charges of imperialism. Thus, the lack of adequate housing or social services and low wages is justified because of the stage of development at which a particular country finds itself; U.S. and British industrialization, it is argued, were based on similar conditions. Here the conflict between universal rights and national sovereignty is sharply drawn.

The formation of regional trading blocs may be diluting the power of this argument in relations between richer and poorer countries. National labor movements and environmental groups in particular have raised charges of unfair competition in cases where trade barriers are lifted between nations of widely varying labor and environmental standards. The argument of economic necessity due to a country's low level of development has been replaced to some extent by that which says conditions should be "harmonized" so as to eliminate unfair advantages for the country that has lower standards. The European example in this area has set a precedent for similar demands for harmonization in a North American free trade area, in spite of the important differences between the two projects. In the case of NAFTA, the Mexican government has downplayed its developing nation status and insisted that it wants "trade, not aid", even though in the negotiation process it has raised the issue of assistance to meet higher environmental standards and it has shown some support for the idea of a North American regional development bank that could help ease the adjustment costs of a transition to freer trade. Mexico's (ultimately successful) attempts to become a member of the OECD and its government's argument that free trade will bring Mexico into the "First World" further undermine claims that Mexico needs an exemption from environmental and labor standards for its economic development

Formal regional integration may lend a further legitimacy to discussions of labor rights and standards, where the process of economic integration or the internationalization of the economy by themselves do not. While the process of Mexico's integration with the U.S. economy has been occurring over a period of decades, traditionally there has been little concern with (and more than a little misunderstanding about) what happened inside Mexico's borders. In particular, U.S. labor, environmental, and other citizens' groups had minimal contact with their Mexican counterparts. Throughout most of the 1980s, members of these groups were more familiar with the politics of Central American countries and the details of U.S. policy in this region than they were with their neighbor to the south, with whom they shared a two thousand mile border. Also during the 1980s, however, the expansion of the maquiladora industry, the restructuring of both U.S. and Mexican industry, and Mexico's unilateral economic opening drove many U.S. companies to Mexico in search of lower labor costs. These developments led some labor unions to begin to search for new collaborative strategies with their counterparts across the border in order to improve their bargaining position with their transnational employers (Middlebrook 1992). There were few such efforts, however, and these were generally undermined by numerous obstacles, not the least of which were mistrust,

146

cultural stereotyping, and the lack of support for such collaboration among both national union leaderships and rank-and-file members.[1]

It was not until Mexican President Carlos Salinas de Gortari proposed the creation of a North American Free Trade Agreement to President George Bush in 1990 that labor unions and numerous grassroots groups in the United States, Mexico, and Canada became truly interested in one another. In particular, Congress's debate in 1991 over granting the president fast-track authority mobilized opposition groups with diverse interests into forming coalitions in order to defeat fast-track and then NAFTA (Thorup 1991).[2] These coalitions adopted a variety of strategies: They lobbied their congressional representatives to oppose fast-track and NAFTA, they educated their own members on what they saw to be the dangers of free trade, and they looked across the borders for allies. Suddenly, cross-border alliances and coalition formation were seen as crucial in the political battle to defeat what had become an important domestic policy issue, and not "merely" an international trade agreement. Canadian opponents of the U.S.-Canada Free Trade Agreement and of NAFTA were especially eager to convince Mexican and U.S. counterparts that they should fight to oppose the agreement, based on their experience with free trade in Canada.

The NAFTA debate has acted as a catalyst to the formation of cross-border alliances. Since 1990, there has been an explosion of contacts between Canadian, Mexican, and U.S. nongovernmental groups.[3] These have taken a variety of forms: site visits, educational tours and workshops, meetings attended by representatives of organizations from the three countries, regular communication and exchange of information (aided by faxes and access to computer networks), joint political strategizing around NAFTA, solidarity actions around specific conflicts, pressuring of government officials and politicians to concern themselves with events in the other country, and so on. Cross-border collaboration has taken place at both the grassroots level of people-to-people contacts and among organization leaders.[4] This development of direct, people-to-people networking in the three countries has been called "citizen diplomacy" and represents a novel dimension in U.S.-Mexican relations. Some have argued that this citizen diplomacy can act as an important, bottom-up check on traditional diplomatic relations and government-to-government exchanges (Thorup 1991; 1993).

This cross-border coalition formation took place in a unique historical context, one in which Mexico's economic and political future had come to depend —as never before—on a decision to be made in the U.S. Congress. At the same time, NAFTA's passage was by no means a foregone conclusion. This meant that the political process in the United States was particularly porous on this issue. Congress was not only bombarded by the lobbying efforts of the Mexican government (producing the most expensive single-issue lobbying campaign by any foreign government thus far), but also by domestic constituencies, especially labor and environmental groups, and by the congressional testimony of Mexican citizens—representatives of popular organizations, Mexican NGOs, intellectuals, and even individuals who felt wronged by the actions of U.S. companies in Mexico.[5] Whereas before the international activities of Mexican NGOs consisted, in the best of cases, of contacts with foundations or other social movements, now they were "lobbying at the centers of political decision making, especially the U.S. Congress," where, increasingly, issues relating to Mexico were being decided (Hernández Navarro 1993:10).

Government officials and legislators have also crossed borders in recent years. U.S. politicians flocked to Mexico, especially the border, to learn more about the concerns of their constituents, both those who favored and opposed the agreement. Mexican government officials have been especially active in the U.S. political arena. Not only did they spend millions on lobbying and influential consultants in Washington, D.C., but they targeted the op-ed pages of major U.S. newspapers and traveled throughout the country to campaign for NAFTA (Dresser 1993). The Mexican government especially tried to win over Hispanics in the United States in the hopes that they could act as a strong "pro-Mexico" lobby in Washington.

The political opposition in Mexico has also campaigned in the United States among Mexican immigrants, and announced plans to lobby the U.S. Congress and President Clinton on electoral and human rights issues (Hughes 1993a:12). Competition between the Salinas administration and the opposition headed by Cuauhtémoc Cárdenas for the hearts and minds of Mexican citizens residing in the United States even prompted the Mexican government to respond with an international version of *Solidaridad*, the government's public works program targeted at the poor (Hughes 1993b:13). However, it was in the political process and debate surrounding NAFTA that the interpenetration of the domestic politics of the United States and Mexico emerged most clearly.

That domestic politics have been "internationalized" by NAFTA is especially visible within Mexico. A country long ruled by strong nationalist sentiments and mistrust for its northern neighbor, Mexico's political leaders have typically bristled at any criticism coming from the United States and felt little compunction to address its concerns. Because of its proximity to the United States and the history of Mexico-U.S. relations, Mexico has clung more steadfastly to notions of national sovereignty than most other Latin American nations. These strong nationalist tendencies made themselves felt in the economic arena as well as in politics, even though Mexico's economy has always been strongly dependent on the United States. However, the gradual opening of Mexico's economy in the mid-1980s and President Salinas's strong support for NAFTA have made it more difficult to sustain the nationalist discourse within Mexico and with other countries. Moreover, economic liberalization and restructuring in Mexico are dismantling the regime's domestic support coalition, affecting organized labor in particular, which constituted the strongest pillar of support during moments of nationalist or statist retrenchment vis-à-vis the United States or even the Mexican private sector.

The NAFTA political process has made the Mexican government uncharacteristically responsive to outside criticism of its domestic policies and has shaped the reform process within Mexico. U.S. concerns with Mexico's environmental problems and lax enforcement of its laws led President Salinas to revise environmental legislation and take a series of strongly visible measures aimed at assuaging these concerns. Complaints about corruption, drug trafficking, and human rights violations—issues that had led to tensions in U.S.-Mexican relations in the past—led President Salinas to step up drug interdiction efforts, clean up the judicial police force, and appoint a former human rights advocate to the position of attorney general. On political issues the Mexican government has been more tentative. Nonetheless, charges of authoritarianism from outside as well as pressure from domestic political opponents have pressured the regime to recognize opposition electoral victories in some states and to propose a series of reforms, including campaign spending limits and the expansion of opposition representation in the senate.[6]

Mexico's authoritarian political system has traditionally constrained the ability of domestic political opponents to influence the political process via elections or other internal mechanisms. In recent years, however, Mexican political reform has increasingly been spurred and shaped by what happens in the United States. In extreme cases, a critical article in the *Wall Street Journal* or the *New York Times* can lead to a speedier change in government policy than years of domestic political pressure. It is little wonder, then, that some Mexican intellectuals, labor groups, human rights organizations, and opposition parties have used the U.S. political arena to press for change in their own country. The Mexican left in particular has overcome historic mistrust in order to build alliances with U.S. and Canadian groups. With these allies, they have learned to use the U.S. media and learned how the U.S. Congress works. These are lessons not likely to fade after the issue of NAFTA passes from the screen. Meanwhile, the NAFTA debate has increased the contact points between international actors and the domestic political process in both the United States and Mexico, and it has expanded the possible arenas available to nongovernmental actors for strategic action on a range of issues, not all of them pertaining strictly to NAFTA.

The Transnational Arena and Labor Strategies

A wide variety of groups have engaged in cross-border networking and the creation of alliances. While labor organizations have also become involved in these kinds of activities, labor's participation is both more complicated and in some ways more important than that of other kinds of groups. Labor is an especially important actor in regional economic integration because one of the chief attractions of Mexico as an investment site for U.S. companies is its low labor costs. Low wages and labor standards are also among the chief reasons NAFTA's opponents fear the agreement. While the environmental question also sparks concern in the United States, no issue is so central to what NAFTA is about as the labor issue.

The central importance of Mexican labor for NAFTA also explains why labor's ability to make use of new arenas for strategic action is more complicated than it is for other groups. For over a decade, Mexico suffered under the burden of an enormous foreign debt, high inflation, and minimal or negative growth. Government leaders implemented a program of economic and industrial restructuring that had devastating consequences for labor. Real wages declined by 66 percent between 1982 and 1990, unemployment and underemployment increased, and government subsidies to basic consumer items were cut (Cornelius and Craig 1991). At the same time, labor protest was more strictly controlled than in the previous decade—many of the more visible strikes were declared illegal or nonexistent; industrial restructuring led to a number of layoffs and plant closings that tended to affect more democratic and militant unions; the political influence of major labor organizations such as the CTM declined precipitously (Cook 1994). Mexican labor organizations thus emerged from the decade of the 1980s greatly weakened by the experience. Under President Salinas, the burden of the slow and unsteady economic recovery has continued to rest with labor, as the government has continued to hold down wages in its fight against inflation.

Not only Mexican unions' economic weakness but their growing political weakness and lack of autonomy also complicate labor's search for new strategies. Most labor organizations are subordinate to the government and the ruling Institutional

Revolutionary Party (PRI). Union registration is regulated by the Labor Ministry and can be highly politicized; determination of the legality of a strike is often a similarly political process.[7] The largest and most important labor confederation, the Confederation of Mexican Workers (CTM), has traditionally operated by elite-level bargaining and by exchanging political support and control of worker demands and dissent for political positions in the party and Congress and privileged access to the government. It has even resorted to violence against its own member unions during labor conflicts. Dissident movements within unions are often quickly repressed or contained. In a context of economic weakness, often brutal restructuring, declining political influence, and weak political opposition, labor unions have become even more dependent on the government (and increasingly, the president). At the same time, while the government has tried to distance itself from traditional labor leaders who historically have supported the regime and has acted to decrease labor's presence in the PRI, it still seems hesitant to break completely with labor's support in the ever more complicated presidential succession process.[8] This continued reliance on labor support therefore gives the labor sector some minimal bargaining power and keeps unions interested in supporting the system rather than in striking out in opposition to the regime.

Because of Mexican labor's dependence on the regime, it has been difficult for most unions to publicly criticize their government's support for NAFTA either in Mexico or abroad.[9] At the same time, NAFTA has been widely touted as something that will be good for Mexico, bringing more investment, more jobs, lower consumer prices and greater consumer choice, better quality products, and eventually, higher salaries. These factors make it extremely difficult for Mexican labor unions to campaign actively against NAFTA. They have also made it difficult for Canadian, U.S., and Mexican unions to find common ground.[10] The AFL-CIO's frustration with the CTM's position on this issue, for example, led them to initiate talks with a much smaller, less influential, but more independent labor federation in Mexico, the Authentic Labor Front (Frente Auténtico del Trabajo, FAT).

Nonetheless, a number of cross-border activities have taken place among labor unions, and labor groups have used this new, transnational arena to expand their range of strategies for protecting their interests.[11] The remainder of this section will examine the types of strategies that various Mexican and U.S. labor organizations have pursued and what factors have influenced their choice of strategies.

National Political Bargaining

Peak labor organizations tend to privilege political bargaining with their governments as their primary strategy. Although such organizations may also use their international alliances, their primary bargaining strength lies in the role these organizations play in the national political arena, especially their role in supporting political parties. Thus, in the United States this strategy is followed by national officials of the AFL-CIO, for whom the Democratic Clinton administration offers more opportunities than in the recent past to wield political influence. NAFTA is one of several issues in which U.S. labor has an interest; the others include health care reform and labor law reform. Because these are issues decided by Congress, national labor strategy tends to focus on the legislative arena.

The CTM in Mexico has also privileged this strategy of political bargaining in the national arena, without generally resorting to the transnational arena in order to exert pressure on the government. In part this is so because the leader of the CTM has a strong aversion to international "intervention" in Mexico's domestic affairs. Other reasons are that the CTM has found little common ground with the AFL-CIO or the Canadian Labour Congress on the NAFTA issue, and because the Mexican labor organization continues to wield some minimal political influence with its own government. Labor continues to play a role (albeit an ever declining one) within the Institutional Revolutionary Party (PRI), in the presidential succession, and in legitimating the government's wage-containment policy. Moreover, state-supported challenges to the CTM's hegemony within the Mexican labor movement by rival organizations such as the Revolutionary Confederation of Workers and Peasants (CROC) and the recently formed Federation of Goods and Services Unions (FESEBES) have led the CTM to redouble its efforts to prove its superior representativeness and capacity for control of worker demands to the regime. While U.S. labor organizations tend to target the legislative arena under this strategy, Mexican labor targets the executive, reflecting Mexico's strongly presidentialist political system.

Whereas the CTM is the key Mexican labor organization that pursues this national political strategy, other organizations have also privileged political bargaining with the state. One of these is the FESEBES, the relatively new labor federation that became a competitor of the CTM for state favors under the Salinas administration. Dominated by the once independent telephone workers' union, the FESEBES traded in political independence for the government's support for the new federation and for its support in the telephone union's bargaining with the newly privatized telephone company. Unions within the FESEBES have also adopted a more varied set of strategies, however. They have participated in trinational exchanges with U.S. and Canadian labor and other citizens' groups. The telephone workers' union signed an agreement with the U.S. Communications Workers of America and the Communications and Electrical Workers of Canada, pledging to defend worker rights in the face of regional integration and to exchange information on changes in the industry.[12] However, such contacts have been driven more by the union's effort to prepare itself for bargaining with Teléfonos de México than to join in a common effort to defeat NAFTA. The telephone workers' union has stated its support for NAFTA, whereas its partners in the agreement are opposed.

The case of another union in the FESEBES further illustrates the important role of domestic political alliances in bargaining with the employer. The Mexican Electrical Workers' Union (SME), one of the founding members of the FESEBES, is a small, 35,000- member union representing employees of the Center Light and Power Company, a parastate firm facing liquidation. The SME was drawn into a close relationship with President Salinas in order to receive his protection and ensure its survival in the creation of a new power company. While the SME did participate in trinational meetings and even developed its version of a bill of workers' rights to be appended to the NAFTA, it did not adopt a strong position on this issue within Mexico because of its need to ally with a more powerful partner in the political battle for its survival.[13]

Because of their location in services dominated by domestic private capital or by the state, most of the unions in the FESEBES are likely to continue in the future to center their political strategy within national boundaries rather than in the transnational arena, in spite of their initial contacts with groups outside of Mexico. At the same time, and perhaps more importantly, both the SME and the telephone workers union lack the political autonomy necessary to build upon external alliances.

Transnational Collective Bargaining

This strategy involves cross-border cooperation in bargaining with a common multinational employer. While there are numerous cases of cross-border solidarity between unions, more concerted strategizing is rare. Nonetheless, one case that has received recent attention is that of the Farm Labor Organizing Committee (FLOC), an AFL-CIO affiliate, and the Sinaloa-based National Farmworkers' Union (Sindicato Nacional de Trabajadores Agrícolas, SNTOAC), a CTM affiliate (Nauman 1993:14; Moody and McGinn 1992). Both have agreed to work together to improve conditions in each union by assisting each other in collective negotiations with their employer, the Campbell Soup Company. According to union leaders, this strategy has proven effective in increasing wages and benefits for members in both countries, although Mexican wages remain far lower than those of their U.S. counterparts.[14]

The FLOC took the initiative to locate its Mexican counterpart in 1987, well before NAFTA had even been contemplated, in response to Campbell's threat to buy its tomato paste from Mexico if U.S workers made it "too expensive" to do so in the United States The U.S. union then developed a strategy that consisted of improving conditions for Mexican workers so that the company could not use the disparity in costs against U.S. workers. The FLOC approached CTM patriarch Fidel Velázquez to secure his assistance in contacting the SNTOAC, and obtained support from both the CTM and AFL-CIO to set up a commission for ongoing talks between the two unions. Support from both the AFL-CIO and the CTM appears to have been crucial in making this transnational cooperation successful.

Transnational Organizing

While U.S. unions do not operate inside of Mexico, there are some initial cases of U.S.-Mexican cooperation in union organizing, most notably in the maquila industry along the border. The maquila sector has the lowest union density of any other manufacturing activity in Mexico. Where unions do operate in the maquila, these tend to be dominated by the official confederations: the CTM, the CROC, or the CROM. In some ways this sector is the most open to organizing by unions, even though there are many obstacles. Employers discourage unions, the workers themselves may even shun them, and the official unions can be extremely powerful and effective at stamping out any efforts to organize workers into more independent or democratic unions.[15]

Nonetheless, one independent labor federation in Mexico has begun to try to make inroads into the maquiladora sector. This is a relatively small labor federation, the FAT, that has been extremely active in the transnational arena.[16] In Mexico, it is one of the founding members of an anti-NAFTA network called the Mexican Action Network on Free Trade (Red Mexicana de Acción Frente al Libre Comercio, RMALC). The FAT and the United Electrical, Radio, and Machine Workers of America (UE) have entered into what they call a "strategic organizing alliance" and have decided to cooperate in organizing maquila workers, targeting those runaway plants that employed UE-represented shops in the United States (Witt 1992; Browne and Sims 1993:5). Although the unions involved are relatively small and the results so far are mixed, the alliance has received a great deal of publicity and has inspired other forms of direct assistance to Mexican unions.

Some indication that transnational organizing is occurring in the agricultural sector has also appeared recently. As part of their cooperative strategy, both the FLOC and the SNTOAC are working to organize nonunion farm labor in Texas and in south-central Mexico. The Teamsters are also contacting employees of U.S.-based agricultural industries in Mexico's south-central farm belt (Moody and McGinn 1992). Teamsters Local 912 from California has been especially active in collaborating with Mexican employees of Green Giant, which transferred its vegetable canning and packing operations from Watsonville to Mexico.

U.S. unions have also launched "adopt an organizer" campaigns to support Mexican union activists who have been fired for their organizing work. The program funds Mexican workers who devote themselves full-time to organizing in the border plants. U.S. unions involved in the campaign so far include the United Electrical Workers, Teamsters, and UAW locals. Thus far the program has been targeted at a Zenith electronics assembly plant in Reynosa and at the Ford plant in Cuautitlán, among others (NAWWN 1993:10; Kalmijn 1994; *Labor Notes* 1994).

Transnational Solidarity/Networking

This strategy encompasses different kinds of activities, from participation in trinational meetings to solidarity actions in response to specific conflicts, to speaking tours and site visits. In the last five years labor organizations throughout the continent have engaged in activities of this type. For most these contacts are a starting point, leading to closer cooperation with counterparts and to the adoption of one of the transnational strategies outlined above. For others, visits and meetings do not lead to more formal communication. In any case, the number of contacts that has occurred is significant, especially when one considers the sparse communication among Canadian, U.S., and Mexican unions prior to 1990, especially at the grassroots level.

For many, a series of trinational exchanges that brought together leaders and representatives from a broad range of unions and nonlabor organizations provided the initial contact. In these trinational meetings participants discussed free trade, what positions groups should adopt, and whether and how they should cooperate in defending their interests (see Eisenstadt 1993).[17] Participants stressed that NAFTA did not only represent a threat to jobs, wages, and working conditions, but also an opportunity to develop trinational connections in order to help shape the continuing process of integration (Trinational Exchange 1991:3). In the first meeting, the Mexican side included top representatives from some of the principal labor organizations in Mexico, including the telephone workers, the electrical workers, the airline pilots' association, and the teachers' union, as well as representatives of the FAT and of the CTM. This meeting marked one of the first in which both official and independent union representatives appeared together. From the labor movement on the U.S. side were representatives from the Communications Workers of America (CWA), United Auto Workers (UAW), Amalgamated Clothing and Textile Workers' Union (ACTWU), International Ladies' Garment Workers' Union (ILGWU), the AFL-CIO, and the Coalition for Justice in the

Maquiladoras, the International Union of Electrical Workers (IUE), and the Farm Labor Organizing Committee FLOC.

Several intra-industry meetings have also been set up in the auto sector, including one by the Chrysler-Ramos Arizpe union and the CTM, to which U.S. and Canadian unions were invited (Middlebrook 1992), and another sponsored by the Transnationals Information Exchange in Mexico in 1991. At the TIE meeting, auto workers from the Big Three (Chrysler, Ford, and General Motors) discussed developing action plans by company and formed a trinational committee to coordinate industrywide cooperation and networking (Moody and McGinn 1992). Canadian, U.S., and Mexican electrical workers' unions also met in Mexico in February 1994 to discuss common concerns. This meeting was significant, given that the International Brotherhood of Electrical Workers (IBEW) and the Sindicato Mexicano de Electricistas (SME) carry more clout in their respective countries than either the UE or the FAT.[18]

Labor conflicts at U.S. auto plants in Mexico have drawn the attention of the UAW and the AFL-CIO and led them to lodge complaints about the handling of such conflicts. Among the most important of these cases has been the ongoing series of conflicts at the Ford plant in Cuautitlán, outside of Mexico City. In 1990, the struggle over union representation left one worker dead at the hands of hired thugs who ambushed workers at the plant.[19] The case revealed the collusion of the Mexican government, Ford Motor Company, and the CTM in the repression of labor dissent and of union democracy in Mexican plants.[20] The publicity this case received and the degree of solidarity shown by U.S. unions was unprecedented. The Canadian Auto Workers and some UAW locals lent their support by publicizing the events in their own countries, pressuring government officials to complain about the matter, and by organizing a trinational day of protest in which workers wore black ribbons on the anniversary of the Mexican auto workers' death. The UAW locals in St. Paul and in Kansas City, Missouri, were especially active in organizing support for Cuautitlán workers; they formed a Mexico-U.S.-Canada Solidarity Task Force and sent members to Mexico to witness union elections in 1991. The national UAW, meanwhile, was initially reluctant to engage in a nationwide campaign (Browne and Sims 1993:6). These UAW locals and other U.S. groups continue to follow events at Ford-Cuautitlán. With the help of the North American Worker-to-Worker Network and electronic networks, supporters have begun to adopt the kinds of international action campaigns (telegrams to Mexican labor authorities and political leaders) that Amnesty International has long engaged in to draw attention to human rights violations around the world (NAWWN 1993:26).[21]

In the Cuautitlán case, Mexican auto workers chiefly received support in their fight for union democracy; collaborative collective bargaining or other kinds of issues were not at the forefront (Middlebrook 1992). Such demonstrations of solidarity nonetheless annoyed the Mexican government and the CTM, both of which threatened the workers and pressured them to abandon their external alliances.[22] However, in subsequent bargaining with Ford, the Cuautitlán union was able to draw on added leverage gained through external alliances. It agreed not to enlist the help of U.S. allies if Ford would meet some of its demands during collective bargaining. Authorities have discouraged similar cooperative measures from being taken by auto workers at the Ford plants in Chihuahua and Hermosillo (Middlebrook 1992).

In another case from the auto industry, workers from the Volkswagen plant in Puebla, Mexico, enjoyed the support of their German counterparts during a long strike in 1987. The German workers refused to step up production to compensate for the loss due to the strike in Mexico (Garza and Méndez 1987b). This solidarity helped the union to escape the fate that befell other auto unions in that year. Managers at the Ford-Cuautitlán auto plant, for example, fired the workers during a strike, closed down the plant, and later reopened, rehiring some of the workforce at lower benefit and wage levels and with new work rules (Garza and Méndez 1987a; Middlebrook 1989:86, 92). Workers at Volkswagen were nonetheless confronted with these same tactics and finally defeated during their 1992 strike (Nauman 1992; Othón Quiroz and Méndez 1992).

During a strike in 1990 at the Modelo Brewery, Teamsters in Chicago supported the strike by refusing to deliver shipments of the imported beer. A boycott of the product saw limited success in the United States, but was somewhat more successful in Canada and Europe. The Modelo workers belonged to a CTM-affiliated union, and their enlistment of foreign support drew the wrath of Fidel Velázquez, who also did everything in his power to defeat the strike (La Botz 1992). Other solidarity actions included a corporate campaign by Teamsters Local 912 against Green Giant products in cooperation with striking Mexican employees of the company (Moody and McGinn 1992:48).

The number of site visits and other kinds of exchanges and collaboration that have occurred in recent years are too numerous to mention here, but some examples include the establishment of U.S. and Mexican "sister schools", arranged between U.S. teachers and Mexican teachers belonging to the National Coordinating Committee of Education Workers, a large dissident current within the National Teachers Union (Witt 1992). Announcements for tours to Mexico for U.S. labor groups and others cover the pages of publications such as the *Free Trade Mailing*, and the Detroit-based *Labor Notes* sponsored a Cross-Border Organizing Strategies School on the Mexican border in May 1994.

The maquiladora region has received particularly strong attention since the NAFTA vote. One maquiladora in Tijuana, Plásticos Bajacal (a division of Boston-based Carlisle Plastics), first received publicity prior to the NAFTA vote when a bus of U.S. union activists and observers tried to visit the plant and were turned away by plant management. In December 1994 human rights and union observers witnessed union elections at the maquiladora plant. The company had signed a contract with a union affiliated with the Regional Confederation of Mexican Workers (CROM); workers only learned of the existence of this union once they sought to organize themselves under the auspices of another labor organization, the Revolutionary Labor Confederation (COR). During the representation election, workers were forced to vote out in the open and made to sign their names beside their vote. Elections were finally halted because it was feared that plant managers would retaliate against the dissident workers. U.S. observers, shocked and frustrated by what they had witnessed, felt that by publicizing the case they were at least able to prevent retaliation against the COR supporters (Bacon 1993; Kalmijn 1994).

A couple of additional cases that received much publicity in the United States during the winter of 1993-94 were the firings of workers who had been trying to organize a union at a General Electric maquiladora plant in Ciudad Juárez and at Honeywell in Chihuahua. In both cases, the organization trying to organize the workers was the independent FAT. Its allies in the United States, the UE and the Teamsters, reacted quickly to the firings. UE leaders wrote to the U.S. Congress and pressed General Electric to reverse its position. Teamsters began carrying out leafleting campaigns at

General Electric plant in the United States; both unions are giving financial support to the FAT. In January 1994, the unions finally succeeded in getting General Electric to reinstate six of eleven workers who had been fired in Ciudad Juárez. Efforts continued to force the company to reinstate the remaining fired workers. Teamsters president Ron Carey wrote President Bill Clinton, warning him that unless the labor violations at the Honeywell and General Electric plants were resolved, they could become "an international symbol of the violations of human rights now that NAFTA has passed."[23] The UE is also trying to get Congress to begin an investigation into the labor practices of U.S. corporations in Mexico (*Labor Notes* 1994:14).

Perhaps most significant, on February 15, 1994, the UE and Teamsters became the first unions to file complaints to the new National Administrative Office (NAO) set up under the terms of the NAFTA labor side agreement (Rose 1994:A2). The U.S. unions argued that by firing the union organizers, the U.S. companies in Mexico were violating the spirit of the trade agreement. In April 1994 the U.S. NAO decided to accept the submissions and planned to hold hearings on the cases later in the year. The evolution of these cases will set an important precedent for subsequent filings, and may indicate whether the new institutions set up by the side accords will complement or complicate grassroots alliances and organizing efforts.

Political Bargaining in the Transnational Arena

Another strategy that some labor groups have adopted involves political bargaining in the transnational arena. This strategy was directly linked to the NAFTA debate, and involved both direct and indirect lobbying of U.S. congressional representatives by Mexican groups. Indirect lobbying occurred through the exchange of information and networking with U.S.-based organizations, which then pressured the U.S. Congress. Direct efforts included congressional testimony by individuals and representatives of Mexican groups who reported on conditions for workers in Mexico. The strategy was largely aimed at defeating NAFTA in the U.S. Congress and with the U.S. public, although it also helped to secure support for side agreements and consideration of compensation mechanisms for likely "losers" of free trade.

At the same time, because of the Mexican government's sensitivity to outside criticism, Mexican coalitions such as the Mexican Action Network were able to gain access to their own government because of the attention they received and the role they played in the United States debate on NAFTA. Under circumstances in which the network would not otherwise have played much of a political role within the country, its use of transnational spaces gave it greater leverage within national boundaries. To the extent that the network has played a role in providing information about Mexican labor and environmental conditions to the U.S. Congress, unions, and other groups, it has also acted indirectly to reform domestic politics in Mexico, precisely because the Mexican government has acted to preempt criticism of Mexican practices by those who would decide NAFTA's fate.

Transnational political bargaining represents a new strategic arena for labor and other groups in Mexico. As with its counterparts in the United States and Canada, the Mexican Action Network is composed of a diverse set of organizations that have come together through their loose opposition to the NAFTA. As such, after the NAFTA vote is over, it is unlikely that much will hold these coalitions together. In the meantime, however, the use of the transnational arena by the Mexican groups has raised their visibility and political effectiveness. This is significant given that the network represents a small but burgeoning set of independent popular organizations and single-issue groups, such as environmentalists and human rights groups. The alliances they have forged and the skills they have learned over the last few years may bode them well in future negotiations with the Mexican government on human rights, the environment, and even democratization. Within this coalition, labor groups are perhaps the most constrained, given the political controls on labor and the current economic vulnerability of unions. In addition, it would appear that only those labor groups with weaker ties to official labor organizations and the government, and which otherwise are too small or nonstrategic to represent a significant political or economic threat, are free to participate in such activities.

NAFTA and the Side Agreements

The concerns of U.S. labor unions, the election of a Democratic president in 1992, and pressure by a host of citizens' groups throughout the electoral campaign led to the negotiation of labor and environmental side accords to accompany the NAFTA. The inclusion of these accords reflected the new administration's efforts to make NAFTA more palatable to opponents by addressing concerns over the deterioration of environmental conditions and lower environmental and labor standards in Mexico. Such lower standards, it was argued, would make for unfair competition, would tend to drive U.S. standards down, and would cause further exploitation of the environment and of Mexican workers.

From the beginning, the negotiation of the side deals was a tricky issue, and one more aimed at assuaging U.S. congressional opponents and key lobby groups than ensuring a commitment to higher standards. Both the Canadian and Mexican governments were opposed to the idea of side agreements and to the need for them, and feared that some of the enforcement mechanisms and institutional arrangements being suggested in side accords would threaten "national sovereignty." U.S. negotiators therefore had a very difficult task: to appease moderate critics of NAFTA in order to secure congressional approval, while not alienating the Canadian and Mexican governments.

Nor had it been made publicly clear what was meant by "labor standards." In a preliminary report on the draft options presented by an interagency subgroup of the National Economic Council, possible scenarios for the side agreements ranged from the inclusion of a broad definition of labor rights and standards, such as tying wages to productivity and securing the right to organize and to collective bargaining, to a minimal treatment of labor standards (or "basic rights"), such as ensuring enforcement of child labor laws and health and safety standards.[24] Similarly, positions wavered regarding the nature of the institutions that would be set up to oversee compliance with these standards, as well as the nature of the enforcement mechanisms. Through it all, U.S. Trade Representative Mickey Kantor repeatedly insisted that the side accords would "have teeth."

The NAFTA debate and discussion surrounding the side accords brought attention to a series of problems that afflict Mexican labor: low wages, lax enforcement of child labor laws and of health and safety standards, and political restrictions on the right to strike, to organize, and the right to choose one's union representatives. The labor side accord offered the possibility to address some of these issues by, ultimately, subjecting allegations of rights violations to a supranational institution for scrutiny. Provided that individual workers and labor union locals as well as unions could file complaints with the commission, such an arrangement offered the promise of institutionalizing a process of external scrutiny that was begun with the NAFTA debate and which has been shown to be more effective than domestic pressure alone. Thus, the final outcome of the labor side agreement—its definition of labor standards, institutional arrangements, and enforcement mechanisms—could be crucial for determining whether it would indeed be able to help improve the conditions of workers in Mexico. If, on the contrary, the labor side accord merely paid lip service to labor standards and contained meek enforcement mechanisms, then the result for Mexican workers could be worse than if no accord existed.

Negotiations among the three governments over labor and environmental side accords were completed on August 13, 1993, and the final text of the accords appeared one month later. Based on this text and available summary analyses, the labor side accord appears to fall far short of what would be required to ensure effective enforcement of laws and respect for labor rights.[25] Labor and environmental leaders and many Democratic politicians indicated that the accords would not affect their opposition to the trade agreement, while business leaders in the U.S. and Mexico expressed satisfaction with the accords (Andrews 1993).

The key problem with the labor side accord is that it is unlikely to address conditions among Mexican workers that constitute unfair competition for U.S. workers. There are several problems with the accord as it is now written that lead me to this conclusion: 1) The restricted scope of the labor side agreement; 2) the lengthy dispute settlement process; 3) weak enforcement provisions; and 4) the limited political autonomy of the commission.

The restricted scope of the agreement is probably its most troublesome aspect. According to the labor side accord, persons or organizations can file complaints relating to a persistent pattern of failure to enforce domestic laws in the areas of child labor, health and safety, and the minimum wage, and in areas that affect trade between the parties. Aspects of industrial relations, such as the rights to strike, organize, and bargain collectively are not subject to the dispute settlement process contemplated in the accord. In addition, the parties to the accord agree to enforce their existing laws; there is no reference to the creation of new legislation nor to harmonization of standards. The problem with this narrower definition of labor standards is that it provides no recourse beyond that which already exists for unions and workers whose rights to organize, strike, and bargain collectively are curtailed by employers and by the Mexican government. These restrictions have long prevailed in Mexico, in spite of labor legislation that prevents it and in spite of Mexico's participation in ILO conventions covering these areas. Violations of rights to organize and to strike are especially common in the maquiladora sector, for instance, but violations have also occurred throughout more advanced sectors, such as the auto industry. Removing industrial relations from the scope of the accord thus protects the Mexican government from external scrutiny of its political control over labor unions, an aspect that it has clearly declared corresponds to "national sovereignty."

Other problems relate to the dispute settlement process and enforcement. The process itself is constructed so as to not reach the point of fines or trade sanctions.

Instead, consultations among ministers will be the likely response for the majority of complaints. Any member of the Ministerial Council may petition the others to create an evaluation committee of experts (ECE) to study a particular issue, as long as it falls under the restricted category of rights described above. A pattern of failure to enforce any of the other domestic labor laws mentioned in the agreement's preamble, which lists a broader set of rights, is technically not subject to investigation. After an ECE submits its final report (a process which can take three hundred days on the outside), the council resorts to consultations. If the matter remains in dispute, then two out of three members of the council may vote to establish an arbitral panel. The arbitral panel would investigate the dispute further and, if it finds that the party violated the agreement, then the Parties would discuss an action plan to be undertaken by the Party complained against. If the action plan is not implemented or does not remedy the problem, then any Party can request that the arbitral panel be reconvened. The arbitral panel could eventually impose a "monetary enforcement assessment," and, if the fine were not paid, it could ultimately suspend NAFTA benefits in an amount no greater than that needed to collect the monetary enforcement assessment. Counting from the time a complaint is first investigated until sanctions are applied, the process can take as long as three years. Mexican Commerce Secretary Jaime Serra Puche assured members of his party that it was highly unlikely that a dispute would ever reach this stage.

Neither the threat of sanctions nor the fine are likely to be much of a deterrent to any of the governments. A fine of up to $20 million can be levied against the offending party; no minimum has been set. The fine is to go into a fund from which the violating government may then draw and apply toward enforcement. The assumption behind this arrangement is that failure to enforce one's own laws is a problem of lack of resources, not of political will.

A final problem mentioned here has to do with the lack of political autonomy of the labor commission. The key institution is a ministerial council, made up of the three labor ministers. It is the ministerial council that calls for investigations and if conditions warrant, sets up the arbitral panels from a previously agreed-upon roster of "experts." Since initiatives for investigation of violations must either come from the ministerial council or be approved by it, the potential for government political interests and foreign diplomacy concerns to intervene, as well as the possibility of retaliation in calling for investigations, is likely to restrict serious consideration of violations by any of the parties. The remainder of the labor commission is to be made up of a trinational International coordinating secretariat, one for labor and one for the environment, which would be set up to carry out the day-to-day work of the commission and would be overseen by the ministerial council. Each government is also responsible for setting up a national administrative office (NAO) in its respective country. Presumably, the NAO would receive complaints ("conduct preliminary reviews") on labor law matters arising in the territory of another party, consult with other NAOs, and distribute information regarding the labor commission. Details concerning the composition and activities of the NAOs are left to each government to work out.

Because the labor side accord's scope is restricted to a minimum definition of standards, it may be much more difficult for complaints regarding other labor rights to acquire legitimacy, even if they have a demonstrable effect on trade. It also appears unlikely that the scope would be expanded any time soon. During the negotiations, the United States might have been able to extract such a concession from the Mexican government. However, after NAFTA's ratification the United States lost the key bit of leverage it had to negotiate —the fact that NAFTA had not yet been approved. While formalized free trade with Mexico may permanently raise international levels of concern over what happens within Mexican borders, it is also true that the NAFTA debate and process opened a limited window of opportunity in which to secure institutional changes that could offer greater protection to workers in all three countries. It appears that, with the final terms of the side agreements, that opportunity has now been lost. The institutional arrangements put in place by the side accords may well restrict the labor strategy of political bargaining in the transnational arena and reinforce traditional domestic strategies. Moreover, unions that try to employ transnational collective bargaining and organizing and that try to carry out solidarity around these issues are not likely to find institutional protection for such strategies at the supranational level.[26]

Conclusion

The internationalization of domestic politics refers to the growing tendency for nongovernmental actors to engage in "international relations," acting in ways that help to shape the practices and policies of national governments. This internationalization also involves domestic interest groups and social movements forming alliances and coordinating strategies with external actors in order to better bargain with their own governments and influence change within their own countries. This confluence of external and internal pressures acting on national governments is especially important in cases of authoritarian regimes, where other, national mechanisms for pressing for reform may be limited. Examples of domestic policies and practices increasingly shaped by international nongovernmental forces can be found in the areas of human rights, environmental protection, and to a lesser extent, labor rights. Formal economic integration such as that occurring in Europe and under NAFTA also expands the opportunities for international actors to shape domestic politics. While the free trade area set out in NAFTA does not go as far as the economic union represented by the European Union, the NAFTA debate has nonetheless expanded the range of nontrade issues under discussion and heightened the Mexican government's sensitivity and responsiveness to external criticism.

The debate surrounding NAFTA has also led to an explosion of cross-border contacts, alliances, and activities among grassroots actors, representing something quite new in U.S.-Mexico relations. What might have started as a search for allies in order to defeat NAFTA, in some cases has developed into cooperation among unions operating within the same industry or sharing the same multinational employer. With the passage of NAFTA, there is an added incentive for these kinds of cooperative relations to continue. Nonetheless, with few exceptions it is not yet clear what outcomes the various activities and strategies described above will produce, nor how effective they will be. Nor is it yet clear whether the end of the NAFTA debate after the vote has closed off an important part of this transnational arena, or whether the institutions and procedures set up by the NAFTA side agreements will displace the kinds of grassroots activities that have been occurring so far. Moreover, numerous factors shape the likelihood that labor groups will pursue a transnational strategy, aside from whether or not there is a counterpart on the other side of the border. We have seen here that such factors as the nature of the industry (for example, the presence of multinationals), the size and organizational structure of the union (for example, small vs. large; autonomy from national union leadership), and the labor organization's political role within the labor movement (and its relationship with the government) shape the likelihood that a particular union will include a transnational strategy in its repertoire. In any case, while NAFTA has greatly concerned labor, environmental, and other citizens' groups throughout North America because of the power it was seen to grant to multinational corporations, the NAFTA debate has simultaneously expanded the arena for strategic action by these groups. What use is made of this new arena is up to them.

Endnotes

1. On the history of AFL-CIO's relationship with Mexican unions, especially its treatment of independent unions, see Browne and Sims 1993.

2. In Mexico, a coalition called the Red Mexicana de Acción Frente al Libre Comercio (Mexican Action Network on Free Trade, RMALC) was formed in 1991. Its U.S. counterparts included the Fair Trade Campaign, Citizens' Trade Watch Campaign, and the Alliance for Responsible Trade (formerly the Mobilization on Development, Trade, Labor and the Environment, MODTLE); in Canada they were the Action Canada Network and Common Frontiers.

3. Where before the focus of Mexican NGO relations had been in Europe, it has now moved to the United States and Canada (Hernández Navarro 1993:4).

4. For a discussion of some of these cross-border efforts, see Thorup 1991; Brooks 1992; the Spring 1993 issue of Enfoque; and Browne et al. 1994.

5. In one case, a woman fired from her job at a General Electric maquila due to prior union organizing activities was brought to the United States to testify before the U.S. Senate; the United Electrical Workers, Teamsters, and Jobs with Justice were active in bringing her to the United States.

6. The Chiapas rebellion on January 1, 1994, is likely to produce further moves in the direction of political reform. The pact among political parties agreed to on January 27, 1994, is an example of the political reform ramifications of the uprising (see Eaton 1994:1A).

7. For some examples during the Salinas administration, see La Botz 1992.

8. For a more detailed discussion of state-labor relations under the Salinas administration, see Cook forthcoming.

9. On the broader political restrictions in debating NAFTA within Mexico, see Aguilar Zinser 1993.

10. See, for example, the various positions expressed by Canadian, U.S., and Mexican labor groups during the first trinational exchange, held in Chicago in 1991 (Trinational Exchange 1991).

11. This essay does not consider the role of international secretariats and focuses instead on direct contacts among national labor organizations, unions, and union locals. On the problems faced by the International Metalworkers' Federation in Mexico during the 1960s and 1970s, see Middlebrook 1992:21-22.

12. A copy of the agreement is reprinted in *Latin American Labor News*, issue 5, 1992, p. 7.

13. See Sindicato Mexicano de Electricistas, "Carta Internacional de Derechos Sindicales y Laborales a Incluirse en el T.L.C." July 30, 1991.

14. Here the unions have been pushing for wage "parity" by comparing the relationship between wages and cost-of-living in each country.

15. On unionization in the maquiladora sector, see Hualde 1994 (this volume).

16. The FAT has the added characteristic of being an independent organization that has NGO status. For these reasons, the FAT does not have the same kinds of political commitments to the regime that other Mexican unions do.

17. An outgrowth of these trinational meetings was a NAFTA congress held in Mexico in 1991 at the same time as official negotiations on the agreement were taking place, sponsored by the Mexican Action Network on Free Trade, during which a "social charter" was developed (RMALC 1992).

18. Reported in SourceMex (University of New Mexico electronic mail news service), February 16, 1994.

19. For an account of this case, see La Botz 1992, and Americas Watch 1990:67-70.

20. See *La otra cara de México*, no. 21, May-June 1991, pp. 4-5.

21. In a "post-NAFTA-vote" strategy session, the North American Worker to Worker Network, a coalition of local unions and labor-related NGOs, decided to support independent union organizing in Mexico through a variety of tactics, including an "Emergency Response Network" of people who will send faxes, telegrams, and take out newspaper ads in the event of illegal firings or harassment of Mexican independent labor organizers.

22. La Botz 1992; "Weekly Commentary," *ARKA Mexico Report,* August 21, 1992.

23. Reported in SourceMex (University of New Mexico electronic mail news service), February 16, 1994.

24. See *Inside U.S. Trade*, Special Report, March 5, 1993.

25. See the *North American Agreement on Labor Cooperation*, and Levinson 1993.

26. Nonetheless, it is significant that the United States NAO accepted to hear complaints filed by the United Electrical Workers and the Teamsters in 1994, even in the face of protests by U.S. business groups and Mexican government officials. In addition, a group of labor rights non-governmental organizations filed a third complaint in August 1994 against a Sony plant in Nuevo Laredo. While these hearings are not likely to lead to fines or trade sanctions, U.S. unions filing these complaints can hope that the publicity will serve to pressure U.S. companies operating in Mexico to alter their practices regarding union organizing by Mexican workers (see Myerson 1994:D1, D4; Davis 1994).

References

Aguilar Zinser, Adolfo. 1993. "Authoritarianism and North American Free Trade: The Debate in Mexico." In *The Political Economy of North American Free Trade,* Ricardo Grinspun and Maxwell A. Cameron, eds. New York: St. Martin's Press.

Americas Watch. 1990. *Human Rights in Mexico: A Policy of Impunity* (An Americas Watch Report).

Andrews, Edmund L. 1993. "Accords Fail to Redraw Battle Lines Over Pact," *The New York Times*, August 14.

ARKA Mexico Report. 1992. "Weekly Commentary,"August 21.

Bacon, David. 1993. "Mexican Union Election Falls Short," *San Francisco Chronicle*, December 24, p. 1A.

Brooks, David. 1992. "The Search for Counterparts." *Labor Research Review*19: 83-96.

Browne, Harry and Beth Sims. 1993. "Global Capitalism, Global Unionism." *Resource Center Bulletin* no. 30 (Winter).

Browne, Harry, with Beth Sims and Tom Barry. 1994. For Richer, ForPoorer: Shaping U.S.-Mexican Integration. The U.S.-Mexican Series No. 4 Albuquerque, NM, and London: Resource Center Press and Latin America Bureau.

Chalmers, Douglas A. 1991. "An End to Foreign Policy: The U.S. and Internationalized Politics." Paper presented at research conference, "Crossing National Borders: Invasion or Involvement," Columbia University, New York, New York. December.

Cook, Maria Lorena. 1994. "State-Labor Relations in Mexico: Old Tendencies and New Trends." In *Mexico Faces the Twenty-first Century: Change and Challenge*, Donald E. Schulz and Edward J.Williams, eds. New York: Praeger.

Cook, Maria Lorena. Forthcoming. "Mexican State-Labor Relations and the Political Implications of Free Trade." *Latin American Perspectives* (Winter).

Cornelius, Wayne A. and Ann L. Craig. 1991. *The Mexican Political System in Transition*. La Jolla: Center for U.S.-Mexican Studies, University of California, San Diego.

164

Davis, Ben. 1994. "Fund Files NAO Complaint against Mexican Government," *Worker Rights News*, International Labor Rights Education and Researrch Fund, issue no. 10 (Summer).

Dresser, Denise. 1993. "Exporting Conflict: Transboundary Consequences of Mexican Politics." In *The California-Mexico Connection*, Abraham F. Lowenthal and Katrina Burgess, eds. Stanford: Stanford University Press.

Eaton, Tracey. 1994. "Mexico Pledges Electoral Reform in Bid for Peace," *Dallas Morning News*, January 28, p. 1A.

Eisenstadt, Todd. 1993. "Helping Grassroots Actors Find a Voice: An Interview with David Brooks." *Enfoque* (Center for U.S.-Mexican Studies) (Spring).

Garza, María Teresa and Luis Méndez. 1987a. "El conflico de la Ford Cuautitlán," El Cotidiano no. 20 (November-December): 384-85.

..... 1987b. "La huelga en Volkswagen," *El Cotidiano* no. 20 (November-December): 381-83.

Grinspun, Ricardo, and Maxwell A. Cameron, eds. 1993. *The Political Economy of North American Free Trade* (New York: St. Martin's Press).

Hernández Navarro, Luis. 1993. "Mexican NGOs in Transition." *Enfoque* (Center for U.S.-Mexican Studies) (Spring).

Hualde, Alfredo. 1994. "Industrial Relations in the Maquiladora Industry: Management's Search for Participation and Quality." In *Regional Integration and Industrial Relations in North America*, Maria Lorena Cook and Harry C. Katz, eds. Ithaca, NY: Institute of Collective Bargaining, New York State School of Industrial and Labor Relations, Cornell University).

Hughes, Sallie. 1993a. "Looking North for Support." *El Financiero International*, September 6-12, p. 12.

..... 1993b. "Poverty Program Serves Up Pork." *El Financiero International*, September 6-12, p. 13.

Inside U.S. Trade. 1993. Special Report, March 5.

Kalmijn, Jelger. 1994. "U.S. Activists Support Organizing Drive: Intimidation Halts Union Vote in Tijuana," *Labor Notes*, February, pp. 3, 14.

Keck, Margaret. 1991. "The International Politics of the Brazilian Amazon." Paper presented at research conference, "Crossing National Borders: Invasion or Involvement," Columbia University, New York, New York, December.

La Botz, Dan. 1992. *Mask of Democracy: Labor Suppression in Mexico Today.* Boston: South End Press.

La otra cara de México. 1991. No. 21 (May-June).

Latin American Labor News. 1992. Issue 5.

Levinson, Jerome I. 1993. "The Labor Side Accord to the North American Free Trade Agreement: An Endorsement of Abuse of Worker Rights in Mexico," Briefing Paper, Economic Policy Institute, September.

Middlebrook, Kevin J. 1989. "Union Democratization in the Mexican Automobile Industry: A Reappraisal," *Latin American Research Review* 24 (2): 69-93.

..... 1992. "Transnational Industrialization and Labor Alliances: Mexican Automobile Workers Confront Industrial Restructuring and North American Economic Integration." Paper presented at the International Congress of the Latin American Studies Association, Los Angeles, California, September.

Moody, Kim, and Mary McGinn. 1992. *Unions and Free Trade: Solidarity vs. Competition* (Detroit: Labor Notes).

Myerson, Allen R. 1994. "Big Labor's Strategic Raid in Mexico," *The New York Times*, September 12, pp. D1, D4.

Nauman, Talli. 1992. "VW Gets Its Way; Workers Get Grief," *El Financiero International*, August 31, 1992.

..... 1993. "Labor Solidarity Crosses the Border", *El Financiero International*, August 9-15, p. 14.

North American Agreement on Labor Cooperation between the Government of the United States of America, the Government of Canada, and the Government of the United Mexican States, Final Draft, September 13, 1993.

North American Worker to Worker Network (NAWWN). 1993. *Free Trade Mailing*, 3 no. 2 (June).

Othón Quiroz, José, and Luis Méndez. 1992. "El Conflicto de Volkswagen: Crónica de una muerte inesperada," *El Cotidiano* no. 51 (November-December): 81-91.

Pastor, Robert A. 1992. "NAFTA as the Center of an Integration Process: The Nontrade Issues." In *North American Free Trade: Assessing the Impact*, Nora Lustig, Barry P. Bosworth, and Robert Z. Lawrence, eds. Washington, D.C.: The Brookings Institution.

166

Red Mexicana de Acción Frente Al Libre Comercio (RMALC). 1992. *Memoria de Zacatecas, La opinión pública y las negociaciones del Tratado de Libre Comercio: Alternativas ciudadanas.* (Mexico City: RMALC).

Rose, Robert L. 1994. "Labor Unions File First Tests of NAFTA Office," The Wall Street Journal, February 15, p. A2.

Sikkink, Kathryn. 1991. "International Human Rights and Sovereignty in Latin America." Paper presented at research conference, "Crossing National Borders: Invasion or Involvement," Columbia University, New York, New York.

..... 1993. "Human Rights, Principled Issue Networks, and Sovereignty in Latin America." *International Organization* 47, no. 3 (Summer): 411-441.

Sindicato Mexicano de Electricistas. 1991. "Carta Internacional de Derechos Sindicales y Laborales a Incluirse en el T.L.C." July 30.

Thorup, Cathryn L. 1991. "The Politics of Free Trade and the Dynamics of Cross-Border Coalitions in U.S.-Mexican Relations," *Columbia Journal of World Business* 26 (Summer).

..... 1993. "Redefining Governance in North America: Citizen Diplomacy and Cross-Border Coalitions." *Enfoque* (Center for U.S.-Mexican Studies). (Spring).

Trinational Exchange. 1991. "Trinational Exchange: Popular Perspectives on Mexico-U.S.-Canada Relations, Summary Report," Chicago, April 26-28.

Witt, Matt. 1992. "Labor and NAFTA," *Latin American Labor News*, Issue 5, June.

Free Trade and Its Implications for Industrial Relations and Human Resource Management

Morley Gunderson and Anil Verma

Summary

The paper analyses the implications of free trade for industrial relations and human resource management, with particular attention to: 1) wages and employment, 2) workplace and human resource practices, 3) unions and collective bargaining, and 4) government legislation, regulations, and adjustment programs. The emphasis is on North America, especially with respect to the recent Canada-U.S. Free Trade Agreement (FTA) and its successor, the North America Free Trade Agreement (NAFTA), which includes Mexico.

The wage and employment impacts of NAFTA are likely to be positive but very small for Canada and the United States, albeit larger for Mexico. They are likely to lead to greater wage inequality in Canada and the United States, but greater equality in Mexico. While the net employment effects are expected to be positive, there will be considerable adjustment consequences associated with the need to adjust from the declining to the expanding sectors, especially because the effects vary considerably by sector.

Free trade will place considerable pressure on employers to strategically adjust their human resource management and workplace practices. For example, more emphasis will be placed on hiring workers with a generic set of basic skills and education that facilitate flexibility and adaptability in rapidly adjusting to ever-changing tasks. Training needs will increase to deal with the adjustment consequences that will occur both on the "downside" (layoffs, plant closings) as well as the "upside" (skill shortages, new job requirements). Subcontracting and contingent workforces will increase so as to facilitate flexibility and adaptability. Mergers, alliances and joint ventures will create issues in areas ranging from compensation to changing job requirements.

Unions will be affected because in countries like Canada and the U.S., those sectors subject to the greatest import competition tend to be unionized, those subject to the least import competition tend to be nonunionized, and the export growth tends to be in nonunion sectors. Unions will increasingly be faced with a variety of strategic choices: to follow a more cooperative strategy or to continue with the more conventional adversarial approach to bargaining; to continue focusing efforts at enterprise level bargaining or at the broader political level; to continue nationalist policies or to focus on international linkages, coordination, and possibly integration.

Trade liberalization will increase the demand for government programs to deal with the adjustment consequences. But, it will also put pressure on governments to restrict adjustment programs, as well as legislative and regulatory initiatives in the labor area, because the cost consequences may adversely affect the countries' competitiveness.

Free trade clearly implies that important strategic choices have to be made by all actors in the industrial relations scene—labor, management, and governments. Free trade, however, is but one of the many interrelated forces that is creating a potential transformation of our systems of industrial relations and human resource management.

Free Trade and Its Implications for Industrial Relations and Human Resource Practices

Free trade currently is a driving force behind the industrial restructuring that is occurring throughout the world. Consequently, free trade is on the top of the policy agenda in many countries. Despite the policy preoccupation with trade issues, the impact of free trade on industrial relations and human resource management practices have received scant attention. This is unfortunate because, in many ways, the accrual of benefits under free trade depends on effective adaptation in labor markets and in the workplace.

All of the strategic actors in the industrial relations scene—labor, management, and governments—have an interest and stake in the impact of free trade on industrial relations and human resource practices. Management needs to know the pressures that will be placed on their workplace practices and how they should respond strategically. Employees need to know the pressures that will be placed especially on their wages and employability, and how they need to respond particularly in areas such as education and, training. Organized labor has an interest in the pressures that will be placed on collective bargaining, and perhaps on their very existence as an institution. Governments have an interest in the conflicting pressures that will be placed on labor adjustment policies, and on their ability to pass legislation and adopt social programs.

Numerous trade arrangements are emerging and being discussed within the Americas. Such "Western Hemisphere" initiatives include the FTA (effective 1989), which was subsequently superceded by NAFTA, between Mexico, Canada, and the United States (effective 1994). In Latin America, the Mercosur agreement, which went into effect in 1991, includes Argentina, Brazil, Paraguay, and Uruguay. There is also the Andean Pact between Venezuela, Colombia, Ecuador, Peru, and Bolivia. The United States has indicated that it would like to examine possible extensions of NAFTA to include Chile, some of the Caribbean countries, and, potentially, to the Andean Pact and Mercosur natioins.

Such trade arrangements throughout the Americas are of particular interest because they involve countries of quite different levels of development and wages; this is somewhat uncharted terrain since most free trade agreements historically have been among countries of similar levels of development.[1] The possible trade arrangements within the Americas also are among countries with different philosophies with respect to the role of governments and regulations in labor markets, as well as social policies in general. The United States is at the "laissez-faire" polar end with a low degree of legislative regulation and unionization (down to 16 percent of the labor force). Canada is more in the middle, with fairly extensive social programs and legislative regulations of the labor market, and with approximately 36 percent of the workforce unionized. Latin American countries, in particular, are concerned about the possibility that the economic forces that accompany free trade will compel them more in the direction of the U.S. model. Some of these countries wonder whether they can follow more interventionist strategies with respect to social programs and labor market regulation, more along the lines of the Canadian model.

The interrelatedness between free trade and human resource policies is of interest to both developed and less developed countries, albeit sometimes for different reasons. For developed countries, there is a growing realization that it is neither possible—nor desirable—to compete with developing countries on the bases of labor cost. Rather, the sensible competitive strategy is to emphasize high value-added production and market niches based on a workforce that is highly productive, flexible, committed, and focused on quality and customer satisfaction. For these countries, their comparative advantage no longer lies in such conventional sources as physical and financial capital, natural resources, access to large markets, or even technology and innovation—all of which are increasingly available on the global market and quickly emulated. Rather, the comparative advantage of the more developed countries lies in their human resource policies and workplace practices, which are geared to high productivity and the growing information-oriented economy.

For developing countries, whose comparative advantage lies mainly (but not only) in low-wage labor, the hope is that free trade will increase the demand for such labor, which in turn will lead to steady increases in wages and employment opportunities, as well as to absorbing labor from the rural and informal sectors. This, in turn, can reduce income inequality. In these circumstances, sustained increases in wages and real living standards and reductions in inequality require that trade liberalization be coupled with substantial investment in human capital—policies that have successfully been pursued in Taiwan and South Korea (Alarcon-Gonzales 1992).

Clearly, trade liberalization and human resource policies are intricately related, and the various industrial relations actors—labor, management, and governments—have an interest in this interrelationship. The purpose of this paper is to analyze the implications of free trade for industrial relations and human resource management—as well as vice versa (i.e.,the impact of industrial relations practices and human resource management for global competitiveness under trade liberalization). The emphasis is on North America, especially with respect to the Canada-U.S. Free Trade Agreement (FTA) and its successor the North America Free Trade Agreement (NAFTA).

Wage and Employment Impacts

Free trade leads to increased exports and increased imports, with the increased exports associated with "job creation" and increased imports with "job destruction." The net effect on employment can be positive or negative depending on the relative growth of exports and imports, as well as their labor content.

Wage changes should occur in the same direction as the employment changes. That is, wages should rise in the growing export sector and fall in the import-impacted sectors, with those wage changes being the market signal to encourage the reallocation of labor from the declining import-impacted sectors to the expanding export sector. For high-wage countries like Canada and the United States, the import competition is likely to come from goods produced by countries with low-wage labor (putting downward pressure on low-wage jobs), and the export expansion is likely to come from high value-added jobs (leading to increased wages in already high-wage jobs). These forces could exacerbate wage inequality in the more developed countries. For low-wage countries like Mexico, the labor intensive exports should increase wages, which should reduce inequality, although it is possible that some wage structures may widen (for example, as semiskilled wages rise but less skilled wages are constrained by the reserve of workers in the rural and informal sectors). Overall, the level of real wages should rise in the countries that engage in mutual trade liberalization, because of the efficiency gains from free trade, although this may occur in the form of declining product prices rather than increases in nominal wages. Obviously, there will be gainers and losers, although the efficiency gains can provide the means to compensate the losers.

With respect to the empirical evidence on the impact of wages and employment on trade liberalization, Gunderson (1992b) reviewed over seventy-five studies, some of which directly pertain to NAFTA as well as to the earlier Canada-U.S FTA. The studies involved eleven different methodologies: 1) trade exposure studies and ad hoc procedures, 2) accounting decomposition studies that relate output changes to exports and imports and ultimately, to employment, 3) input-output studies that measure the indirect as well as the direct effects of trade, 4) industry wage studies that relate industry wage levels to trade measures, 5) augmented "Phillips curves" relating aggregate wage changes to measures of trade, especially import competition, 6) base wages and employment in collective agreements related to trade measures, 7) micro wage equations relating individual wages to measures of trade, 8) studies relating individual wages and wage inequality to trade, 9) job displacement and permanent job loss studies relating wage loss and unemployment durations to trade measures, 10) macroeconomic forecasting models, and 11) computable general equilibrium models.

The studies generally concluded that the wage and employment impacts of NAFTA are likely to be positive but very small, at least for Canada and the United States. For Mexico, they are also apt to be positive but more substantial. They are likely to lead to greater wage inequality in Canada and the United States, but greater equality in Mexico. Even if the net wage and employment effects tend to be positive, there will be considerable adjustment consequences associated with the need to adjust from the declining to the expanding sectors, especially because the effects vary considerably by sector. As well, in Canada and the United States the adjustments can lead to substantial wage losses for many workers, especially those who are older, less educated, blue-collar, unionized, and who have considerable seniority and industry-specific human capital.[2]

Impact on Human Resource Management and Workplace Practices

The impact of trade liberalization on human resource management and workplace practices emanates from the various effects that free trade will have on employers. Those effects include: increased opportunities from export growth and challenges from import competition; pressure for flexibility and adaptability to adjust to the vicissitudes of international competition; pressure for cost cutting and "leanness" to compete on a global basis; pressures to develop market niches both domestically and possibly on a global basis; and the need to consider forming joint ventures and alliances, sometimes on a temporary basis associated with a particular project and sometimes on a more permanent basis to establish global networks. These changing demands on employers will filter down to imply a changing set of demands on their workplace and on their human resource management practices.

When recruiting and hiring, employers will place more emphasis on hiring workers who have a generic set of basic skills and an education that facilitates adapting to ever-changing tasks. Knowledge of specific tasks will be less important than having the foundation to learn—and to relearn by absorbing subsequent retraining. Education and training requirements will also change and will emphasize general education and training that can be used in a variety of ever-changing environments. Especially at the more senior and managerial level, there will also be increased importance attached to language and other skills that facilitate international interactions and communication.

Training needs will increase to deal with the adjustment consequences that will occur both on the downside (layoffs, plant closings) as well as the upside (skill shortages, new job requirements). The problem of skill shortages can be especially acute if they create bottlenecks and inhibit organizations from quickly responding to new market opportunities. Developed countries will want to enhance training at high skill levels to facilitate high value-added production and the establishment of market niches. Developing countries will want to enhance training at basic levels so that they can close the productivity gap between themselves and the more developed countries and ensure that the benefits of trade liberalization get reflected in higher wages accompanying that higher productivity.

The emphasis on general basic training means that employers will continue to face the classic "poaching" problem associated with generally usable training. If employers provide the training, they may lose the trained workers to firms that do not provide training but simply bid away trained workers. To avoid poaching, firms would have to pay the higher wage to keep their trained workforce, in which case they "double pay"—by paying for the training and by paying the higher wage. In such circumstances, employees should be willing to pay for the training (perhaps by accepting a lower wage during the training period). But, they may be hindered from doing so for a number of reasons: the inability to absorb the cost, especially if they are already at a subsistence level; inability to borrow to finance the investment; and a reluctance to absorb the cost of an investment for which they may have little control over the returns. Employers who provide training in such circumstances will be looking for ways to retain their core of trained workers. Possible mechanisms include: paying deferred compensation that comes later in the worker's career; providing small amounts of constant retraining so as to minimize the losses associated with those who leave; training only a core of key workers who then work with subcontractors, contingent workforces, and alliances with other organizations.

The use of subcontracting and contingent workforces will increase to facilitate flexibility and adaptability. Contingent compensation and bonus payment arrangements will also increase so as to tie pay to performance at various possible levels—the individual, the work group, and the organization. These will be used to enhance productivity and to gear compensation to the ability of the individual organization to pay—an increasingly important consideration to ensure survival under global competition.

The job losses that will be engendered by the import substitution mean that employers will increasingly have to deal with termination issues. These include unjust dismissal claims through the courts, grievances over dismissals and layoffs, claims for unpaid wages and accrued vacation time, and legislative requirements that may pertain to such factors as advance warning or severance pay.

Mergers, alliances, and joint ventures also have important implications for human resource policies. The job requirements of the workforce may change, especially if an alliance is formed because an older organization with a highly paid core workforce may find it more cost-effective to expand by forming a joint venture with a newer, more "entrepreneurial" company that does not have such a highly paid "protected" workforce. In such circumstances, the employees in the older organization may find that they are more like employees in a holding company: they are focusing on activities pertaining to coordination, with the associated change in job requirements.

Compensation issues may also arise if the merger or joint venture requires an integration of compensation or other human resource practices. For example, horizontal inequities may arise if employees who were previously in a separate company are now part of a new alliance or joint venture, and they have different compensation or treatment based on their previous employment. Horizontal equity (the equal treatment of equals) may dictate similar treatment, although the differential treatment may have been one of the reasons for the alliance or joint venture in the first place (as discussed in the example above). Prior to the joint venture, employees in the newer company may never have compared their pay to that of the older company; under such an alliance, they may be more prone to make such comparisons. Mergers, acquisitions, and alliances have important implications for integration not only with respect to products, services, technology, capital and other inputs, but also to human resource practices.

Impacts on Collective Bargaining

The same trade liberalization pressures that affect human resource and workplace practices obviously will affect the collective bargaining process of organizations that are unionized. In fact, for reasons outlined subsequently, the impacts are likely to be very substantial in unionized establishments.

The reallocations that will occur from the declining import-impacted sectors to the growing export sectors have obvious implications for collective bargaining and for unionization in general. Import competition can threaten union wage premiums and, in fact, the very existence of unions to the extent that there are additional costs associated with the benefits that unions bring to their membership (Belous 1990; Gunderson and Verma 1992).[3] In order to deal with the potential adverse effects of the job losses from import competition, unions will be under more pressure to bargain over issues like advance notice, severance pay, layoff and recall provisions, and possibly even wage concessions, perhaps in return for job security. They will be under considerable pressure to accept many of the changing human resource policies and workplace practices that are part of the corporate restructuring that is occurring in response to global competition. Unions will also be under more pressure to break traditional pattern bargaining and to bargain according to the particular firm's ability to pay, especially if the survival of that firm is now jeopardized by import competition. Of course, these are issues that unions are facing in response to the broader set of competitive pressures associated with interrelated factors such as global competition, industrial restructuring, deregulation, and privatization. Free trade simply exacerbates those pressures.

Unfortunately, there is little systematic evidence on how unions have responded to the pressures of free trade through altering specific provisions in collective agreements. Some Canadian evidence, given in Gunderson and Verma (1993), suggest that provisions, from 1981 to 1991, in collective agreements did not change much in response to the Canada-U.S. FTA. There was some increase in worker protection as evidenced by increased use of such factors as: restrictions on contracting-out; advanced notice of technological change; and longer notice periods in the case of layoffs. There was a decrease in the use of seniority for promotions, albeit not for layoff or recall, suggesting that there may have been some trade-off between increased flexibility to management in return for some increased protection for workers.

Faced with job losses from increased import competition, unions take little solace in the fact that trade liberalization also leads to job gains from the export expansion. These job gains are seldom in the same firm or even industry. Trade liberalization leads to reallocations according to comparative advantage, and such reallocations tend to be across (not within) industries and the firms in those industries. In Canada and the United States, for example, industries that are at risk because of import competition from low-wage countries include high-wage, blue-collar manufacturing jobs with an older workforce—the heart of traditionally unionized jobs. The export-led job expansion, in contrast, often occurs in sectors that traditionally are not as unionized: high-tech manufacturing, financial and business services, research and development, and the "information-oriented economy." The new businesses that are opening up with these jobs are also often in "greenfield sites" or regions that are less unionized—and, in fact, are often in areas that try to attract new business by fostering a legal and regulatory environment that is hospitable to business and not to the formation of unions. The sectors that are subject to the least import competition include low-wage services, since such "services" conventionally cannot be imported. This is a sector that is conventionally not unionized.

In essence, trade liberalization puts considerable pressure on unions in countries like Canada and the United States, because those sectors subject to the greatest import competition tend to be unionized, and those subject to the least import competition tend to be nonunionized; and the export growth tends to be in nonunion sectors. Hence, unions in Canada and the United States have tended to oppose free trade agreements (Adams and White 1989; Betcherman and Gunderson 1990; Randall 1986).

In the face of increased trade liberalizations and other similar pressures, unions are confronted with a number of strategic choices. While a comprehensive analysis of these choices is beyond the scope of this paper, certain dimensions can be indicated. First and foremost, unions are faced with the strategic choice of whether to follow a more cooperative strategy or to continue with the more conventional adversarial approach to bargaining. Elements of the more cooperative strategy include an acceptance of many of the new workplace practices (broader job classifications, quality circles, and team production, for example) as well as an emphasis on areas of mutual interest to both labor and management (retraining, alternative work time arrangements, and employee participation, for example).

Labor management cooperation can occur at all levels: the individual enterprise, the industry (perhaps through sectoral committees), or at the broader political level. At the political level, unions are also faced with the strategic choice of how much of their effort to focus at enterprise-level bargaining (which is prominent in Canada and the United States) or at the broader political level. At the broader level, their strategic decisions pertain to factors such as whether to try to forge social partnerships with governments, perhaps to bargain over a "social wage" or a broader social charter. A social charter could harmonize labor standards across trading partners and prevent the downward spiralling (so-called "social dumping") that otherwise may occur between trading partners as they seek to enhance their competitiveness by reducing labor standards and regulations.[4]

Faced with the growing internationalization of markets, organized labor is also faced with the strategic issue of international linkages in the labor movement. It is well known that, to be effective, unions have to organize "up to the level of the product market." Otherwise, nonunion firms could likely undercut union firms through lower costs. To "take labor out of competition," it is necessary that most firms in the particular industry be organized or behave in the same fashion—perhaps to avoid the threat of being organized. If trade liberalization and global competition are effective in making the product market an international one, then trade unions may have to think more in terms of international strategies for purposes of organization, cooperation, or perhaps even integration.

Impact on Government Programs and Policies

The same trade liberalization pressures that affect the human resource and workplace practices of organizations and the collective bargaining process of unionized establishments, will also affect the other main actor in the industrial relations system: governments. Their impact will be felt largely through the role that governments play in providing labor market adjustment assistance and in providing the legal environment within which human resource management and collective bargaining takes place.[5]

Governments faced a conflicting set of pressures with respect to adjustment programs. There will be an increased demand for such programs to deal with the adjustment consequences that will result from trade liberalization. The demand for adjustment programs will be fostered by the collective sense of fairness in collective which at least some of the efficiency gains from free trade should be used to compensate the losers. There may even be an efficiency rationale for such compensation, to the extent that it reduces the resistance and opposition that may otherwise block efficiency-enhancing changes.

Although governments will face these pressures to enhance programs to deal with the adjustment consequences of free trade, they face an equally compelling set of pressures to be restrictive. To the extent that a social program subsidizes domestic producers, there is the risk that such programs may be interpreted as unfair subsidies and hence be subject to countervailing duties. Adjustment programs are costly and firms that are required to pay for these costs, (either through higher taxes or more regulations), may alter their location decisions partially in response to the costs.

Capital mobility may be enhanced by trade liberalization through a number of mechanisms. Companies are now more able to locate in the countries with lower legislative and regulatory costs and export into countries that may have higher regulatory costs, once tariffs are reduced. Free trade agreements also usually have provisions that facilitate investment by ensuring that foreign firms will be treated like domestic firms. Increased trade also fosters a more global outlook that may be manifest in investment decisions. It may also provide a signal to the international investment community that a country is embarking on a more open economy with respect to investment as well as trade. The effects may also be cumulative, as globalization "de-couples" businesses with the conventional notion of a "home base."

In such circumstances, capital mobility, or even the threat of capital mobility, can deter countries from instituting legislative, regulatory or social policies that impose costs on organizations that are now more mobile. It is in this sense that concern has sometimes been expressed that free trade will reduce the ability of a country to follow its own independent social and legislative programs. The pressure will be for harmonization at the lowest common denominator—that is, the environment that imposes the lowest cost on business.

Although these forces can exist, it should be emphasized that policymakers should put the most pressure on dissipating regulations and programs that are not cost-effective in achieving their objectives. In many circumstances, such programs and regulations can enhance efficiency (for example, programs that provide education, training, or labor market information). In other circumstances, such policies may save on costs elsewhere (for example, health and safety regulations can save on accident costs, workers' compensation can save on the cost of tort liability, and state-provided medical care can reduce employers' premiums for health and disability insurance). In other circumstances, the policies may simply be ones the cost of which the country is explicitly willing to bear to achieve certain social objectives. The potential for business investment and plant location decisions to be affected by such regulatory costs simply makes the cost of such policies more explicit, at least in terms of affecting those decisions. This, in turn, puts more pressure on governments to ensure that the benefits of such policies outweigh the cost. Free trade enhances competition, including competition between governments for business investment, at least to the extent that such investment is perceived as desirable, perhaps because of the potential for job creation.

This suggests that free trade and increased capital mobility will put pressure on governments to constrain their legislative and regulatory interventions that are costly to business. This restraint may occur in a variety of areas including taxes, investment restrictions, and environmental and industrial policies. It may also occur in the area of labor laws and regulations as well as human resource development policies and adjustment assistance and income-maintenance programs. The extent to which such competition betweeen countries should be regarded as "ruinous competition" or "social dumping" as opposed to healthy competition where governments are simply forced to pay attention to the cost of their policies, is an area in need of more research and analysis.

Concluding Observations

Clearly, free trade can have a wide-ranging set of impacts on industrial relations and human resource practices. These in turn can have an impact on the ability of a country to compete in the increasingly global marketplace.

The impact of free trade in this area is manifest in the actions of all actors in the industrial relations scene, and it compels them to make strategic choices that can have important implications for the future of industrial relations and human resource management. Free trade has implications for the workplace practices and human resource management decisions of organizations as they restructure to compete in the increasingly global marketplace. It also has implications for unions in the collective bargaining arena and in the broader political area, as well as in the area of international unionism and coordination. Free trade and capital mobility also affect government policies, programs, and legislative initiatives in the area of industrial relations and human resource practices. Clearly, the interaction of free trade and industrial relations and human resource management merits increased attention, as countries increasingly embark on trade liberalization.

While free trade has these potentially important effects, it should be emphasized that free trade is but one of the many interrelated forces that is creating a potential transformation of our systems of industrial relations and human resource management.[6] By itself, free trade may not transform our systems of industrial relations and human resource management, but the cumulative effect of the various interrelated forces can cause such a transformation. Free trade is an important factor contributing to the restructuring of our industry and product markets. It may also contribute significantly to the restructuring of our system of industrial relations and human resource management.

Endnotes

1. Within the European Community, the disparity in wages between the highest-wage country (Germany) and the lowest-wage country (Portugal) was in the neighborhood of 5 to 1 when Portugal entered in 1986. In contrast, in the proposed NAFTA, the wage disparity between Canada and the United States on the one hand, and Mexico on the other, is in the neighborhood of 10 to 1.

2. Reasons for these substantial wage losses for trade displaced workers are discussed in Gunderson and Hamermesh (1990).

3. It is theoretically possible for union wage premiums to actually expand in industries that are declining because of factors like import competition. This is so because the declining nature of such industries reduces the likelihood that new firms would enter to compete with existing firms that may have an inflated cost structure. In essence, unions may be able to appropriate a larger share of any economic rents (because of a reduced threat of new entry into the industry), even though overall rents are declining (because of import competition or other competitive pressures). This is akin to the well-known strategy followed, for example, by John L. Lewis and the United Mineworkers in the United States in the face of a declining coal industry.

4. The social charter of the European Community, and the implications of a social charter for NAFTA, are discussed in DeBoer and Winham 1992, Morici 1992, and Weintraub and Gilbreath 1992.

5. These issues are discussed in more detail in Gunderson (forthcoming) in the context of the proposed NAFTA between Canada, the United States, and Mexico.

6. The interrelatedness of free trade and these other forces is emphasised in Flanagan 1992, Gunderson 1992a and Gunderson and Verma 1992.

References

Adams, R., and J. White. 1989. "Labor and the Canada-U.S. Free Trade Agreement." *ILR Report* 27 (Fall): 15-21.

Alarcon-Gonzalez, D. 1992. "Does Free Trade Promote Income Equality? The Experience of Structural Adjustment in Mexico." Vancouver: Fraser Institute.

Belous, R. 1990. "Trading Blocs and Human Resources—The New Wild Card." In *The Growth of Regional Trading Blocs in the Global Economy*, R. Belous and R. Hartley, eds., pp. 43-45. Washington, DC: National Planning Association).

Betcherman, G., and M. Gunderson. 1990. "Canada-U.S. Free Trade and Labor Relations." *Labor Law Journal* 41, no. 8 (August): 454-60.

De Boer, E. and G. Winham. 1992. "Trade Negotiations and Social Charters." *Canada-U.S. Outlook* 3, no. 3 (August).

Flanagan, R. 1992. "NAFTA and Competitive Adjustments in North American Labor Markets." (Vancouver: Fraser Institute).

Gunderson, M. 1990. "Regional Dimensions of the Impact of Free Trade on Labor." *Canadian Journal of Regional Science* 13, no 2-3 (Summer/Autumn): 243-54.

..... 1992a. "Labor Market Impacts of Free Trade." (Vancouver: Fraser Institute).

..... 1992b. "Wage and Employment Impacts of Free Trade." Vancouver: Fraser Institute).

..... 1992c. Forthcoming. "Labor Adjustment Under NAFTA: Canadian Issues." *North American Outlook*.

Gunderson, M., and D. Hamermesh. 1990. "The Effect of Free Trade on the North American Labor Market." In *The Dynamics of North American Trade and Investment: Canada, Mexico and the United States* C. Reynolds, L. Waverman, and G. Bueno, pp. 225-40. Stanford, Calif.: Stanford University Press.

Gunderson, M. and A. Verma. 1992 "Canadian Labor Policies and Global Competition." *Canadian Business Law Journal* 20, no. 1 (March): 63-89.

..... 1993. "The Impact of Free Trade on the Collective Agreement". In *The North American Free Trade Agreement: Labor, Industry and Government Perspectives*, M. Bognanno and K. Ready, eds. (Westport, Conn.: Greenwood Publishing).

Morici, P. 1992. "Implications of a Social Charter for the North American Free Trade Agreement." *Canada-U.S. Outlook* 3, no. 3 (August).

Randall, M. 1986. "Free Trade and Canadian Industrial Relations: a Union View." In *New Pressures in Canadian Industrial Relations*, Proceedings of the Thirty-fourth Annual Conference of the Industrial Relations Centre. Montreal: McGill University).

Reynolds, C. 1992. "Will a Free Trade Agreement Lead to Wage Convergence? Implications for Mexico and the United States". In *U.S.-Mexico Relations: Labor Market Interdependence*, J. Bustamante, C. Reynolds, and R. Hinojosa-Ojeda, eds. Stanford, Calif.: Stanford University Press.

Weintraub, S. and J. Gilbreath. 1992. "The Social Side to Free Trade," Canada-U.S. Outlook 3, no. 3 (August).

The Restructuring of the Automobile Industry in Mexico and the Repercussions for Labor

Arnulfo Arteaga Garcia

What has caused the Mexican affiliates of the North American transnational automobile manufacturers to rank among the principal exporters of the region?[1] No doubt, the answer to this question is related to the strategies pursued by those firms, combined with national economic policies in Mexico. The firms have achieved solid competitive advantages and have successfully penetrated global markets, in particular, the U.S. market.[2]

Firm strategies have emphasized human resource development with a focus on quality objectives aimed at creating a multiskilled work force. At the same time, firm strategies have included the implementation of technological advances that provided qualitative advancements in technical conditions. However, managerial strategies have varied across firms and even across plants belonging to the same company. Strategies have particularly varied in terms of the development of the workforce and modifications made to labor relations. Some firms have developed cooperative relations with their unions and workers (consensual forms) (GM Ramos Arizpe, 1985) while other firms maintained vertical decision-making without the consultation of workers or their unions (Ford Cuautitlán, 1987, 1991, and 1993, Volkswagen 1987 and 1992).

Regarding the development of dynamic local or regional advantages, particular emphasis has been placed on qualitative aspects, especially upon the extent of internationalization and the development of related industries and suppliers that share activities in the value chain.[3] A central objective in these company strategies has been increased integration into a North American regional market.

This paper describes how the Mexican automobile industry has become more integrated into the North American market. The first section describes the evolution of the automobile industry in Mexico. The paper then shows how recent transformations have profoundly affected labor relations and corporate strategies, particularly with regard to the scope of work processes. The third section analyzes how the restructuring of the auto industry in Mexico has led to modifications in labor relations in the factories of two specific firms.

Evolution of the Automobile Industry in Mexico
and its Integration in the North American Regional Market

Table 1 describes the key periods in the development of the Mexican auto industry.[4] As seen in the chart, firms varied in their ability to face the effects of industrial restructuring.

The first period covers 1925-63; the second period covers 1964-80, and the third period extends from 1981 to the present. These period are distinguished by a set of variables that identify the industry's evolution during each period. These variables include the production characteristics, the various government industrial policies, geographic location, technological characteristics (pertaining to either the process or the product), organizational and labor relations strategies, characteristics of the workforce, and the form of union organization.

The Productive Core

The "productive core" refers to the phases in the production processes that were incorporated into the production facilities of the auto industry. The first productive core is auto assembly, the final stage in the automobile manufacturing process. Assembly was initially based on CKD (completely knocked-down) parts that were imported since the beginning of the industry in 1925 until the early 1960s. Then, after the "Decree for the Integration of the Automobile Industry" (1962), which demanded national integration, the assembly stage began to include a high national content.[5] This decree established the requirement of a minimum of 60 percent domestic content. Currently, only two plants solely entail assembly operations. Those plants are the most obsolete: GM (1936) and Chrysler (1937).

The second auto manufacturing productive core in Mexico includes foundry, machining, and engine-assembly operations. The U.S. companies that started their auto assembly operations in Mexico in the 1920s and 1930s did not locate these related operations in Mexico until the 1960s when they opened new industrial complexes (Ford's in Cuautitlán, State of Mexico; GM and Chrysler in Toluca, State of Mexico). The Japanese and German companies (Nissan and VW, respectively), established in the early 1960s, included from the start machining and auto engine assembly, as well as final auto assembly, to comply with conditions imposed by the integration decree.

Industrial Policy and the Legal Framework

In each period there were various types of legislation and regulations associated with industrial policies. These policies express, in general terms, the outcomes of negotiations between the main actors in the auto industry concerning a stimulation policy for the auto sector. The first period lacked a consistent policy. In the second period, industrial policy sought to encourage product diversification based on domestic production, using increased internal integration rates as its main basis (1962, 1969, 1972 and 1977 decrees). Finally, a transition stage, which began with the 1983 decree, sought integration in the midst of the globalization occurring in the industry. This integration was consolidated by the 1989 decree.

The North American Free Trade Agreement reinforced this framework. In effect, NAFTA ratified the integration of the industrial plants in Mexico with the U.S. auto industry, an integration itself that follows from the strategies of the U.S. corporations and the commercial interests of the European firms (Volkswagen and Renault), and the Japanese entrant (Nissan). NAFTA overrules the 1989 decree. For the first time, a decree will be binding for a fifteen-year period until the year 2004, which eliminates the freedom to make decisions domestically without outside pressures.

Geographical Location

The auto industry was geographically concentrated in the Federal District (Mexico City) during the first period.[6] GM's and Chrysler's plants had very important locational advantages until the mid-1980s. They were located within Mexico's principal auto market, that is, the Federal District. Later they expanded into its metropolitan area.[7] They were endowed with services, infrastructure, and a dynamic labor market that included a well-qualified and educated workforce. Nevertheless, the advantages derived from industrial centralization were reversed at the end of the 1970s when acute urban problems appeared in the Federal District, leading to policies encouraging industrial decentralization. What followed were incentives to increase investments in various zones of the country and taxes on the manufacturing activities occurring in the country's central area. These governmental policies slowed when at the end of the 1970s, the companies decided, to construct new industrial complexes in the north of the country. Ford closed its La Villa plant in the Federal District, a plant that had been in operation since the 1920s. GM and Chrysler did the same in subsequent years in their plants in that area.

In the second period, geographical decentralization took place in those states closest to the capital: Dina-Renault in Ciudad Sahagún, Hidalgo; VW in Puebla, Puebla; and the Nissan plant at Ciudad Industrial del Valle de Cuernavaca (CIVAC), Morelos. The three companies had begun their production operations in these locations between the 1950s (Dina) and the 1960s. Meanwhile, the U.S. firms of Ford, GM, Automex (which operated under Chrysler, and which later became a Mexican company) and Vehículos Automotores Mexicanos (VAM, with the participation of American Motors), sited their new plants in the State of Mexico. These new U.S. plants specialized in foundry, machining, and engine assembly, whereas the European- and Asian-owned plants started their operations by including foundry, machining, and auto engine production with auto assembly.

It's important to note that even though plants belonging to the second period were conceived, designed, and implemented in a period when mass industrial production concepts dominated, their production scale was limited because only a small market existed in Mexico. However, the construction of large-scale plants on large plots of land has been an important element facilitating the modernization process for Nissan and VW. VW is currently building a nearby industrial park for its principal suppliers, incorporating just-in-time management.

Industrial decentralization later took place in the north-central part of Mexico. Expanded areas include: Aguascalientes (Nissan, 1985); Durango (Renault, 1983); in the north, Coahuila (GM and Chrysler, 1981) Chihuahua and Sonora (Ford, 1985); and near the northern U.S.-Mexico border, where a huge number of in-bond maquilas are located, some of which are owned by the same U.S. firms operating under different names.

The Technological Features

The technical bases of the auto plants are related to specific manufacturing processes and the work organization on which the development of production is based. The first productive core is associated with body assembly, painting, and fit and trim. The second productive core is associated with foundry, parts machining, and engine assembly. At times, the latter are integrated at the same complex and incorporate the assembly stages of finished units or maintain some of the assembly operations pertaining to the first productive core.

During the first two periods, the basic technology involved the transfer of relatively obsolete technological packages. These packages did not allow production in Mexico to be competitive in foreign markets, although they were technically sufficient for the protected and small-scale market found in Mexico.

In the current period, the transfer of technology involves state-of-the-art technology (such as Ford's Chihuahua and Hermosillo plants and Nissan's Aguascalientes complex), and advanced technological levels (GM and Chrysler at Ramos Arizpe, for instance), which make the subsidiaries competitive at international levels even though they do not always utilize state-of-the-art technologies.

Organizational Structures and Strategies, Organization of Work, and Labor Relations

Tetsuo Abo, proposes a hybrid model that measures and recognizes the particularities of "japanese-style management."[8] This model identifies the most important characteristics of the organizational and labor relations strategies utilized in firms and plants.[9]

Implementation of Japanese management in Mexico has been the result of a long and conflictive process dating back to the early 1980s. The application of this strategy was based on geographical decentralization toward the north of the country. This decentralization converged with the "southern strategy" of the U.S. auto industry. The strategy included union atomization, the elimination of collective contracts, plant closings, and a labor policy favoring the companies whenever labor conflicts arose (GM 1980; VW 1987; Ford 1987 and 1989; VW 1992).[10]

Until the mid-1980s, compartmentalized and very hierarchical organizational strategies (with autocratic leadership) dominated. Work organization followed "Taylorist-Fordist" concepts.[11] That is, there was a segmented production system based on the "one man/one machine/one operation" ratio, with workers specialized in one small fragment of production. These characteristics were particularly strong in those plants belonging to the first two productive cores.

In the third period, spurred by the integration occurring in the third production core, various firms implemented interfunctional administrative strategies based on horizontal decisionmaking and reduced autocratic leadership. With regard to work organization these strategies incorporated work teams (with various names). Work team activities included the organization and administration of production and the workforce. New areas of worker participation concerned daily production, quality control, safety, work environment issues, and training.

The management strategies pursued in the third productive core's plants have encouraged a transformation away from old manufacturing cores. The main innovators are the large international organizations, particularly in those palnts belonging to the new industrial structure. These organizational factors contributed heavily to increases in both productivity and competitiveness.

While most of the new industrial structure is beginning to operate under new organizational strategies, the old industrial structure is under pressure to revamp deeply rooted labor practices. The principal obstacle blocking this organizational transformation is the companies' middle and highmanagement. There is pressure to generate a new industrial culture and a new type of relationship between workers and their supervisors and higher-level managers. New practices substantially alter the definitions of power, and the manner in which power is exercised on the production line. These tensions will be exacerbated by NAFTA.

The Labor Force

The characteristics of the labor force for each of these periods have been affected by specific dynamics in labor markets during each production stage, technology, and unionization. These variables have also influenced the location policies of the firms. During the first period, the industry's labor market was shaped by the integration of the early working-class groups, particularly in large firms. The principal source of these groups was artisan workshops indirectly related to the auto industry.

In the second period the labor force had no industrial consciousness and primarily came from agricultural areas. The average age and education level were lower than those of workers found in the first productive core. The characteristics of the workers who belong to the first two productive cores have changed considerably. Now the labor force has industrial experience, and although family ties still matter, the labor market operates in an increasingly professional manner.

In the third period, with the opening of the new industrial plants, much of the new labor force is without industrial experience and comes from mid-sized urban areas. There is a noticeable drop in the average age of workers. In addition, there is a polarization of formal education levels and heavy female participation, the latter especially evident in the maquilas.

Presently, the first productive core's labor force has the highest average age within the automobile industry. In this sector skills and professional advancements are linked to job classifications and based on seniority in the company.

The Structure and Organization of Unions

The key union issues concern the goals of unions and the strategies they developed toward enterprises. The workers in the first productive core (located in Mexico City) early on tried to obtain legal recognition for their unions, independent of whether they belonged to a confederation or not. This action led to union growth and consolidation throughout the country from the 1930s until the end of the 1950s.

The first industrial geographic decentralization process coincided with the consolidation of official unionization, in particular, the Confederation of Mexican Workers (CTM [Confederación de Trabajadores de México]). All the new plants that started their operations at the beginning of the 1960s signed "protection contracts" with this confederation. These contracts lowered working conditions and benefits, particularily for the pattern-leading workers located in the first productive core in the center of the country. In spite of this type of contract ("Protection Contract"), unionism linked to the Independent Workers Union (Unidad Obrera Independiente) arose in the Volkswagen and Nissan plants. This unionism differed from traditional unionism by promoting new, more aggressive and coordinated strategies. But, union coordination later dissipated and dissolved into single unionism, in large part due to careless union administration.

Antidemocratic practices, as well as certain actions by workers, led the CTM and the Independent Workers Union to split up and become independent. The Volkswagen union became part of FESEBES after the 1992 conflict.

With a second wave of industrial geographic dispersion and the subsequent creation of the third productive core, companies signed a new "Protection Contract" with CTM. In spite of the existence of "National Company Unions" (Sindicatos Nacionales de Empresa) at companies such as Ford and Chrysler, the collective contracts at each company differed in terms of salary, schedule, and other contract items. In general, union administration and negotiations were conducted carelessly. In addition, each plant had a different contract expiration date. GM now has four unions, one located in the capital, which belongs to the Workers' Revolutionary Confederation (Confederación Revolucionaria de Obreros), and another in Toluca (CTM). In the Ramos Arizpe complex a different union exists for each plant (engines and assembly), each having a separate contract.

The last decade saw the dismemberment of Ford's contracts in La Villa and Cuautitlán. Renault closed its Ciudad Sahagún complex, and Dina and VAM did the same in Mexico City and Toluca. The same occurred at the VW, GM, and Chrysler plants.

It should be noted that in each case management has unilaterally imposed greater flexibility to varying degrees. The workers and the unions had little influence on these changes. In part, this is due to the fact that management did not consider unions as legitimate partners. But, moreover, this occurred because workers' representatives did not develop alternative proposals. This union attitude is linked to their historical focus on economic clauses and disregard for direct problems related to production in contract negotiations. Unions, due to the lack of an alternative plan have become passive and serve primarily as objects of the companies' strategies.

The companies are taking the initiative in the reformulation of labor relations. They are also promoting a new labor culture based on collaboration and workers' participation in issues concerning production, quality control, work environment, training, and job security. This participation mandates that the processes be bilateral and negotiated with both the workforce and unions. For Mexican unions to become active counterparts to the companies who themselves are operating in a more integrated manner in the U.S. region, requires the unions to take responsibility for work conditions.

The Three Stages in the Evolution of the Mexican Automobile Industry
and its Integration within the North American Region

The process of regional integration has not been a "natural" one. It has required a considerable restructuring of the automobile sector from the late 1970s to the early 1990s. The following kinds of changes occurred: a) geographical: with dispersion as the industry moved northward; b) technological: with the introduction of new and technologically advanced equipment, machinery, and devices to respond to international competitive pressures; c) organizational: new systems based on the involvement of the workforce in areas such as production, quality, security, working environment, and

186

training; and d) contractual: new collective work contracts providing greater flexibility and managerial discretion.

Companies in the Mexican automobile industry sector invested between $6 and $8 billion from 1979 to 1992 to refurbish old factories and construct new complexes and plants. A total of seventeen new plants were completed. These plants included stamping, engine, foundry, and final assembly plants. The capacity of the industry rose to a little over one million vehicles annually, and over two million engines in the same period.

In spite of a predicted sales slowdown in the U.S., Canadian, and Mexican markets, a sustained increase in investments is expected in the 1990s. One source expects that investments for the 1993-96 period will be around $5,200[12] million dollars, while another source predicts investments of $4,225 million in the auto parts sector alone.[13] The above-mentioned forecasts indicate that the growth trend that began in the late 1970s is likely to persist.

In Mexico, there were three stages in the process of integration into the North American market. The first stage involves productive specialization in the auto parts sector, which is related to the development of an industrial structure for the production of engines. Over the period 1982-92 approximately twelve million engines were exported to factories in the United States and Canada. At the same time, throughout the past decade, an extensive network of maquiladora exporting factories were built along the country's northern border (from Baja California to Tamaulipas). For the most part, these factories are owned by the transnational companies and operate directly under the administration of their parent U.S. corporations. As a result, Mexico contributed 15 percent ($5,285 million) of the total auto parts imported into the US in 1992.[14] Table 2 lists the percentage of various auto parts used in the US in 1991 that were manufactured in Mexican plants.

The second stage in regional integration was characterized by segmented specialization. It began in the middle of the 1980s and was shaped by the strategies of the companies. In 1991, the plants in Mexico exported $2,805 million in assembled vehicles, which represented 5.1 percent of the total number of assembled vehicles imported into the US (as a reference, Canada exported $20,845 million). The three subsidiaries of the U.S. companies—Chrysler, Ford, and GM dominated in assembled vehicle exports. These companies directed their exports mainly to the United States. Volkswagen also restarted exports to the US and Canada. Altogether, during 1992, 87.23 percent (342,113) of Mexican-assembled vehicle exports went to the US or Canada.[15]

Nissan is the only company that directs its exports from Mexico principally to Central and South America. Out of the 40,070 units exported from Mexico to this region in 1991 Nissan had 83.20 percent of the total.

Another novel aspect of this second stage in the integration process was the opening of plans in Mexico dedicated solely to export production (for example, Ford Hermosillo, with a 170-million-unit annual installed capacity). Some existing plants also started up export programs (Chrysler, GM, Nissan). Volkswagen increased the number of its plants for the production of models destined for both the internal and external market.

As a result of these two stages of regional integration, Mexico's contributions to the U.S. auto industry equalled the amounts described in Table 3 in 1991.

The third stage of the regional integration process is characterized by an integrated regional operation and entails the agreements included in NAFTA (See NAFTA, "Annex 300-A: Automotive Sector", in chapter 3, "National Treatment and Market Access." It is also in chapter 4, "Rules of Origin." Both of these are continued in the Part 2: "Trade of Goods." The antecedents of the process, in the case of the relation of Mexico to the US, are in "Decrees for the Rationalization of the Automotive Industry in Mexico," and in "Decrees for the Promotion and Modernization of the Automotive Industry").

The importance of these agreements rests on the fact that the auto companies, together with the governments of the three signing countries, are now attempting to fully direct the integration process described above. The purpose is to promote a deeper penetration into productive and commercial areas and further standardize regional operating norms and produce stronger links between market forces and working conditions in the three countries.

The Effects of Restructuring on Labor Conditions

In this section we will illustrate, by using two cases, the modernization of work processes and labor relations. The two cases provide insights into the change strategies being adopted at both companies and at the plant level.

The Contractual Differences between the GM Plants

To illuminate the restructuring process we describe the core elements of the collective bargaining contracts (CCT) of the four GM plants in Mexico.[16] The first key issue concerns union atomization. The first core plant is in the Federal District, where the union is part of the Confederation of Workers and Peasants (CROC). The union from the second core plant is affiliated to an iron and steel national union, which, in turn, belongs to the CTM. The third core's plants are in Ramos Arizpe (RA) and are located in the same industrial complex, but have different unions and different collective contracts. Two belong to the CTM. This company has three industrial plants and four different unions, each with different CCTs and separate negotiations. This organizational dispersion is sanctioned by the CCTs. (See D.F./CCT. Article 5, "The stipulations of the current CCT extends to all persons who work in the firm's agencies in the Federal District," and RA/CCT, Article 2, "Jurisdiction. Exclusively in the area designated in the attached plan, which corresponds to the Automotive Vehicles Assembly plant, under the topographical data that this contract's attached plan includes.")

Concerning hiring practices in the Federal District, the trial period for a new or reinstated employee has been eliminated, as stipulated in RA/CCT, Article 3 states, "All of those employees who are new or reentering the service of the company, will be submitted to a trial period of 30 days." Likewise, the possibility of hiring minors is allowed in this plant. Article 4 states, "The general requirements (. . .) those who are of eligible age, must guarantee to have completed the mandatory military service" (emphasis added). By not explicitly mentioning the possibility of the hiring of minors, the minimum considerations contemplated in the Federal Labor Law are eliminated. The hiring of minors was induced by the scarcity of manual labor when this plant began operations in 1981.

With regard to labor's positions in terms of category, function, and department in the Federal District/CCT certain specifications exist. Percentages are set for each category, as well as the departments to which they are assigned. No regulations exists in the RA/CCTs. This allows for the workers' unrestrained availability without commensurate renumeration for more qualified positions. Article 12 states, "The company is free to transfer its employees from one department to another, and from one job and/or shift to another according to its need, always and whenever an overload of work is not occasioned in the section or department where the employee is transferred."

In the Federal District, the workweek consists of forty hours for the three shifts RA/CCT Article 13 states, "The workweek will consist of the following <u>discontinuous shifts</u>: <u>48 effective work hours</u> per week for the day shift; 45 per week for the mixed shift, and 42 per week for the night shift." (emphasis added). The starting and quitting times are not mentioned, since these are stipulated in the Internal Labor Bylaw (Reglamento Interno de Trabajo). Thus, there exists an extra eight hours in the workweek along with a few extra work requirements. Since RA has a more recent technological base, hypothetically, it also has increased productivity and more intensive work. Salary and benefits differences do exist in the Federal District. (These are described in more detail later in the paper.) Management has the discretion to rotate employees across distinct responsibilities and positions without corresponding changes in their wages, job, category, or function. The company violates the Federal Labor Law (Article 63) in both contracts by not considering the half hour designated for meals as an official allowance of the working day and by not paying overtime for it.

In the benefit area these contracts also provide substandard terms. For example, while DF/CCT in Article 20 designates seventeen mandatory holidays, RA/CCT in Article 20 designates only eleven days. Although DF/CCT Article 23 regulates vacation time and requires a 164 percent bonus, in addition to the employee's salary, the RA's collective agreement provides only the minimum established conditions in the Federal Labor Law by awarding a 50% bonus. The flexibility in labor conditions at RA allowed the company to undertake the successful organizational transformation described in the next section.

The "Tailored Suit" with a Japanese "Pattern"

As part of the introduction of total quality control (TQC) concepts in its Mexican plants GM began organizational restructuring at the end of 1985.[17] This process began with the administrative fusion of the two plants in Ramos Arizpe, which until then had operated separately. The next step was the promulgation of a strategy including quality concepts at all levels of the complex. It is interesting to note that executives did not explicitly mention the influence of Japanese management approaches during interviews conducted at both the complex and the company's other plants in the country. Rather, special recognition was paid to Deming and Juran as the pioneers of statistical control processes. Nevertheless, Ishikwa's influence in the formulation of a model of organizational transformation is apparent.[18]

"Quality First": The Formation of a Structure that Supports Strategies

Management's fundamental objective was assurance of high quality in each step of the production process, including suppliers and distributors, in order to attain "client satisfaction." To do so a strategy was designed that, through "interfunctional committees," involved all the divisions of each company using the concept of "interfunctional management." At the first level, a quality improvement governing "commission" was created. It is comprised of all plant operations in the Federal District, Toluca, and Ramos Arizpe. The maquiladora plants had no such structure, as they depend directly on corporate headquarters in the US

The corporation's commission is linked to the plants through a similar organization comprised of the five directors of each of the plants: the director of the commercial and suburban assembly plant in the Federal District; the director of the engine machining and assembly plant in Toluca; the director of the machining and engine plant in Ramos Arizpe; and the director of the passenger vehicle assembly plant in Ramos Arizpe. Parallel to this structure is a substructure called the "client satisfaction council." It is presided over by the corporate sales director and is linked to the client satisfaction teams found in each plant. These teams include the plant manager and often also the managers of product quality, service, parts, and supplier quality assurance, for example. Each plant's team reports regularly on the ten principal problems, the manner in which they are being resolved, and on quality levels. All of this is reported on a monthly basis to the council.

This process is informed by a 5 percent sample of production resulting from internal audits and audits by the divisions. (Mexican operations are controlled by the Division of Small Cars within GM's global structure, which is made up of Chevrolet, Pontiac, Canada [C-P-C]).

The five-year plan is one of the noteworthy features of the organizational restructuring. The plan began in 1987 and was managed by the suppliers' quality assurance group. The purpose was to identify and report on the critical aspects of production, based on the statistical control procedures. Plans were developed with GM's supplier companies. It was expected that, on a gradual basis, by the year 1992, plans would implement a "source approval of parts."[19] They were also to eliminate receiving inspection of materials and handling under the "kanban" system so as to decrease "quality costs" from 4.5 percent to .5 percent (the level that Toyota operates on).

The Organizational Transformation Process: Ideology and Practice

The organizational transformation was to be based on the creation of work teams. The first aspect to be developed was the complete alignment of the various hierarchal levels in relation to a "vision." This vision was directed toward "an increase in the standard of living and in the skills of our people" (GM).

The transformation process is directed toward the creation of an organizational structure based on operating units that are integrated through systems and permanent training. The training is directed toward the development of skills, such as statistical process control, techniques for conflict resolution, and leadership development.

The fundamental objective is "client satisfaction." This satisfaction is to be acquired through "quality, productivity, and improvements in the worker's quality of life," based on the regular "communication" of results, a process that depends on the creation of negotiating teams. The goal is to develop a worker who is involved and has initiative. The worker is to be reevaluated based on skills and knowledge of how to resolve daily production problems, even though pay levels are to remain relatively modest. In order to promote this process, the following concepts are promoted during training activities:

The person who performs the job is the one who knows the most about it

Recognition for accomplishments

Compensation for knowledge

An information system for personnel regarding accomplishments

Spontaneous cooperation between the team's members

Training for supervisory personnel to participate in work teams

With more extensive training being provided to the entire workforce and work teams being formed, the new work organization was to delegate conception, supervision, and control functions to production personnel. In the past, these duties were performed directly by middle managers on the shop floor.

This model was implemented successfully in Ramos Arizpe but it has led to significant adjustments in labor relations and to labor conflicts. Conflict was particularly intense with regard to modifications made to pay due to skill and knowledge levels.

Ford: The Fragility of Unilateral Flexibility

In the Cuautitlán plant modernization was particularly advanced in the foundry, machining, body assembly, paint jobs, and the final vestment production. Ford incorporated new technologies to a greater degree than other companies.[20] As a result of this strategy, the Chihuahua and Hermosillo Ford plants are the most automated in Mexico and are even advanced by international standards.[21] But the firm's strategy in this plant has centered on efforts to develop a new labor relations model based on making the work force more flexible.

In the Cuautitlán plant, one of the first projects to modify labor relations policy was the "Active Participation Program for Quality and Competitiveness (PACC). "It had two objectives. First, it was a pilot plan to assess workers' responses with the intention of extending its operation to the entire plant. And second, based on the involvement models set forth in the APPQC, the "bell to bell" system was implemented.[22] This system allowed management to recover control of the foundry process. The PACC internal introduction document claimed that the way to maintain the foundry process was to develop export programs so as to revert the effects of the domestic market's decline and the government-imposed restrictions on the installation of eight-cylinder engines as of 1985. As a result of the decline in demand, employment in the foundry plant had fallen from 909 workers in 1980 to 393 in 1984. If this trend continued the company forecast a decline of up to 173 workers in 1986.[23] For these reasons, the company's document stated that "a harmonious atmosphere and a responsible participating labor environment are essential, we must get involved and support each of the program's actions. In this way, we will become larger and stronger, which, in turn, will make us strong and solid for the goals that time and circumstance set forth for us."[24]

The CCT provided the principal obstacle for the radical transformation of labor relations since, in addition to assuring better benefits for the workers, it guaranteed a relatively strong bilateral relationship. This impeded management's efforts to use labor in a discretionary and flexible manner. On the other hand, the CCT had made significant changes in salaries and benefits and this had a strong demonstration effect on the workers. In the following section, we illustrate some of the most notable differences in salaries and benefits in the former CCT and the current one.

We begin by comparing the average base daily wage, which was about 12 percent above the wage levels in the first productive core plants.[25] This advantage was even high when the Cuautitlán wage is compared to the second productive core plants (up to 28.2 percent). The advantage was up to 53.5 percent when a comparison is made to the third productive core.[26] These differences are more pronounced in the direct comparison of the wages at Cuautitlán with those at Ford's two plants in the third productive core. When compared to the engine plant in Chihuahua, the Cuautitlán wage advantage was about 103.6 percent (4,376.01 pesos) and about 126.5 percent (3,932.79) when a comparison is made with the Hermosillo plant's wage.[27]

The workers also received additional cash payments, like the punctuality bonus, which equaled 46 days of pay. Meanwhile, the average additional payments in the other companies varied between 66 (GM, Federal District, first core) and 0 (Chrysler) days of pay. The vacation bonus was 30 days, varying between 28 days (GM, second core) and 4 (Ford, third core, Hermosillo). When the Christmas bonus, savings fund, provisions coupons, profit-sharing, and social security are included, the total number of additional compensation amounted to 146 days of pay per year. The average in most of the industry's companies and plants was 89.1. The only plant where the total extra compensation exceeded that in the Cuautitlán plant was GM's plant in the Federal District, which had 149.4 extra days of pay. The compensation factor, in the same order, was 40.7 percent, 24.8 percent, and 41.5 percent.[28] The earnings (12,533.33 pesos per day) of the Cuautitlán workers was 19.4 percent, 32.5 percent, and 62.4 percent, respectively, higher than average earnings in the three cores.

Among Ford's plants in the third productive core there were some very prominent disparities. As revealed in Table 4, earnings of the Chihuahua and Hermosillo plants varied substantially.

In terms of worker's annual income considered (see Table 5), the Cuautitlán workers had secured, through the CCT, an amount of 4,047,669 pesos.[29] This was 26.4 percent higher than average earnings in the first core, and 45.2 percent and 149 percent, respectively, higher than earnings in the second and third core. All together, the base wage, cash benefits, and benefits, and benefits in kind yielded a very high labor cost structure, since the first represented 31.5 percent, the second 33.1 percent, and the last 35.4 percent of total earnings.

The strong contract and high wages at the Cuautitlán complex motivated the company, in complicity with the CTM leader, Fidel Velazquez, and Ford's National Union Executive Committee, to drastically modify the CCT. Ford attempted to introduce substantial flexibility and intense conflicts resulted in 1991 and 1993.

There were three stages in the change from the former CCT to the current one. The first stage involved the loss of guarantees and decreases in benefits. The second stage involved the loss of bilateral labor-management relations. Union representatives could no longer intervene in the determination of work conditions. The third stage entailed a "loss of autonomy" for the local union committees.

Table 1

The Periods and Principle Variables in
the Automobile Industry's Evolution in Mexico

Variable Period	1st Period 1925-1963	2d Period 1964-1980	3d Period 1981- present
Productive core	Car and truck final assembly out of CKDs	Foundry and casting of motor parts, machining, and assembly of engines	Engine and car die and die and assembly. Machining auto parts for exports
Industrial policies/legal frame	Partial regulations without industrial policies	1962, 1967, 1972 and 1977 decrees	1983, 1989 decrees, and NAFTA Agreements
Geographical localization	Mexico City, Hidalgo (Ciudad Sahagún)	Estado de México (Lerma-Toluca); Morelos (Cuernavaca); Hidalgo (Sahagún)	Coahuila (Ramos Arizpe); Chihuahua (Chih.); Aguascalientes (Ags.); Durango (Gómex Palacio); Sonora (Hermosillo); Guanajuato (Silao); and north border strip
Technology	Machinery and rigid transfer equipment, internationally obsolete, but in good shape technologically for low-scale production and protected markets	Same	Modern equipment and transfer machinery, competitive internationally, automatized system, CNC, automatic press casting and robots
Production and labor relations	Taylorist-Fordist autocratic hierarchial hard, labor contracts centered on lendings, little participation in regular production	Same	Interfunctional administration, more specialized production, participative, few hierarchic levels, flexible
Labor force features	Urban artisan origin, low education levels	Country origins, low education levels with no previous experience in industrial work	Urban extraction from new industrial zones, higher education; without previous experience; Increase of female participation, mainly in maquilas
Union organization	Without organization at the beginning, CROC, CTM and other unions	CTM, OUI	CTM, independent without unions FESEBES

Table 2

Mexico's Share of Auto Parts in the U.S. Market
(Selected Products, 1991)

Product	Percentage of share
Windshield wipers	83.88
Safety belts	77.00
Brake parts	54.24
Radios	49.95
Air conditioners	32.96
Gasoline engines	35.93
Transmissions	27.51
Radiators	22.54
Suspension systems	15.33

Source: Based on SECOFI information, *La industria automotriz en el Tratado de Libre Comercio*, Mexico, November 1992, Tables 2 and 3.

Table 3

Mexico and Canada's Share of Imports into the U.S. in 1991,
Expressed in Dollars and Percents
(Auto Parts and Assembled Vehicles)

Region	Auto Parts		Assembled Vehicles	
	%	$ (1,000s)	#	$ (1,000s)
Mexico	15.1	5,285	5.1	2,805
Canada	24.6	8,610	37.9	20,845
Others	60.4	21,140	57.0	31,350
Total	100.0	35,035	100.0	55,000

Source: Based on SECOFI information, *La industria automotriz en el Tratado de Libre Comercio*, Mexico, November 1992, Table A.

Table 4

Comparison of the Average Daily Base Wage

Company	Base wage	Cuautitlán advantage in %
Ford (Cuautitlán)	8,907.84	----
General Motors		
Federal District	8,305.90	(7.2)
Toluca	5,992.56	(48.69)
Ramos Arizpe	4,514.74	(97.3)
Chrysler		
Federal District	7,384.46	(20.6)
Toluca	5,322.02	(67.4)
Ramos Arizpe	4,226.29	(110.8)
Nissan		
Cuernavaca	6,395.85	(39.3)
Lerma	5,878.05	(51.5)
Aguascalientes	3,683.64	(141.8)
Volkswagen		
Puebla	7,890.36	(12.9)
Ford		
Chihuahua	4,376.01	(103.6)
Hermosillo	3,932.79	(126.5)

Source: Company's internal documents, compiled by the labor relations staff for the 1987 contract negotiations.

Table 5

Comparison of the Workers' Annual Income at the Ford Cuautitlán Plant
with Earnings at the 1t, 2d, and 3d Production Cores

	Yearly base wage	Liable benefits	Annual taxes	IMSS	Income	Benefits, extras	Income, net	Dif. (%)
Ford Cautitlan	3,521,362	917,508	367,057	----	3,801,813	245,856	4,047,669	----
Cores								
1t	2,609,469	714,618	259,223	48,045	3,179,952	22,104	3,202,056	26.4
2d	2,336,608	703,550	193,778	74,768	2,771,076	15,146	2,786,972	45.2
3d	1,511,688	179,468	34,316	57,988	1,198,967	22,058	1,620,760	149.7

Source: Compiled from data from Ford's staff. The data corresponds to March 1987, prior to the salary or contractual negotiations.

Appendix A

Comparison between 1985-1987 and 1989-1991 Collective Bargaining Agreements (CCT)
(flexibility, guarantees, and reduction in benefits)

1985-1987 CCT

Chapter IV
Permanent, Temporary, and Seasonal Employment
Clause 7. Due to the nature of the Company's operations, it is necessary to intensify production during part of the year, for which the services of temporary and seasonal plant workers are needed; taking into account that these workers will be utilized for part of the season or the entirety of it, the Company and the Union agree to recognize the rights of the workers previously mentioned to all and every one of the workers who are included in this clause. . . . In the event that due to unforeseen circumstances it is necessary to interrupt the period that was defined to the worker upon reentry, *the Company will pay the concerned worker a bonus equivalent to two wage days for each week that said period was reduced, without detriment to such worker's rights for rehiring.*

Chapter V
Rehiring and Vacancies
Clause 12. *The Company agrees to have a number of workers assigned to cover absenteeism,* which shall be equal to the real quantity observed as absent during the former week for each department, adjusting to the statistical increasing or decreasing trend which has been observed.

Clause 10. In the cases of daily absenteeism, all of the positions which are vacant due to absenteeism [sic] will be covered (hiring temporary replacements from other nonproductive

1989-1991 CCT

Chapter IV
Permanent, Temporary, and Seasonal Employment
Clause 6. The figures for temporary plant workers are nullified and those for seasonal and temporary workers are redefined, thus remaining only those for seasonal and temporary workers, affecting the determination of benefits for each of the worker's figures. The company's responsibility to indemnify the worker is nullified when, for reasons not imputable to the latter, the contract under any of the above-mentioned kinds is suspended.

departments and citing temporary replacements in overtime, with the exception of those positions which, due to their nature, do not complicate, nor affect the productive systems, and absenteeism will be covered (hiring temporary replacements from other non-productive departments, citing temporary replacements in overtime or others of similar nature. . .). Likewise, the Company and the Union will periodically review the number of absenteeism which are covered for each department.

Chapter VI
Promotions and Personnel Changes.
Clause 13. In order to cover positions of equal or inferior category, the worker with the least seniority who meets the previously stipulated requirements, and whose wages will not be impaired, will be selected. . . . All of the transfers to a higher category in normal time must be recorded for the purpose of paying benefits of punctuality bonuses, holiday and Christmas bonuses, such benefits will be paid weekly, using 3.53 percent as a factor for hours worked.

Clause 16. In the event of temporary ascensions due to fluctuations in the volume of production or derived from extraordinary operations being temporary in nature, during such period in which the worker occupies a position of higher classification, said worker will be compensated with the corresponding provisional wage (compensation).

In the current contract, the regulations for the promotion and personnel change procedures are eliminated, leaving a wide margin for informal bargaining, limiting themselves to declare the possibility of its existence. On the contrary, with the introduction of the "quarterly feedback system," the supervision becomes more specific and the same union becomes involved in the objectives of the Company.

Clause 11. The Company and the Union recognize that in the normal operations of the plants, personnel are promoted and demoted. These movements will be performed taking into account the corresponding departmental rosters, and the Company and the Union will select the employees based on their competence, efficiency, conduct, attendance, punctuality, and union discipline as reflected in the quarterly feedback system registers.

Clause 13. The Company and the Union will come to an agreement of the changes in personnel from one Plant or location to another when circumstances warrant it. The corresponding provisional wage (compensation) and for the entire duration of the trial period, in which period the company will grant such worker all the facilities for training; once such period has passed, the Company will grant such worker the corresponding base wage without further extension, that is, in a definitive manner.

Clause 21. When the Company needs to transfer personnel from one location to another, the Company and the Union will agree on the arrangement. . . striving to place the worker in a position similar to the previously performed one without affecting the rights of the department's workers, knowing that the worker's wage cannot be detrimentally modified.

Clause 18. The Company and the Union are in agreement that every worker that has been promoted to a higher classification and responsibility, and that such position is considered definitive and permanent, will have a maximum trial period of ninety days, in which such worker will be awarded the corresponding provisional wage (compensation) and for the entire duration of the trial period the former position of the promoted worker can remain vacant for that day. Therefore, the "cover-absenteeism" position, contemplated in the former CCT, is canceled.

Chapter XVI
Fringe Benefits
Clause 69. Those days that correspond to the worker for life insurance in relation to said worker's seniority and which vary between 495 wage days for a year of work, to 1,415 for 44 and 47 years, are included in this clause.

Upon the totality of the workers being liquidated, they will lose their seniority since the new CCT only stipulates life insurance for those workers with one to two years of seniority.

Bilaterality

Chapter III
Clause 4. f) Those candidates who have been selected must pass a medical examination, which must be administered by the Company's doctor.

Clause 4. f) Those candidates who have been selected must pass a medical examination, which must be

In the event that a candidate does not satisfactorily pass said exam, the Union may solicit a written diagnosis by the respective doctor so that such diagnosis can be submitted for a final exam by an official medical institution, obligating both parties to accept this opinion.

h) . . . Those candidates who in the first instance were not accepted by the Company, may be proposed again by the Union.

administered by the Company's physician, which should be satisfactory.

h) . . . Those candidates who in the first instance were not approved by the Company, may be newly proposed for a second exam by the Union. *To give another opportunity to the rejected candidates, a minimum period of six months must pass.*

Chapter VI
Promotion and Personnel Changes
Clause 17. . . . When no assurance exists, either on the Company's part or that of the Union, concerning the worker's competence to perform the vacant position, and if consequently the two parties have not come to an agreement, they jointly will proceed to apply the respective tests previously established by both parties, which must be strictly related to the requirements held by the vacant position; the application . . . must be overseen by the Company and the Union.

Chapter IX
Work, Holidays, and Regular Work Time and Overtime.
Worker's starting time or quitting time is after 11:00 p.m., or before 6:00 a.m. of the following day, either through a regular work day or through overtime, the Company is obligated to cover the workers.

Chapter IX
Work, Quality, and Productivity
In the current CCT, a new chapter has been incorporated which includes the workers in the objectives of the company, as from the establishment of self-control mechanisms assumed as necessary by the Union.

Clause 22. The Union acknowledges the importance of being competitive within the same industrial branch, without allowing such acknowledgment

Clause 31. Changes in shift shall be made invariably in accordance with the practice.

Clause 32. The Company acknowledges the worker's right to develop such worker's duties in a balanced manner during the work day, at a normal work rhythm, which is understood as that performed by an average worker.

It is the Company's obligation to avoid work overloads which are derived from absenteeism, equipment failure or any type of irregularity not caused by the worker.

Clause 33. . . . personnel who work in deferred shifts and as a consequence have to work Saturdays and/or Sundays as part of their official work week, shall receive an additional bonus of 75 percent (seventy-five percent) over the regular Saturday and/or Sunday wage."

Clause 39. When the Company has the need to work complete shifts during either of the two days designated as mandatory rest days (in addition to that which is stipulated in the Federal Labor Law), respective personnel shall receive "a special compensation for work on rest days equal to 14 percent of the income derived from the overtime worked on those shifts."

to implicate the rejection of the legal contractual rights of the workers.

The Company and the Union acknowledge that the involvement and participation of the personnel are the essence of quality and productivity, for which reason they will jointly design and support efforts that encourage individual and collective participation.
In order to promote appropriate communication between the workers and supervisors, the Company and the Union will agree on procedures established in the respective proceedings.

Clause 20. The personnel who work in deferred shifts and as a consequence must work Saturdays and/or Sundays as part of their official work week will receive an additional bonus of 50 percent (fifty percent) over the regular Saturday and/or Sunday wage.

CEL'S LOSS OF AUTONOMY

Chapter III
New Employees and Trial Periods
Clause 4 b). Employment applications will be numbered progressively and will be filled out in duplicate, with a certain amount in the Union's possession and another in that of the Company....Said applications must be signed in approval

Clause 4. b) . . . such applications must be signed in approval by the Labor Secretary of the National Executive Committee.

by the Labor Secretary corresponding to the respective location.

h) The accepted candidate, as well as the Union Representative, shall sign the respective individual work contract before the worker may initiate such worker's duties for the Company.

h) The accepted candidate, as well as the General Secretary, shall sign the respective individual contract before the worker may initiate such worker's duties for the Company, of which a copy will be given to such worker.

Endnotes

1. According to the trade magazine *América Economía*, "the Mexican automobiles..." (sic) the following are among the top ten exporting companies of the Latin American region: General Motors, in fourth place with $2,250 million (3.5 percent less than last year); Chrysler in fifth place with $1,800 (an 18.7 percent increase in relation to last year); . . . the Ford affiliate in Mexico is in [the sixth] 6th place. *La Jornada* August 16, 1993, p. 45.

2. Porter 1990.

3. Arteaga Garcia and Thirión 1993.

4. Gutiérrez 1987; Arteaga and Micheli 1987; and Wilson 1990.

5. For example, the internal report by General Motors de México, *Proceso de Transformación Organizacional (En planta México transformamos el futuro hoy)* s/f., reported that in the mid 1980s, 70 percent of the production cost for the Av. Ejército Nacional plant was generated by suppliers located within the country. This showed the high level of national integration that had been achieved by this plant.

6. Salvo, *Automotriz O'Farrill*, which assembled the brand "Hillman-Minx," in the state of Puebla and "Planta Reo de México," which did the same with "Rambler" and "Toyopet" in the city of Monterrey. The rest of this activity was concentrated in the center of the country. Nevertheless, the participation of both firms can be considered marginal since together their participation included 2.7 percent and 3.8 percent of national sales for 1958 and 1962, respectively.

7. The previously cited study referred to the 70 percent national content, 90 percent of which came from the metropolitan area and is located between 30 minutes to three hours distance. The engines come from the plant of the same company that is located in the city of Toluca, in the state of Mexico. The rest come from outside of the Federal District's urban borders.

8. Tetsuo Abo has developed a model that incorporates 20 characteristics, which he grouped into six categories to analyze the application of the Japanese model of administration and labor organization in the auto industry. These are: 1.) Organization of work, operation, and management. Their components are: system of classification of the workforce, wages, rotation of the work force, training, promotion, and supervision; 2.) Control of the production process: technological process, quality control, and maintenance; 3.) Sense of belonging, including: job security, small group activities, "open office" style, uniformity, socialization, and employee-manager meetings; 4.) Employment situation, related to homogeneity, external rotation rate, and labor union relations; 5.) Local supply; and 6.) Subsidiary companies' relations, decision-making and management styles.

9. As Abo concludes, "One of the principal interests of the Japanese manufacturers in the U.S., who want to maintain the comparative advantages which originate from JM (Japanese Management), is to consider the human factor as a creator of a feeling of involvement (Japanese-style participation), and a the flexibility to adapt to changes. The Japanese companies are probably aggressive in their attempts to reach these human advantages, since the 30,000 parts needed to make an automobile must be assembled by people who must respond to the JM with the highest possible efficiency. In this respect, the factory's environment, particularly defined by the union and by labor relations, is extremely important for the automobile companies" (1994: 339).

10. Kevin Middlebrook focuses on the particular system of industrial relations in Mexico, one of the principal advantages of the enterprises in the automobile industry, which supported the policy of flexibilization and the incorporation of new management strategies.

11. However, there still is no comprehensive analysis of the forms of development of Taylorism-Fordism as a management strategy in the Mexican manufacturing industry. It attempts to identify not only the application of a determined work organization style, but also to what point did management thinking break, rationalize, and take on the production process with a systematic attitude, until it truly became a part of the culture, in order to increase productivity and maintain control over the variable workforce, as other areas of the production process.

12. *El Economista*, November 30, 1993, p. 23. Stated amount is divided by $4,000 million for the terminal industry, and $1,200 million for the auto parts industry.

13. According to the National Auto Parts Industry (INA), an organization that groups together an important part of the sector's companies, this quantity is distributed in the following manner: 1992, $835.1 million; 1993, $849.1 million; 1994, $709.3 million; 1995, $883.8 million; and 1996, $948 million. *El Economista*, November 30, 1993.

14. Another 24.6 percent of the auto parts imported into the U.S. came from Canada.

15. Another 10 percent of assembled vehicle exports went to Central and South America.

16. For a more detailed perspective see A. Arteaga, and J. Micheli, "El nuevo modelo de las relaciones capital-trabajo en la industria automotriz en México," in *Brecha* no. 3, (Spring 1987): 73-86. For a complete comparison of the CCT in DINA, VW, and Ford Hermosillo see: Herrea, Fernando, *Flexibilización contractual en la industria automotriz de México* (Mexico, 1993).

17. A more detailed account is found in *Transformaciones technológicas y relaciones laborales en la industria automotriz*, A. Arteaga, J. Carrillo, and J. Micheli, eds., Work Documents No. 19, Fundación Friedrich Ebert, Mexico, 1989.

18. K. Ishikawa, Que es el control total de calidad? Colombia: Editorial Norma, 1986.

19. The quality cost is determined by the relationship between the cost of quality defects and total sales.

20. Ford's strategy has been analyzed in more detail in A. Artega Garcia, *Reconversión industrial y flexibiliadad en el trabajo en la industria automotriz en México*, 1981-1986, in E. Gutiérrez (coordinator), *Austeridad y reconversión* Siglo XXI Editores and UNAM, 1988). A. Artega Garcia, (Mexico: "Nacido ford, crecido flexible," in Trabajo magazine no. 2 (Spring 1990), and A. Artega Garcia, "Ford: Un largo y sinuoso conflicto," in Graciela Bensusan (coordinator), *Negociación y conflict laboral en México* (Mexico: Friedrich Ebert and FLASCO, 1991).

For background on the Cuautitlán plant, see *Coambios importantes en las instalacioines y proceso en las plantas de ensable and Informe del Subcomité de Fabricación P.A.C.C.,* internal company documents. Please see A. Artega Garcia and J. Carrillo, "Automóvil, hacia la flexibilidad productiva," in *El Cootidiano* no. 21 (Jan.-Feb. 1988).

21.For a more detailed description, see Artega and Carrillo, *Automovil* and Shaiken and Herzenberg. Concerning the plant in Hermosillo, Shaiken and Herzenberg quote the international president of Ford, Donald E. Petersen, "Our stamping and assembly plant in Hermosillo is not only the newest one, it is the most modern one, with our best technology and 'world-class' talent incorporated into its organization and functioning" (p. 10).

22. The "bell to bell" system simply dictates that the workers will have an official work day of eight hours. This leaves out the dead times from the beginning clocked time to quitting time, cancelingwherever possible, the pauses and interruptions, that come from traditional workers' practices.

23. Participación Activa para la Calidad y la Competitividad," Ford-Sitraford, Foundry Plant s/f. Internal company document.

24. Ibid.

25. The daily wage base considered is obtained from the relationship between the distribution of the workers by category and the average wage between the various categories. the comparisons are based on Ford's internal documents, compiled by the labor relations staff, for 1987 contract bargaining. From now on, we will refer to the staff as Ford Staff.

The plants from the first productive core were built between the 1930s and the 1950s. They were dedicated mainly to the final assembly of automobiles. It's important to note that although the Cuautitlán complex belongs to the second productive core, starting the 1960s its wage levels were above average. Since the formation of the national union in this company in 1976, a good part of the gains, including wages, by the workers of the Villa plant were extended also to the workers of Cuautitlán. This did not happen in other companies, due mainly to the fact that the firms with labor contracts were in the second productive core.

26. The third productive core refers to the plants created in the northern states of the country in the 1980s. They supported the export effort for the U.S., Central American, and South American markets.

27. Ford Staff.

28. The compensation factor is the extra cash compensation as a percentage of the base wage.

29. The workers' annual take-home included the annual base wage plus the liable benefits and minus the yearly tax, social security taxes, and untaxed benefits.

References

Arteaga Garcia, Arnulfo. 1991. "Ford: un largo y sinuoso conflicto." In *Negociación y conflicto laboral en México.* G. Bensusan (coord.) Friedrich Ebert y FLACSO, Mexico.

..... 1990. *Nacido Ford, crecido flexible.* In *Trabajo* magazine, no. 2, Spring.

..... 1988. *Reconversión industrial y flexibilidad en el trabajo en la industria automotriz en México, 1981-1986.* In *Austeridad y reconversión.* E. Gutiérrez, (coord.), Siglo XXI Editores and UNAM, Mexico.

Arteaga Garcia, Arnulfo, and J. Carrillo. 1988. *Automóvil, hacia la flexibilidad productiva.* In El Cootidiano, no. 21, Jan.-Feb.

Arteaga Garcia, Arnulfo and Jordy Micheli Thirión, 1993. "La Transición Manufacturera en México." Discussion article for the Social Security and Labor Secretary, Mexico.

..... 1987. *El Nuevo Modelo de las relaciones capital-trabajo en la industria automotriz en México.* Mexico: Brecha.

Arteaga Garcia, Arnulfo, J. Carrillo, and J. Micheli, J. 1989. *Transformaciones Tecnológicas y Relaciones Laborales en la Industria Automotriz.* Work Documents no. 19, Fundación Friedrich Ebert, Mexico.

Gutiérrez E. (Coord.). 1987. *Innovación Tecnológica y Clase Obrera en la Industria Automotriz.* In Reestructuración Productiva y Clase Obrera. Siglo XXI Editores, Mexico.

Herrera, Fernando. 1993. *Flexibilización contractual en la industria automotriz de de México.*

Ishikawa, K. 1986. *Qué es el control total de calidad?* Editorial Norma, Colombia.

Porter, Michael. 1990. *The Competitive Advantage of Nations.* The Free Press: New York.

Tetsuo, Abo. 1994. *Hybrid Factory: The Japanese Production System in the United States.* New York: Oxford University Press.

Wilson, Pérez N. 1990. *Foreign Direct Investment and Industrial Development in Mexico.* Development Centre Studies, OCDE, Paris.

Industrial Relations in the Maquiladora Industry: Management's Search for Participation and Quality

Alfredo Hualde

The Future Of The Maquiladora Industry In The Context Of Nafta

The export-oriented maquiladora industry was a controversial issue in the debate surrounding the North American Free Trade Agreement (NAFTA) and will no doubt remain a matter of discussion in the future. This is so for several reasons: 1) In recent years, employment in the maquiladora industry has counted for a growing share of the Mexican manufacturing labor force.[1] 2) It is likely that low wages in Mexico are attracting foreign investment, thus contributing to unemployment, especially in the United States 3) Maquiladoras are seen as the model of what the Mexican industry will be like in the near future. According to this view, all of Mexican industry would be converted to maquiladora production, spreading all of the ills commonly associated with this industry: low wages, poor labor conditions, environmental degradation, and technological backwardness. This image contrasts sharply with that put forth by NAFTA advocates, who foresee the coming of a new age, signaled by more and better jobs, the upward leveling of wages, and strict regulations concerning the environment and technology transfer (Dornsbusch 1991).

A third position sees NAFTA as a positive agreement, although it foresees a period of adjustment in which the Mexican economy will lose jobs in less competitive sectors and firms. This temporary increase of unemployment would be compensated in the medium term by the creation of new jobs as a result of general growth in the economy. The negative aspects of this scenario have predominated recently because of the 1993 recession, during which unemployment increased substantially in the industrial sector. Even maquiladora growth has been uneven.

On the other hand, speculation on the future of the maquiladora industry is somewhat paradoxical since, at the same time that a large increase of investment in this sector is expected, NAFTA will put an end to the maquiladora as a special legal regime in 2001, when tariffs will be standardized throughout the country. That is, the terms for both imports and exports will be equal and generalized.[2]

Recent studies have described the kinds of technological and organizational processes now occurring in this industry (Carrillo 1989; González-Aréchiga and Ramírez 1990). They have also dealt with prospects for the industry from the perspective of its role in international subcontracting. These studies have concluded that there is not a single kind of maquiladoras. A more detailed picture of the maquiladoras has been drawn, examining such issues as linking economic performance to production methods, the origin of investments, and plant location. These new trends have been associated with what is called "the new maquiladora" or "the post-Fordist maquiladora." (Carrillo 1989; Wilson 1992).

These trends have also been a matter of controversy, and not all of the analyses are optimistic. Some authors maintain that the technological features of this new phase, such as a more intense emphasis on automation, will reduce the number of jobs in relation to units of capital (González-Aréchiga and Ramírez: 1990: 25), and cause some manufacturers to return home. Lack of adequate infrastructure in the border cities is also an obstacle to large investments in this sector.

This essay, however, is concerned with labor conditions and unionism in the maquiladora industry, a field of analysis which has recently become more complex, thereby raising new questions. With respect to wages and labor conditions, the maquiladora industry has traditionally been viewed as the paradigm of cheap labor for exploitation by foreign capital. Some recent studies, however, have uncovered more positive aspects by comparing the evolution of wages and labor conditions in the maquiladora industry with those in the rest of Mexican industry (Carrillo1991). This more positive perception clearly differs from the traditional position, which stresses the existence of a large gap between Mexican, Asian, and North American wages and labor conditions.

Whatever the case, the most convincing argument in favor of maquiladoras is not based on labor conditions but rather on the number of jobs the industry has already generated—about half a million. The future employment potential of this industry remains strong, although not sufficient to meet the demand for employment. Indeed, the maquiladora industry can only create 12 percent of the 1.2 million jobs per year Mexico will need during the current decade (González-Aréchiga and Ramírez 1990: A:29).

The new labor processes have been geared toward the goal of obtaining greater quality in production. The use of new participatory methods such as quality circles and work teams, and the tendency to promote a greater consensus in the workplace, appear to be two new trends in this area (Carrillo1989). Additional data point to the growing number of technicians and engineers being recruited by firms, as well as a tendency for some firms to cooperate with educational institutions in order to expand training of the workforce (Hualde1993b). These studies underscore a perspective that differs in great measure from the common notion that maquiladoras are an unpredictable and temporary industry. They tend to adopt a pragmatic view, taking into account the evolution of the industry during the last thirty years, rather than automatically assuming that maquiladoras are negative phenomena.

However, studies of work organization in the plants have not yielded definite conclusions about the kind of unionism developing in the maquiladoras.[3] On the one hand, some of these processes are relatively recent, so that systematic analyis has not yet been possible.[4] On the other hand, it would be deterministic to assume that changes in the labor process or the automation of labor will automatically bring important changes for union organizations. I would instead argue the opposite: it is the forms of union organization that determine the introduction of certain kinds of work organization under specific conditions. I am not suggesting the existence of a mechanistic relationship between these two elements. However, it is becoming evident that new forms of work organization and, above all, certain participatory aspects of human resource management, are already producing changes in labor relations.[5] This is true not only for the case of the maquiladora industry but for other productive processes as well.

In spite of the new trends mentioned above, the conventional wisdom about maquiladoras remains the same, that is, the notion of an industry that offers disadvantageous labor conditions in comparison to the rest of the national industry. With regard to unionization, the common assumption is that this is one of the weakest sectors. However, it is important to note the following: 1) Data on labor conditions in the maquiladora industry are new and need to be verified by several methods.[6] 2) There are no comparative studies on the maquiladora industry and the rest of national industry, especially small industries. 3) The conventional wisdom on non-maquiladora unionism is probably outdated.

This essay focuses on labor relations by considering the main features of maquiladora unionism and by noting differences between diverse union strategies. I will also consider those features of the labor process and of management strategies that influence industrial relations, especially in nonunionized plants. This last aspect has yet not been analyzed in a systematic way. In my view the central question is how human resource management is performed in nonunionized plants, and whether or not consensus on quality production is reached.

Labor Relations in the Maquiladora Industry

As many studies have pointed out, labor relations in the maquiladora industry have distinctive features with respect to labor relations in the rest of Mexican industry. In addition, maquiladora unions along the northern border display different tendencies depending on the particular labor organization with which they are affiliated. Normally, each of the major labor confederations exercises some hegemony over a particular territory. As a result, each of the areas present certain kind of union practices in accordance with the particular organization that predominates in the region (Hualde 1993a). While it should be mentioned that the maquiladora industry is neither non-unionized nor free from labor claims, my concern is not to verify affiliation, but rather to show the way in which union action is deployed, since in Mexico the presence of a union does not necessarily mean an active and democratic union life.

As I mentioned above, differences in union courses of action are largely due to the labor central organization to which a union is affiliated and to the region in which it is located. The "functional-regressive" or "subordinate" unionism of the Confederación Regional de Obreros Mexicanos (CROM) in Tijuana is far different from the traditional unionism of the Confederación de Trabajadores de México (CTM) in Matamoros. Several studies have already discussed these differences, so I will limit my discussion to their relationship to NAFTA.[7]

Traditional unionism in the maquiladora industry does not differ so much from the unionism that the CTM habitually practices. Its ability to offer certain advantages to workers—better wages and fringe benefits—comes from a political pact with local, regional, and national political forces. To put it more plainly, the union maintains control over workers, thus guaranteeing "social peace" in exchange for these advantages. However, the stability this pact has provided to cities such as Matamoros, on the eastern end of the border, is vulnerable to political developments, such as leadership turnover or changes in overall political strategy, that affect the CTM nationally.[8] This kind of unionism displays the characteristic features of authoritarianism, caudillismo, and patronage, and advances basic union demands such as stable jobs and acceptable labor conditions. Additionally, in Matamoros the CTM has been able to secure the highest wages in the maquiladora industry. Some authors maintain that this kind of union power could begin to diminish as maquiladoras attempt to move toward greater workplace flexibility.[9]

Another kind of unionism could be called "subordinate" or "functional-regressive" unionism since it often accepts labor conditions that are worse than those established in previous labor contracts, or even lower than the minimum standards established by Federal Labor Law. Lack of union activity inside the plants is another of its basic features. This kind of unionism is most commonly found in Tijuana, and has become stronger during the 1980s. Previously, the active presence of other labor organizations used to provoke tension in the city. The CROM's growing hegemony, however, paved the way for a union strategy that favored increased private capital investment. In this kind of unionism labor contracts are often not renewed and the right to set working conditions and determine layoffs is frequently ceded to management.[10]

Whatever the orientation of unions, their affiliates are predominantly young and female, of rural origin, and often with little or no manufacturing experience. In recent years, however, a growing number of male workers has been noted, complicating the sociodemographic profiles of these unions. The biological reproductive cycle of women, as well as the inexperience of the young labor force, account in part for the weakness of unionism in the industry.

We also need to look at *regional labor markets*, in particular the fact that many workers have a background as employees in commerce and services. Some of the labor markets of the border region appear to be "socially flexible" (Contreras 1990) since they offer varied employment opportunities suitable for an unskilled or relatively skilled labor force. The high labor turnover rates in the maquiladora industry are likely due to a workers' sense of their jobs as temporary.[11] In some plants, however, service (three to four years in some cases) has begun to stabilize. In this way, "careers" could be developing in the plants' internal labor markets.[12]

This factor helps us begin to understand the fact that both the CTM and the CROM's tactics are more succesful in the border region than in the rest of the country. We can assume in this sense that the hegemony of the CTM in Matamoros is due to its leadership's political skill in maintaining its power in a heavily unionized region, whereas in Tijuana conflicts between unions, as well as the isolation of labor organizations from local political forces, have given rise to the kind of spurious unionism we have already mentioned (Quintero 1990). These factors and historical circumstances also help us to confirm that unions in this region, especially those labeled "subordinate" or "functional-regressive," have traditionally coincided with the acceptance of "outlaw" labor contracts that contain disadvantageous clauses for workers.[13]

With respect to the new trends in labor relations, it has been said that unionism in the maquiladora industry is already flexible—with the possible exception of the kind of unionism found in Matamoros. Fifteen years ago, this trend toward flexibility was unforeseen. Today, flexible methods have been adopted by the largest Mexican manufacturing firms in spite of worker resistance and labor conflicts. In fact, flexibility is now in place in those industries where labor conditions seemed almost impossible to change only a few years ago. In view of this trend, we can suggest that an at least partial convergence between border and non-border flexibility is now taking place. In this case, we should see a more flexible and generally homogeneous kind of unionism in the future, although its specific manifestations could vary according to conditions in particular sectors and firms.

Less is known about nonunionized plants. Some data suggest the presence of a paradoxical phenomenon: the flourishing of improved labor conditions in nonunionized plants rather than in unionized ones, especially in the automotive parts industry (Carrillo and Hualde 1990). The reason for this is that these firms improve labor conditions in order to avoid the presence of unions in the plants.

Labor relations in nonunionized plants appear to be quite varied and depend on management's view of the potential of the workforce. In some cases, high-quality standards have been achieved by the maquiladora industry. The introduction of techniques such as statistical process control (SPC) provides one example. In spite of the assumption that maquiladora products can be assembled with little or no margin of error by unskilled workers, there are some cases of cross-training aimed at training the workforce in all of the operations in the plant. In addition, there seems to be a growing interest in some firms to cooperate with educational institutions to provide technical training to workers. This early trend appears to support the goal of creating a stable core of workers, or at least to reduce absenteeism by varying the tasks of some employees. The introduction of intensive human relations training programs, the creation of work teams, and the development of professional management staffs, all suggest the appearance of new concepts in labor relations that are far different from the well-known model based on authority and tight control.[14]

I am not suggesting, of course, that the maquiladora industry has become a kind of paradise for the flourishing of democracy and the upgrading of labor force skills. I am simply pointing out, on the basis of field work done in Tijuana and Ciudad Juárez, that some firms are now concerned with fostering labor environments that can increase workers' commitment to their jobs.

These new trends are supported by several management strategies. Some of these underscore the need for joint action between firms and workers in defining the content of labor operations; others recommend limiting participation of workers to marginal issues. Other strategies support the idea that workers should participate in decision making in the administration of firms.[15] Successful implementation of some of these strategies depends on the quantity and quality of information that workers possess, as well as management and labor culture, and the types of unionism present in the regions where plants operate.

In some maquiladoras a controlled and limited participation by workers is now being promoted. The flow of information is still restricted, in part due to a lack of interest by workers. However, some human relations departments are now trying to improve communication between levels. Wage increases are largely blocked, although the introduction of new job categories suggests the emergence of internal labor markets. Awards, parties (dancing and social meetings), and sporting facilities round out the new management techniques.

These methods do not prevent—although they can lessen—high turnover, a phenomenon largely due to legal dispositions that do not guarantee stability in employment. Turnover in this context has a dual consequence. On the one hand, it reflects worker resistance when faced with poor labor conditions, including health risks.[16] Turnover is in this sense negative for plants that demand high-skilled labor. However, during periods of reduced production, high turnover—along with cheap labor contracts—is a key advantage for firms.

These considerations indicate one possible way to link labor relations to both the union movement and firm strategies. To sum up, five issues are key and bear further study: 1) Maquiladora strategies and management culture; 2) labor organizations' strategies; 3) the tradition of unionism in the border region; 4) features of the labor force; and 5) regional labor markets.

After Nafta: The Future of Maquiladora Labor Relations

On the basis of the situation outlined, we can predict that important changes in maquiladora unionism will not arise from an external framework such as the NAFTA. However, some external agreements, such as those contained in the labor side accord, could influence labor conditions in the plants. The maquiladora industry will be exposed to external scrutiny, and perhaps in this way labor conditions could improve incrementally. Though quick solutions are not expected to occur, political pressure exercised by citizens' movements on both sides of the border can also produce advances in this area.

From a different perspective, requirements of quality and more complex technological processes in a competitive globalized environment could encourage investment in training and elementary education in order to develop a quality labor force. This would be an unequivocal sign of long-term commitment to the border plants and one way to substantially decrease turnover. Today, with new human resources techniques, some worker participation in day-to-day operations can be seen. But we still cannot find in the maquiladora plants what we could call a "career" for workers on the line, although the availability of professional careers could increase for technicians and especially for engineers and managers.

The development of NAFTA will bring new challenges and opportunities in the future because of the expected increase in foreign investment and its geographic dispersion. Issues related to labor markets, skilling and deskilling of the labor force, union strategies and changes in unionism, and new topics in collective bargaining will be some of the key issues that all of the actors involved will face.

Endnotes

1. Recent figures from the National Statistics Institute (INEGI) estimated that more than 540,000 workers were employed in 1993 in the maquiladora industry: 170,000 in Chihuahua, 107,000 in Baja California, and 93,905 in Tamaulipas. See INEGI, 1993.

2. The Border Industrialization Program (BIP), dating from 1965, established a special tariff for all of the foreign commercial transactions on the northern border region. This program was designed to attract foreign investment for export-oriented assembly plants. In 1971 legislation was established in order to allow the establishment of maquiladoras south of the border region. At the beginning of the BIP, all maquiladora products had to be exported. From 1983 to 1989, selected maquiladoras were allowed to sell a maximum of 20 percent of production within the country on condition that products contain at least 15 percent of national content, and that they not compete directly against Mexican products, among other conditions. By April 1988, only fifteen of thirteen-hundred maquiladoras had been authorized to sell in the Mexican market.

   With regard to ownership rules, foreign capital in maquiladoras was originally limited to 49 percent. From 1971 on, ownership was allowed to be 100 percent foreign.

   In 1989, the Mexican government set out new regulations on the establishment of plants. Regulations for trade among maquiladoras and between maquiladoras and non-maquiladora industries were simplified. Maquiladoras were also allowed to sell within the country a maximum of 50 percent of their value added out of the annual value of their total exports.

   As Mexican enterprises, maquiladoras are subject to the same tax regulations as the rest of Mexican business. Employer obligations include fees to Infonavit (the government worker housing agency) and to social security. On legal aspects, see Davis 1985 and U.S. Department of Labor 1990.

3. Cirila Quintero has distinguished several kinds of perceptions by workers, but she does not analyze specific productive processes.

4. Plant managers say they have introduced such methods as kaizen, quality circles, statistical controls, and just-in-time inventories. We do not know, however, how these techniques actually operate, and what kinds of consequences they have brought for both technicians and workers.

5. A point to investigate is the possibility that changes in labor relations occur without significant changes in the unions.

6. The *"Encuesta sobre mercados de trabajo"* (Survey on Labor Markets), the largest survey to date, includes data only from management. It would be useful to have a parallel survey from workers comparison. Analysis and data are summarized in Carrillo, coord. 1993.

7. On this aspect, see Quintero 1990 and Carrillo and Hualde 1990.

8. The clearest example was the imprisonment of Agapito González Cavazos, the union boss in Matamoros, in 1991.

9. See Edward Williams and John T. Passé-Smith, "The Unionization of the Maquiladora Industry: The Tamaulipan Case in National Context," Institute for Regional Studies of the Californias, San Diego State University, 1992, p. 33.

10. See María Eugenia De la O and Cirila Quintero: "Sindicalismo y contratación colectiva en las maquiladoras fronterizas. Los casos de Tijuana, Ciudad Juárez y Matamoros." In *Frontera Norte* 8 (July-December 1992).

11. We would qualify our statement by saying that we have detected some cases of workers who have had five or six jobs in maquiladoras throughout their labor careers.

12. In recent fieldwork done in Tijuana we could find a few women who have been working for fourteen or fifteen years in the same maquiladora. Those interviewed were single or divorced and in all cases took care of children or elderly parents. They worked as supervisors who earned a slightly better wage than workers on the assembly line.

13. See the detailed and illuminating analysis by Mónica Claire Gambrill "Sindicalismo en las maquiladoras de Tijuana: regresión en las prestaciones sociales." In *Reestructuración industrial: Maquiladoras en la frontera México-Estados Unidos.* Jorge Carrillo, ed. México: CNCA-COLEF, 1986.

14. On sophisticated management of human resources, see Carrillo and Hernández, 1985.

15. See Marino Regini, (1992): "Los empresarios frente al problema del consenso," **Sociología del Trabajo** 16, (Madrid).

16. Though some hazardouz chemicals have been identified, systematic research on this issue is only now beginning. An environmental approach can be seen in Sánchez 1990.

References

Arrikath, S. 1994. *Maquiladora Industry Outlook 1994-1998*. El Paso, Texas: CIEMEX/WEFA.

Carrillo, Jorge. 1989. "Calidad con consenso: asociación factible? *Frontera Norte* 2 (julio-deciembre).

-------. 1991. "Maquiladoras ¿para quiénes?" *El Nacional*, 107, May 23.

Carrillo, Jorge, coord. 1993. Condiciones de empleo y capacitación en las maquiladoras de exportación en México. El Colegio de la Frontera Norte/Secretaría del Trabajo y Previsión Social.

Carrillo, Jorge and Alberto Hernández. 1985. *Mujeres en la industria maquiladora.* México.

Carrillo, Jorge, and Alfredo Hualde. 1990. "Maquiladoras: la restructuración industrial y el impacto sindical." In Graciela Bensusán Areous and Samuel León, coord. Negociación y conflicto laboral en México.

Contreras, Oscar. 1990. "Relaciones sociales de trabajo en la industria maquiladora; esbozo de un marco conceptual." Paper presented at the symposium "Estructura y perspectivas de la frontera," COLEF, Tijuana.

Davis, L. R. 1985. *Industria maquiladora y subsidiarias de co-inversión. Régimen jurídico y corporativo*. Cárdenas, Editor.

Dornbusch, Rudiger. 1991. *U.S.-Mexico Free Trade: Good Jobs at Good Wages. Testimony before the Subcommittee on Labor-Management Relations and Employment Opportunities*, Committee on Education and Labor, U.S. House of Representatives, April 30.

Domínguez, L., and F. Brown. 1990. "Nuevas tecnologías en la industria maquiladora." In *Subcontratación y empresas transnacionales*, Bernardo González-Aréchiga and José Carlos Ramírez. México: COLEF/Fundación Friedrich Ebert.

Fernández-Kelly, Maria Patricia. 1983. *For We Are Sold, I and My People: Women and Industry on Mexico's Northern Frontier*. Albany: State University of New York Press.

Gambrill, Monica C. 1986. "Sindicalismo en las maquiladoras de Tijuana." In *Restructuración industrial: Maquiladoras en la frontera norte México-Estados Unidos*, edited by Jorge Carillo. Mexico: CNCA-COLEF.

González-Aréchiga, Bernardo and R. Barajas, compilers. 1989. *Las maquiladoras: Ajuste estructural y desarrollo regional*. Mexico: Fundación Friedrich Ebert/COLEF.

216

González-Aréchiga, Bernardo and José Carlos Ramírez, compilers. 1990. Subcontratación y empresas transnacionales. México: COLEF/Fundación Friedrich Ebert.

Hualde, Alfredo. 1993a. "Sindicatos y tratado de libre comercio: de la flexibilidad en la maquiladora a la regulación del mercado de trabajo trinacional." In Sindicalismo, relaciones laborales y libre comercio, AlejandroCovarrubias and Vicente Solís, coordinators. Mexico: El Colegio de Sonora.

..... 1993b. "Mercado de Trabajo y formación de recursos humanos en la industria electrónica maquiladora de Tijuana y Ciudad Juárez: su vinculación con las instituciones educativas técnicas deformación profesional." Mimeo.

INEGI. 1993. Industria maquiladora de exportación. México: INEGI.

Mertens, L., and L. Palomares. 1986. "El surgimiento de un nuevo tipo de trabajador en la industria de alta tecnología: el caso de la electrónica." In Testimonios de la crisis, Esthela Gutiérrez Garza, ed. (México: Siglo XXI), vol. 2.

Montalvo, Carolos. 1992. "Costo ombiental del crecimiento industrial: el caso de la maquiladora eléctrica en Tijuana, B.C." Documents de trabajo 44 (Mexico: Fundación Friedrich Ebert).

Quintero, Cirila. 1990. La sindicalización en las maquiladoras tijuanenses. México: Consejo Nacional para la Cultura y las Artes.

Ramírez, José Carlos, and Bernardo González-Aréchiga. 1989. "Los efectos de la competencia internacional en el funcionamiento de la industria maquiladora de exportación en México." Frontera Norte 1, no. 2 (July-December).

Sánchez, R. 1990. "Otra manera de ver la maquiladora: riesgos en el medio ambiente y en la salud." In Subcontratación y empresas transnacionales, Bernardo González-Aréchiga and José Carlos Ramírez, (México: COLEF/Fundación Friedrich Ebert).

Stillman, D. 1991. "Probable Economic Effect on U.S. Industries and Consumers of the Free Trade Agreement netween the United States and Mexico." Statement before the International Trade Commission.

Tiano, Susan. 1990. "La composición de la fuerza laboral y los estereotipos sexuales en la industria maquiladora." Frontera Norte 157-158, no. 3 (January-June).

U.S. Department of Labor. Bureau of International Labor Affairs. 1990. Workers Rights in Export Processing Zones. Report Sumitted to Congress under the Omnibus Trade and Competitiveness Act of 1988. August, vol. 134.

U.S International Trade Commission. 1991. The Likely Impact on the United States of a Free Trade Agreement with Mexico. USICT Publication 2353. February.

Wilson, Patricia. 1992. *Exports and Local Development. Mexico's New Maquiladoras.* Austin: University of Texas Press.

The Effects on Labor of the Restructuring of Petróleos Mexicanos: 1989-1993

Rafael Loyola Díaz

and

Liliana Martínez Pérez

Until the early 1980s, the Mexican model for development was based on nationalistic economic protectionism, on the state's central and guiding role in the economy, and on political authoritarianism of an exclusive and virtually one-party nature. A further characteristic of this model, and one significant for this analysis, was corporative unionism. This unionism benefited from public policies and from legislation (still in force) that provided for the protection of workers and vested powers in the state to achieve these goals.

This model was very evident in the petroleum sector. From the year 1938, when the industry was expropriated and the resource was nationalized, this model was assiduously applied. In this way, the development of the petroleum sector was guided by public policies. The petroleum sector included exploration, production to marketing, and refinery operations. Petroleum products served as industrial raw materials—basic petrochemicals. These products had to be stored, distributed, and sold. State protection and intervention extended to oil reserves. The Regulatory Law of Constitutional Article 27 stipulated that oil reserves were to be processed through Petróleos Mexicanos, by subsidiary companies or state-held companies "consisting entirely of Mexicans."[1]

This essay focuses on the labor policies and unionism that prevailed in the petroleum sector. The purpose of this essay is to describe the effects of economic restructuring in the petroleum industry on labor and labor relations. The petroleum industry was one of the sectors most protected by the development model prevalent in Mexico up until the early 1980s. After this point a restructuring policy was applied in Petróleos Mexicanos (PEMEX), a policy guided by a new economic policy. This policy entailed the withdrawal of the state from economic activities, the opening to private investors of sectors still dominated by public administration, the relaxation of norms and controls that limited the participation of foreign companies and capital, and integration into international markets.

We first present a brief outline of the labor relations and type of unionism that prevailed in the petroleum sector from 1947 until 1989, when they were abruptly dismantled. This includes a brief account of the political process that made the restructing of PEMEX possible. An analysis of the changes affected in the collective labor contracts (CLC) follows. In addition, we describe the results of the new labor policy in terms of personnel adjustment, reductions in the unionized workforce, and company production cost savings achieved through decreases in wage and salary expenses.

The Corporative, Patrimonial, and Protectionist Union Model

The formation of the traditional model of labor relations in the petroleum industry began in 1947 when the newly elected government of Miguel Alemán Valdez (1946-52) decided to dispose of the petroleum union's executive committee.[2] The traditional model was defined by the following: security of employment; a broad spectrum of social security benefits including medical services, education, housing, recreation centers, and assistance in basic consumer goods; rights to employment, whose prerogatives extended to include inheritance of a job and, as a result, a predominance of family connections as a source of labor recruitment; mechanisms for continual promotion where advancement was determined primarily by length of service; limitations on transfers to other sectors within the petroleum industry; and significant union involvement in the organization of work processes and recruitment of personnel, with the former leading to limited mobility of personnel and equipment. The union had even gained the right to assign personnel to contractor companies performing work for the public company.

Furthermore, through labor contracts or through informal agreements with the company, the union developed a patrimonial culture as a result of the participation granted to it as co-beneficiary of the exploitation of oil. For the same reason, for years the union enjoyed rights to 2 percent of the overall value of the work undertaken by contractors for PEMEX (clause 36 of the CLC). Contractors' personnel provided the union with dues, free labor in the union's numerous production units, and political support for the union's leadership.[3]

Since 1947 the union has also benefited from the right to participate as a contractor to the petroleum industry. From 1977 onward, in the midst of the petroleum boom, the unioin increased its income by reserving for itself 40 percent of the drilling work, as well as the right to subcontract and supply workers to the private drilling companies. The latter right was obtained in exchange for permitting the evasion of clause 1 of the CLC that reserved this type of work for the company.[4] In the same way, the union procured direct contributions from the company to cover expenses for social construction, and union activities and administration. The union also obtained a considerable number of board members and countless economic sinecures for its leaders.[5]

Similarly, union intervention in the work process allowed it to influence the number and duties of nonunion workers. The union's coproprietorial and co-beneficiary role in the exploitation of oil led it to construct its own economic complex and economic interests, which ran parallel to its organizational functions. Finally, the petroleum union acquired a privileged position in the political power structure, both in official union organizations and in the official party. This enabled the union to occupy popularly elected posts, which ranged from the control of municipal presidencies and seats in the chamber of deputies, to seats in the senate of the Republic.

This labor relations system strengthened the union and gave it considerable autonomy with respect to the company and the state. At the same time, this system sustained the influence of a group of union leaders—those of the Ciudad Madero, Tamaulipas zone—within the union. But, this system also placed a considerable burden on the company's operational costs by providing so many benefits to the union. The benefits came either through the union's contractual role, through the share the union received of the value of the works undertaken by third parties for the public company, or through the advantages that accrued to the union from its position as cobeneficiary in the exploitation of crude oil.

For the company, the basic issue that emerged was how to gradually relax the union's controls. Management's claims for a reassertion of its control was strengthened by the perceived strategic importance of the industry. The union had lost sight of its union-related responsibilities in order to dedicate itself entirely to the pillaging of the company, at the same time, disregarding the productivity and profitability of the industry because its energies were directed toward filling its coffers. It did this through the abuse of union rights in the areas of construction work, drilling, transport, support, and maintenance services within the industry.

In this situation lay the crux of the labor problem in PEMEX. These problems explain the efforts that started with the government of Miguel de la Madrid (1982-88) to correct problems in the company, and the radical adjustment policies applied since the beginning of the government of Carlos Salinas de Gortari.

The Breakup of Patrimonial Unionism

After the weak attempts of Miguel de la Madrid's government to incorporate the petroleum sector into the programs of administrative and economic reorganization, the government of Carlos Salinas de Gortari (1988-94) was inaugurated with the intention of eliminating the political problems posed by the leadership of the petroleum union. The government's objectives included modifying the collective contract in those areas that obstructed the modernization and productivity of the petroleum company and laying the foundation for the definition of a new policy within the petroleum sector. The new petroleum labor policy was related to the deepening of economic liberalism throughout the economy. The government's economic policy was later linked to the project for national integration into international markets, in particular the North American market.

The petroleum union, its leadership and the contractual model established in Pemex were perceived as the major obstacles to the government's agenda. The union had blocked the radical restructuring policy, the industry's reorganization, and the redefinition of the regulatory criteria and principles that had been attempted from the time of de la Madrid's administration. As a result, the police and military actions carried out by Salinas's administration against petroleum leaders in January 1989 had legitimacy within various social groups.[6] The actions were perceived to be the beginning of the process of the industry's total reorganization. From then on the workers and the union lost their oppositional force in the face of the rationalizing and modernizing policies adopted by the petroleum industry and the government. The latter, in turn, increased their authority and responsibility within the industry.

On February 2, 1989, Sebastián Guzmán Cabrera took over the leadership of the petroleum union through a maneuver by the secretary of the government (Secretaria de Gobernación). From the beginning of his term, the new petroleum leader defended a policy of complete cooperation with President Salinas de Gortari's government, and full support for the petroleum management's restructuring. From this moment on, the petroleum union's leadership were dedicated to restricting the union's activities to strictly labor-related matters in its relations with the company. In addition, they wanted to eradicate those procedures and extracontractual relations that allowed union leaders to take unfair advantage of casual laborers and to exert pressure on company directors. The union was excluded from management activities and supported all of the reformist and modernizing initiatives proposed by the petroleum administration.

Pemex's labor policies over the last five years have allowed the company largely to dismantle the patrimonialist union model that had existed prior to 1989. This was done through the mobilization, retirement, or sacking of those high- and medium-level individuals linked to "quinismo," by the removal of sinecures for the union, and through the creation of new roles and functions for both the union and the company made explicit in collective labor contracts.[7]

The Restructuring of PEMEX through the CLCs

Despite dissatisfaction among the ranks of labor with the new petroleum union, the government was able to impose policies favoring management's interests, though not without conflicts. An analysis of the last three CLCs signed by the Union of Petroleum Workers of the Mexican Republic (STPRM) and PEMEX demonstrates the new resrictions imposed on the union through governmental and management policies.

The CLC that controlled labor relations between 1989 and 1991 favored a policy of rationalization, efficiency, and cost-reduction through the following mechanisms: the exclusion of the union from fixed contracting, the transfer of some previously union work to nonunion workers, an increase in the mobility of personnel and equipment, and the removal of those contractual clauses that had channeled economic resources to the union. On the basis of these agreements, the company dismissed temporary workers or transferred them to permanent posts (728 posts in 1990).[8] Management also increased its capacity to transfer any worker with managerial, supervision, control or supervisory functions to the category of nonunion employee (between July and August 1989, 9,896 union posts were transferred to nonunion status).[9] Management undertook an ambitious program of redundancies, retirement, and the elimination of posts (see Table 1); thus creating the conditions necessary to structurally reorganize the industry without contractual obstacles.[10]

The CLC in force from August 1991 to July 20, 1993, went even further by enabling the company to increase and consolidate its aspirations to achieve a broad margin of freedom within which to control the industry. The new contractual document canceled the percentage limit of nonunion employees in the company, allowing the transfer of 5,156 union posts to nonunion status during July and August 1991, and the regrouping of 2,055 positions in the same period).[11] The new contract provided the company with the freedom to relocate unionized workers throughout the Mexican Republic.[12] It simplified the procedures for redundancy and early retirement and introduced the possibility of using a drop in job category as a procedure for facilitating the reorganization of the industry and for pressuring people to resign and to take early retirement. With respect to the criteria for contracting personnel and promotion procedures, the company stipulated mechanisms for qualification through competition. It added the criterion of working conduct to that of seniority and aptitude. Working conduct was measured through an evaluation of the discipline, attendance, interest and initiatives, and cooperation demonstrated by workers in their responsibilities toward the company.[13]

The 1991-93 contract also eliminated the union's ability to intervene with contractors to employ its members. This action reduced the union's influence to the level of suggestions, and allowed the company to be free to make recourse to the services of third parties. For this purpose, in line with Clause 34 of the CLC "the employer may, by choice, effect through direct administration or through free contract, those works and services which are not specified in Clause 1 of this Contract, such as exploration and drilling work, including all related work and services; construction work in general. . . ; maintenance in general. . . ; likewise, any extraordinary maintenance tasks within the industry. . . ; and those of distribution and transport.[14]

Another of the powers granted to the petroleum company in the 1991-93 CLC was the right to "issue instructions and orders for the execution and development of all of the Industry's works,"[15] as well as the legal admission that "the employer will have wide powers for the modernization of its plants and the simplification of working systems or methods which might allow an effective increase in productivity."[16] In relation to this latter point and in line with the petróleos mexicanos master plan for productivity (Plan Maestro de Productividad de Petróleos Mexicanos), the parties agreed to the creation of the Joint National Commission for Wage Scales and Promotions (Comisión Nacional Mixta de Escalafones y Ascensos) and the Joint National Commission for Productivity (Comisión Nacional Mixta de Productividad), whose purpose was to standardize the procedures for entry and promotion of personnel, as well as to promote productivity increases through technological means and personnel training.[17]

Finally, the payment to the union of 2 percent of the value of all works carried out by third parties was canceled, along with the company's obligation to give over all unclaimed salaries to the union.[18] Furthermore, with the approval of the new Organic Law for Petróleos Mexicanos (Ley Orgánica de Petróleos Mexicanas) in July 1992, the process of company restructuring intensified. This resulted in, among other fundamental changes, the disappearance of the "Section for Projects and Construction of Works," an area from which the union had culled the greater part of its extracontractual income.

The CLC signed on July 31, 1993, which will remain in force until August 1995, appears to provide the company with even greater freedom to make structural and modernizing decisions, such as is the case with the "Regulation for Wage Scales and Promotions." This regulation establishes that each subsidiary body is responsible for setting corresponding wage scales in those work centers that fall within its domain.[19] Furthermore, the value of the criterion of "seniority" is significantly reduced relative to the criteria of "aptitude" and "working conduct" in the consideration for promotions. Moreover, seniority rights with regard to retirement, labor litigation, dismissal, or readjustment or elimination of posts, are now limited to permanent workers rather than to unionized workers in the general sense established by the previous CLC.[20]

With respect to the reduction of posts and the elimination of departments, the employer's powers to adapt the organization and simplify working methods completely independent of the views of the union have been established. The employer is now free to provide new placements, wherever possible, to any permanent workers and not necessarily to union members. This pattern is repeated in relation to compensation for category demotion.[21] Limiting the number of those who will benefit from the CLC to permanent unionized workers is a new characteristic of the labor policy. It weakens the union administration's areas of activity and reduces the public company's expenditures on social benefits.

In addition, the National Joint Commission for Productivity, created in 1991, is adapting to the new structure of Petróleos Mexicanos and its subsidiary bodies. It is now known as the National Joint Commission for Quality and Productivity and is made up of the joint groups for quality and productivity, that exist in each subsidiary body and in Pemex, and whose functions for stimulating training and implementing rationalizing methods and techniques are maintained.[22]

To summarize, an analysis of the successive transformations of the collective labor contracts signed by the Union of Petroleum Workers of the Mexican Republic and Petróleos Mexicanos confirms that a radical change has occurred in the model for company-union relations in Pemex since 1989. This new model, in contrast to what had been established over previous years, this new model has two basic characteristics. The first concerns efforts to strengthen and make more independent the decision-making powers of management in relation to the union on matters of labor policy and working conditions. The second concerns the collaborative role now played by the union toward management proposals, particularly those that concern reductions in and relocations of petroleum workers as directed by the modernization and productivity plans of PEMEX officials. The reformulation of the roles played by the company and union have not only weakened the latter's presence within labor policy, but has also reduced the union's capacity to represent workers in the new management bodies resulting from the reorganization of the industry according to the law approved in July 1992.[23]

These transformations have permitted the establishment of a labor policy that displays the following tendencies: (a) Consolidation of management's role as the body responsible for productive control, both in matters related to the organization of work and to the behavior of the work force. This includes adjustments in personnel; (b) Exclusion of the union as co-beneficiary in the industry and reduction in its powers and control; (c) A drastic reduction in the income and labor privileges of the petroleum workers, together with termination of their traditional employment security; (d) The rupture of family and union routes of entry into the company and of seniority as a criterion for continuous promotion; (e) Systematic decreases in Pemex's workforce through retirement, liquidations, or the elimination of posts; (f) Accelerated increases in the number of nonunion workers; and (g) Reductions in the number of workers who benefit from the CLC through its restriction to cover only permanently employed union members. All in all, these changes have weakened the union's influence and negotiating capacity and have favored a management policy of cost reduction and productivity increase.

Some Results of the New Labor Model

One of the fundamental effects of Pemex's policy of restructuring and modernization has been the systematic reduction in the size of the workforce over the last five years. Accurate figures on size of between 1988 and 1993 are difficult to obtain in part due to the manipulation of these figures by the company, press, union officials, and opposition leaders. The data included in Table 2 come from primary and secondary sources that have dealt with this topic from 1988 to August 1993. Although the figures are not perfect, they do provide an approximation of the cuts in personnel that have occurred in recent years.

The various sources indicate that, from 1989 to 1993, the workforce was reduced by between 42.8 percent and 50 percent.[24] Some sources indicate that at the present time the company has around 120,000 workers, compared to estimates of a 1989 base employment of 240,000.[25] A high-placed company official who requested anonymity, stated "that the intention is to concentrate the workforce still further, which would bring the current administration down to only 50,000 permanent and nonunion workers."[26] If this turns out to be the case, then PEMEX would have, by 1994, a workforce close to that of 1958, when it had 45,352 permanent and temporary employees, including those involved in building construction, a department that does not exist today.[27]

Another effect on labor of the new policies in the petroleum sector has been a reduction in salary outlays. An analysis of salary costs compared to costs budgeted shows that according to the "Reports to the Administration Board of PEMEX" (see Table 3), from 1989 to 1992, less money was actually paid than was budgeted.

These salary savings, in addition to the personnel readjustments and intensification of labor, achieved a 20 to 30 percent reduction in production cost per barrel, according to the statement of Gustavo Varela, Subdirector of Administration and Finances of the subsidiary company Pemex-Exploración, at the beginning of August 1993.[28]

Finally a significant number of unionized workers have been transferred to nonunion status (15,052 in the CLCs for 1989 and 1991, according to the incomplete Reports to the Administrative Board, Informes al Consejo de Administración). Pemex has been reorganized into four large subsidiary companies, a process that has led to the "federalization" of labor-management contractual relations. The leader of the MNP, Hebraicaz Vásquez, claims that during 1993 nonunion workers have increased by 300 percent.[29] The transfers have allowed the company to impose greater productivity demands on their personnel and achieve reductions in costs through reductions in labor benefits.

Conclusion

The state-owned petroleum company has entered into a state of profound transformation, which should lead it toward a very different configuration than that displayed by the subsidiary, protectionist, supportive, and patrimonial model. The new petroleum company is likely to be characterized by the dominance of corporate administration and the freedom to adjust the dimensions of the industry without being blocked by labor obstacles. Furthermore, the new company will have the power to contract personnel and impose managerial programs concerning promotion and productivity. This new model has been accompanied by the union's exclusion from the organization of work and by the elimination of the union as a beneficiary in the exploitation of oil. The union no longer exercises significant control over the company.

Two further tendencies, still in the process of consolidation, should be noted. The first relates to a form of "federalization" of labor relations which has arisen from the weakening of the previously centralized Petróleos Mexicanos in favor of four subsidiary companies. This has brought a weakening of the union's centralized structure and role. In addition, this federalization has opened the door to union sectors defined by each one of the corporate sections, which could determine, with a considerable level of autonomy, their own contractual conditions. The second tendency concerns the possible re-establishment of a close relationship between petroleum officials and union leaders. Such a relationship may reappear because there are still officials within the company who benefit from the patrimonial system, as well as union leaders who are loyal to "quinismo." Among the latter are Sebastián Guzmán Cabrera, one of the leaders who emerged from the shelter of the Ciudad Madero leadership, as did his current substitute, Carlos Romero Deschamps, who has always been identified as the last of Joaquín Hernández Galicia's men. As a result, rumors flourish within the public company concerning the possible emergence of new riches and new partnerships.

In brief, it is too early to tell whether the federal government can successfully transfer PEMEX and establish efficient, productive, and honorable structures. After the destruction of the old leadership of the petroleum sector in 1989, the state no longer has anyone else to blame for its own inefficiency.

Table 1

Retirements, Dismissals, and Cancellations in Petróleos Mexicanos
(1988-1992)

Year	Jan.-Feb.	Mar.-Apr.	May-June	July-Aug.	Sept.-Oct.	Nov.-Dec.	Total
1988							
Retirements handled[a]	522	525	473	409	531	447	2,907
CLC 1989-1990							
1989							
Retirements handled	478	534	609	592	747	576	3,536
Liquidations agreed	607						607
Subtotal	1,085						4,103
1990							
Retirements handled	498	588	543	711	664	586	3,590
Liquidations agreed	154						154
Posts canceled, reduced, or eliminated							34
Subtotal	622						3,708
CLC 1991-1993							
1991							
Retirements handled	434	2,977	350	493	516	598	5,368
Liquidations agreed	27	4,053		121			4,021
Liquidations & retirements[b]					509		509
Posts canceled, reduced, or eliminated					7,849		7,849
Subtotal	461	7,030	1,123	8,447			17,927
1992							
Posts canceled, reduced, or eliminated	9,353	3,006	17				12,376
Total							41,131

[a] The retirements handled are distinct from retirements handled due to "current state of health and labor ability."
[b] This refers to unionized workers carrying out management, supervision, control and overseeing functions.
[c] These "liquidations and retirements" are not the sum of each separate category, but are data provided in aggregate form.

Note: Data relating to liquidations, retirements, cancellations, and reductions or eliminations of posts were used to calculate "posts cancelled, reduced or eliminated" for a group of workers. Source: Petróleos Mexicanos, *Informe Al Consejo de Administración (bimestral)*, 1988, 1989, 1990, 1991, 1992.

Table 2

Variations in the Petróleos Mexicanos Workforce
(1986-1993)

Years	Number of Workers
1986	186,117 [a]
1987	210,157 [b]
1988	170,766 [c]
1989	170,183 OR 210,000 [d]
1990	182,996 [e]
1991	147,000 [f]
1992	136,207 [g]
1993	120,000 [h]

[a] *Source*: Sub-Management of Information on Pemex, quoted in *El Financiero*, September 19, 1988, p. 14.

[b] Ibid.

[c] *Source*: *Anuario Estadístico de Pemex,* 1988, p. 52. This information does not include employees in the "Section for Projects and Construction of Works."

[d] The first figure comes from the *Anuario Estadístico de Pemex*, 1988; the second from a nonspecified source quoted in *El Sol de México*, September 10, 1992, p. 5

[e] *Source*: Census of Active Workers for Petróleos Mexicanos quoted by *El Universal*, August 8, 1991, p.5

[f] *Ibid*. It should be explained that the same newspaper reported on July 23, 1991, quoting the same source, that the 1991 workforce had been reduced to 122,000 workers, which would imply a variation of around -60,000 workers.

[g] *Source:* A document presented by Petróleos Mexicanos to the Secretaria de Hacienda y Crédito Público, signed by the director of finances, quoted by *Uno Más Uno*, September 10, 1992, p.18.

[h] *Source*: information provided by the corporate administration director of Petróleos Mexicanos, Cuauhtémoc Santa Ana, quoted by *La Jornada*, August 11, 1993, pp. 44 and 14.

Table 3

Wage and Salary Expenditure in Pemex, in Relation to Estimated Budget
1988-1992

Year	Expenditure
1988	3.9
1989	-9.0
1990	-43.4
1991	-34.6
1992	-12.9

Source: *Informes al Consejo de Administración* (bimonthly), 1988 to 1992.

Endnotes

1. *Marco jurídico básico,* Subdirección Técnica Administrativa, Gerencia Jurídica, Petróleos Mexicanos, México, 1988.

2. Rafael Loyola Díaz. 1991.

3. The economic relevance of the 2 percent is reflected by the estimate made for the years 1973 to 1983 where the union earned 14 billion pesos under this provision. See Alonso and Lopez, 1986.

4. To provide some idea of the magnitude of the income that the union received for its participation in contracting, it is informative to note that in February 1989 the deposed "moral guide" of the petroleum workers, Joaquin Hernández Galicia, "la Quina," stated that, in less than five years, 20 billion old pesos had been stored in the union's coffers and over 30 billion had been "invested in houses, saved and re-invested," all of which resulted from work undertaken for PEMEX. See Delarbre and Galvan 1989.

5. Alonso and Lopez 1986; Rafael Loyola Díaz 1990; and Shapira 1979.

6. Loyola Díaz 1990a.

7. Nonetheless, it is worth mentioning that the institution of this policy has not enjoyed the enthusiasm of the workers who yearn for the old days. For example, three years after the destruction of patrimonial unionism, its greatest proponent, Joaquín Hernández Galicia ("la Quina"), still has a significant level of sympathy among union members. According to a survey conducted by the magazine *Este País* and the Movimiento Nacional Petrólero (MNP, which is among the groups traditionally opposed to the leadership of the union heads of Ciudad Madero) 66.7 percent of those surveyed in the northern zone had a "good" opinion of la Quina, compared with 42.4 percent in favor of his successor, Sebastián Guzmán; in the central zone, la Quina obtained 58 percent, compared with 22 percent in favor of Guzmán; and only in the southern zone was the positive opinion of la Quina (42 percent of those surveyed) lower than the number of Guzmán's defenders (45.5 percent). Figures courtesy of the Coordinación Ejecutiva del Movimiento Nacional Petrólero from a document entitled *Programa de estabilidad sindical y productividad S.T.P.R.M.-Pemex* (nueva cultura política organizacional), México, January 1992 (photocopied). *Este País*, in its report on the survey (no. 10, January 1992: 10-11) did not present the data in terms of the percentage of workers in favor of la Quina by region; as for the percentages of those surveyed who were in favor of Sebastián Guzmán, the magazine diverges from the results offered in the document quoted, placing the figures at 19 percent in the North, 6 percent in the central zone, and 41 percent in the south.

8. Pemex, *Informe al Consejo de Administración* (bimonthly) 1990. Between May and June, 400 posts were transferred. Between July and August, 162 were transferred, and between November and December, 166. It is worth clarifying that the source used for this data is incomplete, since at times it refers to the movement and adjustments in personnel within the company without offering quantitative data. Nonetheless, the source

is used because of the possibility of reconstructing the phenomenon by studying it in a bimonthly form from January 1988 to December 1992.

9. Pemex, *Informe al Consejo de Administración* (bimonthly), July-August 1989.

10. Loyola Díaz 1990b.

11. These actions were facilitated by the deletion from the CLC's text of the reference to the company's obligation not to exceed a level of 10 percent permanent nonunion workers and 5 percent of temporary nonunion workers (*Informe al Consejo de Administración* (bimonthly), July-August 1990).

12. STPRM, *Contrato Colectivo de Trabajo*, México 1991, Claúsula 85, p. 84.

13. Pemex and STPRM; *Contrato Colectivo de Trabajo*, Reglamento de Escalafones y Ascensos, Anexo 2, Artículo 21, inciso C, pp. 295 and 296.

14. Pemex and STPRM; *Contrato Colectivo de Trabajo*, México 1991, pp. 31-32.

15. Pemex and STPRM; *Contrato Colectivo de Trabajo*, México 1991, Cláusula 7, p.16.

16. Pemex and STPRM; *Contrato Colectivo de Trabajo*, México 1991, Cláusula 20, p. 23.

17. Pemex and STPRM; *Contrato Colectivo de Trabajo*, México 1991, Cláusulas 15 and 252, pp. 21 and 23.

18. Pemex and STPRM; *Contrato Colectivo de Trabajo*, México 1991.

19. *Informe de la revisión del Contrato Colectivo de Trabajo, Bienio 1993-1995*, photocopy, 1993, p.1. This is the sole source of information since the *Contrato Colectivo de Trabajo for 1993-1995* has not yet been made public.

20. Ibid. p.3.

21. Ibid. p.4.

22. Ibid. p.17.

23. The new Organic Law for Petróleos Mexicanos adapts to the constitutional precepts of the petroleum industry, but it opens up the industry to private capital in the service sector by way of contracting and leaves all those departments that the industry occupies for the fulfillment of its functions, but which are not the preserve of the state constitution, exposed to liberalization or privatization. The new regulation gives the company the flexibility to rid itself of functions that are not fundamental to it, such as the creation or removal of subsidiary or co-investing companies. Furthermore, the law intends to put an end to the massiveness of Pemex by dividing it into four subsidiaries integrated by a corporate center. With these changes, the workers lost power since they now only report to the Board of General Administration while they are in a marginal

position in relation to the boards of each of the subsidiaries. This is in line with the trend to reduce worker influence in those areas where the most important decisions will be made and carried out. *CF Inicativa de Reforma de Ley Orgánica de Petróleos Mexicanos y Organismos Subsidiarios,* presented by Carlos Salinas de Gortari to the Congress of the Union, July 1, 1992.

24. According to other sources consulted—*Informe al Consejo de Administración de Petróleos Mexicanos (bimestral)*, 1988, 1989, 1990, 1991, 1992—the total number of personnel retired, liquidated, or eliminated from January 1988 to December 1992 surpassed 47,787 (see Table 1). Nevertheless, on different occasions this source refers to the retirement, redundancies, or elimination of personnel without offering precise figures. Consequently, we consider the figures provided by this source to be incomplete.

25. During the Seminar "Petróleo: Desarrollo y Perspectivas, Democracia Sindical y Derechos de los Trabajadores," organized by the Universidad Autónoma Metropolitana-Iztapalapa and the Movimiento Nacional Petrolero (MNP), both the leader of this movement, Hebraicaz Vásquez, and other academics and former Pemex officials confirmed the reduction of 90,000 workers in Pemex. Furthermore, Pemex's director del corporativo de administración, Cuauhtémoc Santa Ana, stated to the press that in the last five years the workforce of Pemex had been reduced to 120,000, after a removal of 120,000 workers,which leads one to suppose that in 1989 there were 240,000 workers in the public company.

26. Quoted in *La Jornada*, August 11, 1993, pp. 44 and 14.

27. Pemex, *Anuario Estadístlco de Pemex, 1988*, p.52.

28. Varelo estimated that at the end of 1993, the current cost per barrel in terms of operational costs will be between 40 and 45 percent lower than costs for 1989; in the daily newspaper *La Jornada*, August 7, 1993, p. 29.

29. *Diario de México*, March 10, 1993, p. 4-A.

References

Alonso, Angelina, and Roberto Lopez. 1986. *El sindicato de trabajadores petróleros y sus relaciones con Pemex y el Estado, 1970-1985*. México: El Colegio de México, p. 187.

..... 1989. "La liquidación del feudo petrolero en la política moderna." México.

Loyla Díaz, Rafael. 1990a. *Mexican Studies* 6 (2).

..... 1990b. "Las implicaciones laborales del Neoliberalismo en Petróleos Mexicanos." In Relaciones Laborales en las Empresas Estatales, Graciela Bensusán and Carlos García, coordinators. Mexico: Fundación Friedrich Ebert.

..... 1991. *El ocaso del radicalismo revolucionario*. Edited by Instituto de Investigaciones Sociales. Mexico: UNAM.

Shapira, Marie Fance Prevot. 1979. "Trabajadores del petróleo y podersindical en México," in *Cuadernos Americanos*, 20, no. 2.

NAFTA and AFTA: Regional Integration and Industrial Relations in Southeast Asia

Sarosh Kuruvilla and Adam Pagnucco

Introduction

The recent conclusion of NAFTA, following the successful completion of the internal market program in the (EC) European Community, has spurred debate about the possibilities of similar free trade areas in Asia. Viewed from a Southeast Asian perspective, NAFTA is seen as a threat for two major reasons. The first reason is the fear that the EC and NAFTA will result in the creation of protectionist trading blocs that is, "Fortress North America" or "Fortress-EC" that will significantly impinge on Asian exports to North America.

The second reason concerns the presence in NAFTA of Mexico. In this case the fear is that Mexico will supplant the Southeast Asian economies as a source of cheap labor and manufactured goods. While the Southeast Asian economies in recent years have witnessed impressive growth rates, average monthly manufacturing wages in most Southeast Asian nations are very similar to that of Mexico. In addition, while wages have grown steadily in Southeast Asia over the last five years, they have actually declined in Mexico during the 1980s. A further reduction of tariffs within NAFTA will only increase Mexican competitiveness relative to that of the Southeast Asian region.

In addition, more recent efforts at economic integration in South America such as the Central American Common Market, the Andean Group, Mercosur, and G-3, have also motivated the Asian region to examine the concept of regional economic cooperation.

Although various forms of pan-Asian-Pacific cooperation have been discussed in response to both the EC and NAFTA (notably APEC [Asia-Pacific Economic Community]), the only concrete step has been the effort of the ASEAN countries (Association of Southeast Asian Nations, which includes Singapore, Malaysia, the Philippines, Thailand, Indonesia, and Brunei), who have slowly created AFTA (ASEAN Free Trade Area), a process that began in 1967, but which took a major leap forward in 1992 following EC and NAFTA.

In keeping with the theme of this conference, this paper examines the progress made on AFTA, the degree of economic integration that has already taken place in ASEAN, the prospects for increased economic cooperation, and the role of industrial relations in this integration.

AFTA

AFTA is the product of ASEAN, a twenty-five-year-old regional grouping of countries in southeast Asia. The evolution of AFTA may be traced in three distinct phases. During the first phase (1967-76), ASEAN laid the political foundations for regional economic cooperation, focusing primarily on learning from each other, adopting successful experiments from each other, and fostering a commitment to regular information exchange at the level of different ministries and departments of Southeast Asian governments. The second phase (1976-92) was devoted to experiments in regional economic cooperation. Given the vastly different world trading environment post-EC and the beginnings of NAFTA post-1992, the third phase (1992-present) specified a more concrete program of regional integration.

Taken together, the ASEAN countries comprising AFTA represent a market of 380 million people, a market that is certainly comparable in size to both the EC and NAFTA, but clearly not in purchasing power. Indonesia is the largest member, with 218 million people, while Brunei is the smallest, with 0.3 million people (Singapore has 3 million, Malaysia 22 million, Thailand 61 million, and the Philippines 76.1 million). The per capita income of these countries varies widely; from $11,200 in Singapore, $2,500 in Malaysia, $1,420 in Thailand, to $760 and $560 in the Philippines and Indonesia respectively. However, these economies have also been growing at a rapid pace during the 1980s (with the exception of the Philippines), when average growth rates exceeded 6 percent annually.

The timetable for AFTA calls for tariffs to be reduced to 0-5 percent and all nontariff barriers to be dismantled in fifteen years beginning January 1, 1993. It is envisaged that most tariffs will be reduced to 20 percent within the first eight years, and subsequently to 0-5 percent in the following seven. The implementation of this dismantling scheme is based on the common effective preferential tariff (CEPT), which takes a sector-by-sector approach, in contrast to the preferential trading area approaches used in the EC, which focuses on an item-by-item approach to tariff dismantling. Naturally, the CEPT approach is expected to result in a much quicker reduction in tariffs.

The fast-track CEPT approach covers fifteen different product groupings, including both first-stage processing groups like vegetable oils, rubber products, paper pulp, and rattan products, as well as industrial goods-electronics, cement, chemicals, pharmaceuticals, and finished consumer goods-gems and jewellery and textiles.

There are a number of factors that are responsible for the acceleration of the AFTA program. As Ariff (1992) suggests, the principal reason is externally driven, that is, the end of the cold war, the deepening of the European community from EC to the European Economic Area, the establishment of NAFTA, and the rising tide of economic regionalism in the third world. But, internal factors are also important. The growing regional consensus that a free trade area will benefit the local economies has been spurred primarily by their steady economic growth during the decade of the 1980s. Rapid increases in purchasing power, intra-ASEAN trade, and the structural transformation of deregulation, privatization, and export orientation that has accompanied economic growth in all ASEAN economies have resulted in a stronger political will to continue economic integration. The similarity of the development strategies that these countries have undertaken and the success of these strategies have convinced even free trade laggards such as Indonesia (which once feared a one-way flow of goods into Indonesia) about its ability to compete effectively.

However, it is still Indonesia that will determine the speed of trade liberalization in AFTA since it is the poorest country and also accounts for one-half of the ASEAN market. Ariff (1992) suggests that AFTA will go only as far as Indonesia will allow it to go. Although there is some uncertainty depending on the growth of the Indonesian economy, there are numerous factors that suggest the potential for successful completion of the AFTA program. These include the relative similarity of the development paths these economies have taken, the complementary effects of their relative positions on the typical ASEAN development trajectory, the relatively low percentages of tariffs, the rapid growth in intra-ASEAN trade, and several synergistic cross-country efforts at regional integration that have been initiated by the countries. These factors, which enhance the potential for the successful completion of NAFTA, are discussed in greater detail below.

Prospects for AFTA and Regional Integration

The Similarity of Development Patterns in ASEAN: Complementarity and Competition

In this section, we argue that the similarity of development strategies and the location of countries at different places in the development path promotes both complementarity and competition among the countries. Both result in increased economic growth (a necessary condition for successful integration) as well as in increased intra-ASEAN trade (indicative of the progress towards integration). It is important to note that the development path taken by ASEAN economies (discussed below) has also been used by several other successful Asian countries (for example, South Korea, Hong Kong, and Taiwan) and is a model for newly emerging economies of Vietnam, Laos, and Cambodia as well.

All these economies started out as import-substitution industrialization (ISI) economies in the 1950s. It was easy to sustain such a strategy in the early stages, when with comparatively little investment and technology, the economy could produce simple manufactures to produce local demand. But, their relatively small internal markets quickly became saturated. To expand into more sophisticated products required importing both materials and technology from abroad, at a cost that overshadowed the savings on foreign exchange that ISI implied. Resource crunches caused by various individual problems (for example, the new economic policy in Malaysia and the debt crisis of the Philippines) in these economies led to shifts away from the strategy of ISI to exports oriented industrialization (EOI), largely financed by foreign investment. In many cases the shift from ISI to EOI was based on recommendations by the World Bank and IMF.

The first stage of EOI was characterized by exports of low-cost manufactured goods that capitalized on the advantage of cheap labor and numerous export incentives. Some countries have successfully gone into the next stage of EOI, a stage characterized by the manufacture of more capital and skill-intensive products accompanied by some form of industrial deepening (for example, Singapore and now Malaysia). The effects of this industrialization strategy can be seen in the changes in the economic structure of these countries and, in particular, in the relative increase in the size of manufacturing relative to agriculture over time, as Table 1 shows.

Table 1 suggests the development path characterized by ISI, then simple EOI, then advanced EOI, and finally service-dominated economies (for example, Singapore and Hong Kong). The success of this industrialization path can be seen in several indicators, notably GDP growth rates, and the increased contribution of exports to GDP, which are reported in Table 2. In addition, the trend of increases in foreign investment (see Table 3) witnessed in several ASEAN economies is also a testament to the success of an export-oriented strategy financed by foreign investment.

As Kuruvilla (1994b) notes, both low-cost and advanced EOI strategies followed by the ASEAN nations were predicated on a strong role of the state in facilitating development through the creation of infrastructural facilities, enactment of various incentives to attract foreign capital, and, in the advanced EOI stage, to gear the economy to attract higher technology-based foreign investment. The range of policies in this regard included financial, infrastructural, education, and training, immigration, and other regulatory policies that were common to all nations. (For a brief description of such successful policies, see Kuruvilla 1994b. For a discussion of policies that failed, see Macaraya and Ofreneo 1992 for the Philippines.)

The initial success of all these economies centered around exports in electrical manufactures, electronics assembly, and textile production. In the late 1960s and early 1970s, Korea and Singapore were the largest exporters of these products. In the late 1970s and 1980s, Malaysia, Philippines, and Thailand were the largest exporters of electronic assemblies, and in the 1990s, Vietnam, Cambodia, and Laos are expected to be the largest. For instance, in Korea in the 1970s, these three industries accounted for over 80 percent of exports. In the 1980s, electronics and light manufactures account for over 70 percent of total exports of Malaysia and Thailand. In all these economies, the contribution of manufacturing exports to total exports is above 60 percent (Kuruvilla 1994).

The similarity of development strategies, and the relative place of the ASEAN economies in the stagewise development process identified above, ensures that each economy has a source of competitive advantage, at any given time, and their industrialization strategies are therefore complementary. For example, the Singapore economy is the most developed and is service-based. It increasingly depends on the other three economies for its basic industrial goods. Malaysia is at the verge of a transition between simple EOI and advanced EOI, while the Philippines is still in the simple EOI stage, while Indonesia is just emerging out of its ISI phase.

Foreign investment appears to mirror the stage of development that each economy is in. As Salih, Young, and Rajah (1987) suggest, Japanese investment in electronics is a particular case in point. In the 1970s, the bulk of Japanese investment flowed to Singapore, in the 1980s the bulk of their electronics investments flowed to Malaysia, the Philippines, and Thailand. The nature of Japanese investments differs from country to country. Product development is often located in Japan or Singapore, while production facilities are located in Malaysia, Thailand, and the Philippines. Companies, that follow a low-cost strategy (for example, UNIDEN) have moved factories to areas that provide the cheapest labor (China and the Philippines), while companies that require higher skilled labor and use higher technology processes are moving increasingly into Malaysia.

The complementarity arising from different locations on the development path facilitates not only investment, but also the growth of intra-ASEAN trade. For example,

Singapore, the most advanced country accounts for 73.6 percent of all imports of CEPT goods in ASEAN, followed by Malaysia (12.5 percent), Thailand, (8 percent), Indonesia (3.6 percent) and the Philippines (2.3 percent). In addition, the country shares of intra-ASEAN trade also reflect the development pattern. Singapore accounts for 47.1 percent of all intra-ASEAN trade, followed by Malaysia (26.4 percent), Thailand (12.8 percent), Indonesia (8.1 percent) and the Philippines (3.5 percent) all in 1990. The point is that less developed economies have a ready market for their products within the ASEAN system.

This complementarity has helped reduce, to some extent, the dependence of ASEAN countries on external trade. As Table 4 indicates, all of these countries had a significant increase in trade to other ASEAN countries between 1985 and 1991. The significance of the United States, and Japan, the traditional leading trading partners, is declining based on export figures, although there is some increase in exports to the EC. In the case of Singapore, Malaysia, and Indonesia, the ASEAN share of their total trade has increased, while there have been slight declines in Thailand and the Philippines.

Whereas the complementarity discussed above provides a fillip to intra-ASEAN trade, there is also substantial competition among these countries in relation to their trade with the rest of the world. For instance, Malaysia and the Philippines still compete in the exports of electronics, textiles, and footwear products. The Philippines and Indonesia compete primarily in terms of the export of cheap manufactures, particularly since both economies still view cheap labor as their competitive advantage. This is to a lesser extent true of Malaysia, where rapid growth and the transition to more high-technology-based exports, and the shortage of labor ensuing from its rapid growth has forced it to move away from viewing cheap labor as its competitive advantage. In terms of foreign investments, much of the recent investment into the lower-cost ASEAN countries have been made from the developed countries such as Taiwan, Korea, and Singapore, which have supplanted Japan and the United States as the biggest investors (Kuruvilla 1990). In sum, ASEAN development trajectories create complementarities and some intranation competition, both of which have resulted in increased economic growth.

Tariff and Nontariff Barriers

Current levels of tariffs can also indicate the potential for faster economic integration. Although there is an agreed timetable for the reduction of tariffs (0-5 percent in fifteen years), the fast-track CEPT program is designed to reduce most tariffs in the first eight years. Unilateral trade policy reforms have led to a significant reduction in tariffs in Malaysia, the Philippines, Thailand, and Indonesia. The average tariff levels in ASEAN are lower than those of most developing countries. The average nominal tariffs in Singapore and Brunei are negligible. The objective of reducing tariff levels to 0-5 percent by 2007 appears quite reasonable in the light of existing tariff levels. In overall terms, nominal tariff rate averages are about 16 percent in Malaysia, 26 percent in the Philippines, 22 percent in Indonesia, and 44 percent in Thailand. The offer on tariff reductions under consideration by the Uruguay round of the GATT talks is likely to reduce these figures considerably. An examination of tariffs on critical items falling into the fast-track CEPT program is generally encouraging. Table 5 shows that tariffs are low in most cases, except in a few critical items.

Three issues germane to tariff reduction relate to the policy regarding "politically sensitive items," the importance of tariffs in an environment where they can be easily bypassed, and problems of trade deflection. There is an "exclusion list" of politically sensitive items that are not included in the CEPT program. It is still unclear which items will find their way into this list. How this list will be dealt with is also unclear. With regard to the second issue, Ariff suggests that high tariffs on many items are redundant, either because domestic substitutes are so competitive that they do not really need tariff protection or because tariff barriers are so effectively circumvented that the prices of imported products in the local market do not reflect the official tariffs applied at customs.

The problems of trade deflection, (that is, the possibility of a low-tariff country such as Singapore being used by a third country as an entry point for final destination elsewhere in ASEAN) is a more general one. This is a problem in NAFTA as well, and predominant NAFTA-type methods of rules of origin and local content specifications are likely to be invoked in the short term until all tariffs are removed.

Overall, the low level of tariffs portend well for tariff reduction in AFTA. Other nontariff barriers, however, pose a far bigger problem that has yet to be addressed by the parties. In particular, nontariff barriers such as safety regulations, health standards, industrial relations issues, and customs procedures, tend to constitute a bigger barrier to intraregional trade and investment flows than tariffs. There has been very little discussion on these issues, and an upward harmonization effort similar to that of the EC has yet to be made. On the other hand, many of these systems are reasonably similar (see the later section on industrial relations as an example) given that these countries have been exchanging information about these issues since 1967, and some degree of cross-country learning and cooperation has taken place. Overall, while the issue of tariffs does not appear to pose a problem to the development of AFTA, it is likely that nontariff issues may, and hence require addressing. During the Manila summit of 1987, the countries committed themselves to a standstill and rollback of NTBs although there has been little evidence of efforts to identify and quantify the impact of NTBs.

Another line of argument suggested is that NTBs will not have much of an impact on AFTA because they are not watertight, and can be easily circumvented. This is evidenced by the apparent refusal of different national chambers of commerce to detail their experience with NTBs before the ASEAN secretariat, for fear of giving away trade secrets (Ariff 1992).

The Importance of Industrial Relations in Economic Integration

Although industrial relations can be viewed as a significant nontariff barrier to integration, the close relationship between economic development strategies and industrial relations policies in Southeast Asia noted by many (for example, Kuruvilla 1994 and 1994b) suggests that industrial relations can be a central determinant in the pace of progress of AFTA, has been unlike in the EC and NAFTA. In the EC and NAFTA, IR issues have been significant obstacles. In the EC, till today, there no consensus regarding the harmonization of industrial relations legislation. In North America, NAFTA's lackluster addressing of labor issues generated a potent resistance effort by the labor movement, which hindered passage of the trade pact. In Southeast Asia, IR policies are far more similar across countries than in the EC and in NAFTA, and an important part of the development strategy of Southeast Asian economies. We focus below on the extent of similarity of Southeast Asian IR systems, and thereafter, we examine the close links between economic development, industrial relations, and integration. Our discussion focuses more on Singapore, Malaysia, Thailand, and the Philippines, given the lack of available information on IR practices in Brunei and Indonesia.

Commonalities and Differences in Industrial Relations

In general, these four economies follow the two-planked Asian approach to labor policy. The first plank in Asian labor policy focuses on labor protection, that is, labor standards laws and welfare policies. Table 6 lists these policies. As Table 6 indicates there is a remarkable similarity in labor protection legislation in these countries. All these economies are characterized by advanced legislation mandating annual leave, casual leave, maternity leave, child care (borne by employer), and legislation regarding overtime, working hours, safety and health, restrictions on terminations, severance pay, annual bonus, and retirement benefits. Protective labor legislation is advanced, certainly more so than in the United States, and the commonalities are explained more by the willingness of these economies to follow established ILO conventions with respect to these issues. It would appear that harmonization of labor standards legislation would appear to be a less problematic issue, although enforcement standards vary widely.

The second plank of labor policy concerns labor-management relations issues. Table 7 compares the countries on these issues. As Table 7 indicates, all of these countries are characterized by low union densities (4 percent-30 percent), and the rights of unions to organize in essential industries are limited, plus the range of industries characterized as essential vary. All countries have various restrictions on union formation, with the administrative arrangements concerning registration used to weed out unions that the state does not want. All of these countries started out with craft- and industrial-type unions, but are shifting to enterprise-based unionism, primarily through legislative enactments. In all of these countries (except the Philippines) the scope of bargaining is limited. In most of them unions cannot bargain over job assignments, transfers, promotions or layoffs, and, in some cases, wages. Many of these countries also require collective bargaining agreements to be certified, with the certification agency allowed to send the agreements back to the parties if against the national interest.

In all of these countries there are several restrictions on the right to strike, such as not permitting strikes while a dispute is under conciliation, mediation, or arbitration, administrative practices that circumvent unions' ability to call a strike, and the prohibition of strikes for political purposes and in essential industries (where the definition of "essential" is wide). To promote workplace flexibility, there has been a movement toward adoption of enterprise-based unions, while at the national level, efforts have been made to keep the labor movement fragmented (except in Singapore). What is common across these kinds of strategies is the focus on national-level stability and workplace-level efficiency. Rules have been made in ways that facilitate considerable employer discretion on IR issues, and have been made keeping in mind that the reduction of industrial conflict is essential to economic development, hence the restrictions on strikes, union formation, and the limited scope of bargaining. Frenkel (1993) contains a series of essays delineating the approach to labor-management relations in each of these countries.

The commonalities in institutional methods listed in Table 7 are only a part of the overall labor strategy taken by Southeast Asian governments. Drawing from other work by Deyo (1989), Kuruvilla (1994b), and others, these countries evidence a mix of suppressive and cooptationist approaches. Generally, Thailand, the Philippines, and

Malaysia have several repressive elements in their approach to labor policy, while Singapore has a more cooptationist strategy.

Congruence: Industrial Relations, Economic Development, and Integration

Aside from commonalities and differences, however, there appears to be a basic congruity between labor policy and where a country is on the EOI development ladder. Thailand and the Philippines,which are at the lowest stage of EOI, that is,, low-cost exports based on cheap labor-have industrial relations policies that reflect the priority of cost control. Incidentally, Thailand and the Philippines have two of the most repressive labor policies in the region. Both allow the crudest forms of labor repression to go on unchecked, such as intimidation, violence, bribes, and yellow-dog-style hiring requirements demanded by employers. Neither regime has successfully cultivated a part of the labor movement in order to achieve backing for its labor policies. Rather, the emphasis is on minimizing union power, especially in terms of negotiating wage hikes and shop-floor conditions with employers. This type of labor policy is aimed at preserving the low-cost, cheap labor advantage so critical to first-stage EOI.

Malaysia, having advanced to second-stage EOI with exports of capital-intensive, high-skills-based manufactures, has altered its labor policy to emphasize training and upskilling to increase to increase worker productivity. Although the Malaysian system retains some repressive characteristics, three significant events indicate change. First, the ban on unions in electronics was formally lifted in 1988, even though union formation continues to be difficult (Kuruvilla 1994a). Second, the regime has adopted a somewhat ambivalent stand toward unionization in the public sector, seeking to replace unions with "cultural associations" but not to eliminate them entirely (Ponniah and Littler 1993). Third, the government is taking steps to build up support systems for skills development, such as bold new education policies, encouragement of R&D, and adjustment of immigration policies to ease skills shortages (Kuruvilla 1994a). These IR changes on the part of Malaysia reflect the emphasis of second-stage EOI on capital-intensity, skills-intensity, and high productivity. Since low costs and cheap labor are not as important, union repression becomes less of a priority.

Singapore stands at the top of the development ladder and is currently making the transition to a service-based economy. Its priorities are now to attract corporate headquarters and R&D facilities, build its service and support networks, and diversify its manufacturing base (Wu 1991). As in second-stage EOI, skills development continues to be a priority. But, Singapore's future does not depend on its ability to compete on a cost basis with rival manufacturers; rather, its growth potential lies in supplying advanced service and support capabilities to manufacturers throughout the region. The country's IR policies reflect these needs. Repression of the labor movement is minimal in Singapore, both because labor is dominated by the government-backed federation and because cheap labor is no longer important to the leading sectors of the economy. Skills development is considered a top priority, and is supported by a massive array of government training subsidies and basic skills training programs (Chew and Chew 1993). Because of its educated workforce, relatively high wage base, and lack of domestic capital (the country is dominated by multinationals), Singapore's development path demands economic integration in order to expand and perfect its service industries, particularly financial services, transport and communications, and R&D.

Clearly, therefore, IR policies reflect the development stage, and is a crucial element in the development strategy of Southeast Asian nations (see Kuruvilla 1994b) for a more elaborate discussion). And this congruence does matter, both in terms of attraction of foreign investment and in enhancing regional integration initiatives.

Given that all these Southeast Asian economies have depended on foreign investment for their economic success, the IR strategies of multinational firms are especially important. And typically, multinationals follow IR practices that are congruent with the stage of development of different ASEAN economies. For example, Kuruvilla (1994b) shows that multinational firms (for example, UNIDEN) emphasizing a low-cost business strategy tend to follow IR practices that focus on cost containment and tend to locate in countries that have IR systems that focus on cost containment (for example, the Philippines). In addition, firms that emphasize higher skill and technology-intensive manufacturing of higher quality products (for example, Motorola, Matsushita) tend to locate in countries whose IR systems reflect a skill enhancement focus such as those of Malaysia and Singapore. As integration under AFTA proceeds, countries evolve their own competitive niches based on its stage of EOI development and labor policy, in a way that all countries gain from the complementarity noted earlier.

Industrial relations considerations also drive other regional integration initiatives. One such example is the growth triangle concept. Growth triangles exemplify government and employer cooperation on the basis of industrial relations issues such as labor costs, availability, and productivity.

The "Sijori" growth triangle involves Singapore, Johore (the southernmost state of peninsular Malaysia), and the Riau Islands of Indonesia. The triangle was first suggested by current Singapore Prime Minister Goh Chok Tong in 1989 as a way of providing a complete operating area for foreign investors that would allow each nation to benefit from development. Labor-intensive operations could take advantage of Indonesian cheap labor, intermediate technology operations could operate in Johore in Malaysia, and advanced research and headquarter facilities could find a home in Singapore. What makes this convenient for investors is the mutual proximity of all these areas to each other: Singapore is separated from Johore by a narrow strait, while Batam Island (one of the Riau Islands) is only twelve miles away from Singapore (Stewart and Png 1993). Singapore's advanced seaport and airport provide an outlet for manufactures to the rest of the world (Wu 1991).

The Sijori growth triangle is not a free trade zone. Each country maintains its own tariff structure, its own labor and environmental regulations, and its own taxation scheme. There is no one multilateral agreement that administers Sijori; rather, each of the governments cooperate in order to finance infrastructure projects and attract foreign investors. Currently, cooperative development is under way at two islands in the Riau chain: Batam and Bintan. Companies located in neighboring Singapore are free to locate their labor-intensive facilities at Batam, where production worker wages are up to 80 percent lower. Bintan, twenty-eight miles distant from Singapore, will be based around a jointly financed resort featuring twenty hotels, nine condominiums, twenty-seven villa clusters, and more than a dozen golf courses. While Indonesia supplies the labor, Singapore and Malaysia will supply the tourists. Already the Sijori triangle has attracted several firms, including Sumitomo Electric, which has located wire harness manufacturing operations in Johore and Batam while maintaining a technical support office in Singapore. Smith-Corona, Philips, and Western Digital have similar arrangements (Stewart and Png 1993).

Another example is the growth triangle including southern Thailand, northern Malaysia, and northern Sumatra (Indonesia). This new growth triangle has been centered around Penang, one of Malaysia's premier industrial centers. The regions of Thailand and Indonesia included in the triangle are not heavily industrialized, but possess large supplies of cheap labor which could potentially be utilized by manufacturers based in Penang, given the labor shortage faced by Malaysia. Firms in the region will cooperate with government authorities to attract low-wage, low-skill investment. Because this growth triangle is so new, it is unclear exactly how it will develop or how the member governments will cooperate on its progress (Vatikiosis 1993a).

Another different example of competitive and complementary niches based on labor cost considerations can be seen in the region's automobile industry. ASEAN governments have cooperated extensively to offer subcontracting facilities and production workplaces for Japanese automobile firms. In 1988, ASEAN announced its brand-to-brand complementation scheme (BBC), specifically designed for automobile production. Under the BBC, an automobile company could apply to the ASEAN Committee on Industry, Minerals, and Energy for a host of benefits, including a 50 percent tariff cut on all auto parts fabricated in any ASEAN countries and full local content requirement exemption for all ASEAN-made parts. In order to be eligible for BBC benefits, the auto firm would have to present a detailed production plan illustrating its subcontracting network in ASEAN (Rushton 1990).

Mitsubishi, Toyota, and Nissan have all drawn up regional complementation programs in order to gain BBC benefits. Mitsubishi has at least five complementation schemes. One scheme involves the shipment of Philippine transmissions and Malaysian electrical equipment to Thailand, where they are combined with Thai engines and other parts and shipped to third country destinations, such as Canada, for final assembly. Another scheme involves the shipment of Philippine transmissions, assembled in Thailand, and Thai engine systems, ignition coils, cables, panels, and brakes to Proton, Malaysia's national car company and a partial subsidiary of Mitsubishi. Proton cars, which sell heavily in Malaysia, are also exported to Great Britain, Singapore, Brunei, and recently Indonesia (Vatikiosis, 1993b). Toyota's and Nissan's complementation schemes are similar, though Toyota maintains a local service and support headquarters in Singapore (Rushton 1990).

Though the utilization of local comparative advantages is not immediately apparent, the auto firms occasionally reveal their logic in constructing complementation schemes. Toyota has located its transmission operations in the Philippines despite the fact that comparable Japanese plants are twice as productive because it expects savings through low wages and exchange differentials (Rushton 1990). And high-skill Malaysia invariably shows up as a prime source for advanced, capital-intensive parts like electrical equipment and steering gear.

Conclusion

As the preceding examples show, industrial relations issues have played a crucial role in these experiments that further ASEAN integration. The important point is that industrial relations issues are inextricably linked to the dominant economic development strategies of the government. Countries whose governments emphasize competitive advantage based on high skills, attract firms that also adopt high-skill based industrial relations policies, such as those evident in the Malaysian electronics industry, which are increasingly characterized by team-based production, wages linked to skills development, increased job security, and multi-training of operatives, designed to increase internal flexibility (ee Rajah 1994 and Kuruvilla 1994a for a more detailed discussion of work practices in Malaysia). Where countries emphasize economic development policies based on low costs, such as in the Philippines, the country attracts firms whose industrial relations systems are characterized by low wages, antiunion policies, and the adoption of external flexibility enhancing policies such as extensive layoffs, no job security, increased subcontracting and casualization of labor. (See Ofreneo 1994 for a more detailed discussion of IR practices in the export-oriented sector in the Philippines.)

The progress of AFTA hinges on several issues, of which industrial relations is particularly important. The role of IR policy in Southeast Asian economic integration is to shape and enhance comparative advantage, which ultimately stems from where each nation is on the EOI development ladder. First-stage EOI countries will be viewed as sources of cheap labor by multinationals, but they will only be viewed as viable if IR policy aims to preserve their cheap labor edge. Second-stage EOI countries will be viewed as locations for high-skill, intermediate technology operations, but only if their IR policies help to build workforce skills and enhance productivity. Service-oriented countries will be viewed as potential research and technical support bases, but only if IR policies encourage education, training, high skills, and state-of-the-art infrastructural capacity. Although industrial relations has been viewed as a significant barrier to integration in both the EC and NAFTA, our discussion suggests that industrial relations is a critical factor in ASEAN integration, given its central role in the development strategies of countries. And, given the increasingly wide acceptance of the Southeast Asian development model in other parts of Asia, the role of industrial relations in furthering economic integration will only become more important.

Table 1
Changes in Economic Structure in Asia, 1980-1990

Country	Agriculture		Manufacturing		Services	
	1980	1990	1980	1990	1980	1990
Hong Kong	0.8	0.3	22.3	18.1	54.8	58.2
Singapore	1.2	0.3	29.1	29.1	44.7	53.8
Korea	14.9	9.1	29.7	29.2	27.0	29.1
Taiwan	7.7	4.1	36.0	34.4	35.6	45.2
Malaysia	22.9	18.7	19.6	26.9	22.4	22.7
Thailand	23.2	12.4	21.3	26.1	35.5	38.0
Philippine	25.1	22.1	25.7	25.5	26.2	30.7
Indonesia		17.9		42.9		39.3
Vietnam		38.2		24.6		37.2
Cambodia		49.4		16.3		34.4
Laos		59.8		17.2		23.0

Table 2
GDP Growth Rates, Exports as a Percentage of Gross Domestic Product,
and Foreign Investment Growth Rates in Southeast Asia

GDP Growth Rates
(% per annum)

	1987	1988	1989	1990	1991	1992	Average 1980-91
Korea	12.0	11.5	6.2	9.2	8.4	0.5	9.9
Singapore	9.4	11.1	9.2	8.3	6.7	5.8	6.3
Taiwan	12.3	7.3	7.6	4.9	7.2	6.6	8.5
Malaysia	5.4	8.9	0.2	9.7	8.7	8.0	5.2
Indonesia	4.9	5.8	7.5	7.1	6.6	5.9	5.5
Thailand	9.5	13.2	12.2	10.0	8.0	7.5	7.8
Philippines	4.8	6.3	6.1	2.7	-0.7	0.0	1.0

Source: Asian Development Bank 1993.

Exports (Goods & Service) as Percentage of GDP, 1960-1993

	1960	1970	1980	1990	1991	1992	1993
S. Korea	8.6	29.7	34.0	31.0	29.3	30.9	32.3
Taiwan*	11.2	30.6	48.9	42.1	47.8	47.6	47.9
Singapore	163.1	113.2	207.2	189.0	182.3	173.5	158.6
Hong Kong	82.4	101.1	106.7	134.6	140.5	143.8	150.1
Malaysia	42.5	39.8	57.5	77.3	81.4	78.0	80.3
Thailand	16.5	18.6	24.3	35.7	35.4	36.0	37.0
Indonesia	5.3	20.3	33.0	27.5	27.6	29.3	27.8
Philippines	17.2	24.8	23.6	28.0	30.0	28.9	31.6
Cambodia	13.9	5.8		5.1	6.2		
Laos*			6.5	11.3	12.9	16.2	20.5
Vietnam*	36.6		6.8	29.0	32.6	32.4	28.2
China	4.2	4.6	10.2	17.6	18.7	20.9	22.1
India	3.6	4.3	6.5	7.9	9.3	9.8	11.3

Source: Economic Intelligence Unit 1994.

246

Table 3
Foreign Direct Investment ($ Million)

	1986	1987	1988	1989	1990	1991
Korea	435	601	871	758	715	1,116
Singapore	1,710	2,836	3,655	2,770	3,861	3,584
Taiwan	326	715	959	1,604	1,330	1,271
Malaysia	489	423	719	1,668	2,514	3,454
Indonesia	258	385	576	682	1,093	1,482
Thailand	263	352	1,105	1,775	2,444	2,041
Philippines	127	307	936	563	530	544

Source: Asian Development Bank.

Table 4
Direction of Exports (Percent Share)

	Internal Asian Region		USA		Japan		EEC	
	1985	1991	1985	1991	1985	1991	1985	1991
Hong Kong	38	40	30	22	4	5	12	16
Korea	13	21	36	27	15	18	11	14
Singapore	38	41	22	19	9	8	10	14
Taiwan	16	26	15	20	11	13	5	10
Malaysia	40	44	11	17	25	16	13	13
Indonesia	17	25	21	12	46	36	6	12
Thailand	29	22	19	21	13	18	17	19
Philippines	21	18	35	35	19	20	13	17
Laos	71	61	2	2	9	5	1	27
Vietnam	50	34	--	--	17	37	5	11.3

Source: International Trade Statistics.

Table 5
Average Unweighted Tariffs (in Percent) by CEPT Product

Product	Indonesia	Malaysia	Philippines	Thailand	Average
Pulp	9	3	7	5	6
Textiles	19	6	26	30	20
Vegetable oils	13	1	21	10	11
Chemicals	4	0	7	10	5
Pharmaceuticals	5	0	9	8	5
Fertilizers	0	0	3	0	1
Plastics	15	13	17	25	18
Leather	3	9	19	24	14
Rubber	9	8	23	22	15
Cement	15	55	30	5	36
Glass	20	15	20	18	18
Gems	11	5	24	0	10
Electronics	24	15	18	25	21
Furniture	50	24	33	8	47
Average	14	11	19	19	16

Source: Kumar 1992.

Table 6
Labor Protection

Laws	Singapore	Malaysia	Philippines	Thailand
1. Minimum wages	Yes	No (certain occupations only)	Yes (certain areas only)	Yes
2. Working Hours	44	48	48	48 (56 hrs in commercial establishments)
3. Overtime Pay	1.5	1.5	1.25	1.5
4. Holidays (Paid)	10	10	10	13
5. Annual Leave	Max. 15 days	Max. 22 days	5 days	6 days
6. Sick Leave	14 days w/o hospitalization 60 days w/ hospitalization	22 days		30 days
7. Female Employment	No night work	No night work	No night work (except in occupations where males cannot match dexterity of females)	No night work. No employment in hazardous operations
8. Maternity Benefits	8 weeks	60 days	6 weeks	30 days paid 30 days unpaid
9. Child Labor, Limited Types of Work	12 years	13 years	15 years	13 years
10. Workmen's Compensation for Occupational Injuries	Yes	Yes	Yes	Yes
11. OSHA Laws	Yes	Yes	Yes	Yes
12. Termination, Layoffs	6 weeks notice	8 weeks notice	2 weeks notice	2 weeks notice
13. Severance Pay	Maturity scheme via insurance	20 days pay for every year of service	1 month's pay for every year of service	1 month's pay for every year of service
14. Annual Bonus	Max: 3 months	No	No	No
15. Social Security	Lump sum on retirement. Employer contribution = 10% of monthly pay	Lump sum on retirement. Employer contribution = 10% of monthly pay	Lump sum on retirement. Employer contribution = 6-7% of monthly pay	Lump sum on retirement. Employer contribution = 6-7% of monthly pay

Table 7
Industrial Relations

	Singapore	Malaysia	Philippines	Thailand
1. Union density as a percentage of the nonagricultural workforce.	20% and declining	14% and declining	30% stable	3-4%
2. Union formation, registration and recognition: (administrative procedures significantly impact ability to form unions).	- Minimum 7 persons -Simple majority for union registration and recognition	- Minimum 7 persons. - 51% of majority for registration - Employer must recognize within 30 days - Registrar has extensive powers to disallow registration	- 30% of bargaining unit for registration - Registrar of unions has extensive powers to register or not register	- 20% of enterprise votes necessary for registration - Registration process arduous and a disincentive to union formation. (Procedure takes a minimum of 90 days) - Ban on unions in certain sectors
3. Union structure	- Mix of craft, enterprise, and industrial unions - Since 1987, enterprise unions are the norm - Most unions affiliated with NTUC, only recognized national federation	- Since 1980, enterprise unions encouraged - Unions allowed to affiliate to peak federations in some sectors, not in others (e.g., electronics)	- Enterprise unions - Affiliated to national centers - ISS national federations and 5,600 independent unions	- Enterprise unions.
4. Scope of Bargaining	-Bargaining over wage increases subject to national wages council guidelines -Cannot bargain over job assignments, transfers, promotions, layoffs, retrenchment, and other redundancy issues	-Cannot bargain over job assignments, transfers, promotions, layoffs, and retrenchments. -In pioneer industries, cannot bargain beyond the minimum laid down by employment law terms and conditions beyond the -Explicit ban on union political activity	-Unrestricted scope	-Wages set by tripartite wage boards -Otherwise unrestricted scope

	Singapore	Malaysia	Philippines	Thailand
5. Right to Strike	-Prohibited in essential industries -Essential industries defined. -Strikes for political purposes prohibited	-Prohibited in essential industries -Essential industries *very* broadly defined	-Prohibited for political purposes	-Prohibited in government, public sector, essential industries (broadly defined), and sectors like telecommunications, transportation, education -Strikes banned under military governments
6. Administrative policies and practices that attempt to curtail industrial conflict, by making it difficult for unions to go on strike	- 14-day notice - 2/3 majority vote by secret ballot - Cannot strike if dispute is under conciliation/arbitration - Appropriate gov't immediately refers disputes to conciliation - Registrar can ban strikes if against public interest	- Notice - Cannot strike if dispute under mediation - Minister of Labor actively intervenes to either "enforce" settlement or refer dispute to compulsory arbitration	- Notice to employee and DOL - 30-day cooling off period - Can strike only if conciliation avenue exhausted	- Notice - Secret ballot - Strikers cannot launch boycott of company's products - Strikers cannot publish statements about the company
7. Labor involvement in decision making on IR policy at gov't. level (de facto)	Yes - Full	No	No	Partial involvement in wage boards and labor relations committee
8. Labor Management Cooperative (De Jure)	Labor-management committees	Labor-management committees	Labor-Management Committees	None

References

Ariff, Mohammed. 1992. The Prospects for AFTA. Malaysian Institute of Eocnomic Research: Kuala Lampur.

Asian Development Bank. 1993. Asian Development Outlook. Oxford University Press. April.

Chew, Soon Beng, and Rosalind Chew. 1993. "Impact of Development Strategy on Industrial Relations in Singapore." Nanyang Technological University, April.

Deyo, Frederick. 1989. Bene*ath the Miracle: Labour Subordination in East Asian Development*. Berkeley: University of California Press.

Economist Intelligence Unit. 1994. World Outlook: Forecasts of Political and Economic Trends in over 180 Countries. U.K.: The Economist.

Frenkel, Stephen, ed.. 1993. *Organized Labor in the Asia-Pacific Region*. Ithaca, NY: ILR Press.

Kumar, A. N. 1992. ASEAN Free Trade Area: The View from Malaysia. Paper presented at the Annual MIER Outlook Conference, Kuala Lampur Dec. 3-5.

Kuruvilla, Sarosh. 1994a. "Industrialization Strategy and Industrial Relations Policy in Malaysia and the Philippines." Paper presented at the Annual Meetings of the Industrial Relations Research Association, Boston, Jan. 3-5.

..... 1994b. Southeast Asian Industrial Relations Systems. Implication for Industrial Relations Policy in Developing Economies. *International Labour Review*, forthcoming.

Macaraya, Bach, and Rene Ofreneo. 1993. Structural Adjustment and Industrial Relations: The Philippine Experience. Paper presented at the Conference on industrial relations in Asia and East Africa. Sydney, September 5-7 1992.

Ofreneo, Rene. Forthcoming. Labor and the Philippine Economy. School of Labor and Institute for Industrial Relations, University of the Philippines, Quezon City.

Ponniah, Arudsothy, and Craig R. Littler. 1993. "State Regulation and Union Fragmentation in Malaysia." In Stephen Frenkel, ed., 120-47. *Organized Labor in the Asia-Pacific Region*. Ithaca, NY: ILR Press.

Rushton, Kevin. 1990. "Auto Parts Complementation in ASEAN." no. 23. (Spring/Summer): 1-61

Salih, Kamal, Mei Ling Young, and Rajah Rasiah. 1988. Transnational Capital and Local Conjuncture. The Semiconductor Industry in Penang. Malaysian Institute of Economic Research. 1987.

Stewart, Terence, and Margaret L. H. Png. 1993. "The Growth Triangle of Singapore, Malaysia, and Indonesia." *Georgia Journal of International and Comparative Law*, 23, no. 1 (Spring): 1-61.

Vatikiosis, Michael. 1993a. "Cars Out, Planes In: Malaysia Eyes New Market in ASEAN." *Far Eastern Economic Review* (August 26): 54.

..... 1993b. "Three's Company: Malaysia, Thailand, Indonesia Forge Development Zone." *Far Eastern Economic Review* (August 5).

Wu, Friedrich. 1991. "The ASEAN Economies in the 1990s and Singapore's Regional Role." *California Management Review* (Fall): 103-14.

Appendix

Workshop on

REGIONAL INTEGRATION AND INDUSTRIAL RELATIONS
IN NORTH AMERICA

School of Industrial and Labor Relations
Cornell University

October 1-2, 1993

SUMMARY OF PAPER PRESENTATIONS
AND DISCUSSION

Prepared by Kate Anderson
School of Industrial and Labor Relations
Cornell University

Contents

List of Conference Participants 256

I. Changes and Trends in Industrial Relations Systems 258
Harry C. Katz, "Taking Stock of the Transformation of U.S. Industrial Relations"
Enrique de la Garza Toledo, "Trends in Mexican Labor Relations and
    Collective Bargaining"
Mark C. Thompson, "Trends in Canadian Labor Relations"
Discussion

II. Labor Law and Institutions 261
Graciela Bensusán Areous, "Trends in Labor Law and Institutional Change in Mexico"
Gilles Trudeau and Guylaine Vallée, "Economic Integration and Labor Law Policy"
Katherine Stone, "U.S. Labor Law and Its Prospects"
Discussion

**III. Impacts of the U.S.-Canada/North American Free Trade
Agreements (NAFTA)** 266
Roy Adams, "The Social Dimension of Freer Trade"
Ian Robinson, "How Will the North American Free Trade Agreement Affect
    Worker Rights in North America?"
Alberto Aziz Nassif, "Mexican Political Party and Labor Union Responses to the
    North American Free Trade Agreement"
Maria Lorena Cook, "Transnational Labor Strategies and Economic Integration"
Discussion

**IV. Sectoral Trends in Labor Relations and
Collective Bargaining: Part 1** 271
Anil Verma, "Industrial Relations in the Canadian Steel and
    Telecommunication Industries"
Arnulfo Arteaga Garcia, "Labor Relations in the Mexican Automobile Industry"
Harry C. Katz, "Collective Bargaining in the U.S. Auto Assembly Sector"
Discussion

**V. Sectoral Trends in Labor Relations and
Collective Bargaining: Part 2** 276
Michael Belzer, "Inter-City Trucking in the United States"
Alfredo Hualde, "Labor Relations in the Maquiladora Industry"
Robert Hebdon, "Public Sector Labor Relations in Canada"
Rafael Loyola Diaz, "Labor Relations in the Mexican Petrochemical Industry"
Discussion

VI. Comparative Perspectives 281
Lowell Turner, "Cross-National Labor Collaboration and the Battle for a Social
    Dimension in the European Single Market"
Sarosh Kuruvilla "NAFTA, AFTA, and Labor Relations Trends in Southeast Asia"
Marcus Rebick, "Japan"
Discussion

LIST OF CONFERENCE PARTICIPANTS

Roy J. Adams
Faculty of Business
McMaster University
Hamilton, Ontario, Canada

Graciela Bensusán Areous
Universidad Autónoma Metropolitana-
Xochimilco
México, D.F.

Michael Belzer
School of Industrial and Labor Relations
Cornell University
Ithaca, NY

Maria Lorena Cook
School of Industrial and Labor Relations
Cornell University
Ithaca, NY

Rafael Loyola Díaz
Facultad Latinoamericano de
Ciencias Sociales (FLACSO)
México, D.F.

Arnulfo Arteaga Garcia
Universidad Autónoma
Metropolitana-Iztapalapa
México, D.F.

Morley Gunderson
Faculty of Management and Centre
for Industrial Relations
University of Toronto
Toronto, Ontario, Canada

Robert Hebdon
School of Industrial and Labor Relations
Cornell University
Ithaca, NY

Alfredo Hualde
Colegio de la Frontera Norte (COLEF)
Tijuana, México

Harry C. Katz
School of Industrial and Labor Relations
Cornell University
Ithaca, NY

Sarosh Kuruvilla
School of Industrial and Labor Relations
Cornell University
Ithaca, NY

Alberto Aziz Nassif
Facultad Latinoamericano de Ciencias
Sociales (FLACSO)
México, D.F.

Marcus Rebick
School of Industrial and Labor Relations
Cornell University
Ithaca, NY

Ian Robinson
Institute of Labor and Industrial
Relations
University of Michigan
Ann Arbor, MI

Katherine Stone
Law School and School of Industrial and
Labor Relations
Cornell University
Ithaca, NY

Mark E. Thompson
Faculty of Commerce
University of British Columbia
Vancouver, BC, Canada

Enrique de la Garza Toledo
Universidad Autónoma
Metropolitana-Iztapalapa
México, D.F.

Gilles Trudeau
Ecole de Relations Industrielles
Université de Montréal
Montréal, Quebec, Canada

Lowell Turner
School of Industrial and Labor Relations
Cornell University
Ithaca, NY

Guylaine Vallée
Ecole de Relations Industrielles
Université de Montréal
Montréal, Quebec, Canada

Anil Verma
Faculty of Management and Centre for
Industrial Relations
University of Toronto
Toronto, Ontario, Canada

I. CHANGES AND TRENDS IN INDUSTRIAL RELATIONS SYSTEMS

"Taking Stock of the Transformation of U.S. Industrial Relations"
Harry C. Katz, School of Industrial and Labor Relations, Cornell University

The changes and trends in the industrial relations systems in the United States can best be understood as a response to broad pressures that the unionized sector is facing. Both economic trade and the growing nonunion sector have had a strong impact on the state of labor relations in this country. By the 1970s, much of U.S. industrial relations focused on collective bargaining. Attempts to understand what was happening to unions focused on management tactics to thwart union efforts. Moving beyond this narrow focus, to look at the impact of the nonunion sector, allows for a historical perspective of the state of labor today. In the 1980s, the transformation of industrial relations could best be understood by following the patterns of concession bargaining and by exploring the new experiments with employee involvement and team systems. In some cases there has been a radical alteration in the role of unions in the company with the introduction of participatory programs. While cooperation has had its successes, the adversarial labor-management relationship has often led to criticisms that these are management attempts to co-opt the union.

Perhaps the best way to understand industrial relations today is through the diversity that exists. While there have been many cases of decertification and aggressive anti-unionism, there are also some positive developments, for example, the relationship between Saturn and the UAW. Katz explains that there is something going on that is not traditional or co-optive, that is, the expansion of unions into the strategic business issues of the company. Of course, there is the obvious decline in overall numbers, with only approximately 11 percent of the workforce in the United States unionized. Fundamental changes have taken place in the structure of collective bargaining. Labor relations has seen a decentralization of negotiations away from the national unions. That is, more and more decisions are being made at the plant or even work group level. In sum, the American industrial relations system is in a period of significant transformation.

"Trends in Mexican Labor Relations and Collective Bargaining"
Enrique de la Garza Toledo, UAM, Iztapalapa

Enrique de la Garza sets out four general characteristics to define the industrial relations system in Mexico: the shared responsibility of unions for the smooth operation of the state, the concentration of labor relations principally at the state level, the subordination of labor negotiations to the economic policies of the state and the existence of the relationships between trade unions, the electoral system, and the social security system in the context of weak union democracy and repression of opposing parties. Overall, approximately 28 percent of salaried workers in Mexico are unionized, with rates varying considerably across industries.

The year 1982 can be seen as a significant reference point for labor relations, according to de la Garza. The key aspect that defined this year was the increased use of flexibility in firms. Management has generally defined this as a reduction in obstacles to hiring and firing employees, and the use of workers in work processes that may, to

259

a limited extent, lead to tying wages to productivity. The fundamental characteristics of flexible contracts included the elimination of obstacles to internal mobility in collective bargaining; the use of "a multivalue system"; an increase in the use of contractors, subcontractors, and temporary workers; and the elimination of strict promotion criteria and seniority procedures. Flexibility became more intense in the larger, older, and export-oriented firms and in certain geographic areas, particularly along the border with California. The strategy that corporations pursued was further defined by the characteristics of past collective bargaining agreements, the type of trade union (official, independent, or "white") and the policy of the government in relation to labor, which often differed by sector. Behind these developments, one must understand that the economic crisis that occurred in Mexico was seen as a crisis in productivity which could be overcome with flexibility.

After 1992 a new situation began to develop. The previous ten years had been characterized by declining union power and the unilateral setting of the terms and conditions of employment. In order to achieve needed flexibility the state defined a new unionism whose ideology was social liberalism. The central axis for new industrial relations had to be industrial democracy, not in the European sense, but limited to the involvement of unions in productivity enhancement efforts and worker training. As a result of this a 1982 national agreement to increase productivity was approved by the state, management representatives, and the unions. This appeared to be a new direction on the part of the state.

The pact has not resulted in decreased vigilance by the state. Within production a polarization has occurred, with one extreme characterized by low standards and technological obsolescence and the other by competitiveness. In general the union has been pushed aside as a partner. Overall, total quality has left little power to the workers and is often used as a control mechanism.

"Trends in Canadian Labor Relations"
Mark E. Thompson, Faculty of Commerce, University of British Columbia

Mark Thompson notes that, with some differences, the Canadian industrial relations system fits fairly well into the Wagner model. The unions' fundamental role is collective bargaining and is primarily entrenched in the heavy industrial sector and public sector. Canadian employers are reluctant but law abiding, that is, they are "relatively comfortable" with unions. The government is removed from day-to-day industrial relations and is distanced from the terms of bargaining. Industrial relations takes place in a decentralized system.

At the strategic change level, there hasn't been much change. Union membership has remained relatively constant at approximately 36 to 38 percent of the labor force, with only minor shifts in proportions from the private to the public sector. In contrast to trends in the United States, recent legislation has favored labor, particularly in British Columbia and Ontario. While overall, labor unrest as indicated by the occurrence of strikes has decreased, by international standards, Canada ranks high in conflict. As in the United States, Canada has seen a growth in concession bargaining, with 1993 characterized by a dramatic increase in negotiated wage freezes.

Many smaller shifts are occurring in Canadian industrial relations, according to Thompson. For example, participatory practices and employee involvement schemes have been on the rise. The response of labor to these developments has typically been opposition at the national level, with the local level making a pragmatic decision. As noted above, there has also been a decentralization of bargaining structures with the result that wages are increasingly being put into competition. Similar to the United States, there has been a strong emphasis on flexibility through the use of part-time employees and a shift to fewer job classifications.

While competitive pressures and low economic growth in Canada have resulted in struggles for both the public and private sector, the former is where significant developments have been taking place. Recent government attempts to negotiate wage freezes and other concessions have resulted in public discontent and reaction. This has created tension between labor and the New Democratic Party, which claims to represent the interest of unions. Thompson feels that the most significant arenas for future change in Canadian industrial relations will be the public sector, rather than the private, and at the workplace level.

Discussion

Anil Verma suggests that, despite the historical relationship between the state, labor, and employers, the future of industrial relations in Mexico might better fit into a decentralized model in which employers and unions negotiate terms based on the conditions prevailing in the industry. Enrique de la Garza notes that while such a form of labor relations would be preferable, it is almost inconceivable given the strong involvement of labor in politics and because employers show no signs of removing their support for the centralized approach.

It is clear from the above that the industrial relations systems across the North American bloc created by NAFTA varies considerably by country. Perhaps the most difficult task is to attempt a comparison of Mexico, the United States and Canada when there are basic disparities even in the use of terms. For example, Alberto Aziz points out that although the discussants may be premising their discussions on similar concepts, for Mexico there is a very different way of filtering these ideas. The maquiladoras were used as an example to demonstrate this point. Due to the crucial contribution of this region to the GDP, the government has adapted a special labor policy that has tended to favor the employer over democratic trade unions and their members. Enrique de la Garza explains that there is a type of trade union in Mexico called a "protectionist trade union." These organizations are created out of an arrangement between management and the trade union. In fact, they are established without the election of leaders and often without the knowledge of the workers altogether. The purpose of these "unions" is to preempt workers from forming their own representative body. The Ministry of Labor not only allows for the existence of these organizations but, one could go so far as to suggest, it supports their formation. Also permitted in the maquiladoras are predatory contracts, which allow for standards below what is mandated by Federal law, and the subjective prohibition of strikes by the Ministry of Labor.

Arnulfo Arteaga emphasizes that we must note these differences when we consider what impact economic integration will have on labor relations. That is, there is no one model of labor relations and the passage of NAFTA will clearly have varying implications for industrial relations in each of the three countries. While the parallel agreement is meant to some degree to regulate these differences, he suggests, it is questionable what impact they will have in concrete terms.

II. LABOR LAW AND INSTITUTIONS

"Trends in Labor Law and Institutional Change in Mexico"
Graciela Bensusán Areous, UAM - Xochimilco

Graciela Bensusan explains that in the first phase of the negotiations of NAFTA the labor or social dimension was completely excluded. Because the Mexican labor laws were understood by the Bush administration as being very advanced, this area was ignored in the negotiations process. Afterward, there were some attempts made within NAFTA to regulate labor issues in Mexico through the creation of the side agreement. While the side agreements call for a combination of national enforcement of laws and provides for tri-national supervision, this model is very limited.

The key problem in reference to Mexican labor regulations is not the lack of enforcement. If this were the principal concern more resources could simply be allocated for more inspectors, and so forth. The real issue concerns the political context in which the labor legislation operates. In order to have enforcement, it is essential to have a government or state system that is supportive of upholding the written law.

The Mexican model of industrial relations is one of "anticipated institutionalization" embedded in the 1917 Constitution. That is, the notion of flexibility of the state to alter labor regulations did not arise out of the crisis surrounding economic integration, but rather had already been in place. The mounting pressure to become competitive will continue to result in government intervention and adjustment in labor laws. An example to illustrate this point is the new model proposed by the Salinas administration. It is based on industrial democracy, which allows both parties to be active in negotiations. Ironically, however, at the same time this was imposed, the state intervened in a strike at a Volkswagen plant and imposed a final settlement without the input of either labor or management. Bensusán also suggests that the labor law system in Mexico is being strongly impacted by the process of integration. Primarily this means a convergence with American labor law.

"Economic Integration and Labor Law Policy"
Guylaine Vallée, Ecole de Relations Industrielles, Université de Montreal
and Gilles Trudeau, Ecole de Relatións Industrielles, Université de Montreal

The assumption of the paper by Guylaine Vallée and Gilles Trudeau is that economic integration between the United States and Canada and between the United States and Mexico is not the result of NAFTA or FTA, rather it confirms a relationship that has already existed and therefore labor law has already been significantly impacted. The Canadian economy is largely dependent on its commercial relationship with the United States, demonstrated by the fact that more than 75 percent of its exports entered the United States in 1989. The United States is Mexico's most important trading partner with 75 percent of Mexican imports coming into this country. Direct commercial exchanges between Canada and Mexico, however, are very limited. It appears from these figures, and from the fact that there is a rising similarity between the types of exports entering the United States from Canada and Mexico, that the two are competitors for the American market in this new economic alliance and that rather than being a trilateral negotiation, it has been a bilateral process between the United States and the other two parties individually.

Despite the fact that Canadian labor relations and legislation is more decentralized and considered more "labor friendly," overall the American and Canadian systems are very similar, with the Canadian system drawing from many of the provisions of the 1935 Wagner Act. That is, before existence of NAFTA or the FTA the relationship of Canadian labor law and collective bargaining to that of the United States was well defined.

According to Vallée and Trudeau, labor law exists as a protective conscience that aims to protect the worker through social legislation and minimum standards and rights and also insures stable conditions for the production of goods and services. These original reasons for the raison d'être of labor law are not taken into account in NAFTA, the parallel accords, or the FTA, explain Vallée and Trudeau. Labor is viewed as a commodity in the context of these agreements, with labor regulations seen as obstacles to free trade among the participating countries. Commercial competition has been placed over the importance of social legislation or labor standards. If a country fails to impose its laws, unfair subsidies to trade may be claimed by any of the parties. That is, labor law will be seen in the light of its impact on competitiveness and therefore will most likely lead to a more "cost-effective" diminishing of standards. There is a fear of downgrading or a "race to the bottom" when there is a stark difference between labor standards and regulations across countries. In the arena of collective bargaining, the threat of moving to Mexico to pursue lower wages has been presented by many companies to force unions to accept certain contract terms.

Finally, the parallel agreement contains major flaws that contradict the very purpose for which it was negotiated. The side accord addresses only matters related to basic human dignity, including health and safety, child labor, and minimum wage standards, and omits many other crucial subjects. Overall, there is no guarantee preventing any of the three countries from deregulating their labor markets on social issues. Without an enforcement mechanism to ensure upgrading, the agreement in fact promotes competition on the basis of labor costs. The logic of the market will prevail in the formation of the social dimension of NAFTA.

"U.S. Labor Law and Its Prospects"
Katherine Stone, Law School and School of Industrial and Labor Relations,
        Cornell University

Since the 1930s, according to Katherine Stone, there has been a two-tiered structure of labor relations in the United States. The first tier has included social welfare legislation that establishes minimal standards for an employment contract, for example, minimum wages, health and safety standards, and bans on discrimination, and the second tier has included the National Labor Relations Act that protects and empowers unions. Protection for individual employment rights are somewhat minimal with moderate provisions for unemployment benefits, retirement or disability benefits or health insurance. Overall, in comparison to the protections provided in Canada, Mexico, and Europe, American workers exist in a quite unmitigated labor market.

Established in the 1930s, the federal labor law was created to protect and empower labor through the right to organize, strike and by requiring the employer to bargain with union representatives. Many of the protections that were provided to unions in this labor law however, have been dismantled in the last twelve years. The National Labor Relations Board, which administers labor law, has begun to permit employer business judgments and business rationality to justify actions that abrogate workers' rights. What has occurred is a reinterpretation or use of the law that has permitted the loss of its original protections. According to Stone, this has meant that "regulations have been reduced to a proxy for the market and the regime of regulations has been replaced with a regime of market rationality." During this time, however, there has been an improvement in individual rights, particularly at the level of the state. This has included the rights of workers in unjust dismissals, minority protections, health and safety and takeover protections. Overall, there has been a shift from regulations that sought to protect collective rights to one focused on individual rights. This differs from Mexico, Canada, and Europe primarily because the United States lacks a labor party to defend, enforce, or enhance those individual rights in the future.

With the new administration there are some positive signs for the future of labor and employment law. It is predicted that the trend toward a strengthening of individual rights at the state level will continue and there is a possibility of reversing some of the decline of collective rights. This may be reflected in the reform in the legislative arena at the federal level or on the administrate level of the NLRB.

The side agreements to NAFTA are not a harmonization law but rather state that each individual party to the agreement must enforce its own laws. The language dealing with labor principles promotes the right to organize, to strike, equal pay for equal work, and so on, but these impose no enforceable authorizations. According to Stone, even the enforceable areas surrounding health and safety, child labor and minimum wage laws are "watered down by qualifiers" that basically allow for exceptions to all cases of non-enforcement. There are questions as to whether NAFTA will freeze countries at their present level of labor regulations or even force a downward trend in standards. Within the agreement there seems to be a bias to raising the standards in the name of "discriminatory burdens and indirect barriers to trade." NAFTA does not have a direct impact on collective bargaining system but it may make it impossible for U.S. labor law to apply extraterritorially and, even if labor laws are not harmonized, unions will be impacted by any harmonization that may occur in corporate law, bankruptcy law, or any other commercial law that affects them. On a positive side, this may give an incentive to American unions to work together against the power of transnational corporations.

Discussion

Enrique de la Garza offers that "flexibility" is nothing new. Mexico previously defined this as the manipulation of the law according to political and economic interests but since 1980 a different flexibility is found within the changes to collective bargaining agreements. The limits set within the parallel agreements dealing with minimum wages and child labor, he notes, do not really impact foreign investment. Standard wages in Mexico are low enough to attract investment and the supply of labor is large enough so that companies do not have to resort to employing children. In addition, if the government perceives that the preferable way to attract foreign investment is through a low minimum wage, it can and will maintain it at a low or reduced level. Also, the government has traditionally regulated inflation by controlling the minimum wage. In conclusion, the government, through unions and collective bargaining agreements, will maintain wage levels as part of its economic policy.

In reference to the maintenance of rights, Stone suggests that while the parallel agreements "protect" the right to strike, the problem is this notion "has many dimensions to it." In the United States, for example, this right exists with the simultaneous ability of the employer to permanently replace strikers. In some provinces of Canada and in Europe, employers are not legally permitted to replace strikers and workers may receive unemployment benefits during a dispute. Therefore, while we may have consensus on allowing for the right to strike, it is much harder to agree on what this means in the context of an international agreement. While the parallel accord dictates the enforcement of the right to strike, it is unclear how one defines enforcement. In the United States, the NLRB has discretion over which cases to hear and also has budgetary constraints that limits its power. Because of these factors, should the right to strike be considered unfair practice under NAFTA? The question becomes what is baseline versus what should be considered a burden or subsidy to trade. If, in fact, some action may be found in violation of labor standards, the maximum penalty allowed is defined as 1/7,000th of 1 percent of the amount of trade between the countries. In conclusion, how one defines the terms and the enforcement under NAFTA is not clear and if determined will be of questionable impact.

Bringing the issue of the "race to the bottom" in the context of the United States, one can see that even among regions there has historically been a conflict between those states that have, for example, more stringent health and safety standards and those that are more relaxed. What has occurred is that those states that have offered some incentive to corporations in the form of lower standards have been able to lure them to locate in their area. As a result, unions have pushed for federal regulation of higher standards across states. The construction industry in the Maritimes, Quebec, and Ontario, however, has moved toward deregulation to meet the standards of other provinces.

Some suggest that the reference to the micro level within the countries that reveals a harmonization of standards downward will likely occur at the international level with the passage of NAFTA. Others predict that the agreement will have a minimal impact on the labor laws of the three independent countries. Mark Thompson concludes that labor law is deeply embedded in the values and cultural systems of a country and to expect countries with mature systems of labor law to yield sovereignty or transform significantly is unreasonable. That is, industrial relations structures in fact tend to be quite stable and unsusceptible to change. Ian Robinson disagrees, arguing that the drastic decline in American union density since the 1950s, and the instability of Mexican labor relations and the role of the Mexican state in that regime, indicate anything but a stable system of industrial relations in these countries. Katz goes further to suggest that the evidence seems to show that "the law has never really mattered that much and that the systems are actually moving in ways that are not very well determined by the law." What does seem to be of significance, in addition to the subtle and qualified influences of the law, are the larger economic trends, developments, and forces that are occurring in these countries.

One must be careful not to overestimate the significance of wages as a determinant of competitiveness. Many other economic forces occurring that are not in the direction of a search for lower wages. It is not clear to Katz that low wages are the dominant factor in any of the countries, nor is there any one pressure that dominates in one country--the pressures differ by industry and company. Economic strategies, he claims, can not simply be defined by low wages. Perhaps, Ian Robinson states, the search for low wages is not the prime mover of all economic change but the nature of economic restructuring, and how this alters priorities in the aggregate sense can best be analyzed by further exploring how productivity and low wage priorities will be played out with NAFTA. Enrique de la Garza suggests that certain characteristics of the maquiladoras, for example the low wages it offers, may be viewed as very attractive to some international corporations, while others may find that the environment is not conducive to a high- technology strategy involving new work processes.

III. IMPACTS OF THE U.S.-CANADA/NORTH AMERICAN FREE TRADE AGREEMENTS (NAFTA)

"The Social Dimension of Freer Trade"
Roy J. Adams, Faculty of Business, McMaster University

Roy Adams finds that the key labor issues that continuously come up in trade agreements include adjustment, social dumping (within a trade agreement a party will manipulate labor standards in order to gain an unfair advantage), sovereignty, and equity, that is, capital always comes out at the top to the detriment of labor. Sovereignty is of particular concern, as any particular country may lose its ability to regulate federal codes with the result that member countries may be whipsawed against one another. Each of the above characteristics can exist with or without the possibility of free trade; therefore, some argue a social dimension to trade should not exist at all.

One position that has emerged from the corporativist research in Europe is that if a free trade area is to operate to its optimum it is necessary to get a social consensus and without it there will be continuous conflict that will inhibit the efficient functioning of the market. In Europe, a social charter, which sets out the basic rights of workers within the European Community, was ratified. Because the enforcement mechanism for these principles are not powerful, some suggest that such a dimension is not valuable.

Adams believes that the social dimension established in Europe stands as a symbol. It is a clear signal that companies not living up to these standards are behaving in a manner that is not acceptable. The existence of this type of symbolic statement permits continual pressure to be exerted by unions, the government, and the public. While the mechanisms in the parallel agreement to NAFTA were modeled, to some extent, on the European example, it is unlikely that the enforcement powers or influence will come anywhere near that of European agencies. Adams suggests what is needed in the context of NAFTA, even over strong enforcement powers, is a high profile standard setting, value-setting agency.

"How Will the North American Free Trade Agreement Affect Worker
Rights in North America?"
Ian Robinson, Institute of Labor and Industrial Relations,
University of Michigan

The question that Ian Robinson tackled was the extent to which different forms of economic integration would impact workers' rights. He found that capital mobility was one of the primary trends that will take place with free trade. Mobility will increase, he suggests, due to the elimination of tariffs over time, the reduction of risks to corporations as a result of new property rights, and the expansion of the capacity to challenge government regulations through the argument that they violate national treatment. Two kinds of immediate impacts are likely to occur with the passage of NAFTA. First, it will encourage employers or the government to adopt a low wage/high productivity competitive strategy, and second, it will reduce the bargaining power of labor in all three countries because of the "exit" threat of corporate investors and the declining union density associated with NAFTA-induced economic restructuring.

National and corporate competitive strategies that combine high productivity with low wages will require employer or state repression of basic worker rights to make them work. Otherwise, workers will act collectively to capture a substantial share of the gains from productivity increases, thereby undermining the competitive strategy. Reduced bargaining power will make it more difficult for unions to resist that repression. So will increased public acceptance of the view that workers who seriously assert their collective bargaining and strike rights are undermining national competitiveness. Robinson argues that in this regard NAFTA only intensifies a process that has been underway since the early 1970s. In Canada and the United States, employer unfair labor practices have increased dramatically since then. In Mexico, the Salinas administration's assault on the teachers' and petroleum workers' unions received considerable attention, but repression in the maquiladoras has been more systematic and extensive. One result of the Mexican manufacturing sector, despite the higher average productivity levels that prevail in the maquilas. Finally, Robinson argues that the income polarization that will result from further repression of workers rights will reduce the quality of democracy in Canada and the United States, and make high-quality democracy more difficult to achieve and sustain in Mexico. Since worker rights fare much better in high quality democracies, this sets in motion a political vicious circle that will reinforce NAFTA-related downward economic pressures on workers rights in the three countries.

"Mexican Political Party and Labor Union Responses to the North American Free Trade Agreement"
Alberto Aziz, CIESAS

Aziz agrees with Robinson that, particularly in Mexico, there is a clear and direct relationship between the quality of democracy and the quality of the rights of workers. The side agreements serve to cover up the lack of workers' rights. The relationship between the labor movement and the political system has undergone significant changes during the negotiation of NAFTA. Despite the lack of explicit changes in norms, new rules exist in the relationship between the state, agriculture, the church, and the worker.

The 1980s were seen as an era of defeat for workers in their relationship with the state. The status of these ties went from that of equality to one of subordination. For example, although the right to strike was seen as a privilege granted by the state, the union was involved in the decision to strike. Now, there is a lack of any sort of bilateral exchange and the right to strike has been fundamentally taken away. This change has caused a tense and conflict-ridden situation between trade unions and the government.

The push toward labor flexibility has resulted in the destruction of collective bargaining agreements. Also, the new political discourse in favor of competitiveness, productivity, and flexibility in practice has meant drastic wage controls and wage adjustments that have served to deter from the stated objectives. As a result, the labor movement has been pushed from an influential position within the political system to one that is subjugated to the directions of the state. The CTM has lost governorships and the right to participate in the distribution of housing for workers. Given these fundamental changes, there is much uncertainty as to where labor unions will end up.

"Transnational Labor Strategies and Economic Integration"
Maria Lorena Cook, School of Industrial and Labor Relations,
      Cornell University

The number of cross-border activities between labor, environmental, and community groups is a positive development that has expanded as a result of NAFTA. According to Maria Cook, several factors have driven the proliferation of these alliances and contacts including, most importantly, the efforts by NAFTA opponents to expand their alliances across borders in order to defeat the agreement, to develop strategies to address capital mobility, and to shape political reform within Mexico. Two key aspects have made these activities possible. These include the process of economic integration that has been occurring between Mexico and the United States, particularly since the 1980s, and the openness of domestic political processes to international actors as a result of the debate surrounding NAFTA. Within the United States an unprecedented number of Mexican citizens groups, political leaders, and government officials have been trying to shape public opinion. Mexican representatives testifying before Congress at the governmental level and grassroots discussions at the community level have stimulated discussion in many different forums.

In the United States, debate and criticisms directed at Mexican policies in the areas of the environment, human rights, labor rights, and democracy, have actually resulted in much of the recent reform in Mexico, in spite of the fact that Mexican groups had been pushing for these same reforms for many years. Through this "internationalization of domestic politics," Mexican citizen groups have increasingly been able to rely on external scrutiny to push for domestic reform. This has meant greater leverage in an authoritarian political system that typically does not allow for critics to effectively lobby their positions. Labor unions have also attempted these cross-border strategies, but they have not been as successful due to their weak position as a result of the economic restructuring of the 1980s and the subordinate position they hold under the influence of the government. The contacts that have been made take many different forms. The key labor organizations in Mexico have maintained their bargaining with the state as their main strategy while the smaller unions, with weaker political ties, have been more apt to pursue cross-border alliances. The tactics that have been used include transnational solidarity, which usually exists in the form of publicity of labor rights violations, "transnational organizing, commonly translating into assistance in collective bargaining," and political bargaining, which has taken the form of U.S. congressional pressure on Mexico to make improvements in the enforcement of labor standards. NAFTA has acted as a catalyst for this collaboration across borders. The question remains as to what extent these developments will be affected now that NAFTA has passed; that is, will NAFTA create an environment that will facilitate and institutionalize pressures to transnational alliances or hinder them?

Discussion

One aspect that the three countries appear to have in common is the simultaneous existence of low wages and salaries with high or rising productivity levels. It was often assumed that new technology and higher productivity would necessarily raise the standard of living of workers employed in those corporations. Enrique de la Garza notes that workers in the maquiladora are attracted by the higher wage rates that may be found in that region. Instead of comparing themselves with the income levels of workers in the United States or Canada, Mexicans tend to base their comparison on other regions within the country. De la Garza draws a contrast with Sweden, where it is unlikely that the relationship between productivity and wages would be so disproportionate.

Perhaps in the area of the social dimension the laws are not so important as the historical and cultural traditions of the country and the response of the individual actors at the microlevel. For example, Anil Verma suggests that while there was general consensus among governments in the EC over directorates dealing with the social objectives, the real impact came from meetings held by personnel directors across countries. Perhaps this is in line with Roy Adams's argument that some sort of international standard in the form of a social contract is very important in setting a basic vision that clearly communicates valued behavior. That is, the intent of the law changes the perceptions of the economic actors, including individual corporations, of what is acceptable, and therefore necessarily impacts their actions. At present, Adams suggests, we are not "doing a very good job" at communicating what sort of behavior is appropriate for corporations, particularly with regard to free trade. Ian Robinson contends that what is needed is a counter vision of how economies should be organized that is not defined by stringent national regulations but rather by a vision that unites people and in part is the source of labor movement commitment to pursue social policies.

In one sense the transnational alliances and the goals that have been pursued stand as an informal charter of social objectives and rights. While in the 1970s there was much discussion regarding the possibility of transnational bargaining and international collaboration between labor unions, nothing dramatic had come of this. NAFTA provided the immediacy that has resulted in the proliferation of transnational strategies particularly over the past five years. While Canadian and European counterparts were reasonably receptive to contacts with Mexican labor and community groups, only the recent NAFTA debate has brought the United States into these coalitions. What is most significant about these developments is not necessarily the obvious successes but rather the contact itself. The dialogue that has been initiated by free trade opens the door to deeper collaboration and networks. So far, those initiating these contacts are local unions and nonlabor groups rather than the national unions.

Katz suggests that the passage of NAFTA may in fact be positive for unions because NAFTA gives them a rallying point that will sustain mobilization. It is doubtful that the narrow, weak, and questionably enforceable side agreements will replace the efforts of the labor movement, environmental groups, and citizen organizations to push for higher and enforced standards. Michael Belzer states that while NAFTA is a historical event with debatable consequence, the force driving it is not temporary or dubious. The search for profit on a global scale is a permanent characteristic of modern economies. Unions in all three countries must recognize this and should rally for social concerns as driving the process, not profits. Ian Robinson notes that the NAFTA is only one agreement supporting free trade. The GATT and other inevitable future accords will continue global integration. He suggests that with the passage of NAFTA there will be a demoralizing effect on some groups that have been trying to think of alternatives to globalization contemplated by this agreement. This will result in various parties dropping out while others may have fewer resources to devote to a continuing battle.

Roy Adams points out that, for the last several years, employers in Mexico have been petitioning for the removal of the 1917 standards. Salinas's response has been that once NAFTA passes, the issue will be discussed further. Adams suggests that if the labor side agreements were emphasized and given significant power, they would make it difficult for the government to remove the 1917 rules and would in fact give workers a base from which to fight.

Morley Gunderson suggests that NAFTA will have a negative impact on two other significant areas: for Mexico, the agricultural sector will be hard hit by imports and, for Canada and the United States, the import competition will affect the low wage sectors and will increase and exacerbate the wage polarization that already exists. Within NAFTA, agriculture is dealt with on a bilateral basis, that is, between the United States and Mexico on the one hand, and the United States and Canada on the other. A mechanism exists to temper uninhibited free trade for the next fifteen years with a schedule protecting certain agricultural products that may be adjusted annually.

Empirical evidence on the impact that NAFTA will have on the economy in each of the three countries has varied in conclusion. Morley Gunderson finds that the studies done on the impact of the 1989 Canada-U.S. Free Trade Agreement are not able to clearly disentangle the impact of free trade itself. Some suggest that it has had minimal impact and that it has simply accelerated or aggravated what would have occurred anyway. Employment forecasting models in the United States suggest that there will be a limited impact on the aggregate level. As suggested above, however, there will be some sectors, especially low wage sectors, that will be substantially effected, contributing to wage polarization. Alberto Aziz notes that while Salinas's NAFTA has been promoted as a vehicle of job creation, no similar quantitative studies on NAFTA's impact on employment in Mexico have been done.

IV: SECTORAL TRENDS IN LABOR RELATIONS AND COLLECTIVE BARGAINING: Part 1

"Industrial Relations in the Canadian Steel and Telecommunication Industries"
Anil Verma, Faculty of Management, University of Toronto

Anil Verma suggests that one means by which sectoral trends can be analyzed with free trade is in the context of a model of industrial relations premised on increased competition. With an intensification of competition, the market will become more cost- and quality-conscious and driven by innovation. As a result, there will be a demand for a more skilled, trained, and adaptable workforce. Firms will respond and change in four general areas: flexible work organization, compensation innovation, employee involvement, and workplace governance and job security, which includes training. The process of industrial relations will also adapt. At the first level, the rising pressure of competition will force management to seek concessions. Rather than changing the actual structure of collective bargaining, the focus will be distributive and short-term. The second stage, occurring as a result of further competition, is that of strategic bargaining. The issues will be expanded to include new investments, job security, and other elements including traditional items, thus moving from distributive to integrative bargaining. There is no guarantee that strategic bargaining will take place in subsequent rounds. The mechanism that institutionalizes this process is the formation of strategic alliances.

Verma uses this model in order to describe developments in the Canadian steel industry. This sector is small relative to U.S. standards, with approximately 15 million tons of output per year. Due to a small domestic market, 25 to 35 percent of the domestic production is exported. In 1980, the industry could best be described as relatively stable with modern technology and a predictable and established labor-management relationship. By the late 1980s, however, pressures on steel intensified, making it clear that change was needed. The industry strike of 1990 can be attributed primarily to the fact that the parties were being forced to realign their relationship. The resultant contracts varied across companies. While there was slow progress made in the area of workplace reform or employee involvement, there were attempts to introduce gainsharing plans. In some cases, negotiations resulted in strategic bargaining and alliances while in other instances, concession bargaining occurred. At the industry level, federal government money was allocated to a joint labor-management council to deal with the issue of dislocated workers and job retraining.

"Labor Relations in the Mexican Automobile Industry"
Arnulfo Arteaga Garcia, Maestria en Sociologia del Trabajo,
UAM-Iztapalapa

Arnulfo Arteaga describes the characteristics of the integration process between Mexico and the United States and how it has impacted the automobile industry. Over the years, this sector has undergone a significant transformation process within collective bargaining agreements and in general working conditions. The subsidiaries of the major American automobile companies, with a competitive advantage stemming from governmental policies focused on competitiveness, have become the principal exporters of the Latin American economy.

As a result of NAFTA, the industry as a whole has begun to restructure. American auto companies are realigning their strategies, causing Mexican subsidiaries to adapt. For example, in order to respond to the demand of the American parts market, the automotive industry has begun to export totally assembled cars. Together with the maquila industry, this has become the proof that Mexico can be a trustworthy supplier.

Since the 1920s the Mexican automobile industry has undergone a major transformation. The characteristics of the production process; industrial policy; geographic location as it relates to the industrial process; and the collective bargaining process have all shifted during this period. During the first sixty years the automobile industry was concentrated in the center of the country. In the 1980s, however, a major relocation toward the north took place. The relocation focused plants on serving American markets, particularly in the production of engines and car assembly. Overall, the installed capacity in Mexico increased during this decade.

Arteaga notes two different types of industrial relations patterns. The first is characterized by a single union that covers the entire industry under one contract while the second, exemplified by the maquiladoras, is defined by a decentralization of contract negotiations at the plant level. New industrial structures will have a significant impact on the technology, workplace organization, collective bargaining agreements, and wages of the older industrial base. Centralization of the auto industry to the north will result in major plant closings in the center of the country. Already, 50 percent of the workforce of firms located in Central Mexico have been laid off. Most of the eliminated jobs had higher wages and benefits. While there may be an increase in overall employment in the Mexican automobile industry, the quality of these jobs appears to be lower. Union fragmentation has resulted from this shift and, in some cases, collective agreements exist even before workers are hired in these new locations. Quality circles and work teams have been introduced as elements of this transformation. As examples, General Motors has been relatively successful in imposing the above shifts while Ford has run into significant difficulties in the transition.

"Collective Bargaining in the U.S. Auto Assembly Sector"
Harry C. Katz, School of Industrial and Labor Relations, Cornell University

In the last ten years, there have been substantial inroads and expansion of foreign auto production capacities in the United States from Germany and most significantly, Japan. This recent expansion, notes Katz, has been spurred by foreign exchange fluctuations that have made the American market more financially attractive. A second observation that is important to the analysis of the auto industry is the substantial variation that exists across American automobile corporations. While Ford and Chrysler appear to be doing quite well, General Motors is suffering a considerable loss of market share. A final key economic trend in the industry is the geographic recentralization of assembly and major parts production to the Detroit region and the area surrounding Tennessee, and the decentralization of parts supply. According to Katz, this bifurcation in the production system has meant that, while assembly plants are remaining in the United States, parts plants seem more likely to locate outside the country.

The industrial relations systems in the United States, as noted earlier, is best characterized by its diversity. While the "low end" is distinguished by management practices of firing at will and demanding substantial concessions, the opposite is described by worker participation schemes and employee involvement in which the union may be centrally involved in business decisionmaking. Katz explains that these employee involvement developments may be the result of "pure and simple experimentation" or management's belief that participation is necessary to achieve flexibility and higher quality. Other characteristics of the American model of industrial relations are the decentralization of collective bargaining and the incredible variation inside unions as to the political response to new workplace organization. The New Directions movement within the UAW, for example, has taken a position that resists all joint actions with management, while at the other extreme, some portion of the UAW is involved in the progressive workplace arrangements at Saturn.

Katz states that NAFTA will accelerate the trends that are already underway in the auto industry--for example, the bifurcation in industrial development discussed above. He does not believe that the agreement poses a threat to the assembly capacity of the United States. The parts industry may move to Mexico as it has already begun to do, but he sees little evidence that U.S. companies have plans to move assembly capacity as they are, in fact, recentralizing this component of the industry. What this bifurcation means for the labor movement in the future is unclear. It is probable that NAFTA will increase the diversity in industrial relations, the decentralization in collective bargaining, and the debates that occur within unions.

Discussion

Two general reactions of labor to the actions of firms were noted: cooperation or resistance. In the case of cooperation, Katz explains that unions do get increased involvement in decision making but wages themselves are not clearly linked to cooperation or militancy at the plant level. There is considerable debate as to whether these new forms of employee involvement translate into a faster work pace. Although there is no consensus on this issue, we do know that these initiatives have resulted in a different form of work organization, including more use of teams where unions are cooperating, an increase in information being passed to employees and the union, and union involvement in workplace issues, work organization decisions, and in influencing business decisions. At Saturn, for example, the union participates in discussions, chooses parts suppliers, plans adjustments, and even holds positions throughout the management hierarchy.

One area in which it is clear to see a difference as a result of increased union involvement is in work organization. Adjustment strategies are more frequently employed where unions have a strong voice. At Saturn, there is a system that plans much further in advance for the entrance of new workers into the plant. More time is committed to interviewing candidates and counseling workers before they start the job. Also, the union has not allowed the use of temporary workers in assembly or in independent parts suppliers.

A key concern that was voiced by labor and other groups throughout the NAFTA debate in the United States was the likelihood of a large exodus of corporations from the United States to Mexico. Gunderson voices this as a strong possibility where productivity in Mexico is approximately 80 percent of U.S. levels and wages only 10 to 20 percent. The fact that Mexican workers can often be trained to achieve comparable skill levels to that of the American workforce further supports this movement. Katz, however, feels very confident that the assembly capacity in the auto industry is unlikely to move to Mexico despite findings of high productivity rates in some Mexican plants. First, the level of political instability in industrial relations in comparison to the United States is quite high. That is, despite the recent trend towards concessions, labor relations in the American auto industry are relatively stable. Second, the recentralization of production in the United States is driven by the demand for skilled electrical workers, by the importance of a close link between assembly and parts components, and because it is felt that corporations will not be able to find the number of skilled workers that they could in the United States. Quick response in the industry translates into redesigning whole plant complexes, not through moving just one plant.

Arnulfo Arteaga explains that when there are plant closings in Mexico, there are few protections for the individual worker and that adjustment policies are nonexistent. For example, in 1980, General Motors announced that it was planning to close a plant in central Mexico and to open a new operation in northern Mexico. The union responded with a strike that lasted 106 days. Not only did they lose the strike but over 50 percent of the workers were fired. In a similar situation at Renault, workers struck but the company began to form deals with workers on an individual basis, offering them money or other rewards. The labor movement has not developed a strategy to deal with these shifts and collective bargaining has not been able to address the issue.

While the decentralization of collective bargaining has caused a shift in power relations to lower levels and has in some cases fragmented labor, it leaves open the opportunity to establish cross-national union relationships at the plant level. Arnulfo Arteaga offers examples of this occurring as a result of two different strikes at auto plants in Mexico. In the first case, a UAW local in Minnesota supported Mexican workers in their conflict. When workers at Volkswagen went out on strike on another occasion, German VW workers agreed not to pick up lost production. Katz offers the contrasting example of the Canadian Automobile Workers split from the UAW to illustrate that a transnational alliance many be overwhelmed by individual differences, varying perceptions, cultures and ideologies, and exposure to different economic realities. The American and Canadian Communications Workers, however, have started a formal exchange of people and bargaining agendas. Recently a conference was organized to discuss how to deal with the changes taking place at Northern Telecom. Dialogue up to this point has concentrated on unfair labor practice issues and other nonmonetary topics. The real test comes, Anil Verma emphasizes, when a company decides to move facilities across borders. Can two unions concerned with jobs for their members maintain a cooperative relationship? Mark Thompson notes that the American labor movement is very protectionist. Cooperation is problematic because unions don't want production to go to Mexico. At the same time, Mexican labor sees NAFTA as an opportunity for its members. The division between Canadian and U.S. members of the International Woodworkers occurred because the United States was trying to keep Canadian products out of the market.

The phenomena of new workplace organization occurring at the micro level is another key development calling into question the future strategy of the labor movement in the three countries. Arnulfo Arteaga questions what these new forms represent. While there is increased delegation of decision making to the individual worker management is intervening at other levels. The modification of the relationship between the worker and management has meant some displacement of the union. Arteaga is concerned that initiatives between workers and unions are not being developed.

Enrique de la Garza points out that there is still a high degree of labor conflict in some of the new plants where total quality programs have been introduced. For example, the Ford Hermosillo plant was designed from the beginning under the Japanese model. The firm has dealt with high turnover and labor unrest by training more workers than they need and by rewarding workers for good attendance records. Ford has been able to use this flexible labor force to maintain its quality standards.

V.   SECTORAL   TRENDS   IN   LABOR   RELATIONS   AND   COLLECTIVE BARGAINING: *Part 2*

"Inter-City Trucking in the United States"
Michael Belzer, School of Industrial and Labor Relations, Cornell University

Government deregulation of the trucking industry in the 1980s caused a dramatic transformation in this sector, explains Michael Belzer. Before this period, general freight firms carried both truckload (TL) and less-than-truckload (LTL) freight (high- and low-revenue freight) allowing trucks to remain loaded in both directions. This arrangement resulted in reasonable and sustaining profits. Economic deregulation unleashed economic forces that compelled firms to specialize in either less-than-truckload or truckload freight (high revenue per pound or low revenue per pound). Significant growth occurred among carriers that handled nothing but truckload freight, while the number of less-than-truckload carriers declined.

The segmentation of industry structure caused a bifurcation of jobs into two classes. Well-paying employment with good working conditions remained in the LTL sector, while poor jobs, characterized by low pay and inferior working conditions, developed in the growing TL sector.

The Teamsters remain the most powerful force for higher wages. While the union has lost control over the TL sector, it still maintains command over much of LTL.

Another significant effect of deregulation on the trucking industry has been concentration. For example, United Parcel Service alone is bigger than all the general freight carriers represented by the Teamsters National Master Freight Agreement combined.

The trucking industry is important in the debate surrounding NAFTA because trucks carry much of the trade between the United States and Mexico. While trucking can be expected to expand between the two countries, this may not translate into more jobs for American workers, although it may create new opportunities for Mexican workers. However, Belzer does not believe that this job growth for Mexican drivers will mean higher wages than those in the Maquiladora labor market.

NAFTA allows Mexican carriers access for international traffic to border states within three years, with full access to the United States permitted in six years. NAFTA permits U.S. companies to own 49 percent of Mexican carriers between three to seven years after the passage of the agreement, 51 percent between seven to nine years after passage, and up to 100 percent after ten years. However, NAFTA permits Mexican companies to own 100 percent of U.S. trucking companies after three years. Belzer predicts that, despite legislation favoring Mexican ownership, eventually most cross-border trucking companies will be U.S.-owned. American companies are stronger financially and are eager to pursue what appears to be a potentially very profitable expansion.

U.S. regulations in the industry probably will continue to support low wages. There is no minimum wage law or overtime law covering interstate trucking and the maximum hours of service law that does exist is very difficult to enforce and violated regularly. It is likely that Mexican drivers will be used for TL work, possibly pushing down already low wages, in the U.S. labor market. American workers may be relegated to ancillary activities such as dock work, bookkeeping, clerical work and supervision.

The effect on regional LTL is uncertain. Belzer expects LTL carriers in the border states to create Mexican subsidiaries, creating redistribution centers to which carriers feed cross-border traffic. Thus LTL road operations will develop characteristics similar to the TL sector. It is even possible, Belzer suggests, that cross-border integration of LTL carriers will cause the restructuring of transportations. Carriers may save money by hauling in a circuitous fashion from the United States to a Mexican terminal for long-distance transshipment back to points in the United States. Finally, in a few years the pressure may be strong enough that U.S. carriers may demand that the government eliminate the prohibition against the use of Mexican subsidiaries in domestic cabotage, thus eliminating much of the LTL industry.

"Labor Relations in the Maquiladora Industry"
Alfredo Hualde, El Colegio de la Frontera Norte (COLEF)

Alfredo Hualde discusses academic critiques of the maquila industry in the 1970s. From an economic point of view, maquilas were criticized because they had few links with the local economy, no transfer of technology and no local assimilation of that technology. Also, the organizations located there were considered volatile because of the total subordination of decision making to corporate headquarters, which were typically foreign. In relation to labor conditions, the maquila was viewed as an area of repression based on a system of capitalistic exploitation of labor demonstrated by low wages, weak labor unions, poor working conditions and labor contracts negotiated below labor standards. The feminist perspective saw the maquilas as a form of exploitation of women because 80 percent of those employed were female. Yet another critique offered is that the work was so unskilled that no training was required. Finally, from a nationalistic perspective, the maquilas were seen as running counter to the import-substitution program and were considered to unduly exploit the environment and the infrastructure of the country.

In the 1980s, the most advanced sector of maquiladora industry saw the introduction of new sophisticated technology (robots, computerized numerical control machines, and so on), new techniques for the organization of production and changes in human resources management addressed to motivate the labor force. Hualde offers two basic models of labor relations that can be found. The first, traditional unionism, is defined by government involvement in unions. The CTM, as an example, has organized all of the maquilas and has brought some improvements in the conditions of employment due to the stability they offer. Secondly, "subordinate" unionism exists. These labor organizations are not known to the workers and the contracts contain extensive management prerogatives and standards below those set by law.

In part as a result of Japanese investment in the Maquilas, there have been interesting changes in the management of human resources. Perhaps this has translated into an improved organizational climate characterized, above all, by better communication channels. Functionally this has meant an increased emphasis on quality improvements and error detection, product development on location, and hiring of more engineers. In addition, some links have been made to local educational institutions. Hualde concludes with the question of whether we will see the future Mexican assembly industries as one of growth, linkages in local economy (as in South Asian countries), and better labor condition, or as one more closely related to the model of the maquilas in the 1970s.

"Public Sector Labor Relations in Canada"
Robert Hebdon, School of Industrial and Labor Relations, Cornell University

Two bills in Ontario are particularly significant in the context of Canadian labor relations: the Social Contract Act, 1993 (Bill 48), which suspends all bargaining on compensation issues until March 1996, and the pending Bill 49 which introduces legislation designed to significantly reform collective bargaining for employees of the crown. Robert Hebdon explains that Ontario's NDP government attempted to deal with intense economic pressures by extracting two billion dollars from the payroll of approximately one million public sector workers under Bill 48. Although the financial objective was achieved, Hebdon explains, it caused tremendous divisions within the labor movement, a weakening of support for the NDP, and public condemnation. Flaws in the content of the process occurred because the provincial government was unsuccessful at convincing the unions of, and creating consensus around, the gravity of the financial situation. The process itself utilized poor collective bargaining procedures. Overall, the action by the government, in what could have been a model of the use of collective bargaining to address financial crisis, appeared as unilateral and authoritative.

Bill 49 is a signed agreement that covers Crown employees and commits the government to some form of labor reform that will likely be a movement toward the private sector form of collective bargaining. According to Hebdon, the current law for direct employees of the Canadian government is a "model of conflict suppression." It takes away the right to strike, limits the scope of bargaining, and restricts the unions' political rights. Bill 49 will grant the right to strike with safeguards for essential services and will allow unions to engage in political action. Public sector workers will be placed under the private sector law for most purposes.

There is no doubt that the public sector is impacted by the forces of globalization and economic integration taking place in North America. The finances of provincial and federal governments have been weakened by the Free Trade Agreement and undoubtedly NAFTA will influence these conditions. Each of the ten provinces is presently suffering from a financial crisis that has resulted in wage restraint legislation and programs, and privatization. Given the forces of increased competition that have shown up in the public sector in the form of wage controls, limits on collective bargaining, social contracts, contracting out, TQM, privatization, and the above examples of what has occurred in Ontario as a result of these pressures, it is difficult to predict the future consequences for collective bargaining.

"Labor Relations in the Mexican Petrochemical Industry"
Rafael Loyola, Facultad Latinoamericano de Ciencias Sociales (FLACSO)

The petrochemical industry is a sector where the changes reflect the new economic and labor relations policies of the government, states Rafael Loyola. The changes that have occurred in this industry began in the second month of Salinas's administration, that is before the negotiations of NAFTA began, with strong measures against the union's leadership. The old model of organization and administration in the industry, characterized by a paternalistic welfare policy and government control, ended in 1989.

The model that characterized Pemex before 1989 was one of a closed and protected industry with its share and control of the petrochemical industry going well beyond what was established in the national constitution. In the past, the unions promoted a highly regulated work process. The employer was restricted, by contract, from moving any workers or machinery. The collective agreement also stipulated that only 10 percent of the Pemex workforce could be management. The union power went so far as to provide contract services. It in fact appeared for some time that the trade union was co-owner of the oil industry.

The new model of labor relations provides a drastically different picture. The unions have retreated to a traditional stance of collective bargaining with enormously reduced powers and stability. Wages and benefits for the workers have dropped significantly and the union has even lost jurisdiction in some areas. The emphasis has now shifted to the subordination of workers to management, Loyola explains. Without seniority protections, employees are recognized on the basis of their competence. While the number of employees that have been laid off is unclear, some estimates are that, at its peak, approximately 210,000 to 240,000 workers were employed by this sector. Predictions are that this will be down to 40,000 workers in the near future. Over time, all those areas of the petrochemical industries that are not classified as strategic will be privatized and many areas will be contracted out.

Discussion

Alfredo Hualde finds that in the maquiladora, management complains of turnover because in many cases they are attempting training. At the same time, however, training programs are a mechanism that helps the company adjust to the fluctuating demand for workers. In companies with training programs, managers often try to make an example of workers with good attendance records to motivate others to achieve similar records. For the workers, turnover is used as a form of passive resistance and is a way of facing certain labor conditions. At present, with the high demand for labor, workers are able to move from job to job with little problem. If employment decreases this trend may change. Turnover in the maquiladora in some plants is more that 100 percent per year, although there is no general data to verify this. Overall, there is not much upward mobility of workers within the firm.

From the point of view of the legal framework, the maquiladora will disappear as such in the year 2000. As a production center in international subcontracting, the mquiladora is expected to grow substantially in the next year. Because NAFTA will require up to 60 percent local content from Japanese companies in Mexico that don't have subsidiaries in the United States, the maquilas will change from simply being a source of assembly to playing a larger production role.

The union in the petrochemical industry had become so important it was almost "a state within a state." Salinas abruptly broke the union because there didn't appear to be any possible form of negotiation. The union at this moment is under almost complete control by the state and the company. Because the downsizing that has been announced is so dramatic there is little hope that the weak union will have any impact. The state has been very careful that the new corruption-related wealth of officials is not publicized because previously the company could blame the union for its failure to introduce reforms. At present however, the state can no longer shift blame or responsibility to the union.

VI. COMPARATIVE PERSPECTIVES

"Cross-National Labor Collaboration and the Battle for a Social Dimension in the European Single Market"
Lowell Turner, School of Industrial and Labor Relations, Cornell University

From the mid-1980s to the 1990s what appeared to be a rather smooth integration is now, after the cold war, getting "quite messy" Lowell Turner explains. With the fall of the Berlin wall, neighboring European countries stand at radically different economic levels. There is cross-national union collaboration to a historically unprecedented degree as a result of integration within the European Community; yet it is still not enough. The social dimension, which was an extraordinary accomplishment, still falls short.

The EC was initially a Franco-German alliance, a deal between French agriculture and German business. The purpose of the alliance was to prevent future world wars and to maintain stable political democracy. Throughout the 1970s and 1980s, the community expanded to its present twelve members. This period was marked by social activism with Social Democratic parties in Great Britain and Germany stimulating some progress. In 1979, what was popularly called "Eurosclerosis" set in. This was the notion that the welfare states could no longer compete in globally competitive markets. The response of the actors to this was to relaunch efforts towards a single market with the Single European Act. The role of key political leaders and the notion to "complete something already started" were instrumental to these efforts. It is important to note that this initiative lacked any input from labor; business unilaterally pushed the deregulation process. The strategy of the European labor movement was to aggressively promote the social dimension.

At the highest level, the European Trade Union Confederation (ETUC) is pushing for legislation along the social dimension. ETUC and UNICE (the All-European Employers' Federation) negotiated a social chapter in Maastricht that allows for majority voting in the European Council on social and workplace issues. At the sectoral level unions are pushing for European industry committees to get started on cross-national collective bargaining. European Works Councils are the goal at the level of the firm. These councils allow for cross-national collaboration and information-sharing.

Unfortunately, Turner notes, the European social dimension has been somewhat of a "fish story." There is considerable debate over whether these developments are exaggerated hopes or truly the groundwork for future accomplishments. Since the initiation of the social dimension, the strength of the efforts has diminished. For example, while the original emphasis was on the harmonization of standards, it is now based on the notion of "subsidiarity." Decision making has been pushed to the lowest level. Overall, the accomplishments have been limited because supporting institutions are weak; there is great difficulty in building institutions of international regulation when the actors themselves have overriding national preoccupations. For example, the CGT, the dominant labor federation in France, still does not belong to ETUC, opposes European integration, and has weakened the ability of unions to collaborate. The almost total preoccupation, since 1990, of German unions with unification has diminished power at the very core of the labor movement's efforts in the EC. As the most powerful player among trade unions, the German unions need to play a central role in supporting cross-national union collaboration, particularly in pursuing codetermination rights, for this to be successful.

Turner is optimistic "that prospects for labor developments in the EC are open." He contends that there is, and will continue to be, enormous pressure on national systems of industrial relations and national union rights and that labor's primary effort will continue to be to defend its position at that level. Cross-national union collaboration will continue and increase and European works councils appear to be on the horizon. This whole process has been complicated by the end of the cold war. There are many new actors and parties at the bargaining table and will be more in the future, as the EC opens up to the north and east.

"NAFTA, AFTA, and Labor Relations Trends in Southeast Asia"
Sarosh Kuruvilla, School of Industrial and Labor Relations, Cornell University

Although Sarosh Kuruvilla feels that Asian integration is far away, or at least unlikely in the next ten years, the passage of NAFTA is a strong signal for Asia to speed up developments. Although several forms of Pan-Asian integration have been discussed (for example, Hong Kong-China-Taiwan, North and South Korea) the most concrete steps toward integration have been taken by the Association of Southeast Asian Nations (ASEAN, comprised Malaysia, Singapore, Indonesia, the Philippines, Thailand, and Brunei) who have instituted AFTA (ASEAN Free Trade Area). AFTA, when completed, will form a market of 380 million people by the year 2000.

AFTA aims at integration with a reduction of tariff barriers within fifteen years beginning 1993. The potential for such integration is great, given the relatively low level of current tariffs between countries, and the similarity of their economic development strategies. The commonalities in economic development strategies can be seen in their economic structure and how this has changed over time. All countries commenced with an import-substitution industrialization strategy. Given a shortage of foreign exchange needed to sustain imports of technology for domestic industry, these countries then shifted to an export-oriented economic strategy. A view of where these economies are today reveals that Hong Kong and Singapore have moved away from export orientation to service-oriented economies; Korea and Taiwan are advanced export-oriented economies; Malaysia and Thailand are in the transition period from low-cost export orientation to more advanced export orientation; while the Philippines and Indonesia are the low-cost exporters. Kuruvilla argues that the relative place of each economy in this development ladder provides each with a competitive niche in the region. Evidence of this niche can be seen in the patterns of foreign investment, as well as in the increased intra-ASEAN trade over the last decade.

A second major similarity is the labor law system. ASEAN countries have a two-pronged approach to industrial relations. The first component is solid labor protection with advanced legislation mandating annual leave, maternity leave, overtime pay, working hours, bonuses, retirement benefits, and a host of other working conditions. The second component is policy on labor relations, which have largely focused on several restrictions on the ability of unions to organize, strike, and bargain collectively. Union density is low, and ranges from 4 to 5 percent in Thailand, to 20 to 25 percent in Singapore.

However, industrial relations is a critical component of the development strategy in ASEAN, and extremely relevant in the creation and maintenance of competitive niches for economic growth. Two general approaches can be seen in the ASEAN countries. One option available to countries and firms, notably the more advanced ones, is an industrial relations system that focuses on upskilling, characterized by new approaches to work organization, human resource management, new compensation systems, and teamwork. This model has increased employee participation in a nonunion environment. The second approach, more common in countries with a low-cost export strategy, focuses on cost containment through low-wage policies, employment of female workers, some repression of unions, and increased flexibility through the use of temporary, part-time, and casual employees, and subcontracting. Overall, the role of unions in Southeast Asia is declining in all ASEAN countries.

"Japan"
Marcus Rebick, School of Industrial and Labor Relations, Cornell University

Mark Rebick offers two explanations for the long-run trend in Japan of a production push to other countries. The domestic factor that has driven this transition is the rapid aging of the Japanese population, which has surpassed the rate of all other developed countries. In addition, labor costs in relation to world markets has increased significantly, due to the appreciation of the yen. Japanese capitalism has traditionally been more focused on expansion, that is, achieving market share has been their key strategy. With the rising yen, firms have had to drop prices, but the Japanese share of world markets has started to decline, resulting in the search for new ways to cut costs, including the movement of manufacturing.

The increased internationalization of trade has led to many changes in the internal economy of Japan. One example of this is the decline in union density from 35 to 25 percent. The drop can partly be attributed to growing internal pressures and the holding down of costs. The present environment has made it very difficult for many workers to increase wages and wage differentials by firm size have increased since 1975. In addition, the bottom end of this hierarchy of firms in the Japanese subcontracting system is facing growing competition from the move of production abroad.

Several short-run trends have also impacted the Japanese economy, including a deep depression. This has resulted in significant layoffs in the ranks of middle management in the white-collar workforce primarily through forced retirements. Rebick offers that this may be an acceleration of a trend that would have occurred anyway with the aging of the population. That is, many companies simply can't afford to support as many upper-level workers. Overall, the unemployment rate has remained less than 3 percent, leaving the blue-collar workforce relatively unaffected. A final trend detected by Rebick is the rising demand for political reform. Rather than continue to pursue the expansionist strategy that is working against the interests of Japanese consumers and the national welfare, there is a growing sense that it is desirable to reform the entire economic system and the political system along with it.

A structural issue that is creating problems with the internationalization process is the organization of production based on a subcontracting system. Small firms are typically under the control of the larger companies to whom they supply parts. Through this relationship, larger companies are able to divide labor within the overall organization

284

and, through a system of enterprise unionism, pay lower wages. Complications arise when the Japanese move production to other countries. Unable to maintain the same subcontracting structure due to protectionist pressures and the rising yen, Japanese firms in the United States have been forced to purchase from American parts suppliers. In turning to these new sources, the Japanese have found that the same long-term contractual relationships based on flexibility are more difficult to maintain and that managing and controlling the quality of inputs is problematic. As a result, Japanese companies have been forced to accumulate inventories and bear greater risks than they have in the past. This has been a problem for the Japanese in various countries and perhaps is one reason why it is believed Japanese firms will rely less on lean production systems and will loosen group structures and hierarchies in the future.

Because content requirements are higher under NAFTA than under the FTA, this causes some concern for Japan and will certainly impact production decisions. At the same time, this may mean an increase in Japanese investment in Mexico. Japan may react to the passage of NAFTA by accelerating coalition forming and investment in Southeast Asia and therefore pursuing a similar bloc formation.

Discussion

There is some speculation that NAFTA will lead to trade diversion from Asia to Mexico. While the net impact on trade may not be large, it seems clear that NAFTA will stimulate more interest in low-cost Mexican production than in Southeast Asian sources, particularly since many of these areas have begun to witness rising wages. Rebick proposes that, regardless of NAFTA, protectionist attitudes toward Japan will remain and that Mexico will become more attractive to the Japanese entrance into the U.S. market. Overall, rising quality standards, lower production costs, and access to American markets make Mexico attractive to investors.

Verma notes that Southeast Asian countries, rather than fight NAFTA, have increased trade within the Asian region. The implications for the Asian Pacific Economic Cooperative (APEC) are unclear, but with the passage of NAFTA, it is likely that President Clinton will go further to pursue arrangements with Chile, Argentina, and other countries. Meanwhile, intraregional trade in ASEAN will expand. Also, individual countries, for example, Malaysia, will attempt to follow the growth model that has been so successful for South Korea.